D1187432

JUSTICE AND VIOLENCE

Ethics and Global Politics

Series Editors: Tom Lansford and Patrick Hayden

Since the end of the Cold War, explorations of ethical considerations within global politics and on the development of foreign policy have assumed a growing importance in the fields of politics and international studies. New theories, policies, institutions, and actors are called for to address difficult normative questions arising from the conduct of international affairs in a rapidly changing world. This series provides an exciting new forum for creative research that engages both the theory and practice of contemporary world politics, in light of the challenges and dilemmas of the evolving international order.

Justice and Violence
Political Violence, Pacifism and Cultural Transformation

Edited by

ALLAN EICKELMANN
University of Southern Mississippi, USA

ERIC NELSON
University of Southern Mississippi, USA

TOM LANSFORD
University of Southern Mississippi, USA

ASHGATE

Published by
Ashgate Publishing Limited
Gower House
Croft Road
Aldershot
Hants GU11 3HR
England

Ashgate Publishing Company
Suite 420
101 Cherry Street
Burlington, VT 05401-4405
USA

Ashgate website: http://www.ashgate.com

British Library Cataloguing in Publication Data
Justice and violence : political violence, pacifism and
    cultural transformation. - (Ethics and global politics)
    1. Violence - Political aspects 2. Justice 3. Globalization -
    Social aspects 4. Just war doctrine
    I. Eickelmann, Allan II. Nelson, Eric III. Lansford, Tom
    303.6

Library of Congress Cataloging-in-Publication Data
Justice and violence : political violence, pacifism and cultural transformation
    / edited by Allan Eickelmann, Eric Nelson and Tom Lansford.
        p. cm. -- (Ethics and global politics)
    Includes bibliographical references and index.
    ISBN 0-7546-4546-0
    1. Political violence. 2. Pacific settlement of international disputes.
3. United States--Military policy. 4. United States--Foreign relations.
I. Lansford, Tom. II. Eickelmann, Allan. III. Nelson, Eric, 1970-   .
IV. Lansford, Tom. V. Series.

JC328.6.J87 2005
303.6--dc22

2005015267

ISBN 0 7546 4546 0

"A Political Calculus of Apology: Japan and Its Neighbors" was previously published in Girma Negash, *Appologia Politica: States and Their Appologies by Proxy* (Lanham, MD: Lexington Books, in press). The essay is reprinted here with the permission of Lexington Books.

Printed and bound in Great Britain by MPG Books Ltd, Bodmin, Cornwall.

Contents

Part 3   Beyond Justice and Injustice

List of Contributors

Neal Allen is a doctoral candidate and assistant instructor at the University of Texas at Austin. His research interests include the American Supreme Court, American Political History, the Presidency, and Political Science pedagogy. He has published articles on presidential responses to foreign policy challenges and the history of third-party presidential candidacies.

Edmund F. Byrne, J.D., Ph.D., is Emeritus Professor of Philosophy, Indiana University–Purdue University at Indianapolis. His current research interest is philosophical critique of pro-violence reasoning. Most of his books and articles address various issues regarding either technology and work or business ethics, both of which come together in *Work, Inc.: A Philosophical Inquiry*. Byrne is Section Editor: Work for *The Journal of Business Ethics*. His latest publication is "Work" in *The Encyclopedia of Science, Technology and Ethics*.

Helena Cristini, Ph.D., is a professor of Political Science in International Relations Theory at the International University of Monaco. Half Spanish and half French, she came to the United States at the age of nineteen to attend university, earning a BA in Spanish Literature and an MA in Latin American Studies from the University of Texas. She went on to earn an MA in Political Science at the University of Massachusetts. Eager to research how spiritual and philosophical solutions might solve political conflicts, she went to India to pursue her Ph.D. at the University of Bombay. While in India she completed a comparative study of religions in order to pursue her thesis topic. Out of this research sprang her interest in debates concerning the West and the Orient – its cultures and its identities.

Chris J. Dolan earned his doctorate in 2002 from the University of South Carolina. Currently he is an Assistant Professor of Political Science at the University of Central Florida. His research focuses on US foreign policy and national security and the American presidency. He is the co-editor with Betty Glad of *Striking First* (Palgrave, 2004) and the author of *In War We Trust* (Ashgate, 2005). His research appears in *International Politics, Policy Studies Journal, Congress and the Presidency, White House Studies, Politics and Policy*, and in numerous edited volumes on US foreign policy and the presidency. Chris also serves as a guest lecturer at the Fulbright American Studies Institute hosted by the US Department of State and at the Lou Frey Symposium hosted by the Institute of Politics at the University of Central Florida. He and his family currently reside in metropolitan Orlando.

Tobias T. Gibson is ABD in political science at Washington University in St. Louis. His primary research interest is in American politics, with focus on the judicial and executive branches. His recent work has appeared in the *Encyclopedia of Law and Society*, *the Encyclopedia of Civil Liberties*, and *the Encyclopedia of the Supreme Court*. His dissertation focuses on the ability of the federal judiciary to affect the actions of the president.

Angela Gordon is a Ph.D. candidate in the Department of Anthropology at Washington University in St. Louis, specializing in archaeology. Her academic interests include the prehistory of agriculture in Eastern North America and Mexico, the conservation of agricultural biodiversity, and alternative farming systems. Her non-academic interests include American politics and political protest. She has published in the *Journal of Archaeological Sciences* and *American Anthropologist*.

Carol Hunter, Ph.D., is professor of U.S. history, peace and global studies and African/African–American studies at Earlham College in Richmond, Indiana. Her research interests are social movements for peace and justice and alternative framings of history. Her most recent book, co-authored with Jim Juhnke is *The Missing Peace: The Search for Nonviolent Alternatives in United States History* (Kitchner, Onatrio: Pandora Press, 2004).

Hans Küng was born in Sursee, Switzerland in 1928, and later studied philosophy and theology in Rome and Paris. He was Professor of Ecumenical Theology at Tübingen University, Germany, from 1960 to 1996. He has also taught as a visiting professor in New York, Basel, Chicago, Ann Arbor, and Houston. He currently serves as president of the Global Ethic Foundation located in Tübingen, Germany, a position he has held since 1995. Over the course of his career, Dr. Küng has received numerous awards and honorary degrees. Among his many books are *Global Responsibility: In Search of a New World Ethic* (1991), and *A Global Ethic for Global Politics and Economics* (1998).

Brian D. McKnight earned his doctorate degree in history from Mississippi State University and is a member of the Department of History and Philosophy at the University of Virginia's College at Wise. Trained as a scholar of the American Civil War, much of McKnight's work focuses on the conflict as it played out along the Appalachian Mountains.

Valerie O. F. Morkevicius is a graduate student in political science in the Department of Political Science at the University of Chicago. Morkevicius' contribution to this collection relates to her larger dissertation project, which examines the types of frameworks (including various *just war* traditions) used by state elites to justify wars and questions whether these norms constrain their behavior in actual wars. She is particularly interested in whether norms regarding justice in warfare are shared across cultures and religions. Although *just war* theory is her primary concern, Morkevicius' other scholarly interests include classical realist theory, military strategy, and the development of national identity.

Girma Negash, Ph.D., is professor of political science at the University of South Carolina Aiken. His current research efforts relate to apology and forgiveness in international relations and the nexus between politics and the arts in political theory. In the first area, he is completing a book, *Apologia Politica: States and Their Apologies by Proxy* (Lexington Books, forthcoming). He just published an article in the second area, "Art Invoked: A Mode of Understanding and Shaping the Political" in the *International Political Science Review*. His publications have also appeared in *Peace Review; International Journal of Politics and Ethics; Social Identities; Journal of African Cultural Studies*; and *Scandinavian Journal of Development Alternatives.*

Robert J. Pauly, Jr., Ph.D., is Lead Instructor of Conflict Resolution and Post-Conflict Reconstruction in the context of the Master of Diplomacy Distance Learning Program at Norwich University in Northfield, VT. His research interests include U.S. foreign policy generally and American-European and American-Greater Middle Eastern relations specifically. His most recent book is *US Foreign Policy and the Persian Gulf: Safeguarding American Interests Through Selective Multilateralism* (Ashgate Publishing Limited, 2005).

Susan Weldon Scott is a graduate student in political science at the University of Southern Mississippi. Her research interests include American foreign policy, specifically the function of democratic principles in American foreign policy.

Fred C. Smith is a doctoral candidate in history at the University of Southern Mississippi. His work has appeared in *Agricultural History, The Journal of Mississippi History, Southern Historian,* and most recently in *Mississippi History Now*, the on-line journal of the Mississippi Department of History and Archives. In addition to labor, agricultural, and southern economic history, Smith has a particular interest in the Mississippi River alluvial plain. He is currently researching toward the completion of his dissertation on those issues.

Will Watson is Associate Professor Of English at the University of Southern Mississippi, Gulf Coast. He is the first in his family to attend college and holds a Ph.D. from Louisiana State University. Watson was a Chicago-area steel worker, longshoreman, electrician and truckdriver in the ten years before beginning college. He is a founding member of the Green Party of Mississippi and Mississippi United for Peace. His essays have appeared in *College Literature* and *Women's Studies Quarterly* among other places; his most recent poetry is in "Blue Collar Review," "Pemmican" and "Living Forge."

Introduction

Allan Eickelmann, Tom Lansford, and Eric Nelson
University of Southern Mississippi

In *Globalization and Fragmentation*, Ian Clark discusses the way in which the twin phenomena of globalization and fragmentation established the international agenda of the Twentieth Century.[1] Other scholars have described why, in the Twenty First Century, increasing globalization has led to increasing fragmentation.[2] In one sense, these twin forces are not new to the international scene, for it can be truly said that as colonialism was the precursor to globalization, that ethnic unrest was the precursor to fragmentation. However, under the old colonial system, the colonial powers were able to contain the fragmenting forces that were systemically inherent. The era of national independence, coupled with high speed information technology, has signaled a time when it is highly unlikely that the forces of fragmentation can be successfully contained. The result is a state of increasing international chaos.[3]

Every article in this anthology carries with it significant implications for the dual phenomena of globalization and fragmentation, as correspondingly these phenomena have significant implications for the concepts of justice and violence. In the Twenty First Century, questions relating to the just use of violence are taking on new meaning, precisely at a time when the use of any form of violence is being called into question in a way that would have been unimaginable prior to the emerging of a global consciousness. No doubt, the decades that lie ahead will determine to what extent violence and to what extent nonviolence will define the nature of international justice.

Historically, the legitimate use of violence has always been the right of whatever governing entity was deemed authoritative within a given geographical territory. Starting with the tribe and proceeding to the city state, the kingdom, the empire and the nation state, this has led to both border conflicts, as well as to expansionist conflicts, as some governing entity has claimed for itself the right to enforce its will in the name of imperial superiority, divine right, manifest destiny, or ethnic and racial purity. As Hobbes pointed out in *The Leviathan*, the limiting of the use of violence to some recognized governing body has, to a large extent, defined the social contract.[4]

With the rise of the modern state, the paradigm was transformed, so that only sovereign nations were seen as having the legitimate and just authority to enforce their will through the use of violence, and to do so only under strict international standards, such as those of the Geneva Convention. With the rise of globalization, two new paradigms are in contention, as both international bodies as well as ethnic and religious groups are claiming this right over against sovereign nations, doing so in the one instance in the cause of globalization and in the other instance in the cause of fragmentation. All of these contending forces have had to make certain accommodations to one another, as nations states have sought some form of international authority to legitimize their use of violence, and as international authorities have had to take into consideration extra-national groups and movements, such as the United Nations recognition of the PLO as an authoritative voice for the Palestinian people. A nation's recognition of some form of international authority, as well as an international authority's recognition of certain extra-national groups, may be given only begrudgingly, but in both instances there is a realization that the current global reality demands such an accommodation.

At the same time, there is a fledgling movement that is proposing its own paradigm that would insist that the use of any form of violence is, by its very nature, unjust. Although it is a political movement, this movement has both explicitly religious, as well as quasi-religious overtones.

To a large extent, religion has become the key player in the current dynamic, in a way that would have been inconceivable in the middle of the Twentieth Century, when it was blithely assumed that the forces of secularization would continue to erode the primacy of the religious phenomena. In recent decades, scholars such as Peter Berger have had to reverse their previous position and concede that religion is not a phenomenon that is going away any time in the near future.[5]

For example, India has witnessed the reassertion of traditional Hinduism, a tradition that possesses the possibility of both pacifism and justifiable violence. Since it is very difficult to separate the religion of India from the nation of India, it is also very difficult to separate Hinduism from Indian nationalism. Although Gandhi emphasized the passive way that permeates the Hindu notion of dharma, there is also within that same tradition a caste structure that empowers the warrior caste to exercise its karma by fulfilling one's destiny in the service of warfare. This understanding of dharma has helped to fuel sectarian strife, leaving open the question as to which element in this tradition will prevail.

Originating in India, only Buddhism, of all of the major world religions, has an unbroken history of nonviolence, given its idiom of "do no harm." However, even within Buddhism, such a completely passive stance seems to be relegated to the Samgha, the Buddhist monastic order.

As in India, the Japanese situation proves especially instructive. The reconstruction of Japan under Douglas McArthur served as a secularizing and globalizing force. Perhaps no nation has more vigorously adapted itself to the new global economy than Japan, and no economic power has been more adverse to development of military power than Japan. However, in recent decades there has been an upsurge of traditional Shinto ideology, including a glorification of the military cult. Once again in the Japanese context traditional religion is serving as a force for fragmentation.

The three religions of the Abrahamic tradition offered varied views of justifiable violence and of pacifism. Christianity certainly finds itself fragmented with regard to the question of justice and violence. In the first two centuries, of what has become known as the Common Era, Christianity celebrated passivity, not as a political statement, but as an expression of pious faithfulness to the way set forth by Jesus of Nazareth. No serious thought was given to violent resistance to the forces of Rome. Such resistance was considered to be both futile as a practical matter and unnecessary in the face of the coming Parousia. The Constantinian accommodation changed all of that, leading Augustine to set forth the principles of just war as an accommodation to human sin. For this reason, perhaps it could be better tagged as justifiable war theory.[6]

Therefore, there has remained within Christianity the notion that ultimately human warfare runs counter to the divine will. From the early decades of the Protestant Reformation, some fringe sects, such as the Mennonites, the Brethren and the Society of Friends, revived passivity as tenant of pious, filial devotion to the way of Jesus. However, it was not until the Twentieth Century that such passivity was seen as the way for Christians to forward a political agenda. Correspondingly, passive resistance has started to win adherents from among those who are in denominations and churches that historically have not claimed pacifism as part of their doctrinal stance. This is evident in the United States within certain segments of several major denominations, such as the United Methodist Church and the United Church of Christ. At the same time, there are those on both the extreme left wing of Christianity, such as Liberation Theology Movement in Latin America, and the extreme right wing of Christianity, such as the Aryan Nations Church of Jesus Christ Christian who seem to view violence as a necessary means in the fulfillment of Christ's vision.

In a similar fashion, the emergence of Islamic fundamentalism has also led to a collision with those forces within Islam that desire some form of global accommodation. This has led to the clamor for Holy War, in which violence is justified as a divine imperative. Within Islam, however, there appears to be no corresponding trajectory toward nonviolence. In fact, of all of the major founders religions, Islam is the only one in which a prize possession of the founder, and correspondingly a significant religious symbol, was the sword. This was certainly not the case for either Jesus of Nazareth, or for Siddhartha Gautama, and it may help to explain why there has been no significant nonviolent movement within Islam. Although, as Carol Hunter points out in this volume, during the struggle for Indian independence, there was a nonviolent Islamic movement that paralleled that of the Gandhi's movement.

Of course, Judaism also does not have a significant model for passive non-resistance, and given the Jewish experience of the Holocaust, it is hard to imagine how such a model could emerge anytime in the near future. Therefore, the battle for the Jewish soul seems to be a battle between the forces of Zionism that advocate Jewish nationalism, on the one hand, and the forces of secularism and humanism on the other. Perhaps this secular form of Judaism is best given expression in the Jewish Reconstructionist Movement.

Given the reality that neither Islam nor Judaism embraces a conceptual framework that would celebrate nonviolence as a means to either glorify God or to evoke social change, it is highly unlikely that any resolution to the current Palestinian question will arise without some reliance on the use of force. This is made all the more complicated given both religions' understanding that retributive action is required to ensure a proper measure of justice.

In this religious landscape, the forces of globalization and fragmentation are confronting one another around the globe. To a large extent, the emerging nonviolent movements can be seen as being lined up on the side of globalization, in that they appeal to an ethic that transcends racial, ethnic, national and religious differences. On the other hand, an appeal to religious fundamentalism and or to nationalism tends to lead the way to fragmentation.

Reinhold Niebhur lamented this state of fragmentation in his classic *Moral Man and Immoral Society,* in which he questioned if there could ever be a truly transcendent ethic that positioned the social order in such a way that political entities could arise above the mere claim of allegiance to one's clan, tribe or nation.[7] Niebhur's lament proved to be almost prophetic, being written as it was in 1932, just prior to the rise of fascism in both Europe and in Japan. It was only after World War II that nonviolent resistance emerged as a political alternative to the forced unity of such totalitarian regimes, and only in the last decade of the Twentieth Century were voices being raised, like that of Hans Kung, calling for a new global ethic that would engage both nations and religious movements in the process of seeking common ground through true dialogue.[8]

All of this has led to a redefining process, in which the old calculus of traditional Just War theory is being reworked by those who would claim that the use of violence still has some utility in the realm of international relations, over-against those who would claim that, given the current global landscape, any use of violence is, in itself, unjust. This is no more obvious than in the debate about military technology. In a previous era, military technology played little if any role in the formulization of Just War theory. This is no longer the case. The advent of weapons of mass destruction has raised the question of how it can make any sense to talk about the just use of violence. On the other hand, these same developments have also led the proponents of the just use of force to claim that modern military technology provides the means to accurately target combatants and avoid collateral damage to innocent noncombatants. This development potentially overcomes several powerful ethical challenges to the less discriminate uses of force associated with modern warfare.

Since its inception, Just War theory has found itself embroiled in an internal means-ends struggle that belies a certain logical inconsistency with the very notion of just war. Beginning with World War I, authors such as Eric Maria Remarque have raised the question as to whether or not the notion of just war is nothing more than an oxymoron.[9] This raises a further question as to whether or not this theory can be adequately reframed for the post modern world. If the answer to that question is yes, then how is that reframing process to take shape, and by whom? If the answer to the question is no, then what if any paradigm is there to replace it that would still allow for the legitimate use of force. All of this is made even more complicated by the fact that originally Just War theory was envisioned to apply only to conflicts among sovereign governments. How, if at all, can it be applied in an era of transnational religious and ethnic movements?

Given the geopolitical landscape, set forth by Clark, this volume has been edited to engage in this key debate over whether there is an appropriate utility for political violence. This collection of essays will be of interest to anyone who is concerned with the ethical mandates and dilemmas inherent in the use of both political violence and pacifism, as strategic vehicles for the advancement of a given political agenda. Also addressed are the larger cultural issues that transcend any political strategy.

Justice and Violence is organized into three thematic sections. The first, entitled "The Justice of Violence", focuses on the dual problems of justifying the use of violence and addressing the injustice of violence after the fact. In her wide-ranging contribution "Just War: An Ethic of Restraint or the Defense of Order", Valerie Morkevicius explores the concept of just war in the Hindu, Muslim and Christian traditions. Morkevicius, in her analysis, emphasizes the shared idea amongst all three traditions that the preservation of the community and the social order provide key criteria for the just use of violence. She uses this insight to advance the possibility that a stable social order is a basic human right and that as such force could justly be used in peace keeping and humanitarian operations to maintain social order. However, she at the same time notes the danger inherent in this shared view by claiming that if the idea is taken in a utilitarian fashion then there is a danger that the community will be taken as an ideal good that must be preserved at all costs. Key to this danger is that while the maintenance of a stable social order lay behind the use of violence in all three traditions, the traditions do not agree on what constitutes the 'good life' that this stability is meant to ensure.

Chris Dolan, in "Moralizing the Violence or a Just Response? The Dimensions and Limitations of the Bush Doctrine", addresses the same general question of justifying violence but focuses specifically on a particularly problematic dimension of the question, the just use of violence in offensive war. He takes as his topic American foreign policy after 9/11 in order to examine whether the threat of terrorist attack has transformed long-standing ideas about the just use of preemptive violence. The key problem that he identifies is whether the new threat of terrorism alters the traditional split within the notion of preemptive war theory between, the justifiable use of violence as a vehicle to preempt an immanent threat where no other means is possible, and the unjustifiable use of such preemptive means, which involves the use of violence to prevent a possible threat in the future. After reviewing the concepts, he establishes that while the terrorist threat leads to new challenges, it still remains desirable to avoid preventive wars, because they are often both avoidable and counterproductive as they destabilize international relations. Dolan recognizes the difficulties inherent in the threat of terrorism and the desirability of preemptive offensive military action in some cases. However, he emphasizes that over use of offensive military action will prove counter-productive and argues that the need for good and timely intelligence is paramount in avoiding preventive wars. Thus, Dolan ultimately upholds the long-standing parameters for the just use of violence in offensive wars by limiting, even in the case of terrorist threats, the use of violence to preemptive rather than preventive operations.

Susan Weldon Scott, in her contribution entitled "The President and the Congress in Concert: Declaring and Making War in the United States", takes up the question of just violence from yet another perspective when she reexamines the war powers clause of the United States Constitution. She explores its provisions through examinations of both the intent of the founders and the War Powers Resolution of 1973, and concludes that the clause has become almost meaningless, as has the formal declaration of war that lay at the center of the war powers clause. She then argues for a re-conceptualization of the war powers clause, first proposed by Brian Hewlett, which would require the congress to use its power in the constitution to write its own reasoned declarations of war independent of the executive branch. She argues that in so doing Congress would ensure that America only entered into clearly defined wars with clearly defined grievances and objectives – hereby avoiding the worst excesses of American foreign policy over the past century. Moreover, she argues that, although this role was not clearly envisioned by the founders, that it would help to address the Founder's original intent to ensure democratic accountability in all areas of government.

Finally, in his contribution entitled "A Political Calculus of Apology: Japan and Its Neighbors", Girma Negash alters the parameters of the debate by focusing on the question of how a state atones for unjust violence after the fact. In this essay, Negash addresses the requirements and problems associated with states apologizing and reconciling themselves to their victims. To explore these issues Negash considers the case of Japan, and especially the problem of comfort women who were forced into sex slavery during World War II. He considers both the stages of apology necessary to reach reconciliation and the difficulties states have in offering complete apologies. The contingent circumstances that shaped Japan's apologies to comfort women offer a particularly revealing consideration of the difficulties surrounding state apologies. Collectively, these four contributions address, in different ways, the timeless problem of if or when violence, which clearly is part of human interaction, can be justified or atoned for.

The second section entitled "Violence as Injustice" explores the related issues of the mandate of pacifism, the utility of pacifism and the moral dilemmas that arise as a result of using violence to advance political goals. Carol Hunter, in her contribution "Power to Destroy, Power to Heal: Violence, State Power and Paradigm Shifts for Peace", examines the current institutional and cultural support in the United States for the base belief in "redemptive violence" – the idea that war can be a force for good. Through a wide-ranging examination of cultural, political and religious examples, she shows how American society promotes the assumption that violence and war, under the right circumstances, are considered good. She argues that to overcome this inbuilt predisposition to violence, as a means of achieving political aims, requires a massive paradigm shift. As a society, we need to expand our understanding of power as coercive force to the idea that power lay with the people, and that even tyrants and dictators cannot exercise power without the acquiescence of the people. To accomplish this paradigm shift, Hunter argues that people need to be reeducated by actively teaching the population about political non-violence, using examples of successful non-violent action. Hunter laments the lack of attention to successful non-violent movements, and argues that through careful consideration of their accomplishments, activists can develop even more sophisticated tactics for non-violent action in the future.

In his contribution "The Ethics of Living American Primacy, or, Towards a Global Jim Crow, and Its Discontents", Will Watson takes a similar approach to Hunter in order to argue that "American primacy" and "global ethics" are ultimately opposed. For Watson, the very language of modern American primacy reveals a coded imperialism that historically has led to an inequality detrimental to the lives of peoples influenced by the dominant power. Watson argues that inequality is unethical and therefore global primacy cannot be ethical – no matter how American policy makers try to frame their dominance in the language of freedom and equality. Watson identifies an alternative language that unlike the language of American primacy would provide a genuine global ethics. It would privilege cooperation, consent and consensus in such a way that it would ensure the restraint of governments as much as those governed. In exploring his theme of double talk in the language of American primacy, he compares the language of global capitalism with the realities of global exploitation. In the end, Watson views the relation of the concepts of global ethics and American primacy as ironic, through comparisons to both the Jim Crow South and the realities of Soviet Socialism. Through these comparisons, Watson draws out the idea of extra-ethics promoted by the powerful and harmful to society as a whole, but especially for certain groups in society. In the case of American primacy, Watson sees a two tiered set of global ethics: one for the population in general and another for the military and financial aristocracies that define the system.

Angela Gordon and Tobias Gibson, in "The Fist of Pacifism", provide an ethnographic case study of the peace movement in Saint Louis Missouri against the United States-led invasion of Iraq in 2003. They use this case study as an opportunity to explore the usefulness of both moral and pragmatic rationales for and against the use of violence. They then explore the increase in the use of violent means of protest amongst Saint Louis peace activists in the months leading up to the invasion of Iraq, in order to argue that any benefits that accrued from this violence were short-lived due to increased suppression by civil authorities, made possible in part by the ideological (and sometimes physical) rift among peace-seekers. Within this one revealing case study Gordon and Gibson are able to examine both the utility of pacifism and the moral dilemmas inherent in the use of violence in the pursuit of peace.

In his essay entitled "Violence and Non-Violence as Constitutional Argument: An Analysis of the 1963 Civil Rights Demonstrations in Birmingham, Alabama", Neal Allen addresses both the utility of non-violent action and the political cost of using violence against non-violent protesters. Allen argues that both the non-violent protestors and the violent police reaction against their protests were in fact extensions of the constitutional arguments following the *Brown vs. Board of Education* decision of 1954. He argues that this transformative ruling by the Court changed the legal landscape and set the terms for the debate to follow, but that much of the debate took place in a broader less Court-controlled process. In part, white southern segregationists used the press to construct an alternative constitutional defense of their positions. But these constitutional arguments spilled violently into the streets when white segregationist officials were faced with an alternative constitutional argument in the form of rights-based non-violent protests of demonstrators. The violence unleashed on these protestors constituted a political argument in support of segregation, but the horrific scenes caught on television resulted in legislation in the form of the 1964 Civil Rights Act that settled the political debate opened by the *Brown* ruling. Here the utility of non-violent action is placed in a wider context to show how the violent suppression of peaceful protest led to success for the non-violent activists in the wider political and legal arena.

Fred Smith, in "Jack Rocks, Earrings and the Occupation of Moss #3: Emblems of the Struggle for Decency in the Appalachian Coal Fields", offers a revealing case study of the adoption of non-violent political action in the face of the failure of violent acts. He takes as his subject the transformation of miner strike tactics from the violence that punctuated previous unsuccessful strikes to the aggressive non-violent tactics adopted by Appalachia miners in the late 1980s. The miner's change of tactics proved important as they found that their non-violent occupations of mine sites garnered sympathetic support from the local population and positive media attention that brought outside arbitration of the dispute. Through this case study Smith brings new insight into the utility of non-violent tactics to secure change in a context where violence had failed in the past.

The final section entitled "Beyond Justice and Injustice", gives voice to questions that transcend the categories of justice and injustice, violence and pacifism. Bryan McKnight in his contribution entitled "A Case of Communist Indoctrination and American Enticement during the Korean War", focuses upon the experience of twenty-three American soldiers who in September 1953 initially chose to remain with their captors rather than accept repatriation. By tracing the American government's campaign first to entice these prisoners to return and later its efforts to punish those prisoners who in the end opted to return, McKnight explores the conflicting natures of liberty and power during the McCarthy era. McKnight's assessment shifts the question of the justice of violence beyond its usual limits, as the liberty of these American citizens to embrace the communist system of their captors became an unexpected outcome of the use of force by the United States in an ideological war against communism.

Robert Pauly's "From Rollback to Preemption: A Comparison of the Reagan and Bush Doctrines" also takes a historical approach to the subject when it reassesses the last two shifts towards activist United States foreign policy. He leaves behind the philosophical and ethical issues of justice and injustice, which are so prominent in this volume, in order to focus on the practical effectiveness of activist foreign policies in increasing the security of the United States. He notes that, while both Reagan and Bush used similar rhetorical justifications for their activist policies, the political and military threats that the United States faced during these two administrations varied significantly. Nevertheless, despite these differences, he concludes that Ronald Reagan's activist policy was an overall success; and, while recognizing that it is too early to offer a full assessment of Bush's policy, Pauley argues that Bush's use of violence in his war on terror and his preemptive invasion of Iraq have contributed positively to America's domestic and international security.

In his contribution entitled "The 2003 U.S. Invasion of Iraq: Militarism in the Service of Geopolitics", Edward Byrne also addresses Bush's activist foreign policy as an ethical issue, when he asks whether it is possible to assess the justness of a war before its outbreak. Byrne argues that there was a disconnect between the justification for the preemptive war on Iraq, as presented by the Bush administration, and the underlying geopolitical and economic motivations that provided the real driving forces. This problem of rhetoric masking unjust motives provides a pressing need for ethicists to find ways of judging the rationales for war, despite problems of securing information and the active subterfuge of leaders before a war begins. While he admits that the challenge to the ethicist is significant in these circumstances, Byrne urges them to seek information beyond what a government offers by analyzing the broad strategic papers commissioned by the government in the past. In the case of the preemptive war in Iraq, Byrne notes with hind sight that the United States government had for decades declared its willingness to use its military forces preemptively to secure the Middle East oil supply. He also cautions that Ethicists must seek to neutralize the rhetoric of righteousness that can shape an ethicist's opinion of the struggle. While he offers hope that real time analysis of just wars can be developed, he accepts that philosophers are still refining their methods of reaching these decisions before violence begins. Here Byrne, like the other contributors to this section, seeks to reshape the question to move beyond the justice of violence to the assessment of just war before it has occurred.

Helena Cristini, in the final contribution to this section entitled "Beyond Politics", argues that violence arises not just from political and economic factors but existential causes as well. The key problem for Cristini is that secularized culture no longer provides the necessary values that are required for both personal and corporate peacemaking. Through this argument, she moves beyond justice and injustice to argue that a cultural transformation is required in order to overcome political considerations that mandate violence. Cristini offers more than just a diagnosis of the problem, as she argues that a transformation in the current secularized educations system is required to bring about this cultural transformation. Because ethics are the foundation of any political philosophy, she argues that the promotion of spiritual values found in the Judeo-Christian, Islamic and Indian religious traditions can provide individuals with the values needed to live happily and ultimately to transform social relations in such a way that the need for violence is obviated. Through this line of argument, Cristini seeks to redefine the parameters of debate by placing potential actions in the broader context of the ethical and spiritual state of a society.

A concluding note is provided by Hans Kung in his article, "No Clash, but Dialogue Among Religions and Nations: Towards a New Paradigm of International Relations". Here Kung begins by discussing the historical basis for such a new paradigm, beginning with the vision set forth by Woodrow Wilson in 1918. Next he explains why this new paradigm necessitates an end to political violence and a board consensus on shared values, resulting in an international political and religious ethic of humankind. In essence, Kung is seeking the common ground of a new global ethic, based on a shared human consciousness, which can overcome the ethical split lamented by Niebuhr. As Kung sees it, such an ethic requires a consensual participation and a consensual development that can only be acquired through non-violent means. Therefore, Kung criticizes the administration of G. W. Bush for trying to enforce such an ethic through the use of military force. Kung sees such an approach as being doomed to failure. According to Kung, first and foremost, a new global ethic will require serious dialogue among the world's major religions, for as he puts it, "peace among the religions is a presupposition of peace among the nations." Finally, Kung outlines why he feels there is sufficient ground for such an ethic, based on the shared values of the world's major religions.

As we move deeper into the Twenty First Century, the contradictory forces of globalization and fragmentation will make it increasingly crucial to give serious consideration to the issues that have been raised in this volume. The beginning of the century has been witness to increasing sectarian unrest, intertribal warfare, ethnic cleansing, and a reassertion of various national sovereignties backed by military might. Whether or not these trends will continue to the end of the century remains to be seen. In any event, it should be clear to all that a new ethic of political violence, as well as a new ethic of nonviolence will be in contention for global primacy. May the reader find this current work a helpful guide in approaching the ethical issues that will shape political, historical, social, philosophical and religious discourse in the decades that loom ahead.

Many hands have gone into the creation of this volume. The editors would especially like to thank the following people Mark Sedgwick deserves special recognition for his diplomacy and attention to detail in the compilation of the final manuscript. We must also recognize Rick Meyers and Robert Jordan who labored many hours with Mark. Alice Nelson needs to be recognized for her computer savvy. She displayed a skill that helped to unfray the nerves of these perplexed editors. Finally, Kirstin Howgate of Ashgate Publishing needs to be recognized for her prompt response to any of our enquiries and also for her encouragement and support of this project. A final note of appreciation is given to Ms. Joan Ford, the recently retired admistrative assistant for the college of Arts and Letters at the Gulf Park Campus of the University of Southern Mississippi. This volume is dedicated to Ms. Ford who served USM for over twenty years, providing incomparable support to the faculty, including the editors of this volume. She graciously treated us far better than we deserved.

Notes

1 Ian Clark, *Globalization and Fragmentation: International Relations in The Twentieth Century* (Oxford, Oxford University Press, 1997).

2 Geir Lundestad "Why Does Globalization Encourage Fragmentation" (*International Relations*, 41/2 (June 2004): 265-276.

3 In a lecture delivered at the Gulf Park campus of the University of Southern Mississippi on 2 November 2002, David Lowry described the process by which the conflict between globalization and fragmentation leads to an increasing state of chaos that he believes can only be resolved through a system of democratic values that win global acceptance.

4 For Hobbes the exclusive reason for establishing civil society was for the protection of the individual who would find life apart from such a society absolutely intolerable. This meant that the individual could rely on the force of governing authority to control the chaos that would most certainly erupt if each individual were to engage in the futile process of attempting to guarantee their own security.

5 Berger's shifting viewpoint can be first detected in Berger, Peter *A Rumor of Angels: Modern Society and the Rediscovery of the Supernatural* (Garden City, New York: Doubleday, 1970).

6 Augustine had a dual concern; first to protect the faith against a barbarian onslaught and second to provide a vehicle that would justify the full participation of the Roman

military in a new Christian state. Given his notion that one's attitude was paramount in determining one's state of grace, it was a natural progression for him to deem that an attitude of peace was more significant than the mere act of peace. For fuller treatment see Roland H. Bainton, *Christian Attitudes Toward War and Peace* (New York: Abingdon, 1960), especially pp. 91-100.

7   Reinhold Niebuhr. *Moral Man and Immoral Society* (New York: Charles Scribner's Sons, 1932).

8   In a paper presented as the conclusion to this volume, Kung sets forth his vision as to how such a new paradigm might take shape.

9   Remarque reflected on his own experience following World War I, and in so doing he struck a cord that resulted in an international pacifist movement among an intellectual core. The first English version of his classic polemic against modern war was published in 1928. Erica Maria Remarque. *All Quiet on The Western Front* (London: Putnam Books, 1928).

PART 1

The Justice of Violence

Chapter 1

Just War

An Ethic of Restraint or the Defense of Order?

Valerie O. F. Morkevicius
University of Chicago

> Holy community and holy war are related ideas – not necessarily because holiness
> makes for hostility toward foreign nations, more likely because community does.[1]
>
> Michael Walzer

The defense of social order seems to lie at the heart of the just war traditions in all
of the world's major religions. Domestic stability is perceived as one of the highest
values, for it is only within a well-ordered, stable society that human spirituality
can reach its highest potential. Such domestic stability is predicated on two types
of order. Order within society – in terms of a just socio-political system, usually
unified under one legitimate ruler – is necessary so that the human community may
flourish and that the religion in question can be practiced most faithfully. Likewise,
some sort of ordered relationship between societies (or states) is necessary to
ensure the survival of the domestic community itself.

When the importance of order is highlighted, the logic behind just war thinking
takes on a different cast. Customarily, just war regulations are seen as attempts to
limit the evils of war, alleviating some of war's destructiveness. Perhaps because
of the excessive brutality of wars in the twentieth century, we tend to conflate
war's destructive nature with the high toll on human life. But death may not be the
worst evil of war. Rather, the concern with restricting the frequency and scope of
wars via just war principles may instead reflect an interest in ensuring that a
particular social order and stability are not destroyed during the course of the war,
so that a war for the defense of the community does not result in the destruction of
the community's potential to live up to its ideals.[2] Prevention or reduction of
violence may not serve only as a good in itself, but rather as a means to an end –
the defense of a just social order. This is not to say that human life is not seen as
sacred or worthy of protection, but rather that the life of the community as a whole
may be of an even higher priority. When the preservation of a certain society is the
base, the focus of the theory then becomes self-defense and the meting out of "just
punishment" when others' infringe on the society's rights.

This paper will explore this perspective on the just war tradition.[3] It will begin firstly by drawing on insights from Hindu and Islamic thinking about war, where the emphasis on protecting domestic stability and order is emphasized to a greater extent. Second, it will re-examine Christian just war in light of these new ideas, judging to what degree the same logics might be operative in this case. Finally, it will discuss the possible implications of understanding just war theory in terms of its emphasis on social order rather than on its violence mitigating aspects.

It was in reading Hindu and Islamic philosophers' discussion of just war that the centrality of defending the community first occurred to me, although the idea can also be found in such canonical Christian just war authors as St. Augustine. Since the concern with protecting the community, and thus ensuring the possibility of a just social order, is more evident in Hindu and Islamic thinking, it seems like a good place to begin exploring this concept. Each of the subsections below will begin by establishing the centrality and importance of the concern with order, before examining how this concern shapes each tradition's classification of the just causes and means of war.

Hinduism: Order as the Foundation for Any Just Society

This concern with stability and order is perhaps the most evident in Hinduism.[4] Man's relation with society is "the basic social relation," morally prior and superior to all other relationships.[5] Order itself is intimately connected with force and violence: "the existence of all fine and noble life, of higher morality, or all happiness, of all order, depends entirely on the basis of force."[6] In nature, stronger animals prey upon the weaker. The same would be true in human society if it were not for force justly used on behalf of the weaker. As one Hindu text reads, "Force was ordained by the creator himself, for protecting religion and wealth, for the happiness of all the four orders, and for making them righteous and modest."[7] The preservation of order is so important that "non-destruction of the wicked is as great a sin as the destruction of righteousness."[8]

Although the internal life of contemplation, understanding and ultimately enlightenment are of the utmost importance, men (and gods) must act relentlessly to maintain order. Philosophy and discipline, renunciation and action, are not inherently contradictory – wise men must avoid such a simplistic duality and apply both correctly, according to the circumstances. In fact, at some points action may even be superior to contemplation.[9] As Lord Krishna reminds Arjuna in the *Bhagavad Gita*: "These worlds would collapse if I did not perform action; I would create disorder in society, living beings would be destroyed." [10] Following in his footsteps, "wise men should act with detachment to preserve the world."[11]

The use of force to ensure order is not only a right (as in the Christian *jus ad bellum* tradition of self-defense), but also a *duty*. In traditional Hindu ethics, duties are delegated to different social classes, and the duty to protect society falls to the warrior class, the ksatriya.[12] Inherent to men of this class are "heroism, fiery energy, resolve, skill, refusal to retreat in battle, charity, and majesty in conduct."[13] As the highest representative of the warrior class, it is the king's duty to use force against those internal and external enemies who would threaten the just and righteous order of society. This concept is expressed in numerous Dharmasutras, or ancient Hindu law codes. These laws were not simply secular, but also carried religious sanction.[14] For example, the Dharmasutra of Vasistha states that while "a Brahmin or a Vaisya may take up arms to defend himself and to prevent the mixing of classes, a Ksatriya, on the other hand, should do so all the time, because it is incumbent upon himself to protect the people."[15] Likewise the Code of Manu lists the ksatriya's duties as "protection of the people, study of Veda, offering sacrifices and bestowing of gifts and abstention from attaching himself to the sensual pleasures;" since their function is to protect the people – indeed all of Creation, warriors and kings come from this class.[16] In modern times, the caste system is outdated, and the injustices that too easily stemmed from it prevent any nostalgia. But it is not too much of a logical leap to imagine that the modern political elite could be seen as taking on the ksatriya mantle, as a way of modernizing the theory.

The ksatriya's duty to act to restore order is emphasized in Hindu mythology. In the *Bhagavad Gita* chapter of the greatest Hindu epic, the *Ramayana,* Lord Krishna exhorts Arjuna to "look to [his] own duty; do not tremble before it; nothing is better for a warrior than a battle of sacred duty."[17] Classifying the battle ahead as a "sacred duty," Krishna warns that abandoning such a duty would not only lead to shame and slander among men, but would also be in itself a morally evil act.[18] If men fail to perform their sacred duty and do not act to preserve order when "chaos prevails," then Krishna appears to inspire men of virtue to their duty, and to protect them while destroying men who do evil.[19] Indeed, the *Bhagavad Gita* itself, as a conversation between Krishna and Arjuna, is meant to encourage Arjuna to do his duty and to fight the battle without fear or guilt.

The fact that the use of force is married to the defense of order can also be seen in the way that wars are classified in several important Hindu texts. The types of wars that are considered just reflect the importance of defending the community, for the sake of upholding a just order. In Kautilya's *Arthasastra,*[20] for example, Indra divides just wars into four classes: "(1) wars caused by invasion of one's territory, (2) wars caused by something done by others prejudicial to the exercise of the regal powers, (3) wars resulting from some dispute about boundaries, and (4) wars caused by some disturbance in the *mandala*."[21] Each type of war relates in some way to the restoration (or preservation) of order. It is important to note that while there is religious sanction for the preservation of order via force, there is no mention of wars of religion in the sacred texts, and thus no justification for fighting in order to propagate Hinduism abroad.[22]

Furthermore, although war may be necessary for the sake of order, it should always be the last resort. In the words of the *Arthasastra*, "Even when the advantages of peace and war are equal one should prefer peace, for war causes loss of power and wealth and is troublesome and sinful."[23] War inevitably tears at the fibers of a well-ordered society. It is also evident that for Kautilya "peace is the very basis for the existence and continuation of any political system," and that peace is the best means for obtaining the ideal of progress.[24] Peace is the environment in which human goodness and spirituality thrive; peace is the necessary foundation for the development of society, which is seen in Hinduism as one of the highest goods. But true peace only exists when there is order – therefore, in times of extreme need force may be used for the sake of order and peace.

The need for order is not only reflected in the just causes for war in the Hindu tradition, but also in the means by which wars may be justly fought. In general, Hindu sacred texts and philosophical and legal treatises on war uphold the principle of non-combatant immunity. Helpless people cannot be slain, whether they be innocent civilians, prisoners of war, or even combatants who have lost their weapons or are running away. In the *Sauptika*, it is asserted that "one should not cast weapons upon kin, Brahmins, kings, women, friends, one's own mother, one's own preceptor, a weak woman, an idiot, a blind man, a sleeping man, a terrified man, one just risen from sleep, an intoxicated person, and one that is heedless."[25] Additionally, the severity of the violence should be limited, and kings should not take advantage of their military superiority. The *Mahabharata* suggests, "the victor should protect the land newly conquered, from acts of aggression. He should not causes his troops to pursue to much the routed foe ... Warriors of courage do not wish to strike them that run away with speed."[26] There is a deep-seated concern with fighting fairly, in particular that both parties should be more or less equally matched, and that "no unfair advantage is to be taken of the opponent's weakness."[27] Together, these restrictions on combat have the effect of ensuring that certain basic social norms are upheld even during battle. By preventing the killing of those who are unable (for whatever reason) to defend themselves – and thus not really a threat to others – these norms morally separate killing during war from murder and treachery, which would clearly upset the social order.

Finally, it is worth noting that the caste system was to be upheld during wartime as well. The divisions between the major classes were viewed in traditional Hinduism as playing an important role in ensuring a well-ordered society that functions well as a unit, while simultaneously protecting the interests and rights of each class. For this reason, there was (in ancient times) a prohibition against mixing classes, as that could lead to disorder. Likewise, in wartime each class had a different set of responsibilities. As mentioned earlier, the kingly class is entrusted with the duty of protecting the community; so ideally, killing is only supposed to be done by kings – and only kings should be the victims. Because Brahmins are responsible for preserving and upholding the religious traditions, laws and rituals, they are to be protected as much as possible; therefore the killing of a Brahmin is the greatest crime. For without the Brahmins, the ethical order of society would be undermined. These roles as *castes* may no longer be relevant today, but in so far as these roles reflect different, valuable segments of society that still exist (albeit in far more flexible forms), it could be fruitful to imagine how these special profession-based responsibilities and protections could be added into our understanding of just war thought.

Islam: Preserving and Extending a Just Order

This concern with preserving an ideal social order is predominant within Islamic thinking as well. As in Hinduism, there is a tacit understanding that force may be necessary in order for justice to prevail. Ibn Taymiya, an eighth century scholar, argued "God does not permit, in effect, to put to death certain creatures except in view of the public good. He said: 'Discord is more frightening than death.' (II, 214) In other words: killing is a source of evil and disorder, but evil and disorder, which give birth to the discord engendered by the infidels, are even more grave."[28]

Consequently, an important duty of the just leader is to enforce the laws and provide incentive for obedience and restraint. Ibn Khaldun, perhaps the world's first critical historian, wrote that "evil is the quality that is closest to man when he fails to improve his customs and when religion is not used as the model to improve him ... evil qualities in man are injustice and mutual aggression. He who casts his eye upon the property of his brother will lay his hand upon it to take it, unless there is a restraining force to hold him back."[29] If the incentive to obey does not prove strong enough, and the law is violated, the transgressor must be punished. In the words of Al Farabi, when an individual "harms the city, he is also unjust and is [to be] prevented. To prevent many [from doing that], there is need to inflict evils and punishments ... So, when the evildoer gets a portion of evil, that is justice. When it is excessive, that is an injustice upon him personally; and when it falls short, that is an injustice upon the inhabitants of the city."[30]

One fundamental goal of Islam, in contrast to Hinduism, is to spread not only its message, but also its system of social and political organization. Classical Islamic thought distinguishes clearly between the *dar al Islam*, the world of peace where Islam has taken root, and the *dar al harb*, the outside world of war. The word Islam itself means peace. As Khadduri points out, "the territory of war was the object, not the subject, of Islam, and it was the duty of the Imam, head of the Islamic state, to extend the validity of its Law and Justice to the unbelievers under the Islamic public order.[31] It is important to note the distinction between spreading the social and political order of Islam and spreading the religion itself. The Koran makes it quite clear that there can be no compulsion in matters of faith. Therefore jihad is not strictly speaking about converting people to Islam: "God commanded the believers to spread His word and establish his Law and Justice over the world ... Religion, however, was and still is to be carried out by peaceful means, as there should be no compulsion in the spread of the word of God. The expansion of the state, carried out by the jihad, was an entirely different matter."[32]

Furthermore, Kelsay argues that in Islam, peace is the product of order with justice, not just the absence of strife.[33] Fundamental to the Islamic understanding of just war is the "notion of the community of believers (*umma*), that the Muslims considered to be the most perfect entity in the world;" this community is seen as so special and valuable that "God assigned it a function, a mission: to establish its rights on the earth, to install the supremacy of the true religion."[34] It is important to note, however, that the meaning of peace is understood differently in the Sunni and Shiite communities. In Sunni Islam, peace refers to an attempt to discover the way of God, and is thus associated both with shari'a (and making decisions consistent with religious law) and with the establishment of a "political entity that acknowledges Islam provides the best and most secure peace available to humanity."[35] In Shii'a thought, only defensive wars are considered just. Thus, technically speaking, there can be no jihad to expand the realm of Islam, but only wars to protect it.

Consequently, in addition to the more well-known domestic shari'a legal system, Islamic jurisprudence also developed the siyar, a special branch of sacred law outlining the just conduct of relations with non-Islamic states (and non-Islamic religious communities within its own territory). The *siyar* covers not only rules of war, but also laws regulating peaceful relations with other nations, revealing Islam's efforts to "cope with the problem of constructing a stable and an ordered world society."[36] Conceptually, the *siyar* was meant to be only temporary, until the message of Islam had become universal. Accordingly, "if the ideal of Islam were ever achieved, the *raison d'être* of a Muslim law of nations … would be non-existent."[37] In general, the argument is that stability and a just social order can best be established through Islam, thus the need for expanding the reach of the Islamic community. In many ways, Islam represents a melding of religion with social and political organization, making defense of one tantamount to defense of the others. Indeed, early Islam did not make a clear distinction between society and state.[38]

In Islam, the primary acceptable cause for war is to defend (or possibly expand) the Muslim community. With all the emphasis in recent times on martyrdom and the glories awaiting the individual martyr, it is easy to forget the purpose of jihad is to serve the community as a whole. Ibn Taymiya argued that among all the works that bring merit, jihad is the greatest as "jihad presents a utility of general order, for he who does it *as for the others*, as well as from both a spiritual and temporal point of view."[39] Al Farabi makes a similar point: "And the warrior killed in warfare is singled out to be praised for sacrificing himself on behalf of the inhabitants of the city and for his boldness before death."[40] The lives of individual members of the community are valuable, not to be wasted or thrown away chaotically. Thus, one should only risk death when "there is greater usefulness to the inhabitants of the city by his dying than by his surviving."[41] Indeed, when the community is threatened, jihad becomes an even greater obligation. Ibn Kudamah lays out this distinction quite clearly: "Legal war (*jihad*) is a duty of social obligation (*fard-kifaya*); when a group of Muslims assure it in a satisfying fashion, the others are dispensed of it ... *Jihad* becomes a duty of strict personal obligation for all Muslims who find themselves in the lines or whose country is [invaded] by the enemy."[42] Ibn Taymiya similarly argues that "when the war is offensive, it constitutes a duty of collective obligation (*fard kifaya*): part of the Muslims assure its execution while the others find themselves free ...When Muslims are attacked, the war becomes a defensive war; it constitutes a duty of individual obligation (*fard'ain*) for all the believers, even if they are not personally attacked. It is considered like a duty of solidarity and cooperative help."[43]

Thus, just wars are fought for the good of the community of faith. In addition to defense, legitimate causes for war include "sympathetic" wars aimed at aiding Muslims under foreign dominion, punitive wars for punishing hypocrisy, apostasy, rebellion and other internal crimes, and idealistic wars for permitting Islam to triumph over other religions and to establish a worthy community.[44] In the words of Ibn Taymiya, "the basis for permissible fighting is jihad which strives to uphold religion, and make the word of God supreme ... Nonetheless, some have argued that the status of unbelief, in itself, merits execution ... The first opinion, however, is more correct because we fight those who fight us when we seek to spread the word of God."[45] What all these various types of wars have in common is that they all are protective in nature.

A closer look at Al Farabi's discussion of just wars makes this clear. Just as a ruler must punish individual lawbreakers in his own city, he must also defend the city's rights against outsiders. Wars may be fought with just cause for the sake of "earning a good for the city," ensuring that others give the city "justice and equity," to "punish them for a crime they perpetrated – lest they revert to something like it and lest others venture against the city in emulation of them," and of course for defense.[46] Interestingly, even mass killing may be justified, if it is necessary for the safety of the people: "warring against them to annihilate them in the entirely and to root them out thoroughly because their survival is a harm for the inhabitants of the city is also earning a good for the inhabitants of the city."[47]

Secular wars, fought not to defend the religion, but to accomplish some other political or strategic goal, are not considered just. Al Farabi describes unjust wars as those fought by a ruler "against a people only to humiliate them, make them submissive," out of desire for more power or honor, or out of sheer capriciousness, or out of fury.[48] Ibn Khaldun also rules out jealousy, envy and hostility as legitimate causes for violence.[49] This is parallel in many ways to the Christian concept of right intention in war fighting.

Because a just war is fought for the sake of universalizing or defending Islam, the way it is fought must reflect those high ideals. First of all, war must be declared openly, and if the war is fought against unbelievers, they must be offered the chance to surrender and (literally) join the world of peace by accepting Islam. As Ibn Taymiya explains, "Whoever has received the call of the Prophet, inviting him to embrace the religion which God charged him to transmit, and who refuses it, must in fact be fought until there no longer exists any schism and the entire religion is God's."[50] This serves to emphasize the fact that the purpose of jihad in Islam is to unite humanity under a particular social and religious system.

Order and discipline must be enforced within the Muslim army: "Prescriptions must be carefully observed and strictly executed. War is not made, in Muslim law, for the purpose of destroying goods, nor for killing human beings."[51] Thus, Khadduri argues that jihadists are forbidden to shed more blood or destroy more property than is absolutely necessary; going to extremes would compromise the true mission, which is to spread a just socio-political order.[52] Al Shaybani cites the behavior of the Prophet Mohammed, and explains that fighting in the "Path of God" prohibits cheating, or committing treachery, as well as mutilating anyone or killing children.[53] Soldiers violating these rules of engagement may be subject to stiff punishments themselves, including the death penalty.

Just as there is a distinction in Islamic thought between the world of peace and the world of war, there are separate rules applicable to wars in each contact. Wars against Muslims (*harb al-bugha*) are to be fought differently than wars against non-believers (*harb al-kuffar*). There are binding regulations governing wars amongst Muslims that are not necessarily applicable when fighting unbelievers, such as not executing fugitives, wounded enemy combatants, prisoners of war, and women and children; in wars against Muslims, property may not be taken as spoils, nor may means of mass destruction be used, unless absolutely necessary.[54] Nonbelievers, on the other hand, once they have rejected a fair invitation to adopt Islam, are judged to "wrongfully and inexcusably rejected the truth, and waived away some of their rights."[55] But not all of them. Noncombatant immunity generally remains, but prisoners of war may be executed if they would be an encumbrance on the army.[56] Although wars against nonbelievers are to be conducted in accordance with Islamic virtues, Kelsay explains that "if it is important to fight, than it is important to win. And, if strategic conditions lead to actions that appear to violate the rules of war, then the necessity of winning provides an excusing condition for the Muslim armies. Indeed, one could say that the fault for excessive enemy casualties devolves upon the enemy leaders."[57]

Christianity: A Troubled Arrival at the Defense of Order

Although this concept of security and the need for social order has been a theme in Christian just war thinking since St. Augustine's times, it has been downplayed in favor of an emphasis on the presumption against killing. Nonetheless, just as in the Hindu and Islamic theorists discussed thus far, early Christian just war thought became deeply concerned with the preservation of the community. Augustine himself argues that "true justice is found only in that commonwealth whose founder and ruler is Christ."[58] God is the source of all justice and order, and thus these values can only truly flourish in a community that has a right relationship with God. For Christian just war thinkers, however, the relationship between the state and the faith is more problematic and complex than in Islam, for example. The state was seen with suspicion, only needed because of man's separation from God and inherently likely to be corrupt and persecutory. Ultimately, "the legitimacy of the power of the State is only a function of its capacity to do good, that is to say, to make reign an order propitious for the accomplishment of the divine will."[59] Perhaps at the root of the distinction between Christianity and Islam on the question of just war is indeed the different ways in which each faith viewed the state from the very beginning. Although Muhammad "did not establish any distinction between religious action and political or military action," Jesus suggested that the two should be held separate (give unto Caesar what is Caesar's).[60]

Although even the fundamental texts of Christianity (i.e., the New Testament) develop the idea of a godly society, they also stress a policy of non-violence, and the reality of an oppressed and stateless faith inside a powerful (and militaristic) empire reinforced this tendency towards pacifism. It is not until Christianity becomes a powerful force within the Roman Empire that the question of a just war really emerges. In a sense, "the notion of the just war ... is nothing but a concession accorded to the State acting for the common good."[61]

The tension between this essentially pacifistic beginning and the realpolitik of a dominant religion in a large state is clearly evident in Augustine, and in later thinkers as well. Thus, the original purpose of war in Christian philosophy was not to extend a Christian state and re-order the world according to its principles, but instead to protect the state against the incursions of outsiders who would threaten to destroy it. Indeed, Augustine was forced to overcome his pacifist tendencies and admit "the real and concrete danger which the barbarian invasions presented, threatening to destroy roman civilization and the institutions of the Church."[62] This concern persisted into the Middle Ages, leading Aquinas to assert that "it is sometimes honest and meritorious to wage war; for it is said that 'if someone die for the true faith and the salvation of his country, or in defense of Christians, he will receive from God a heavenly reward.'"[63]

After all, a sort of domestic peace is necessary to permit the development of higher order values, such as faith. Consequently, Augustine points out that just as "the earthly city, whose life is not based on faith, aims at an earthly peace, and it limits the harmonious agreement of citizens concerning the giving and obeying of orders to the establishment of a kind of compromise," the Heavenly City "must needs make use of this peace also, until this mortal state, for which this kind of peace is essential, passes away."[64] Likewise, Aquinas views preserving the health of the commonwealth as essential "to prevent the slaughter of many and innumerable other ills both temporal and spiritual."[65] The community is a "special kind of good," which must be defended; consequently war may sometimes be just but sedition cannot be.[66] This attitude persists in modern just war thinking. Michael Walzer, for example, asserts "when states are attacked, it is their members who are challenged, not only in their lives, but also in the sum of things they value most, including the political association they have made."[67] Ultimately, if people were "not morally entitled to choose their form of government and shape the policies that shape their lives, external coercion would not be a crime."[68]

Augustine also clearly associates peace with order. In his view, peace arises out of right relationships and good order. Thus:

> peace between mortal man and God is an ordered obedience, in faith, in subjection to an everlasting law; peace between men is an ordered agreement of mind with mind; the peace of a home is the ordered agreement among those who live together about giving and obeying orders; the peace of the Heavenly City is as perfectly ordered and perfectly harmonious fellowship in the enjoyment of God …; the peace of the whole universe is the tranquility of order – and order is the arrangement of things equal and unequal in a pattern which assigns to each its proper position.[69]

Augustine's concern for order is evident in his argument that war is a tool of punishment. He writes, "God's providence constantly uses war to correct and chasten the corrupt morals of mankind, as it also uses such afflictions to train men in a righteous and laudable way of life."[70] Similarly, "the violence which assails good men to test them, to cleanse and purify them, effects in the wicked their condemnation, ruin and annihilation."[71] Just as Al Farabi would later argue that a good leader has an obligation to punish lawbreakers, Augustine asserts that although it may be justifiable to refrain from correcting wrongdoers if to do so would make them worse or make it more difficult for weak but good people to live a godly life, it is not acceptable for the good and the wise members of society to be "nevertheless indulgent to the sins of others, which they ought to reprehend and reprove, because they are concerned to avoid giving offense to them, in case they should harm themselves in respect of things which may be rightly and innocently enjoyed by good men, but which they desire more than is right for those who are strangers in this world."[72] Likewise, if one fails to correct another because of fear that one's "safety and reputation might be endangered or destroyed," one is selfishly acting out of self-interest instead of caring about the well being of others.[73] Ultimately, "the duty of anyone who would be blameless includes not only doing no harm to anyone but also restraining a man from sin or punishing his sin, so that either the man who is chastised may be corrected by his experience, or others may be deterred by his example."[74]

Just as one has the duty to punish the individual wrongdoer, wars must be fought to undo or punish wrongs committed on the scale of states. "For it is the injustice of the opposing side that lays on the wise man the duty of waging wars," writes Augustine.[75] Aquinas shares this view, asserting that war is only just when "those against whom war is to be waged ... deserve to have war waged against them because of some wrongdoing."[76] This belief was widely held in the Middle

Ages, when "warfare was seen as a function of divine providence designed to punish sin and crime."[77] Aquinas, for example, asserts that just as God may slay sinners in order to protect the good, "this also human justice imitates as far as it can; for it slays those who are dangerous to others."[78] Ultimately, "the notion of justice became assimilated to that of legality, and war was seen as an extraordinary form of a lawsuit."[79] Sidgwick, writing at the turn of the last century, similarly asserts that "the deepest problems presented by war, and the deepest principles to be applied to dealing with them, are applicable also to the milder conflicts and collisions that arise within the limits of an orderly and peaceful community."[80]

Thus, although "it is an established fact that peace is the desired end of war," it should be kept in mind that when men do go to war "their desire is not that there should not be peace but that it should be the kind of peace they wish for."[81] It appears to Augustine to be human nature of a sort:

> all men desire to be at peace with their own people, while wishing to impose their will upon those people's lives. For even when they wage war on others, their wish is to make those opponents their own people, if they can – to subject them, and to impose on them their own conditions of peace.[82]

This is true even for Christians: "It comes to this, then; a man who has learnt to prefer right to wrong and the rightly ordered to the perverted, sees that the peace of the unjust, compared with the peace of the just, is not worthy even of the name of peace."[83] Thus, wars must be fought for the sake of justice and order. As Sidgwick would argue much later, war among humans is "not a mere conflict of interests, but also a conflict of opposing views of right and justice."[84]

Thus far, I have focused largely on Augustine, both because of his centrality to the Christian just war cannon, and because his *ad bellum* logics for war clearly reflect the concern with order that we have been exploring in Hinduism and Islam. But Augustine is certainly not the only Christian just war thinker to have such a perspective. Since Augustine says little about the just means for waging war, our discussion of other Christian thinkers will focus on *in bello* ethics.

Aquinas seems to be of the view that "when a war was just because it was necessary, logically it should be fought by any means and at all times."[85] Vitoria too asserted, "in war everything is lawful, which the defense of the commonweal requires. This is notorious, for the end and aim of war is the defense and preservation of the State. Also, a private person may do this in self-defense ... A prince may go even further in a just war and do whatever is necessary in order to obtain peace and security from the enemy ... Therefore it is lawful to employ all appropriate measures against enemies who are plundering and disturbing the tranquility of the state."[86] Michael Walzer also starts down this risky slope toward total war: "We don't call war hell because it is fought without restraint. It is more nearly right to say that, when certain restraints are passed, the hellishness of war drives us to break with every remaining restraint in order to win. Here is the ultimate tyranny: those who resist aggression are forced to imitate, and perhaps even to exceed, the brutality of the aggressor."[87] Walzer goes much farther than traditional just war theorists, and even suggests a "utilitarianism of extremity," which asserts, "do justice unless the heavens are (really) about to fall."[88] If the losing the war would result in a situation worse than the unconscionable means used to fight it, perhaps normally impermissible means and tactics must be allowed for the sake of the greater good.

Such a view is really radical in just war thinking, which has historically advocated restraint and a certain proportionality.[89] Because a just war is essentially a matter of punishment, those who are innocent must not be intentionally targeted. In the broadest of terms, the guilt or innocence of a person or group of persons "and hence their status as legitimate objects of attack or as immune from direct attack, should be contingent upon an objective, material fact: their participation or nonparticipation in unjust activity."[90] Women, children, and others unable to bear arms clearly fall into this category; others such as ambassadors and religious personnel are also not liable to punishment so long as they refrain from fighting themselves. This concept is pervasive, found not only in Vitoria, but also in Suarez, Grotius and Vattel, among others.

Conclusions and Implications

After examining these three religious perspectives on war, it becomes clear that they all see the preservation of the community as extremely important. Without a peaceful and well-ordered domestic community, the faith cannot develop and flourish. Thus, occasionally wars must be fought to protect the community. Likewise, the means by which the war is fought must not fundamentally upset the normal values of the community. The first reason for this principle is quite obvious: because the community itself claims to represent a sort of ideal social system, and because it often hopes to live in a world with more communities similar to itself, it must not fight in a way that would jeopardize its values or make those values seem undesirable or hollow. The second reason is subtler. Those who fight to defend the community will, once peace is re-established, return home to their ordinary lives. If the means they use to fight the war are utterly opposed to the normal values of the community, when they return they may be somehow tainted or corrupted by the experience, and therefore pose a risk to the community themselves.

One of the most obvious conclusions to be drawn from this exploratory study is the striking degree of similarity in Hindu, Islamic and Christian just war thinking when seen from the point of view of preserving order. While they differ in the specifics, all three traditions share a common concern with creating and defending a faith-based just social order. The concern with order in all three traditions also suggests a different means for approaching conflict resolution. Since much conflict may, at its root, be about different conceptions of justice and how best to order not only domestic but also international society, it may be wise to try to understand how various issues are other stood in other ethical systems. As Sidgwick argues, we must try to see whether "when we look at the opponent's case from the inside, there is not more to be said for it than appeared when we contemplated it from the outside."[91] Additionally, "if there seems to us to be a real difference of principles, then comes the more difficult duty of endeavoring to place ourselves in an impartial position for contemplating the different sets of principles, and seeing if there is not an element of truth in the opponent's view which we have hitherto missed."[92] The more we understand what a just social order is in the eyes of faiths outside our own (and the more conscious we become of our own assumptions on that subject), the more able we could be to negotiate a world order that would permit all of our communities to flourish. Surely there must be some way to integrate these concerns with internal autonomy and order, as well as with the creation of an international structure to preserve these values, more fully into international law. At the very least, reference to these traditional concerns could conceivably be used to pressure states and institutions into more rigorously enforcing the laws already in existence.

Another possibly positive implication to be drawn from emphasizing the importance of order in the just war tradition is that it would seem to reinforce the justification for humanitarian interventions. Although there have been numerous humanitarian interventions, especially since the 1990s, in places such as Bosnia, Somalia, Rwanda, and Kosovo, the legality of these missions has been questioned, providing yet another disincentive to intervening to protect human rights and prevent genocides. The legal problem is that the creation of safe havens (and other forms of intervention more generally) represents a *de facto* succession of a contested region, often against the will of the state or states that claim it, which obviously raises acute sovereignty concerns.[93] An additional problem is that such good will may backfire: the establishing and enforcing of safe zones will almost certainly generate a potential for armed conflict between the intervening powers and the local military groups. The tragedy of the Bosnian safe havens arose directly from this problem; intervening states felt that their hands were tied and refrained from using force to protect the refugees who had fled to their zones for protection.

But just as the violence-restraining aspects of just war theory have been absorbed into international law, perhaps some of the order-enforcing aspects could also be adopted, giving such humanitarian interventions a stronger legal footing. Indeed, Chapter VII of the United Nations Charter gives special powers to member states to intervene when "any threat to the peace, breach of the peace, or act of aggression" threatens international peace and security: the problem, however, is that what defines a threat to international peace is not explicitly laid out. Looking closely at the need for a stable social order as a human right could be a useful starting point for establishing a systematic set of definitions and situations as to when intervention is justified. The understanding that violence may sometimes be more just than refraining from violence may also "add teeth" to humanitarian interventions, permitting intervening powers to take more forceful action to protect innocent people on the ground.

But not all the implications of this perspective are so hopeful. If just war prohibitions are primarily concerned with preserving a just social order for the sake of the home community, then there seems to be a great risk that these principles will be treated as utilitarian. As mentioned before in reference to Walzer, there is a danger in seeing the community as an ideal good that must be preserved at all costs. In the heat and furor of war, how easy is it to rationally and objectively determine whether the opponent is really so evil that any means may be employed to defend the community against it? Are there instances when losing – even if that means the community will no longer be autonomous, or may be completely annihilated – may be more just than continuing to fight using morally troubling (but militarily necessary) means?

Likewise, while it may be tempting to suggest that the states that can intervene should intervene when genocide or other horrible human rights violations loom, there are still moral risks. Yes, a stable social order may be something worth protecting. But who decides what social orders are worthy of protection? While Hinduism, Islam and Christianity all advocate the establishment and defense of a stable social order, they do disagree as to what that social order should look like. In essence, while there is agreement on the need for order, there is not agreement on what constitutes the "good life" that such stability is meant to ensure. There are no simple answers to these questions, but they certainly merit careful reflection in the future.

Notes

1   Michael Walzer. "The Idea of Holy War in Ancient Israel," *The Journal of Religious Ethics*, 20/2 (Fall 1992): 225.
2   Societies may disagree as to *what* such a social order should look like, but all hold some type of social order dear. The nature of this just order – and subjective judgments about its worth – are beyond the scope of this paper.
3   It is important to note that this perspective is not entirely new. The ongoing debate over whether there is or is not a prima facie presumption against harm in the work of Thomas Aquinas, for example, results in some theorists, such as James Turner Johnson, arguing that there is a conflict in just war theory between the duty not to harm and the duty to protect innocent persons, while other theorists, notably James E. Childress, assert that just war theory shares pacifism's presumption against killing. For a lengthier discussion of this debate, see Richard B. Miller, "Aquinas and the Presumption against Killing and War," *The Journal of Religion*, pp. 173-204. My paper, however, goes farther in two respects. First, it presents an overarching view of the presumption against harm, beyond the scope of the

Aquinas-centered debate. Second, it offers a cross-religious perspective, suggesting that this concern is not unique to the Christian just war tradition.

4   A small caveat is in order here. In comparison to Christianity or even Islam, Hinduism is many ways a more fluid tradition, and while there are many texts (such as the *Mahabharata* and the *Ramayana*) which have universal importance, the tradition lacks a centralized or formalized "canon." This makes it difficult to quantify the faith's position on any given matter; the discussion here is drawn largely from my own readings of the two major texts already mentioned, as well the analyses of more minor religious, philosophical and legal texts discussed in the work of other scholars.

5   S.S. More. *The Gita: A Theory of Human Action* (Delhi, India, Sri Satguru Publications, 1990). p. 167.

6   Madanlal A. Buch. *The Principles of Hindu Ethics* (Baroda, India: "Arya Sudharak" Printing Press, 1921), p. 353.

7   Shanti. 15. In Buch, p. 354.

8   Buch. p. 354.

9   *The Bhagavad Gita: Krishna's Council in Time of War.* Barbara Stoler Miller, trans. (New York, NY: Bantam Books, 1986), p. 57. (V.2)

10 Ibid. p. 44 (III.24) The Bhagavad Gita is the mythicized account of the Kurukshetra war, believed to have taken place in the 10th century B.C., between two branches of the same royal family. At the opening of the text, the main protagonist, King Arjuna, has just arrived at the battlefield. Seeing both armies arrayed before him in all their splendor, he is suddenly struck by the horror of war and the realization that such beauty, strength and heroism will be killed during the battle. At the moment when he loses his courage, Lord Krishna reveals himself to be the incarnation of God, and through the dialogue presented in the text demonstrates to Arjuna that fighting this battle is his sacred duty, and that he will bear no sin for the loss of lives, even those of his family members on the opposite side. See R.K. Chatterjee, *The Gita and its Culture* (New Delhi, India: Sterling Publishers Private, Ltd., 1987).

11 Ibid. p. 44. (III.25)

12 This system of social stratification, also known as the "varna system" consists of four varnas, or classes: the Brhamana (philosophers), Kshatriya (warriors), Vaisya (traders) and Sudra (laborers). See Ankush R. Sawant. *Manu-Smriti and Republic of Plato: A Comparative and Critical Study* (Bombay, India: Himalaya Publishing House, 1996), pp. 44-48.

13 *Bhagavad Gita.* p. 149. (XVIII.43)

14 H.S. Bhatia. *International Law and Practice in Ancient India* (New Delhi, India: Deep & Deep Publications, 1977), p. 23.

15 Patrick Olivelle, ed. and trans. *Dharmasutras: The Law Codes of Apastamba, Gautama, Baudhyana and Vasistha* (Oxford, UK: Oxford University Press, 1999), Vasistha Dharmasutra: 3.24-25.

16 Sawant. p. 47.

17 *Bhagavad Gita.* p. 34. (II.31) Consider also Krishna's argument: "Your own duty done imperfectly is better than another man's done well. It is better to die in one's own duty; another man's duty is perilous." p. 46. (III.35) This concept is repeated again later for emphasis: "Better to do one's own duty imperfectly than to do another man's well; doing action intrinsic to his being, a man avoids guilt." p. 149. (XVIII.47)

18 Ibid. p. 34. (II.33)

19 Ibid. p. 50. (IV.7-8)
20 The *Arthasastra* most likely dates to 321-300 B.C. The title literally means 'the science of wealth or economics.' See Bharati Mukherjee. *Kautilya's Concept of Diplomacy: A New Interpretation* (Calcutta, India: Minerva Associated (Publications) Pvt. Ltd., 1976), pp. 15-19.
21 Bhatia. p. 88.
22 Ibid. p. 87.
23 Ibid. p. 82.
24 Mukherjee. p. 30.
25 (Sauptika. 6:21-22) In Buch, p. 357.
26 Bhatia. p. 100.
27 Buch. p. 355.
28 Ahmad ibn 'Abd al-Halim ibn Taymiya. *Le Traité de Droit Public D'Ibn Taimiya: Traduction annoté de la Siyasa sariya*. Henri Laoust, trans. (Beirut: Institut Français de Damas, 1948), pp. 128-129. My translation.
29 Ibn Khaldûn. *The Muqaddimah: An Introduction to history*. Franz Rosenthal, trans. (N.J.Dawood, ed. Princeton, NJ: Princeton University Press, 1967), p. 97.
30 Al Farabi. *Alfarabi: The Political Writings; "Selected Aphorisms" and other texts*. Charles E. Butterworth, trans. (Ithaca, NY: Cornell University Press), p. 41. It is imported to note that Al Farabi is seen by many Muslims to hold heretical views. In my view however, although he may express non-conventional views on specifically theological issues, his stance on just war does not seem particularly unusual.
31 Majid Khadduri. *The Islamic Conceptions of Justice* (Baltimore, MD: The Johns Hopkins University Press, 1984), p. 163.
32 Khadduri. p. 165.
33 John Kelsay. *Islam and War: a study in comparative ethic*. (Louisville, KY: Westminster/John Knox Press, 1993), p. 30.
34 Jean Flori. *Guerre sainte, jihad, croisade: violence et religion dans le christianisme et l'islam* (Paris: Éditions du Seuil, 2002), p. 108.
35 Kelsay. p. 34.
36 Muhammad ibn al-Hasan al-Shaybani. *The Islamic Law of Nations: Shaybani's Siyar*. Majid Khadduri, trans. (Baltimore, MD: The Johns Hopkins Press, 1966), p. 2. Shaybani's siyar represents a compilation of his teacher Imam Abu Hanifa's lectures, representing perhaps the earliest formulation of Islamic international law.
37 Majid Khadduri. *War and Peace in the Law of Islam* (Baltimore, MD: Johns Hopkins Press, 1955), p. 44.
38 Khadduri, 1955. p. 7. Later thinkers, such as ibn Khaldûn and particularly al-Farabi, do recognize a distinction between a (more or less) secular state and society itself, which they see as more religiously governed.
39 Ibn Taymiya. p. 127. Italics added.
40 Al Farabi. p. 52.
41 Ibid., p. 50.
42 Muwaffak al-Din Ibn Kudamah. *Le Précis de Droit d'Ibn Qudama*. Henri Laoust, trans. (Beirut, Lebanon: Institut Français de Damas, 1950), p. 150.
43 Ibn Taymiya, p. 133.
44 Muhammad Hamidullah. *Muslim Conduct of State* (Lahore, India: Sh. Muhammad Ashraf, 1945), pp. 154-159.

45 Ibn Taymiya, in Khaled Abou El Fadl, "The Rules of Killing at War: An Inquiry into Classical Sources," *Muslim World*, 89/2 (April 1999): p. 152.

46 Al Farabi. p. 44.

47 Al Farabi. p. 44. While Al Farabi does not give his sources for this idea, it is possible that his inspiration comes from ancient Jewish thinking, as in the Old Testament it appears that in certain cases the ancient Israelites were ordered to kill all the inhabitants of certain cities, such as those that were idolatrous or that were to be part of their inheritance. See James E. Priest, *Governmental and Judicial Ethics in the Bible and Rabbinic Literature* (Malibu, CA: Pepperdine University Press, 1980); Robert A. Freund, *Understanding Jewish Ethics* (San Francisco, CA: Edwin Mellen Press, 1990), and also Michael Walzer, "The Idea of Holy War in Ancient Israel," *The Journal of Religious Ethics*, 20/2 (Fall 1992): pp. 215-228.

48 Al Farabi. p. 44.

49 Khaldun. p. 224.

50 Ibn Taymiya. p. 123.

51 Raafat Chambour. *Les Institutions sociales, politiques et juridiques de l'Islam* (Lausanne, Switzerland: Éditions Méditerranéennes, 1978), p. 216.

52 Khadduri, 1955. p. 102.

53 Shaybani. p. 76, 91.

54 El Fadl. p. 144.

55 Ibid., p. 151.

56 Khadduri, 1955. pp. 204-207. This practice was certainly not unknown in Europe, despite being a violation of just war principles.

57 Kelsay. p. 36.

58 St Augustine. *City of God*. Henry Bettenson, trans. (London: Penguin books, 1984), p. 75. (Book II: chapter 21)

59 Pierre Crepon. *Les religions et la guerre* (Paris: Éditions Albin Michel, 1991), p. 74.

60 Flori. p. 76. Likewise, David Little argues in his introduction to *Religious Perspectives on War* (USIP, 2002) that "because just war thinking is something of a compromise for many Christian thinkers, and therefore sits rather uneasily in the tradition, doubts and reservations about it abound."

61 Flori. p. 45.

62 Crépon. p. 82.

63 St. Thomas Aquinas. *Political Writings*. R.W. Dyson, ed. (Cambridge, UK: Cambridge University Press, 2002), p. 243. (Summa theologiae IIaIIae40: On war, article 2)

64 St. Augustine. p. 877. (Book XIX, chapter 17)

65 St. Thomas Aquinas. p. 247. (Summa theologiae IIaIIae40: On war, article 4)

66 St. Thomas Aquinas. p. 248. (Summa theologiae IIaIIae42: On war, article 1) The exception, of course, is sedition against tyrannical regimes, unless "the tyrant's rule is disrupted so inordinately that the community subject to it suffers greater detriment from the ensuing disorder than it did from the tyrannical government itself." (IIaIIae42: article 2) Again, note that order vs. disorder is the dominant concern.

67 Michael Walzer. *Just and Unjust Wars* (New York, NY: Basic Books, 2000), p. 53.

68 Ibid., pp. 53-54.

69 St. Augustine. p. 870. (Book XIX: chapter 13)

70 St Augustine. p. 6. (Book I: chapter 1)

71 St. Augustine. p. 14. (Book I: chapter 8)

72 St. Augustine. pp. 15-16. (Book I: chapter 9)

20 *Justice and Violence*

73 St. Augustine. p. 16. (Book I: chapter 9)
74 St. Augustine. p. 876. (Book XIX: chapter 16)
75 St. Augustine. p. 862. (Book XIX, chapter 7)
76 St. Thomas Aquinas. p. 240. (Summa theologiae, IIaIIae40: On War, article 1)
77 Frederick H. Russel. *The Just War in the Middle Ages* (Cambridge, UK: Cambridge University Press, 1975), p. 292.
78 St. Thomas Aquinas. p. 254. (Summa theologiae IIaIIae64: On War, article 2)
79 Russel. p. 297.
80 Henry Sidgwick. "The Morality of Strife," *International Journal of Ethics*, 1/1 (October 1890): pp. 1-15. p. 3.
81 St. Augustine. p. 866. (Book XIX: chapter 12)
82 Ibid., p. 867.
83 Ibid., p. 869.
84 Sidgwick. p. 5.
85 Russel. p. 272.
86 Richard Shelly Hartigan. *The Forgotten Victim: A History of the Civilian* (Chicago, IL: Precedent Publishing, Inc., 1982), p. 81.
87 Walzer. p. 32.
88 Ibid., p. 231.
89 Interestingly, it is on this argument of proportionality that Walzer bases his claim. The idea is that if the injustice perpetrated by the opponent is severe enough, normally forbidden means may actual be proportionate to that evil. To me, this seems like a very dangerous and very slippery slope.
90 Hartigan. p. 93.
91 Sidgwick. p. 14.
92 Ibid., p. 14.
93 Barry R. Posen. "Military Responses to Refugee Disasters," *International Security*, 21/1 (Summer 1996): p. 94.

Chapter 2

Moralizing Violence or a Just Response
The Dimensions and Limitations of the Bush Doctrine

Chris J. Dolan
University of South Carolina

A cornerstone of President George W. Bush's foreign policy strategy is the assertion of a right to wage offensive war in the form of preemptive military force and preventive war. Directed mainly at obviating the spread of weapons of mass destruction and eradicating terrorist activities, the doctrine and its policies are distinguished from previous presidential initiatives in that they reject deterrence, power balancing, and are grounded in terms of moral clarity and varying notions of self-defense. However, are preemptive military force and preventive war adequate responses to the twin threats of WMD proliferation and terrorism or unjust methods of violence that only appear legitimate due to the 9/11 terrorist attacks? The purpose of this chapter is to establish legitimate parameters around which scholars can more fully understand the exercise of offensive force as it is delineated in President Bush's strategic first strike doctrine.

September 11th and Offensive Warfare

The 9/11 terrorist attacks provided the U.S. with the political opportunity to transform America's strategic national security doctrine away from what some perceived as a Cold War-era strategy of containment and deterrence toward one that emphasizes offensive warfare. For one observer, 9/11 represented a "long-standing call for the U.S. to develop a comprehensive strategy that finally spoke to the challenges of the Post-Cold War era.[1] National Security Adviser Condoleezza Rice described the political opportunities for strategic alteration of U.S. national security policy by comparing 9/11 to the immediate post-W.W.II period that provided fertile ground for the assertion of the Truman Doctrine:

> I really think this period is analogous to 1945 to 1947 – that is, the period when the containment doctrine took shape – in that the events so clearly demonstrated that there

is a big global threat, and that it's a big global threat to a lot of countries that you would not have normally thought of as being in the coalition. That has started shifting the tectonic plates in international politics. And it's important to try to seize on that and position American interests and institutions and all of that before they harden again.[2]

President Bush himself perceived the 9/11 attacks as the initiation of a new permanent war that required both defensive and offensive capabilities. On September 20th, in a speech before a joint a session of Congress, he argued:

Our response involves far more than instant retaliation and isolated strikes. Americans should not expect one battle, but a lengthy campaign ... It may include dramatic strikes, visible on TV, and covert operations, secret even in success.[3]

The attacks of 9/11 also allowed the president to expand the U.S. military response to include terrorists and state sponsors of terrorism in a world that for Bush was now clearly defined:

And we will pursue nations that provide aid or safe haven to terrorism ... Every nation, in every region, now has a decision to make. Either you are with us, or you are with the terrorists. From this day forward, any nation that continues to harbor or support terrorism will be regarded by the United States as a hostile regime ...[4]

Bush also expanded the war on terrorism to include preemptive and preventive action against states that both sponsor terrorism and/or pursue WMD In his 2002 State of the Union, Bush stated, "First, we will shut down terrorist camps, disrupt terrorist plans and bring terrorists to justice. And second, we must prevent the terrorists and regimes who seek chemical, biological or nuclear weapons from threatening the United States and the world."[5] Bush also linked North Korea, Iran, and Iraq as states that sponsor terrorism and pursue WMD and hinted at US action against Iraq:

North Korea is a regime arming with missiles and weapons of mass destruction, while starving its citizens. Iran aggressively pursues these weapons and exports terror, while an unelected few repress the Iranian people's hope for freedom. Iraq continues to flaunt its hostility toward America and to support terror. The Iraqi regime has plotted to develop anthrax and nerve gas and nuclear weapons for over a decade. This is a regime that has already used poison gas to murder thousands of its own citizens, leaving the bodies of mothers huddled over their dead children.

This is a regime that agreed to international inspections then kicked out the inspectors. This is a regime that has something to hide from the civilized world.[6]

Bush also made a case that all three states served as imminent threats to the U.S.:

States like these, and their terrorist allies, constitute an axis of evil, arming to threaten the peace of the world. By seeking weapons of mass destruction, these regimes pose a grave and growing danger. They could provide these arms to terrorists, giving them the means to match their hatred. They could attack our allies or attempt to blackmail the United States. In any of these cases, the price of indifference would be catastrophic.[7]

Bush made his most forceful public case for striking first on June 1st, 2002 in his graduation speech to Army cadets at West Point. He stated that "our security will require all Americans to be forward-looking and resolute, to be ready for preemptive action when necessary ..."[8]

The publication of the 2002 *National Security Strategy* (N.S.S.) cemented these ideas into a formal presidential doctrine. It states, "today, our enemies will use weapons of mass destruction as weapons of choice ... We cannot let our enemies strike first." It also goes on to justify the need for preemption based on the concept of self-protection:

We will not hesitate to act alone, if necessary, to exercise our right of self-defense by acting preemptively against such terrorists; to prevent them from doing harm against our people and our country... nations need not suffer an attack before they can lawfully take action to defend themselves against forces that present an imminent danger of attack.[9]

The N.S.S. also claims the power to engage in preventive war:

The greater the threat, the greater the risk of inaction – and the more compelling the case for taking anticipatory action to defend ourselves, even if uncertainty remains as to the time and place of the enemy's attack.[10]

Furthermore, it asserts U.S. global primacy by stating "our forces will be strong enough to dissuade potential adversaries from pursuing a military build-up in hopes of surpassing, or equaling, the power of the United States."[11]

Bush's embrace of preemption and preventive war against terrorists quickly became known as his "first strike doctrine." Preemptive military force or preemption involves striking first at an imminent and ominous threat, believing that an attack is going to occur. Preventive war is the use of force against non-imminent threats in the hope of preventing against future attacks. This highly controversial method of using force dismisses the utility of deterrence and containment, is based almost exclusively on unilateralism, and places considerable faith in guessing at the future intentions of states and non-states. Both preemption and preventive war are premised on the belief that terrorists which combine suicidal attacks with other deadly tactics and states that support terrorism and pursue WMD cannot be contained and deterred. The NSS spells out in detail the case for striking first for the sake of self-defense:

> For centuries, international law recognized that nations need not suffer an attack before they can lawfully take action to defend themselves against forces that present an imminent danger of attack. Legal scholars and international jurists often conditioned the legitimacy of preemption on the existence of an imminent threat – most often a visible mobilization of armies, navies, and air forces preparing to attack.

The moral premise of Bush's doctrine of striking first rests on an expansive interpretation of the traditional right of self-defense. The right of self-defense as a morally legitimating factor on the road to war has a long history in international law, dating to Hugo Grotius in 1625.[12] Historically, the legitimate claim of self-defense included the right to preemptive use of force. This moral right was not absolute, however. In 1842, U.S. Secretary of State Daniel Webster helped to clarify in the *Caroline* case with England, the conditions under which America could exercise the right to preempt an attack with military force in self-defense. Preemptive military force had clearly defined moral limitations and could only be justified in cases in which "the necessity of that self-defense is instant, overwhelming, and leaving no choice of means and no moment for deliberation."[13] To the requirement of necessity then is added the additional requirement of proportionality of the response.

Chapter VII, Article 51 of the United Nations Charter preserves for member states the right of individual or collective self-defense, only if, "an armed attack occurs against a Member of the United Nations, until the Security Council has taken measures necessary to maintain international peace and security."[14] Like any legal text, the exact meaning and scope of what constitutes legitimate self-defense is open and has been subject to debate. However, the intent seems clear, resort to self-defense is legitimate only in cases of real, looming, and imminent attack. In essence, distinctions between unilateralism and multilateralism, states and non-states, and deterrence, preemption, and preventive war are fundamental. A denial of these distinctions is politically and morally unacceptable.

Therefore, on the whole, the Bush administration's expansive version of self-defense and its arguments in favor of a first strike doctrine rest on the larger view that warfare has been transformed by terrorism in general and September 11th in particular. As Colin Powell argues, "It's a different world ... it's a new kind of threat."[15] And in several important respects, war has changed along the lines the administration suggests, although that transformation is nothing new as terrorism has been an ongoing threat to the US for a number of decades. Prevailing wisdom suggests that non-traditional enemies, namely terrorist groups and their state sponsors, are prepared to wage modern warfare by concealing their movements, weapons, and intentions by attacking civilians, military personnel, technologies, and infrastructure. The logic today for American policymakers is driven by the fear that of nuclear, chemical, and biological weapons might fall into the hands of terrorists and tyrannical rogue states. President Bush contends in his 2002 *National Security Strategy* that Americans face enemies who "reject basic human values and hate the United States and everything for which it stands."[16] Although vulnerability could be reduced, it is impossible to achieve complete immunity.

As the argument goes, such vulnerability and fear means the US must assume more offensive military measures. The character of potential threats becomes extremely important in evaluating the legitimacy of the new first strike doctrine, and thus the assertion that the US continues to confront rogue or dangerous states and terrorist groups that oppose everything America represents. There is certainly evidence to believe that Al-Qaeda has always desired to harm Americans. As Osama Bin Laden declares:

> We – with God's help – call on every Muslim who believes in God and wishes to be rewarded to comply with God's order to kill the Americans and plunder their money wherever and whenever they find it. We also call on Muslim *ulema*, leaders, youths, and soldiers to launch the raid on Satan's U.S. troops and the devil's supporters allying with them, and to displace those who are behind them so that they may learn a lesson. The ruling to kill the Americans and their allies – civilians and military – is an individual duty for every Muslim who can do it in any country in which it is possible to do it ... [17]

Indeed, the threat of terrorism, as manifested in 9/11, has contributed to a political environment that allowed Bush to significantly alter America's strategic national security doctrine. According to Yale historian John Lewis Gaddis:

> It took a shock like 9/11 to produce something that was this dramatic ... I have to say that 10 years into the Post-Cold War era, there was very little sign of a comprehensive grand strategy. There were strategies toward particular countries and with regard to particular issues, but very little effort to pull it altogether. 9/11 forced us to get our grand strategic act together. And this is the way it normally happens, it seems to me, in history.[18]

But while 9/11 may have justified America's right to use force as a defensive retaliatory response against terrorism, the Bush Administration makes a questionable and controversial moral jump when it assumes that "rogue states" not directly affiliated with anti-US terrorist activity or 9/11 desire to harm the U.S. with WMD and pose an imminent or future military threat. Does the president blur the distinction between "rogue states" and terrorists and erase the difference between terrorists and those states in which they reside with the following: "We make no distinction between terrorists and those who knowingly harbor or provide aid to them."[19] Any tentative answer must acknowledge, in the first place, that such distinctions make a difference.

Identifying Legitimate Parameters

To effectively explain the exercise of preemptive and preventive use of force, decision makers and attentive international publics must have an interest in promoting an ethical and moral understanding, as well as a political interest, in exercising offensive force. Building on the contributions of realism and just war theory, legitimate offensive force must be exercised within the following set of parameters.

Putting the 'Self' Back in Self-Defense

On the surface, any nation's self-defense criterion can be easily understood. When innocent lives are threatened or attacked, governments are justified in using force to counter enemies and protect citizens. But a nation's self-defense may have another meaning, one in which the "self" is expressed not only in response to specific threats, but one characterized by more broadly defined concepts, such as individual freedom and liberation, property ownership, worker rights, democracy, and survival. How far does "self defense" extend? When conceptual and economic interests are understood to be global and when democracy and human rights are defined more broadly than ever before, the notion of self-defense expands and enlarges. But a broad conception of the self is not necessarily legitimate and neither are the values to be defended completely obvious.[20]

Since WW II, America's interpretation of the self became more broadly defined. The Japanese attack at Pearl Harbor and the Cold War demonstrated that America was confronting global enemies and threats, such as the Soviet Union, its Eastern allies, and Communism and the spread of nuclear technology and weaponization.[21] For many, 9/11 reaffirmed the ideas that America's national identify and survival continue to be under assault by tyranny and terrorism on a global scale. Others agree but temper such beliefs with the reality that Al Qaeda is the specific threat. President Bush's *National Security Strategy* is reflective of the former as it only embraces nations that conform to America's broadly defined goals.

> In the 21st Century, only nations that share a commitment to protecting basic human rights and guaranteeing political and economic freedom will be able to unleash the potential of their people and assure their future prosperity. People everywhere want to be able to speak freely; choose who will govern them; worship as they please; educate their children – male and female; own property; and enjoy the benefits of their labor. These values of freedom are right and true for every person, in every society – and the duty of protecting these values against their enemies is the common calling of freedom-loving people across the globe and across the ages.[22]

Since the American perspective of the world is defined so broadly, at what point does self-defense begin to look like aggression? As Richard Betts has argued, "When security is defined in terms broader than protecting the near-term integrity of national sovereignty and borders, the distinction between offense and defense blurs hopelessly ... Security can be as insatiable an appetite as acquisitiveness –

there may never be enough buffers."[23] The projection of the self-conception of the US onto the world by American leaders could lead to interventions in a number of countries at the expense of being looked upon by the world community as an aggressor nation with imperial designs. Thus, any self-defense conception must be narrowly confined to immediate risks to life and health within borders or to the life and health of citizens abroad.

Based on narrow definition of self-defense, preemption can be legitimated only in cases of actual or imminent attack. Take, for example, the following two cases involving Israel and its Arab neighbors. On June 7, 1981, Israeli Prime Minister Menachem Begin launched what his government argued was a preemptive air strike against the Osirak nuclear facility near Baghdad that was being developed by French and Italian contractors. Israel justified the assault on the notion that Iraq considered itself to be in a permanent state of war with the Jewish state and that it continued to deny Israel's right to exist, and that its nuclear program was for the purpose of developing weapons capable of destroying Israel.

The members of the UN Security Council quickly responded with a unanimous (including the United States) condemnation of the Israeli action as an act of aggression. There was no convincing evidence that Israel acted preemptively out of the necessity of responding to a threat that was imminent, immediate, and overwhelming. The UN Security Council also concluded that the Osriak facility was not the type of threat that left Israel without a choice of means and moment for deliberation.[24] The action represented a case of preventive aggression and was not viewed as legal under international law and the UN Charter.

In order to make the point explicit that international norms were not evolving in the opposite direction, now consider another case involving Israel a decade-and-a-half earlier, during the Six Day War between Israel and Egypt, Iraq, Jordan and Syria in 1967. Raymond and Kegley describe the case well as a classic case of preemption:

> Tensions between Israel and its Arab neighbors had been growing throughout the spring of 1967, and reached their zenith in May when Egyptian president Gamal Abdel Nasser undertook a series of actions that raised fears in Tel Aviv of an imminent attack. Besides mobilizing his troops and cementing military ties with Syria, Jordan, and Iraq, Nasser ordered the United Nations Emergency Force to leave the Sinai ... Furthermore, he announced a blockade of the Straits of Tiran, Israel's vital waterway to the Red Sea and Indian Ocean, and proclaimed that his goal in any future war with Israel would be the destruction of the Jewish state. Assuming an invasion was forthcoming and survival doubtful if Egypt landed the first blow, the Israelis launched a surprise attack on June 5, which enabled them to win a decisive victory.[25]

Again, this was a classic case of preemption, characterized by a threat that was *instant*, *overwhelming*, and *leaving no choice* of means and no moment for deliberation. In this context and cutting through all the maneuvering and mumbo-jumbo of legalistic arguments, where do the new Bush preemptive (read, preventive) war doctrine and the U.S. attack on Iraq fit?

International norms allow states to exercise the right of "anticipatory self-defense." Thus, the exercise of legitimate preemption could only occur if several necessary conditions were met. First, the right of self-defense cannot be invoked to protect imperial interests or to promote hegemony. Second, in which threats must be assessed in terms of immediacy and strong evidence must be identified that an attack is inevitable and likely in the instant future. Moreover, immediate threats should be clearly manifest within days or weeks unless action is taken to thwart them. This demands indisputable and incontrovertible intelligence demonstrating that a potential aggressor has both the real and actual capability and intention to do immediate harm. Third, preemption should succeed in reducing the threat. Specifically, there should be a high likelihood that the source of the military threat can be found and the damage that it was about to do can be greatly reduced or eliminated by a preemptive attack. If preemption is likely to fail, it should not be undertaken. Fourth, military force is necessary, however, only after all legitimate policy options have been exhausted in due time.

Threshold of Credible Fear

The Bush Administration is justified in emphasizing America's s vulnerability to terrorist attacks and the immediate threat of WMD proliferation. The administration has also argued that it cannot wait for a smoking gun if it comes in the form of a "mushroom cloud." There may be little or no evidence in advance of a terrorist attack using nuclear, chemical, or biological weapons. Yet, under this view, the requirement for evidence is reduced to a fear that the other has, or might someday acquire, the means for an assault. However, President Bush seems to have set the bar for preemption quite low in his *National Security Strategy* because his strategic doctrine fails to ask how much and what kind of evidence is necessary to justify preemption and downplays the importance of what credible fears should justify the flexing of preemptive military force?

As Michael Walzer has argued, simple fear cannot be the only criterion. During the Cold War, fear of nuclear warfare deterred the world's major powers from risking even conventional war, not to mention the use of nuclear weapons because of the danger of an uncontrollable nuclear exchange. The fear of nuclear annihilation was allayed when both just war theorists and realists realized that containment and deterrence were the only morally and politically acceptable strategies to employ against the Soviet Union and the East. In essence, containment and deterrence became easy to live with as a workable defense.[26]

However, fear is omnipresent in the context of America's current anti-terrorist campaign. And if fear was clearly justified during the Cold War on the grounds of morality, rationality, and strategy, when and how will we know today if terrorist threats and attacks have been significantly reduced or eliminated? Could we ever know that we have eliminated the terrorists' desire to accumulate nuclear, chemical, or biological weapons technology? The moral and political nature of fear may be that once a group has suffered a terrible surprise attack, a government and its people will justifiably vigilant. Indeed they may, out of fear, be aware of threats to the point of hypervigilance – seeing small threats as large, and squashing all potential threats, no matter how minor they may in fact be, with enormous brutality.[27]

The threshold for credible fear is necessarily lower in the context of contemporary counterterrorism war, but the consequences of lowering the threshold may increase instability and elevate the prospect of prematurely exercising force. If this is the case, if fear justifies assault, then the occasions for attack will potentially be limitless since, according to the Bush administration's own arguments, we cannot always know with certainty what the other side has, where it might be located, or when it might be used. If one attacks on the basis of fear, or suspicion that a potential adversary may someday have the intention and capacity to harm you, then the line between preemptive and preventive war has been crossed. Again, the problem is in perceiving and judging the capabilities and intentions of potential adversaries.

A fine balance must be struck. On the one hand, the threshold of evidence and warning cannot be too low, where simple apprehension that a potential adversary might be out there somewhere and may be acquiring the means to attack the US could trigger the exercise of offensive force. This is not preemption, but aggression driven by paranoia and fear. The US and its citizens must be prepared to accept vulnerability and a minimum level of casualties and uncertainty. We must also avoid the tendency to exaggerate the threat, which almost always heightens our own fear. Although nuclear weapons are more available than in the past, as are delivery vehicles, these forces are not yet in the hands of hundreds of terrorists.

On the other hand, the threshold of evidence and warning for justified fear cannot be so high that those who might be about to do harm that they cannot be stopped or the damage limited. What is required, assuming a substantial investment in intelligence gathering, assessment, and understanding of potential advisories, is a policy that both maximizes our understanding of the capabilities and intentions of potential adversaries and minimizes our physical vulnerability. While uncertainty and risk can never be eliminated, they can be reduced.

Fear of possible future attack is not enough to alone claim a right to exercise preemption. Aggressive intent coupled with a capacity to do immediate harm is the right threshold for legitimate preemption. Preemptive force should be judged by considering two questions: first, have potential aggressors harmed us in the recent past or said they want to harm us in the near future? And second, are potential adversaries moving their forces into position to do significant and ominous harm? While it might be tempting to assume that secrecy on the part of a potential adversary is a sure sign of aggressive intentions, it may simply be a desire to prepare a deterrent force that might itself be the target of a preventive offensive strike. Prior to September 11th, taking the war to Afghanistan to attack Al-Qaeda camps or the Taliban would not have been justified preemption unless it was clear that such action could have thwarted imminent terrorist attacks. After all, potential adversaries may feel the need to look after their own defense against their neighbors or the US. It simply unrealistic to assume that the forces of the world are aligned and aimed so offensively at the US that all want to broadcast their defensive preparations, even if that means they might become the target of an offensive American strike.

Plausible Threat Assessments: Preemption versus Preventive War

The conduct of preemptive actions must be limited in purpose to reducing or eliminating the immediate threat, and nothing more. Therefore, offensive security policies must not only be judged on grounds of legality and morality, but also on forethought. But should preemption evolve into a regular practice, the exercise may become indistinguishable from preventive war and therefore increase instability and insecurity. While capability may not be in dispute, the motives and intentions of a potential adversary may be misinterpreted. Specifically, states may mobilize in what appear to be aggressive ways because they are fearful or because they are aggressive.

A preventive war doctrine of eliminating potential threats that may materialize at some point in the future is likely to create more fearful and aggressive states. In response, other states may defensively arm because they are afraid of a state's preemptive or preventive war doctrine or policy; others may arm offensively now that a precedent for preventive war has been set. In either case, instability is likely to grow as offensive force might create a mutual fear of attack. In the case of the U.S. attack on Iraq, instability may likely to increase because the doctrine is coupled with its goal of maintaining global "supremacy" and building military force "beyond challenge."

Therefore, preventive war undermines morality, international law, and diplomacy because it eliminates deterrence, containment, and economic means of solving problems. More important, the line between preemptive military force and preventive war is ambiguous. If all states reacted to potential adversaries as if they faced a clear and present danger of imminent or future attack at any time, global tensions would escalate and the last resort principle therefore becomes non-existent. Article 51 of the UN Charter would also lose its legitimacy. In sum, preventive war moves us closer to anarchy than a state of international law. While preventive war assumes that today's potential rival will become an adversary sometime in the future, diplomacy or some other factor could work to change the relationship from antagonism to accommodation, from competition to relative cooperation.

One can understand why any U.S. administration would favor preemption and why some would be attracted to preventive wars if they think a preventive war could guarantee security from future attack. But the psychological reassurance promised by the exercise of preventive war is illusory and a recipe for falsely justifying aggression. Preventive wars are imprudent because they bring wars that might not happen and increase resentment. They are also unjust because they assume perfect knowledge of an adversary's ill intentions when such a presumption of guilt may be premature or unwarranted. Preemption can be justified, on the other hand, if it is undertaken due to an immediate threat, where there is no time for diplomacy to be attempted, and where the action is limited to reducing that threat. There is a great temptation, however, to step over the line from preemptive to preventive war, because that line is vague and because the stress of living under the threat of war is great.

If preemption may sometimes be legitimate, is the Bush administration right to extend the case of justified preemption to preventive wars? If all threats are considered imminent and unavoidable without the use of force, then yes. But, in reality, not all threats are immediate and unavoidable. This does not mean that the threat posed by terrorism is not significant. Unconventional adversaries prepared to wage unconventional "asymmetric" war can conceal their movements, weapons, and immediate intentions and may conduct devastating surprise attacks. While nuclear, chemical, and biological weapons are not widely held, the components of these weapons seem more readily available than they were in the recent past. And of course the "everyday" infrastructure of the US can be turned against it, as were the hijacked planes on September 11th 2001. Terrorists in particular are extremely flexible. Unlike conventional militaries they can project power with great efficiency: they do not have to develop weapons and delivery vehicles; they may live among their target populations; and they require comparatively little in the way of logistical support. It is also true that although physical risk to terrorism could certainly be reduced in many ways, as Donald Rumsfeld acknowledges, it is impossible to achieve complete invulnerability. And though the United States was open to serious threats in the past, Americans are perhaps more emotionally aware of that exposure today since, as Condoleeza Rice says, "9/11 crystallized our vulnerability."[28] In sum, when combined with the advantage of surprise, terrorism is a formidable threat.

However, the dual threats of terrorism and the spread of WMD do not mean that preventive war is the only solution. For example, terrorists' sources of funding, often tied to illicit transactions and black market economies, are vulnerable to disruption through determined law enforcement. And while terrorists can piggyback on the infrastructure of their targets, they are also vulnerable to detection via that same infrastructure as they use phones, faxes, the Internet, and other electronic media. Finally, many WMD are still relatively expensive to acquire and difficult to produce and reproduce in any quantity. Still, if we imagine all possible scenarios, the potential for devastation seems limitless and it ostensibly makes great sense to get them before they get us.

There must also be a clear differentiation between threatening intentions and actual capabilities. In estimating potential threats, the intentions of a likely adversary are much more important than capabilities that "might" be employed by someone. So the assertion that the US faces rogue enemies who "hate everything" about it must be carefully evaluated. While there is certainly compelling evidence that Al Qaeda seeks to kill all American citizens, the *National Security Strategy* makes a questionable leap when it assumes that "rogue states" also desire to harm the US and pose as imminent military threats. Moreover, the administration blurs the distinction between "rogue states" and terrorists, thereby erasing the difference between terrorists and those states where they reside: "We make no distinction between terrorists and those who knowingly harbor or provide aid to them."[29] But these distinctions make a difference when a country is deciding whether to initiate offensive force.

However, current US foreign policy does not respect these distinctions. As President Bush said at West Point:

> We must take the battle to the enemy, disrupt his plans and confront the worst threats before they emerge ... Our security will require ... a military that must be ready to strike at a moment's notice in any dark corner of the world. And our security will require all Americans to be forward-looking and resolute, to be ready for preemptive action when necessary to defend our liberty and to defend our lives.[30]

Indeed, since 9/11 and the administration's gradual articulation of its new security doctrine, the US has sent troops to fight terrorists not only in Afghanistan but in the Philippines, Yemen, Indonesia, and Georgia and has used force against Iraq over alleged pursuit of WMD. Limitless preventive war entails an expanding list of force commitments that might spread US military forces thin at the same time that it risks escalating military conflicts. Such uses of force, while seeming sensible in an atmosphere of perceived heightened vulnerability, may be unnecessary. At worst, there is risk of backlash fueled by fear and resentment, not because discrimination between combatants is difficult during war; indeed, it is because they have not yet made an aggressive act that nearly all those killed or injured by a preventive war will be noncombatants.

To see how the Bush Administration has blurred the distinctions between preemption and preventive offensive war, consider their arguments about the threat posed by Iraq's potential to acquire WMD. Vice President Cheney argues that Iraq poses a threat to the US: "Many of us are convinced that Saddam Hussein will acquire nuclear weapons fairly soon ... Deliverable weapons of mass destruction in the hands of a terror network or murderous dictator or the two working together constitutes as grave a threat as can be imagined. The risks of inaction are far greater than the risks of action."[31] But here we must recall the distinction between preemptive war and preventive war. In 2003, did Iraq meet the definition of an imminent threat? Does it even need to?

Moreover, while other so-called "rogue states" present more imminent nuclear threats, the administration insisted that Iraq's potential future capability justified offensive action. As one Bush administration official told the *New York Times* after North Korea announced that it would remove monitoring equipment on both its nuclear reactor and plutonium stockpiles – enabling it to produce several more nuclear weapons within a few months – "We still think Saddam is the bigger threat, but there is no question that the North Koreans, who already have superior firepower, may soon be in a position to threaten to deploy or sell its nuclear capability. Iraq is a long way from that." Did the Bush Administration's arguments about Iraq reveal a strong tendency to lump preemption and preventive war in the same category of first strike initiatives when in fact they are quite different offensive strategies? If so, does this reveal a weakness in Bush's legal and moral claim to invade Iraq in order to safeguard America's self-defense?

The Bush Administration, Moral Conviction, and Moral Contradiction

George W. Bush's national security agenda taps America's deep moral roots and its messianic mission. But instead of promoting Wilsonian liberal values, the missionaries driving U.S. foreign policy today are more comfortable with stark moral contrasts, linking America's post-9/11 mission to an apocalyptic conflict between good and evil. The grand moral scale of the Bush approach has been driven by the simplistic goal of conquering evil and its dismissal of concerns about the means employed.

The moral convictions and contradictions of the Bush Administration are also consistent with the idealistic image of America as a shining "city upon a hill," an image seen in stark contrast to the evil forces it is attempting to eradicate. Tom Barry emphasizes, "Over the past five centuries, American society has continued to believe in its own moral transcendence, but the city on the hill has experienced major urban renewal."[32] At the initiation of the Cold War, the moral values of the city were commonly regarded as Western principles. The collapse of the USSR led many to believe in the perfection of the American democratic ideal. For Barry, "neoconservative 'end of history' and 'clash of civilization' interpretations of history fortified the American conviction that its Judeo-Christian transatlantic culture constituted the epitome of civilization." He goes on to suggest that those who dissent from this ideal, namely Western Europe, are regarded as "moral relativists, political opportunists, and weak-kneed partners afraid to speak evil's name."[33]

The end of the Cold War left U.S. foreign policy without a defining legacy but began a process toward building a political environment in which moral absolutism under Bush Jr. would flourish. In the absence of the anticommunist core, no political sector – left, centrist, or right – could persuasively occupy the moral high ground and articulate a new vision for U.S. global engagement. The "New World

Order" of the Bush Sr. administration was met with derision from the right, as were the "assertive multilateralism" and revived liberal internationalist policies of the Clinton administration. The left focused almost exclusively on backlash politics opposing the new liberal-conservative consensus on free trade, while alternately supporting and critiquing the liberal-centrist consensus around humanitarian interventionism. Also focused largely on backlash politics against the perceived liberalism of the Clinton presidency and largely bereft of their core Anti-Communism, the Right abandoned Cold War-style multilateralism of "West against the Rest" and accepted a new U.S. foreign policy of "America against the Rest."

This coherent yet simplistic moral vision of U.S. foreign policy brought together the traditionalist concerns of the social conservatives, military/industrial complex advocates, and unilateralists bent on declaring American global supremacy. This troika, today known as neo-conservative foreign policymakers and thinkers, forms the core of Bush power base. Dismissive of arguments about new transnational threats to global stability (climate change, resource scarcity conflicts, infectious disease), the new vision was at once simple and grandiose. Simple in that U.S. foreign policy should not get bogged down in conflicts and humanitarian crises that have no direct bearing on U.S. national interests and grandiose in that policymakers should assert global hegemony. This agenda was morally legitimized and politically justified in the minds of neoconservatives quickly on September 11th 2001.

So what is really new about Bush? After all, the U.S. has a long history of throwing its weight around, intervening militarily, sidelining at times with the U.N., at other times allying itself with dictators and human rights abusers, and always asserting for itself the high ground of morality and the blessing of the almighty. According to Howard Fineman of *Newsweek*, "Every president invokes God and asks his blessing. Every president promises, though not always in so many words, to lead according to moral principles rooted in biblical tradition. The English writer G.K. Chesterton called America 'a nation with the soul of a church,' and every president, at times, is the pastor in the bully pulpit." But Fineman describes Bush as occupying a unique position in this tradition: "it has taken a war, and the prospect of more, to highlight a central fact – this president and this presidency is the most resolutely 'faith-based' in modern times, an enterprise founded, supported, and guided by trust in the temporal and spiritual power of God." Bush's personal friend and Secretary of Commerce Donald Evans contends that moral vision "gives him a desire to serve others and a very clear sense of what is good and what is evil."[34]

Bush's new first strike strategy against the "evildoers" incorporates many of the operative and cultural features of American exceptionalism and interventionism while dropping the notion that U.S. leadership should operate within a framework of rules, norms, and institutions designed to promote international security. As a result, its leadership is increasingly seen as less benign. Under Bush, the salient features of U.S. global engagement are its aggressive anti-multilateralism, renewed militarism and disdain for diplomacy, and strict moral interpretation of right and wrong, good and evil, and us or against us. Underlying and fortifying these currents is the language of anti-terrorism, which has replaced Anti-Communism as the organizing and unifying principle in Post-9/11 American politics.

Thus, the emerging Bush strategy is an agenda of preemption and preventive war distinguished by a "moral simplicity," that according to Bush justifies America's "endless" war against "evildoers." Bush's moral simplicity and warning that you are "either with us or with the terrorists" reflect a one-dimensional approach to foreign policy. The president's morally simplistic worldview also relegates realism to the backburner. For example, in a key foreign policy speech at West Point in June 2002, Bush outlined a supremacist or neo-imperial agenda of international security. Not only would the U.S. no longer count on coalitions of great powers to guarantee collective security, it also would prevent the rise of any potential global rival – keeping U.S. "military strengths beyond challenges." As for the "the moral clarity" that Bush's supporters say he uses to interpret world politics, we should welcome the valuable words of Bryan Hehir, former head of the Harvard Divinity School:

> The invocation of moral reasoning for any contemplated policy decision is to be welcomed as long as the complexity of moral issues is given adequate attention. Moral reasoning can indeed support military action, at times obligate such action. It also, equally importantly, can restrain or deny legitimacy to the use of force. To invoke the moral factor is to submit to the full range of its discipline.[35]

The Imperial Temptation

Has an imperial temptation invariably gone to the head of the Bush Administration? While today's dream of a benevolent hegemony is sustained by the notion that the world owes the U.S. gratitude, it rests on America's ever more flattering self-image. Given its preponderance in all forms of power, the U.S. is bound to remain the most important state actor in the world. But, as Pierre Hassner contends, the U.S. has a choice "between an attempt at authoritarian, global U.S. rule tempered by anarchic resistance, on the one hand, and, on the other, hegemony tempered by law, concert and consent."[36]

Offensive wars against terrorists and rogue states have been legitimized by Bush as a necessary means of protecting America's most sensitive moral and cultural values, namely democracy, freedom, and safety. From America's perspective, those obstructing the global war on terrorism are not only evil doers such as Saddam Hussein, Osama bin Laden, and Kim Jong Ill, but also France, Germany, Russia, and China since they did not fully support the policy means with which President Bush was building a case for war against Iraq. Collectively, these nations feared the absence of a global counter-weight or buttress to U.S. global power. Thus, global opposition to America's invasion of Iraq in March 2003 was more about expressing fears concerning the scope and range of U.S. hegemony and the exercise of offensive military force, rather than about the potential of illicit W.M.D. in Iraq.

One can understand why any administration would favor preemption and why some would be attracted to preventive war if they think these offensive measures would guarantee invulnerability. But this psychological reassurance is at best illusory and the effort to attain it may be counterproductive. The temptation to slide over the line from preemption to preventive war is great because that line is vague and because of the extraordinary stress of living under the threat of terrorist attack or war. But that temptation should be resisted as vulnerability is a fact of life.

Even more, have offensive war measures added to a world image of the U.S. as a unilateralist power driven by the desire to maintain global hegemony? According to Stanley Hoffman, U.S. foreign policy can produce "an activism that others see as imperialistic: for we expect them to join the consensus, we ignore the boundaries and differences between 'them' and 'us,' we prod them out of conviction that we act for their own good, and we do not take resistance gracefully."[37]

Notes

1 Rice is quoted in Jay Tolson, "The New American Empire?" *US News and World Report*. (13 January 2003): 39.
2 Rice is quoted in Nicholas Lehmann, "The Next World Order: The Bush Administration May Have a Brand-New Doctrine of Power," (1 April 2002), 1.
3 Ibid.
4 George W. Bush, "Address to a Joint Session of Congress and the American People," 20 September 2001, http://www.whitehouse.gov/news/releases/2001/09/20010920-8.html
5 Bush, "State of the Union," 29 January 2002.
6 Ibid.
7 Ibid.
8 George W. Bush, "Graduation Speech at West Point." 1 June 2002.
9 George W. Bush, The White House, "The National Security Strategy of the United States of America," 17 September 2002, pp. 12 and 19, http://www.whitehouse.gov/nsc/nss.html. Herein referred to as the "National Security Strategy."
10 Ibid, 19.
11 Ibid, 33.
12 Hugo Grotius, *The Rights of War and Peace*, book 2, chapter 1-2, section 1, trans. AC Campbell (Washington, DC: M. Walter Dunne, 1901), p. 1625.
13 Daniel Webster, in a letter to Lord Ashburton, August 6, 1842, set out in John Bassett Moore, *A digest of International Law*, Vol. II (1906), p. 412.

14 See Charter of the United Nations, signed in San Francisco on 26 June 1945. http://www.unhchr.ch/html/menu3/b/ch-chp7.htm (accessed 10 February 2004).

15 Colin Powell, "Perspectives: Powell Defends a First Strike as Iraq Option," *New York Times*, 8 September 2002, p. 18.

16 George W. Bush, The White House, "The National Security Strategy of the United States of America," September 17, 2002, Chapter V, http://www.whitehouse.gov/nsc/nss.html. Herein referred to as the National Security Strategy.

17 See the International Information Program at the Department of State: http://usinfo.state.gov/products/pubs/terrornet/12.htm (accessed 11 February 2004).

18 John Lewis Gaddis, Interview, *PBS: The War Behind Closed Doors*. Public Broadcasting Corporation. 2002.

19 *National Security Strategy*, Chapter III.

20 See Neta Crawford, "The Slippery Slope Toward Preventive War," *Carnegie Council on Ethics and International Affairs*, 2 (March 2003). http://www.cceia.org/viewMedia.php/prmTemplateID/8/prmID/868 (accessed 20 February 2004).

21 For thorough and compelling accounts of American foreign policy during the Cold War (1945 to 1989), see: Stephen E. Ambrose, *Rise to Globalism*. (Middlesex, England: Penguin Books, 1997); John Lewis Gaddis, *Strategies of Containment*; Steven W. Hook and John Spanier, *American Foreign Policy Since World War II*. (Washington DC: Congressional Quarterly Press, 2000); and Mead, *Special Providence*. Several studies are concerned with the use of preemption in response to nuclear proliferation during the Cold War. See: Marc Trachtenberg, *History and Strategy* (Princeton: Princeton University Press, 1991), 103-18, 132-46; C. L. Sulzberger, *An Age of Mediocrity: Memoirs and Diaries, 1963-1972* (New York: Macmillan, 1973), 463; Robert S. Litwak, "The New Calculus of Pre-emption," *Survival* 44 (Winter 2002-03), pp. 61-62; Robert M. Lawrence and William R. Van Cleave, "Assertive Disarmament," *National Review*, 10 September 1968, 898-905; Richard K. Betts, "Nuclear Proliferation After Osirak," *Arms Control Today* 11 (September 1981): 1-7; William Burr and Jeffrey T. Richelson, "Whether to 'Strangle the Baby in the Cradle': The United States and the Chinese Nuclear Program, 1960-64," *International Security* 25 (Winter 2000/01): 54-99.

22 Ibid.

23 Richard K. Betts, *Surprise Attack: Lessons for Defense Planning* (Washington, DC: Brookings Institution, 1982), pp. 14–43.

24 The Israel air strike has been compared with the claim of preemption by President Bush in the development of his strategic national security doctrine. See: Jonathan Steel, "Bush Doctrine Makes Nonsense of UN Charter," *The Guardian*, 7 June 2002, 1.

25 Gregory A. Raymond and Charles W. Kegley, Jr., "International Norms and Military Preemption: Implications for Global Governance." Presented at the International Symposium on "International Norms for the 21st Century," Aix-en-Provence, 11-14 September 2003, 8-9.

26 Geoffrey Goodwin, *Ethics and Nuclear Deterrence* (New York: St. Martins Press, 1982); Michael Walzer, *Just and Unjust Wars*.

27 Chris Brown, *International Relations Theory: New Normative Approaches* (New York: Columbia University Press, 1992).

28 Crawford, "The Slippery Slope Toward Preventive War."

29 *National Security Strategy*, Part III.
30 George W. Bush, "President Delivers Graduation Speech at West Point," 1 June 2002, http://www.whitehouse.gov/news/releases/2002/06/20020601-3.html (accessed 20 February 2004).
31 Richard Cheney, "Vice President Speaks at VFW 103rd National Convention," 26 August 2002, http://www.whitehouse.gov/news/releases/2002/08/20020826.html (accessed 20 February 2004).
32 Tom Barry, "The U.S. Power Complex: What's New," *World Policy Journal* (November 2002).
33 Ibid. See also: Robert Kagan, "Power and Weakness," *Policy Review* (June/July 2002).
34 Howard Fine, "Bush and God," *Newsweek* (10 March 2003), 25.
35 Quoted in Stanley Hoffman, "The High and the Mighty," *The American Prospect* (13 January 2003).
36 Pierre Hasner, "Friendly Questions to America the Beautiful," *The National Interest* (Fall 2002).
37 Stanley Hoffman, *Gulliver's Troubles, or the Setting of American Foreign Policy* (New York: McGraw-Hill, 1968), p. 195.

Chapter 3

The President and
the Congress in Concert
Declaring and Making War
in the United States

Susan Weldon Scott
University of Southern Mississippi

The simplicity of the Constitution in regard to the war powers of the executive and legislative branches is both striking and deceptive. Congress has the authority to declare war and grant letters of marque and reprisal. The president acts as the commander-in-chief of the United States armed forces in times of war. In comparison to other sections of the Constitution in which competing interpretations are plentiful, the untutored mind might naively assume that the war powers clause would be exempt from heated debate and collective confusion.

The exact opposite has proven true. Simplicity should not be confused with clarity with regard to the war powers clause; many are the constitutional debates surrounding the proper scope and role of executive and legislative power in war-making. Although the Framers themselves took a solid collective stance on war-making in favor of the legislative branch, the historical record indicates some individual confusion and concern on just exactly how the democratic delineation of roles in war-making would work in practice. Taken together with the enthusiastic assertion of presidential power in the foreign policy arena and frustratingly sporadic moments of congressional interest, the question of who has the power to go to war and how war is to be conducted remains an enigma.

Perhaps no other public document embodies the confusion and conflicting opinions of the debate than the War Powers Resolution of 1973. To understand its complexities, a careful examination of the War Powers Resolution (WPR), especially the circumstances of its drafting and passage, is in order. The WPR is but one document on the spectrum of this debate, and it should be noted that political and scholarly opinions often come down hard in overwhelming favor of either the president or Congress; there are almost no advocates for a fair and practical middle ground. Rare indeed is the politician or scholar who attempts a justification for war powers that goes beyond the Framers' original intent to identify grander theories of executive and legislative war powers in American government. This, of course, is not to suggest that the Framers' intent is an irrelevant point of reference; however, for many the debate ends there and perhaps that is misguided. Many factors guided the framing of the Constitution. The Framers were engaged in a brave but uncertain experiment, and they were influenced by both the great political thinkers and the political necessities of their day. The same way in which the timing of the drafting and passage of the WPR helps to explain the intent of the legislation more so than its actual prescriptions, so too must the war powers clause of the Constitution be read with an eye toward its historical perspective.

Underlying the war powers debate is an arguably more important problem to consider. The challenge is ultimately to pinpoint a function and role for the legislative branch in war-making that is practical and meaningful, satisfying both the demands of the Constitution and the exigencies of 21st century warfare. The Constitution is a blueprint for government fueled by the ideals of republican democracy, and more than lip service and ceremonial observance of its prescriptions is required of our branches of government if our system is to retain its spirit and survive. Unfortunately, lip service and ceremonial observance is what has characterized the war powers clause, and whether or not our government can move beyond mere ceremony is tied directly into the success and failure of the American democratic experiment.

The War Powers Resolution of 1973

A thorough examination of the War Powers Resolution of 1973 serves as a helpful springboard in a discussion of the war powers debate. Before delving into the meat and bones of the WPR, it is instructive to note the official functions of the president and Congress in war-making, per the Constitution.

Constitutional Functions of Congress and the President

The Constitution vests the legislative branch with the following responsibilities: "to declare War, grant Letters of Marque and Reprisal, and make rules concerning Captures on Land and Water;" raise and support armies; provide and maintain a navy; makes rules and regulations of the land and naval forces; "to provide for calling forth the Militia to execute the laws of the Union, suppress Insurrections, and repel Invasions;" "to make all Laws which shall be necessary and proper for carrying into Execution the foregoing Powers and all other Powers vested by this Constitution in the government of the United States, or in any Department or Officer thereof;" and the power of the purse ("No money shall be drawn from the Treasury, but in Consequence of Appropriations made by law.").[1]

The Executive is made responsible for the following functions: "The President shall be Commander in Chief of the Army and Navy of the United States, and of the Militia of the several states, when called into the actual service of the United States;" and the president "shall receive Ambassadors and other public ministers."[2] In addition, the president has the constitutional authority to repel sudden attacks against the United States without prior congressional approval or declaration of war. Presidents have claimed "war powers" as part of their foreign affairs powers; and they have derived that authority from their status as commander-in-chief. By repeated exercise and without successful opposition, presidents have established their "authority" to send troops abroad probably beyond effective challenge, but the constitutional foundations and the constitutional limits of that authority remain in dispute.[3] It was not until 1973, however, that a congressional discussion took place on whether the president's "war powers" were exclusive, in the sense that presidents have typically regarded military activity as just one of the many instruments to be found in his foreign policy toolbox, so long as his actions stopped short of war.[4] Constitutional scholar Louis Henkin sums up this lack of clarity in the Constitution's instructions:

> That the Constitution is especially inarticulate in allocating foreign affairs; that a particular power can with equal logic and fair constitutional reading be claimed for the President or for Congress; that the powers of both the President and Congress have been described in full, even extravagant adjectives ('vast,' 'plenary'); that instead of a 'natural' separation of 'executive' from 'legislative' functions there has grown an irregular, uncertain division of each – all have served and nurtured political forces inviting struggle ... Conflict has been compounded also by the blurry bounds of 'Executive power' and the uncertain reach of the authority of the Commander in Chief, in war or in peace. Since, generally, these 'boundary disputes' between Congress and the President have not been resolved in Court, they remain unsolved in principle ... [5]

The Drafting and Passage of the WPR

It is not uncommon to hear critics of the WPR characterize it as a response to presidential abuse of war power in the aftermath of Vietnam, but WPR critic Louis Fisher asserts that the "resolution is better described as a slow, evolutionary culmination of institutional struggles and constitutional debate than as a narrow preoccupation with the Vietnam War."[6] Initially, however, it was a pervasive sense of betrayal in the wake of an unpopular war that served as the incentive for Congress's reassertion in foreign policy, particularly war-making. Irrespective of whose authority one seeks to maximize (Congress's or the president's), many regard the WPR as a disastrous, ineffective piece of legislation that only further muddies the waters. Commenting on the final product, Senator Tom Eagleton cynically remarked that the Purpose and Policy section was "no more binding than a 'whereas' clause in a Kiwanis Club resolution."[7]

The main purpose of the WPR was to circumscribe the president's authority to use armed forces abroad in hostilities or potential hostilities without a declaration of war or other congressional authorization, yet provide enough flexibility to permit him to respond to attack or other emergencies.[8] Louis Fisher and David Gray Adler note that although the WPR is generally considered the high water mark of congressional reassertion in foreign affairs, the resolution itself was "ill conceived and badly compromised from the start, replete with tortured ambiguity and self-contradiction."[9]

From the very beginning, the House and the Senate "marched down separate and distinct roads, almost irreconcilable roads."[10] Indeed, the House and Senate had competing visions of the bill, and perhaps the reason for the ambiguity and overall ineffectiveness of the WPR is the lack of common ground on which a compromise was brokered between the two houses. Members of the House were willing to concede that the president, in certain extraordinary and emergency conditions, had the authority to defend the United States and its citizens without prior congressional authorization. Rather than spell out such scenarios, the House relied on procedural safeguards, such as mandatory consultation and reporting to Congress, and the House version gave the president 120 days to carry out unauthorized military action.

The Senate remained staunchly opposed to the spirit and language of the House version, largely because it refused to give the president such unilateral authority to make war whenever and wherever he liked for whatever reason for up to 120 days. The Senate took the opposite approach from the House, outlining certain scenarios for unilateral presidential action rather than relying solely on procedural safeguards. The Senate version also ordered the president to cease military action within thirty days unless Congress specifically authorized the president to continue.[11]

As Fisher and Adler note, these efforts to codify presidential war powers carried a number of risks. Imprecise legislation may widen presidential power rather than restrict it, and executive interpretation of its language (terms such as "necessary and appropriate retaliatory actions," "imminent threat," and "endangered citizens") was subject to a myriad of viewpoints, all sympathetic to executive power.[12] There were also other complications, primarily political pressure to "defeat" President Richard Nixon.

The politics of the day were crucial contributing factors to the WPR, and they should not be understated. At the same time congressmen were literally debating the conference version of the bill, the houses were abuzz with the news that Vice President Spiro Agnew has resigned. Shortly thereafter, Nixon's presidential career began to visibly unravel and the WPR was caught in the crossfire. The "Saturday Night Massacre" (Nixon's firing of Special Prosecutor Archibald Cox) had left many angered and dismayed, and popular disgust for Nixon was only reinforced when he announced that he would veto the WPR on the grounds that it was unconstitutional and that it would "seriously undermine this Nation's ability to act decisively and convincingly in times of international crisis." The hypocrisy of Nixon's constitutional regard was blatant, and it only strengthened the resolve of Congress to achieve passage of the WPR, despite a certain presidential veto.[13]

Nixon issued his veto as promised, and the fight was on for an override in Congress. Nixon had vetoed eight bills in the 93rd Congress, and Congress had failed to override him each of the eight times. As Senator Tom Eagleton noted, it was an embarrassing record for Democratic leadership, and the WPR override would be its best shot at evening the score. Also underlying the eagerness for an override was the belief that it would quicken Nixon's inevitable impeachment. The final vote in the House was 284-135, achieving an override by a four-vote margin; the Senate won an easier override, the final vote 75-18. In his recollection of events, Senator Eagleton (a proponent-turned-avid-opponent of the WPR) recounted instances in which other senators approached him after they override vote to explain how they voted:

> One Senator came up to me after the debate and said, "I heard your argument. I agree with you. I love the Constitution, but I hate Nixon more. Another said, "You were right as a matter of policy. But what you failed to recognize was that this had become a symbolic issue insofar as the public's perception of limiting the President's warmaking."[14]

The intended spirit and purpose of the WPR were consistent with Congress's original desire to put the president in his proper constitutional place, but WPR's prescriptions fell miserably short of its high expectations. Efforts to score short-term political points at the cost of long-term constitutional and institutional interests characterize its passage, although many legislators took comfort in the resolution's symbolic value rather than its contents.[15]

Major Criticisms of the WPR

Absolutely no aspect of the War Powers Resolution is safe from virulent and impassioned criticism. Treatises can be written on the constitutional issues that it highlights, but technically speaking the practicality of the WPR's statutory provisions (consultation, timing, reporting) has been challenged on many grounds, with a plethora of politicians and scholars offering potential solutions and amendments. Criticism comes from all directions, both legislative and executive, and so long as the Courts remain silent, the controversy is unlikely to be resolved.

Proponents for maximum congressional power such as Senator Eagleton argue that the final conference product "did not just simply water down the bill; it turned the Constitution on its head. By failing to define the President's powers in legally binding language, the bill provided a legal basis for the President's broad claims of inherent power to initiate war." Eagleton also attacks the disclaimer on the bill that stated that the WPR was not "intended to alter the constitutional authority of the

Congress or the President," saying that such a disclaimer was meaningless since no court has been willing to tackle the issue, citing "political question" grounds as justification.[16]

The mindset of President Nixon best embodies the criticisms of the pro-president camp. First and foremost, he believed that the WPR encroached upon the president's constitutional responsibilities as commander-in-chief, and this attitude is certainly in line with the prevailing view of proponents of maximum executive authority. Nixon also thought it was impractical and dangerous to fix in a statute the procedures by which the president and Congress would share the war power. He told Congress that the "only way in which the constitutional powers of a branch of the Government can be altered is by amending the Constitution – and any attempt to make such alterations by legislation alone is clearly without force."[17] In any case, Congress failed miserably in its objectives, primarily because it became so mired in detail and attempted to account for every possible scenario while attempting elasticity in the statutes. Nixon's warning about the dangerousness of fixing constitutional limitations through statute should not go unheeded, despite the irony of the source. At the heart of the WPR and the war powers debate is a struggle between branches, and the third branch of government – the Courts – would be the only appropriate source from which constitutional legitimacy could be derived.

Criticisms of the WPR's Statutory Provisions

As it relates to consultation, U.S. foreign policy expert Ellen Collier asserts that the primary controversy is whether or not the WPR is an effective and appropriate instrument for assuring that the president and Congress share in decisions to send U.S. forces into conflict abroad.[18] The president is to consult with Congress "in every possible instance," but this leaves considerable discretion to the president even though it does emphasize inter-branch cooperation. The legislative history of the WPR makes clear that consultation is supposed to constitute more than presidential notification of hostilities, but the statutory definition of consultation is nonetheless vague and ambiguous.[19] Critics of the WPR cite the ambiguity of the consultation section as a serious constitutional dilemma, because Congress cannot delegate away the power to decide for war.[20]

In addition, the WPR does not define "hostilities," and it is unclear whether the term is applicable to circumstances that constitute war or scenarios that are short of war. The conceptual difficulty of Section 2 (c), as scholar Brian Hallett perceives it, is that it envisions the congressional war powers as principally the "statutory authorization" of the commander-in-chief's power to "introduce United States Armed Forces into hostilities, or into situations where imminent involvement in hostilities is clearly indicated by the circumstances." Hallett continues:

Not only is the possibility of Congress's declaring war a subordinate concern in the act, but one has the strong impression that it was viewed by the Ninety-Third Congress as but a different statutory form for authorizing the introduction of U.S. armed forces into hostilities ... [T]he phrase *statutory authorization* appears to be but a euphemism for rubber-stamping a fait accompli. Whatever the congressional war powers might be, they must surely constitute something more substantial that statutory authorization.[21]

Hallett's concerns are lent credence by those of Henkin, who asserts that it is definitely within the realm of congressional authority to determine what constitutes "hostilities" and "war." Congressional acquiescence in presidential military engagements did not, through custom, atrophy congressional power and deprive it of authority to regulate for the future.[22]

Not surprisingly, the reporting requirements are confusing and ambiguous as well and contribute greatly to the overall impracticality of the WPR. If the president introduces troops into hostilities he is to remove them within sixty days unless Congress approves further action; the president can extend the deadline an additional thirty days if he determines such an extension is necessary to protect and remove the troops. This sixty-to-ninety day clock does not start ticking, however, unless the president reports under a very specific section, Section 4(a)(1).[23] For fairly obvious reasons, most presidents have chosen not to report under Section 4(a)(1) and choose to report to Congress more generally. The net result, then, is that the president can wage unilateral warfare until Congress successfully adopts statutory constraints, vis-à-vis a concurrent resolution.[24]

Clearly, there are many aspects of the WPR that are shrouded in ambiguity and confusion. As long as the courts refuse to arbiter the dispute, debates about the legality and practicality of the WPR are sure to continue. To that end, it is likely that Congress will continue to create and dismantle its role in war-making in a piecemeal fashion. However, these brief, energetic spurts of congressional activism, combined with larger periods of inertia, point to related and equally significant questions – questions that are more complex than debating the merits and faults of a piece of legislation like the WPR. Did the Framers have a grander design for Congress than the one realized when the penned those instructions centuries ago? If so, can the rigorous standards of democracy survive the equally rigorous demands of 21st century world politics? If the answer to the latter question ultimately proves to be negative, then perhaps it is time to reevaluate our perceptions of acceptable democratic behavior, revising it to function in a globalized world and within a constitutionally acceptable framework.

The Framers' Intent

Obviously, the Framers' collective intent is reflected in the words of the Constitution. The war powers clause of the Constitution is remarkably precise and unambiguous, yet it is also the genesis for some of the most heated and impassioned constitutional debates. Perhaps more so than with any other part of the Constitution, the Framers' intent with regard to war powers is heavily referenced during the debates over the scope and limits of congressional and executive authority in war-making. Scholars and politicians on both sides of the debate frequently find and cite support under the catch-all heading "Framers' intent." However, the minutes of the debates of the Constitutional Congress and the personal letters and papers of the Framers reveal a subtly splintered version over how the new nation's approach to war-making should function.

Although the individual opinions of the Framers were many and mixed, there is general agreement that their primary intention in the wording of the war powers clause was to avoid placing too much power in the hands of one person.[25] The fact that the power for war and peace was historically associated with the monarchy was repeatedly addressed at the convention, and the deliberations at the convention demonstrate that the delegates embraced the principle of collective decision-making and the concept of shared powers in foreign affairs. Many were for a vigorous executive but remained fearful of vesting too much power in the president, especially the power to make war, as wars were viewed as one of many monarchial oppressions. Alexander Hamilton, a strong proponent of executive power, proposed that the Senate would have the "sole power of declaring war" and that the president would act as commander-in-chief, authorized to have "the direction of war when authorized or begun."[26]

The war clause was considered in debate on 17 August 1787. Charles Pinckney opposed placing the war power in the full Congress, reasoning that its proceedings were too slow and the Senate would "be the best depository, being more acquainted with foreign affairs, and most capable of proper resolutions." Conversely, Pierce Butler was the only person who argued for vesting the war power entirely with the president, who by nature would have all the requisite qualities and would not make war unless the country supported it. James Madison and Elbridge Gerry were dissatisfied with the draft proposal to vest the legislature with the power to make war, and they consequently moved to substitute "declare" for "make," leaving the president the power to repel sudden attacks.[27]

In *Federalist No. 74*, Alexander Hamilton explained part of the purpose in making the president commander-in-chief, reasoning that the direction of war "most peculiarly demands those qualities which distinguish the exercise of power by a single head," and that the power of directly war and emphasizing common strength "forms a usual and essential part in the definition of the executive authority." In *Federalist No. 69*, Hamilton offered a modest definition of the commander-in-chief's powers, professing that the office "would amount to nothing more than the supreme command and direction of the military and naval forces, as first general and admiral of the Confederacy."[28] Whatever the conception was of the president's role, the power to initiate war clearly lay with Congress.

Despite the clarity of the Constitution's text, the Framers themselves expressed doubt and concern for the exercise of the war powers as the fledgling new nation began to assert itself abroad, and in 1836 John Quincy Adams lamented, "The respective powers of the President and Congress of the United States in the case of war with foreign powers are yet undetermined. Perhaps they can never be defined."[29] Although the Constitution had been written and ratified, confusion and debate still continued over which branch was more suitably able to respond and contend with the pressures and surprises of foreign policy. The Helvidius/Pacificus debates between James Madison and Alexander Hamilton, respectively, are an illustration of that controversy. Madison, a fervent proponent of plenary congressional power, challenged Hamilton's support of President Washington's "power" to proclaim neutrality in the war between Great Britain and France. Henkin describes the theoretical construction of the Helvidius/Pacificus debates:

> Madison argued that Congress is the principal organ of government and has all its political authority, in foreign affairs as elsewhere, except (and to the extent that) the Constitution explicitly granted authority to the President (alone or with the Senate)... Further, the Constitution gives Congress the most important foreign affairs power, the power to declare war, which can effectively terminate all relations with the enemy and modify relations with other nations. The power surely included the power to decide not to go to war, as by a proclamation of neutrality; it must include also the power to determine national policy generally, for those might determine war or peace.[30]

In addition, John Quincy Adams reflected in his memoirs on "that error in our Constitution which confers upon the legislative assemblies the power of declaring war, which in the theory of government, according to Montesquieu and Rosseau, is strictly an Executive Act."[31] The Framers, while no doubt devoted to the principles of republicanism, clearly were divided over the proper division of war powers in the republic, even after the drafting and ratification of the Constitution.

Alexander Hamilton's private correspondence lends itself to even deeper reflection. Writing privately in 1798, he declared that the president's constitutional war power did not extend beyond repelling force with force, leaving any further response to Congress under the "idea of reprisals."[32] Reprisals, or "imperfect" wars, could easily develop into general or "perfect" wars (as it had for England in 1652, 1664, 1739, and 1756), and as such, the Framers deliberately vested control over reprisals in the same body that had control over declarations of war.[33] Although letters of marque and reprisal are relics of the past, the notion that Congress possesses control over wars of all scales is intriguing.

Taking into consideration the Constitution, custom, and modern day world politics, the allocation to Congress of the power to decide for war while foreign relations are conducted largely by the president has led to a competition for power and has generated doubts about the viability and wisdom of the constitutional distribution of war powers. That the Constitution grants Congress the power to decide for war does give it legitimate claims of authority to certain other closely related areas, for example, the authority to end war or proclaim neutrality. Congress could also regulate presidential foreign policy and his conduct of foreign relations, as those things could plausibly lead the United States down the path to war. Inasmuch that presidential foreign policy has historically been filled with armed conflicts and undeclared wars, congressional oversight and the regular exercise of its constitutionally ordained rights appears all the more imperative. Further, there are arguably two standard definitions of war, one constitutional (i.e., a state of war exists when Congress declares it), and the other is codified into international law by the Geneva Convention.[34] If one examines U.S. military activity through the lens of the Geneva Convention definition, it is easy to ascertain that the United States has been in states of war, even if the U.S. government does not declare the situation as such. The pervasive view in America's collective historical consciousness is that our country is not one of war-making, as evidenced by our infrequent declarations of war. However, war should not always be judged on scales similar to the World Wars, and the military's track record of late suggests that the U.S. has constantly been and out of a state of war, even if government officials and the news media are not reporting it as such.

Examination and reflection of the Constitution, the debates of the Federal Convention, and the personal papers of key figures in the early republic suggest that the reliance upon "Framers' intent" is perhaps just one more confusing factor compounding this important constitutional issue. The Framers were clearly not united on this issue and had fuzzy ideas as to whether a democratic body could or should manage the country's foreign policy with regard to war. However, scholars and politicians are often able to pick and choose the words of certain Framers to manipulate and enhance their own arguments for either congressional or executive dominance.[35] By deliberately relying on certain Framers to lend credibility to a particular viewpoint, the weight and significance of the argument is greatly increased, perhaps only because one is referencing a giant in American history and offering their words as incontrovertible "proof" of how the war powers are to be construed. Thus, when an author begins bandying about the phrase "Framers' intent," readers beware. The challenge that confronted the Framers is still before us today; namely, how to conceive of a democratic theory of foreign policy that is viable in practice.

A Clausewitzian Constitution?

Central to this important debate is the realization that the United States has not always behaved democratically in the formation and execution of its foreign policy, and this has been especially true with respect to the war powers clause in the Constitution. Executive power in this arena has consistently grown stronger, and Congress has done little but to weakly acquiesce to these presidential advances.[36] Without the president's actions and behavior in foreign policy actively being checked by the legislative branch, democratic principles in war-making have ceased to be meaningful and are largely ceremonial. Congress's most important foreign policy role – its sole authority to declare war – had not only been compromised by its own inertia but also by the exigencies and changes of modern day warfare. In his book *The Lost Art of Declaring War* (1998), scholar Brian Hallett notes additional historical reasons that have contributed to the problem of congressional inactivity in war-making. In Hallett's view, the problem is located primarily in the changes that occurred in international law and custom, not in the silence of the Constitution, or the conflicting notions of the Framers, or the precedents and disputes of the 19th and 20th centuries.[37] Hallett bases his argument on the historical development of Congress's two powers to create a condition or state of war, namely its authority to declare war and its power to grant letters of marque and reprisal. Hallett identifies a possible solution to the tension between democracy and war that is grounded in the theoretical works of a familiar but unexpected source, Karl von Clausewitz.

Marque and Reprisal and Declarations of War

Discussions of the power to grant letters of marque and reprisal lead in one of two directions. On one hand, throughout the 16th, 18th, and early 19th centuries, the law of war provided that "big" or "perfect" wars were to be initiated by a formal declaration of war. "Imperfect" or "little" wars (today's armed conflicts) were to begin by issuing letters of marque and reprisal. Thus, one could extrapolate that since Congress has the power to grant letters of marque and reprisal, although an antiquated practice, the spirit of marque and reprisal retains a residual significance for proving that the Federal Convention intended the congressional war powers to encompass all types of war. Conversely, as a matter of international practice, the issuance of letters of marque and reprisal was outlawed by the 1856 Declaration of Paris.[38] Nonetheless, Congress's power to grant letters of marque and reprisal is a power that warrants further examination, primarily because it is customarily overlooked. Although the practice of issuing letters may be obsolete, perhaps the spirit of marque and reprisal was intended to remain.

The power to declare war, however, has never been outlawed by international convention. Article 1 of the Convention 3 of the 18 October 1907 Hague Peace Conference, Relative to the Opening of Hostilities, mandates that war must be declared before it can be commenced. This convention was ratified by the Senate under the leadership of President William Howard Taft, so the United States has two sources of law which bind it to declarations of war before its commencement. However, the historical record shows that despite the Constitution and the Hague convention, Congress has declared war only two or three times a century; the historical record also shows that the United States has been involved in hostilities more than two or three times each century. Hallett is quick to assert that despite this track record, the U.S. is not a democratic failure. He compares the United States to other parliamentary regimes, concluding that they have been no more successful in involving the full legislature in the decision to go to war. This dilemma is something that is inherent to democratic governments:

> In both systems the executive never requests or promulgates a declaration of war unless it is absolutely certain that Congress or Parliament will endorse it. As a result representative democracies in general and U.S democracy in particular have never lived up to their democratic pretensions, and unlike a direct democracy or a monarchy, representative democracy has always been a sometimes thing, functioning tolerably well in peacetime but reverting back to previous feudal forms during wartime.[39]

Hallett cites several reasons for congressional sterility in exercising its power to declare war. First and foremost, Hallett argues that the custom of formally declaring war had gone out of fashion at least a hundred years before the Federal Convention met in Philadelphia. By 1789, no nation was regularly and consistently declaring war formally, and the realities of international practice and custom had already rendered the power to declare war with due ceremony vacuous. Alexander Hamilton admitted as much in *Federalist No. 25* when he observed that "the ceremony of a formal denunciation of war has of late fallen into disuse." Despite the waning of this international custom, the Constitution vested Congress with the power to declare war. Further, the United States is a country that typically respects and upholds the rules and customs which govern international relations. Since the nation's inception, those rules and customs have dictated that wars be declared formally on only the rarest of occasions, and the U.S. has followed accordingly. Hallett suggests that had Congress declared war more frequently than two or three times a century, the United States would have been seen as a disruptive oddity in the eyes of the world community.[40]

Hallett has also found policy reasons to support his thesis that formal declarations of war are viewed as unnecessary. For example, John Adams was the first president to wage an undeclared war as a matter of conscious policy in his case against revolutionary France in 1793. Further, a 1971 State Department document articulates the perceived impediments of a formally declared war:

> Formal declarations of war are often deliberately avoided because they tend to indicate both at home and abroad a commitment to total victory and may impede settlement possibilities. The issuance of a formal declaration can also have certain legal results: Some treaties may be canceled or suspended; trading, contracts, and debts with the enemy are suspended; vast emergency powers become operative domestically; and the legal relations between neutral states and belligerents can be altered.[41]

Hence, formal declarations of war create the potential for hazardous policy consequences. However, the propensity to avoid declarations of war is obviously in conflict with the Constitution's instructions:

Who, after all, would dare to advocate openly that representative democracy must be sacrificed to international custom during times of war? Alternatively, who would dare to state frankly that the United States must violate the norms of international relations merely to abide by the legal dictates of the Constitution and the philosophical requirements of representative democracy? As a consequence, the principal method for resolving this conflict since 1789 has been to ignore it. When the abstract philosophical demands of the Constitution conflict with the practical realities of the well-established principles and conventions of international relations, pragmatic people prefer settled practices to unsettling philosophies – and change the topic.[42]

By adding an international law and custom perspective into the war powers debate, Hallett has incorporated the final necessary factor crucial to developing a solution to the problem that has plagued the Constitution and American war-making. Congress must reinvent its role, and since the WPR is the best example of such an attempt, it is safe to say that Congress has heretofore failed miserably and desperately needs another approach.

Hallett's Solution

In Hallett's estimation, Congress must reinvent its power to declare war. It remains empty and vacuous, despite the resort to functional equivalents (i.e., joint resolutions and the like), and their attempts have seriously lacked teeth. Congressional declarations of war are, in many ways, rubber-stamping a fait accompli. The Federal Convention clearly envisioned a separation of powers with regard to war; the commander-in-chief was to repel sudden attacks and to conduct all wars, and Congress was to deliberate and write declarations of war. It is self-evident that one cannot declare war until after the declaration has been written and the declaration cannot be written until after suitable deliberations. However, the need for Congress to deliberate or write its own declarations of war has not been self-evident at all. For example, the two 20th-century declarations, those of 1917 and 1941, were both written by the State Department, and the 1941 declaration passed without any deliberation whatsoever. Hallett argues that when one misconceives of the congressional war powers as an injunction for the commander-in-chief to consult with Congress (as did the 93rd Congress with the WPR), it makes sense for the executive to provide the texts of declarations since the president initiates the process and controls the information given to Congress. Under this construction of war powers, it logically follows that commanders-in-chief have always submitted unreasoned declarations of war for congressional approval because, by doing nothing more than declaring war, a blank congressional declaration allows for the widest possible latitude in conducting war.

Hallett's ingenuity lies in his recommendation that Congress's power to declare war be conceived as autonomous congressional power to deliberate and write its own reasoned declarations of war, independently of the commander-in-chief. Congress could not simply declare the brute fact of war as it has for over 200 years, but devote itself instead to analyzing the grievances that called for the resort to arms and the conditions that would restore peace. In order to accomplish this, Hallett realizes that collective sensibilities would have to move beyond modern conceptions of the power to declare war as a mere formality and identify the military and moral functions of a declaration of war. Reasoned declarations of war have an important military role, in that they logically justify the resort to war and establish the meaning of peace and victory; these are the war aims and articulate a grand strategy for the war. The moral purpose of a reasoned declaration of war to clearly argue a grand strategy that articulates the reasons for going to war, but it could also provide for sensible remedies or peace terms to end the war.

This understanding of congressional war powers follows not from the logic of Locke or Montesquieu or another democratic theorist, but Karl von Clausewitz and his theories of war. In Clausewitz's view, reasoned declarations of war (or their functional equivalent) are absolutely essential in the proper conduct of all wars. This grand strategy is crucial because, as Clausewitz stated: "No one starts a war – or rather, no one in his sense ought to do so – without first being clear in his mind what he intends to achieve by that war and how he intends to conduct it. The former is political purpose; the latter its operational objective."[43] The need for clearly defined war aims is one of the painful lessons learned from the Vietnam War, and Hallett observes that the *AFM 1-1, Basic Functions and Doctrine of the United States Air Force* was revised accordingly in 1984 to read: "The fabric of our society and the character of our national values suggest that the decision to employ US military forces depends on a clear declaration of objectives and the support of the American people."[44]

Thus, it is as Clausewitz famously claimed: war is merely the continuation of politics by other means. The political purposes enumerated within a reasoned declaration guide and direct the operational objectives, which is precisely the sort of control Congress has sought to exercise over the executive. It would be controlling the means used by dictating the ends sought. This is not to suggest, however, that Congress would micromanage the conduct of a war down to its smallest detail. By articulating a specific purpose, Congress has controlled through its own edict the size and nature of the military operation, leaving the professional military to deal with operational detail.

Hallett also notes that Clausewitz understood the conduct of war "depends on the particular character of the commander and the army; but the political aims are the business of government alone." Hallett interprets this to mean that Clausewitz understood that the business of war naturally divides strategy into the power to conduct war and the power to declare the political purposes of the war, and that these functions would require the qualities of different agencies of government. This delineation between the power to conduct war and the power to declare war appears to be completely in tune not only with the Constitution's instructions, but also some Framers' understanding of what they had inscribed into perpetuity. Again, one is reminded of Alexander Hamilton's words in *Federalist No. 69*:

The President is to be Commander in Chief of the army and navy of the United States. In this respect his authority ... would amount to nothing more than the supreme command and direction of the military and naval forces, as first General and Admiral of the confederacy; while that of the British King extends to the declaring of war and to the raising and regulating of fleets and armies; all which by the Constitution under consideration would appertain to the legislature.[45]

Hallett's solution satisfies both the demands of democratic theory and the demands of modern day world politics. The only problem, as he perceives it, is that the delegates to the Federal Convention were not versed in the theories of Karl von Clausewitz, and this compromises the notion of original intent. (Clausewitz was a young boy in 1787 and died in 1831. His famous treatise *On War* was published posthumously.) When congressional war powers are conceived as the power to deliberate and write reasoned declarations of war, the blessing of the Founding Fathers cannot be claimed.

Nonetheless, Hallett's solution to the tension that has pervaded the war powers clause since its inception is provocative. Hallett recognizes that "[c]learly something has been lost over the last 400 years, something that has rendered the congressional war powers hollow and ineffectual a hundred years or more before the Federal Convention met in Philadelphia, something that must be recovered ..."[46] Perhaps he has realized such a solution.

Conclusion

Centuries ago, the French philosopher Alexis de Tocqueville warned that the "tyranny of the legislature" would be replaced by a tyranny of the executive. His words echo eerily in this important debate. Foreign policy, especially war, fundamentally tests a nation's commitment to democracy, and in ways that perhaps other features of government do not. From a technical standpoint (best characterized by the WPR), the war powers clause of the Constitution is a struggle between two branches of government, and the principle of checks and balances mandates that the courts as the third branch arbiter the dispute and ordain the dueling branches with meaningful roles in this crucial function of government. The courts, however, have stubbornly remained silent, leaving Congress and the president floating aimlessly and arguing unproductively.

The Constitution is a contract between the government and the people that enshrines the principles of republican democracy. The drafting of the Constitution was an act undertaken by some of the brightest and best minds of the day, individuals who envisioned a better, kinder government and hoped that the Constitution would be a document for the ages, both theirs and ours. History instructs us that empires, even democratic ones, will not last forever. Political entropy, the tendency of things to fall apart, is an historical fact of life. Once something is put into effect, such as the Constitution, it begins to fall apart unless it is carefully overseen and safeguarded. The war powers clause of the Constitution has not been carefully safeguarded, and there have been unintended consequences that have eroded the democratic legitimacy of the Framers' experiment. Whether or not that legitimacy can be recaptured is a critical task facing American democracy.

Notes

1   Louis Fisher, *Presidential War Power* (Lawrence, KS: UP of Kansas, 1995), p. 209.
2   Ibid, 209.
3   Louis Henkin, *Foreign Affairs and the U.S. Constitution, 2nd ed.* (Oxford: Clarendon Press, 1996), p. 49.
4   Ibid, 89, 49.
5   Ibid, 84.
6   Fisher, 1995, p. 128.
7   Thomas F. Eagleton, *War and Presidential Power: A Chronicle of Congressional Surrender* (New York: Liveright, 1974), p. 207.
8   Ellen Collier, "The War Powers Resolution: A Decade of Experience" (1984).
9   David Gray Adler and Louis Fisher, "The War Powers Resolution: Time to Say Goodbye," *Political Science Quarterly* 113/1 (1998): 1.
10 Ibid, p. 2.
11 Ibid, p. 3.
12 Ibid, p. 3.
13 Eagleton, 1974, pp. 210-214.
14 Ibid, p. 220.
15 Fisher and Adler, 1998, p. 4.
16 Eagleton, 1974, p. 203.
17 Fisher, 1995, p. 130.
18 Collier, 1984, p. 172.
19 Two things are unclear about the consultation section of the WPR: (1) whether consultation requires a formal consultation with the 535 members of Congress (not merely designated leaders or committee members); and (2) whether the consultation provision is applicable only when the president involves the U.S. in hostilities without having constitutional or congressional authority.
20 Fisher and Adler, 1998, p. 3.
21 Brian Hallett, *The Lost Art of Declaring War* (Urbana, IL: UP of Illinois, 1998), p. 7.
22 Henkin, 1996, p. 108.
23 The sixty-to-ninety day time clock was a Senate capitulation to the House conferees.
24 The constitutionality of concurrent resolutions as a form of congressional control has come under serious fire as well. The State Department has asserted its belief in the inherent unconstitutionality of concurrent resolutions, especially in view of the Supreme Court's decision in *INS v. Chadha* (1989). Others such as Louis Henkin have an alternative understanding of concurrent resolutions as it pertains to the WPR. Henkin asserts that the unconstitutionality of the legislative veto only applies to congressional efforts to control the executive branch, not its own internal proceedings. Since Congress

has the sole authority to declare war, Henkin interprets concurrent resolutions as being constitutionally permissible.

25 Hallett, 1998, p. 31.
26 Fisher and Adler, 1998, p. 7.
27 Jonathan Elliott, *Debates on the Adoption of the Federal Constitution in the Convention Held at Philadelphia in 1787* (New York: Burt Franklin Reprints, 1974), pp. 438-439.
28 Fisher, 1995, pp. 9-10.
29 Peter Raven-Hansen, "Constitutional Constraints: The War Clause," in *The U.S. and the Power to Go to War: Historical and Current Perspectives*, eds. Morton H. Halperin and Gary M. Stern (Westport, CT: Greenwood Press, 1994), p. 29.
30 Henkin, 1996, pp. 77-78.
31 Ibid, p. 384.
32 Raven-Hansen, 1994, p. 35.
33 Ibid, p. 31.
34 The Geneva Conventions of 1949 are the codified international law pertaining to the conduct of war and hostilities, and it identifies two scenarios in which a state of war exists. The first is a case of declared war or of any other armed conflict, even if the state of war is not recognized by one of the parties. The second case applies to scenarios in which there is a partial or total occupation of a territory, even if the occupation meets with no armed resistance.
35 For example, an advocate for plenary congressional power could easily focus on the words of James Madison, Framer and U.S. president, to propagate his or her aims. Conversely, supporters of rigorous executive authority could rely upon Alexander Hamilton and John Quincy Adams, both Framers and distinguished members of government, to advance their claims.
36 The 1973 War Powers Resolution is the obvious exception to that rule, but that legislation is riddled with impracticality and ambiguity.
37 Hallett, 1998, p. 35.
38 Ibid, p. 27. Interestingly, the United States never signed the 1856 Declaration of Paris.
39 Ibid, p. 29.
40 Ibid, pp. 34-35.
41 Ibid, p. 37.
42 Ibid, p. 47.
43 Ibid, p. 45.
44 Ibid, p. 45.
45 Ibid, p. 47.
46 Ibid, p. 63.

Chapter 4

A Political Calculus of Apology: Japan and Its Neighbors

Girma Negash

University of South Carolina, Aiken

Many have asked me whether I am still angry with the Japanese. Maybe it helped that I have faith. I had learned to accept suffering. I also learned to forgive. If Jesus Christ could forgive those who crucified Him, I thought I could also find it in my heart to forgive those who had abused me. Half a century had passed. Maybe my anger and resentment were no longer as fresh. Telling my story has made it easier for me to be reconciled with the past. But I am still hoping to see justice done before I die.

Maria Rosa Henson, *Comfort Woman*[1]

These concluding words of an autobiographical account of long suffering, reveal not only the endurance of compassion and faith but also a yearning for justice typical of those neighbors of Japan who were victimized by colonialism and the wars of aggression. Considering that most of the so-called comfort women, who were forcibly taken as sex slaves by the Japanese army in World War II, have now reached the mature ages of 70s and 80s, justice as a dying wish makes their claim so much more ethically potent and transhistorical. As the last demanding voices for justice or calls for apology and reparation are fading, a new generation of activists has taken up the banner in Korea, China, the Philippines, Taiwan, Singapore, and Japan itself, with the emergence of universal norms of human rights. On the other side of the equation is the Japanese political elite, barely removed from the first generation of Japanese leaders who survived the Tokyo Trials, and those who received the blessing of the American occupation powers to build a stable and peaceful Japan. Hence the politics of dealing with the injurious past is especially salient in Asia.[2] The following pages introduce an apology mode that applies to such a past and examine Japan's readiness and political calculus in response to the rising calls for apology and compensation for war crimes by its neighbors and the international community. This case is illustrative of the complexity of relationship in a process of collective apology that involves individuals, civil society, and neighboring states bound by the legacies of colonialism and war. I will start by determining the bounds of collective apology.

Collective Apology

Do collectivities, groups and corporate entities act and respond differently from individuals in their approach and disposition to conflict resolution. At first glance there seems to be no distinction between the individual and corporate level in apology. Yet as we move from individual to group, to corporate entities, and finally to nation-state, reconciliatory acts such as apology are differentiated by representation and affectivity.

By way of representation, the requisites of apology apply to groups as they do to individuals except that group to group apology needs to be delegated by leaders or appointed delegates. Such groups (i.e. villages) are less formal compared to corporate groups like a church and its members. Corporate groups have legal personalities as they can be held legally accountable and responsible for any apologizable transgression. The present inquiry is about collective apology or political apology that directly involves nation-states or those in which states have taken interest in apologizing on behalf of many, or are on the receiving end on behalf of victims of grievous transgressions.

There is something distinctive about collective apology, apology between states in this instance, that differentiates it from one rendered between groups and among individuals. Specifically, apologies between individuals are direct and unmediated compared to apologies between collectivities, requiring the acceptance or rejection by the recipient for the most part free from external considerations. As soon as apologies are given in front of witnesses, established norms and the expectations of others transform them into public acts. Thus when the apology is socially sanctioned and linked to more universal moral standards it becomes exclusively public in nature. Even when leaders engage in ritual contrition, in public apology, especially collective apology in which states are the main players, emotions are lacking.

An Ethic of Apology

The set of principles that constitutes the apology mode directed towards reconciliation derives from two sources. The first is internal to the normative and what we have come to understand as its essential meaning. The second part is external to that in the sense that there are instrumentalist expectations of what an apology is going to accomplish. I thus start with the first element of an apology: that it begins with the reckoning of wrongdoing. This account of wrongdoing, normally associated with guilt, is inscribed in an apologetic act for a transgression. Such speech act is normally expressed with sorrow and remorse the sincerity of which, as in the case of guilt, can always be questioned. While these two elements of apology, reckoning and remorse, are subsumed as part of any form of apology, a full apology goes further, aimed at seeking forgiveness and thereby redemption at first. And then, in order to attain forgiveness, coming clean that entails being openly accountable and responsible for one's transgression and preparing to pay one's debt. Those who apologize are also prepared to confess the facts of the transgression or crime, often in response to the demands of survivors and victims. Truth-telling and accountability then go beyond the first utterances of an apology to meet the mutual needs of reconciliation of perpetrator and victim. I thus suggest four criteria for a successful public apology that are necessary in bringing about healing and reconciliation.[3] These are acknowledgement, truth-telling, accountability, and public remorse. Not to be fulfilled in any order, these four requisites require to be met by perpetrators of mass crimes and wrongdoing whether or not victims demand them and forgiveness is given. Let us consider each in turn.

An apologetic discourse may commence with reckoning. There is the temptation to see acknowledgement as an end in itself rather than a step toward reconciliation. Nevertheless the simple recognition and public admission of a wrongdoing can be of crucial symbolic significance to those affected by past wrongs. Theologian Donald Shriver goes even further by contending that acknowledgement can effectively mend broken human relations if it derives from empathy when he notes "acknowledgement of fellow humanity lays a groundwork for both the construction and the repair of any human community."[4]

Truth telling is the second important element of a successful public apology. The offending party may acknowledge wrongdoing but not acknowledge the extent of the injury. The reasons for not accounting fully for past deeds vary according to the willingness of the perpetrators to take full responsibility for their actions. In apologies involving nation-states, requirements of declaratory apologies and official status are not conducive to openness and spontaneity. In the affairs of states the performative use of power and symbolism weighs heavily. Thus a detached public apology may intentionally or otherwise prevent the offender from taking full responsibility and reckoning with the details of what may have occurred during the period of the alleged wrongdoing.

The third imperative for an apology proper involves the expression of remorse by the transgressor. The expression of collective sorrow on behalf of a people or its government seems to be an unattainable. A remorseful apology can be extended from one individual to another.[5] How can the same be extended between collectivities and nations? When the deputies of these collectivities are expressing public remorse are they merely performing rituals? While a leader can be personally remorseful for his actions, how can he or she express collective remorse? Some argue that the effectiveness of public remorse cannot be measured by the depth of remorse, if one can determine it. Nicholas Tavuchis for one asserts "the major structural requirement and ultimate task of collective apologetic speech is to put things on record, to document as a prelude to reconciliation."[6]

The last imperative in the evaluation of public apologies involves clarifying who the relevant partners are and determining their accountability and responsibility for wrongdoing. It is not always clear who exactly is apologizing to whom in many instances of public apologies. When political leaders apologize for historical crimes whom are they addressing? The descendents of those who suffered and died? The survivors, the society of the survivors, the leaders of the victim's society or its government? On the other side, on whose behalf are the leaders speaking, the government, the society at large, or for several generations of people? Such doubts call for clarification because only then can we address problems of responsibility and accountability. One can think of a political identity that comes into being to morally account for grievous misdeeds.

Apart from these prerequisites for a successful apology, there are other conditions that contribute to this goal. First, an apology is affected by who initiates it, who responds to it, and who accepts responsibility. In recent instances of public apology, participants have included victims, perpetrators, activists, advocacy groups, and political leaders as individuals and as agents of the state. Second, questions of agency raise issues of power relationships, the most problematic of which is the asymmetrical relationship between the perpetrator state and its agents, on the one hand, and individuals and groups seeking the apology, on the other. This overemphasis on the performative acts of leaders overshadows the democratic legitimacy – that an apologetic act should be representative of the victims and their families. The agency of victims is prominent in the initiative taken by individual citizens, advocacy groups and a few visionary political leaders. Third, the ethics of apology makes it necessary that participants in the apology project identify with each other morally, defying the conventional geopolitical map, constitutional communities and generational divides. This also implies that citizens assume political responsibility for past wrongs while resisting identification as guilty subjects.[7] Finally, a consideration that is closely tied to the above three is the degree of proximity or distance between perpetrators and victims. The temporal and spatial distances between perpetrators, victims, and events of past wrongs raise complex issues of responsibility and eventually have impact on the efficacy of public apologies. This last point requires further elaboration.

Proximity and Responsibility

At the core of an apology proper is the acknowledgement of a wrong and expression of sorrow on the part of the offenders, ideally facing the victim. This direct confrontation demands humility. The ritualistic acts of bowing, kneeling, and prostrating in seeking forgiveness amount to humbling oneself while morally elevating the victim. It takes a great deal of courage to take that first step forward because the offender is taking risks that could be avoided if he or it, in the case of a corporate entity, chooses to be unrepentant for the wrongdoing. For one thing, the apology may not be accepted and forgiveness is not readily given. There is also the risk of losing one's reputation or being tainted and publicly stigmatized. This is not always the case of course especially when we consider those whose apologies result in social acceptance, at least, or praise for their moral courage. But offering an apology always makes one vulnerable or invites revenge. In certain legal systems the apologizer risks legal liability.[8]

Proximity, i.e. being in the presence of the injured party, entails the risk of being vulnerable to the offended party. Levinas's notion of face in its "upright exposure" that simultaneously invites and forbids violence subtly delineates this notion.[9] In such apologies by proxy or when the apology itself is delivered by a delegate, we need to extend the meaning of face-to-face presence to its metaphorical level – images of the sufferers or victims conjured up from memories and narratives. We can imagine the apologizer facing an apparition who can be interchangeably indifferent, pathetic, haunting, or an accusing figure. Face can also mean a reflection of self as in a mirror. In contemplating an apologetic act the apologizer is expected to seek self-knowledge and introspection in order to come clean, to be redeemed, or be restored into the community from which it has fallen. "Facing" in this context is looking into one's conscience and through self-analysis perceive and admit culpability. It is in this context that the question of proximity, both literally and figuratively is related to the important issue of guilt and responsibility.

Face-to-face presence in this apology mode ushers in accepting or facing one's responsibility to the Other. Beginning with the most proximate parties of perpetrators and victims, guilt and responsibility can be extended to their families and communities, to their nation and even to the international level in which we can all be implicated by virtue of our common humanity. The moral thread that ties the parties within each circle is human empathy for each other, empathy that can be extended even to one's enemy.

This ethic of apology should be flexible enough to recognize the moral distance between an aggrieved individual, a survivor and the modern national state on the other. It should also accommodate the most proximate acts of reconciliation between perpetrators and victims, on one hand, the corporate apologetic modes, at the middle, and the most bureaucratic apologetic accommodation between two states in diplomacy.

The Political Calculus of Apology

In most cases of apology and reparations victims seek apology and compensation from the perpetrator-state responsible for the violence and the consequences. Thus an apology process cannot exclude the state from its moral discourse as the political calculus is unavoidably tied to the "high" politics of the statecentric international order. How can a state or its agents work toward doing justice by the victims and their representatives and move toward reconciliation? Can the distance between the victims and those leaders who claim to represent collectivities in an apology process be bridged?

It is rather difficult to express genuine repentance in public communication, and even more untenable to separate the image-saving rhetoric and those of narrow political utility from the more serious contrition necessary for reconciliation. In spite of the gap between private and public morality, further reflections are needed on the nature and difficulties involved in the use of public remorse in apology. We can begin by drawing out certain characteristics and problems associated with it. First, it needs to address and influence the victim even when forgiveness is not forthcoming. Secondly, office-holders can not represent the body politics of emotions, turning atonement by proxy into a politically creative challenge. Thirdly, public remorse directed toward reconciliation or seeking forgiveness needs to be publicly witnessed, politically negotiated, and be put on record. Finally, public remorse is of more weight and lasting impact when it is accompanied by an affective performance on the part of the apologizing agent.

Japan's relations with its neighbors since World War II have been difficult and are illustrative of the unevenness and contradictions of collective apology that involves individuals, civil society, political leaders and the government and politics of neighboring states bound by the legacies of colonialism and war.

Reluctance to Acknowledgement

Lingering political tensions remain in Asia. They do not emanate from the legacies of the Cold War, the historic balance of power among major regional powers like China, Japan and Russia, or from new economic rivalries. The wounds of the last world war have provoked continuous minor crises since the 1960s. In 2001 there was that shocking story about Korean protestors who ritually chopped off the tips of their little fingers in protest against Japanese Prime Minister Koizumi's visit to the shrine honoring the dead together with his refusal to order revisions of middle-school history textbooks.[10] The festering anger by surviving victims and their advocates only intensified with the continued reluctance of the Japanese authorities to acknowledge alleged wartime crimes perpetrated by the Japanese military. The Chinese government has delayed high-level diplomatic visits of Japanese officials until a "good atmosphere" has been created by Japan. The "bad atmosphere" had been instigated by the visits of Prime Minister Junichitro Koizumi in October 2003 to the Yasukuni Shrine – the memorial for Japan's war dead. This is the controversial shrine where 2.5 million Japanese dead, including fourteen Class A war criminals, are worshipped and commemorated.[11] Visits by Japanese Prime Ministers since the 1970s have brought protest against the violation of religion and state as well as protests from Asian countries that see the shrine as a symbol of Japanese militarism and ultra-nationalism. More recently visits to the shrine by Japanese officials are followed by a routine press release from the Japanese government expressing profound remorse and sincere mourning for all victims of the war. The controversial shrine visits and the political posturing of Japanese officials comes to head in 2004 when the Japanese Supreme Court ruled that the prime ministers' official visits to the Yasukuni Shrine are unconstitutional based on Article 20 of the Constitution that stipulates separation of state and religion. In spite of that ruling Prime Minister Junichiro Koizumi pledged that he continue visiting as he has done since 2001. During the litigation the state argued the Prime Minister's visit was personal even though Koisumi had signed the visitors' book as "Prime Minister Junichiro Koizumi." This conflation between the "private" and the "public" is best illustrated in Koizumi's response under fire: "I don't know. I'm a public figure and private individual at the same time. Junichiro Koizumi, an individual who is also the prime minister, paid the visit."[12] Such purposeful mixing and separation at will between the private and the public became part of the political calculus of Japanese apology as we will see shortly. The political reflexes of the Japanese elite just as much as the protestors are tied to the painful legacies of war.

Hence the slow-in-coming acknowledgement of guilt on the part of the Japanese can be attributed to several factors beginning with the nature of the Japanese defeat. Understandably the devastating defeat after the Hiroshima and Nagasaki nuclear bombing, the first and last use of such weapons that killed 100,000 civilians in each city, created a culture of victimization. Those horrors along with the Tokyo War Crimes Tribunal supervised by the Americans, which brought swift justice to leading Japanese war criminals, and the associated disarming treaties, had all brought history to an end – at least as far as the Japanese political elite were concerned. Hence, in response to some of the first demands for apology and redress, the Japanese government's pet answer was that Japan had settled its obligations through the several treaties it had signed since the end of the war. One such treaty was the Treaty of Basic Relations Japan and South Korea signed in 1965. Under that treaty, "Japan agreed to provide South Korea with a total sum of $800 million, which consisted of: a) an outright grant of $300 million, to be distributed over a 10-year period; b) a $200 million loan to be distributed over a 10-year period and repaid over 20 years at 3.5% interest; c) $300 million in private credits over 10 years from Japanese banks and financial institutions."[13] For over twenty years until the 1965 agreement, the normalization talks between Japan and South Korea provoked strong emotions in both countries. The credit, grant and loans received under that treaty were "for claims made for debt owed, unpaid wages, savings held in Japan, and other specific damages."[14] Thus it was easy for Japanese leaders to hide behind such treaties and declare that they had no obligations toward their Korean neighbors, and thereby exonerate themselves from any responsibility. Also, because of their sense that they had paid the price, strongly reinforced by the trauma of Hiroshima and Nagasaki, the Japanese elite, unlike their German counterpart, were unburdened by a sense of guilt for Japan's war crimes. Furthermore, the events and the memories thereof were far removed from the daily lives of the Japanese since most of the horrendous war crimes took place far from home. For the Japanese leaders as well as the Americans who had forced their surrender, stability had priority over any dispensation of apology and compensation at the end of the war and the beginnings of the Cold War.

A secondary factor that contributed to Japanese reluctance to acknowledge wartime wrongs was the carryover of virulent Japanese nationalism as represented by unrepentant social conservatives and the revisionist right. Also the fact that General Douglas MacArthur chose to spare Emperor Hirohito from being brought to trial, and that the emperor refused to acknowledge Japanese wrongdoing, may have contributed to a continuation of the prewar mentality.[15] Couple this with the carryover of political leaders from the war into post war Japan; as Shuko Ogawa points out:

> Significantly, of the seven Class A war criminals (those tried for the crime against peace of waging an aggressive war) sentenced to death at the Tokyo War Crimes Tribunal, only one, wartime Foreign Minister Koki Hirota, was a civilian. Thus, the mindset of civil servants and emerging political figures was changed little as they set about the task of reconstructing the country. Mamoru Shigemitsu, another wartime foreign minister who was sentenced to prison at the Tokyo War Crimes Tribunal, later even re-emerged to serve as foreign minister in 1954.[16]

Conservative members of the Japanese political elite, mostly present in the Liberal Democratic Party (LPD), the party that had dominated Japanese postwar governments, had for the most part downplayed and denied Japanese complicity in such war crimes as the Nanjing Massacre and the exploitation of "comfort" women. Japanese right-wing revisionists and conservatives inside and outside the LDP argued that Japan had already apologized and paid for the war damages. Further, social conservatives were unwilling to admit to any wrongdoing because they believed that the whole story of Japanese aggression "robs children of pride in their country. Children should be allowed to have pride in their country, and thus not be overexposed to Japanese wartime atrocities."[17]

Third, the politics of denial and the status quo were established from the very beginning with the silence of returning soldiers and wartime censorship. That status quo was enabled by a silent generation ready to forget the war and a younger generation protected from the harsh truths of the war atrocities.

Finally, Japanese reluctance to come to terms with the war and apologize to their neighbors can be tied to an identity crisis of the new Japanese generation caught between the influences of neonationalist revisionism and the pressures of globalization. The young also happen to be the innocent consumers of commodified images of Japan and thus could not be in tune with the long-seated grievances of neighboring countries.[18]

When the Japanese authorities were finally coming around to acknowledging some of the crimes perpetrated by the Japanese military, their admissions came out only in fits and starts. In 1992, after fifty years of denial, the Japanese government finally admitted its involvement in the comfort women system. The system involved an organized racket by the Japanese army that forced approximately 200,000 women from China, Korea, the Philippines and other Asian countries into sexual slavery to serve the Japanese Imperial Army between 1931 to 1945. Euphemistically called "comfort women," or Jugun Ianfu, these women were forced to have sex on the average with thirty to forty men a day. They were raped, tortured, mutilated and sometimes killed in the process. The Japanese authorities acknowledged Japanese government involvement only after incriminating documents were uncovered and made public. According to the new findings, the Japanese government, not private businesses, ran and regulated these comfort stations.[19] A statement by the Chief Cabinet Secretary in 1993 announced the findings of a government study in which it hedges to admit Japanese culpability: "The then Japanese military was, directly or indirectly involved in the establishment and management of the comfort stations and the transfer of comfort women. The recruitment of the comfort women was conducted mainly by private recruiters who acted in response to the request of the military."[20]

After years of hedging on the part of Japanese authorities, the momentous acknowledgement of the country's guilt in World War II came from Prime Minister Tomiichi Murayama on the morning of the 50th anniversary of Japan's surrender. He told journalists that Japan had followed a "mistaken national policy" of "colonialism and aggression" that caused "tremendous damage and suffering to the people of many countries." His admission to Japanese guilt of "aggression," which had never been admitted by any Prime Minister before, brought praise from the West. His choice of the term "apology" or *owabi* instead of the habitual "regret" was also significant.[21] On its worth as a public remorse, I shall return to later. Muruyami's apology paved the way for Japanese leaders to soften the diplomatic discourse in the steps to be taken for normalization and cooperation between Japan, the two Koreas and China. When President Kim Dae Jung of South Korea visited Japan in 1998, a joint declaration read: "Prime Minister Obuchi regarded in a spirit of humility the fact of history that Japan caused, during a certain period in the past, tremendous damage and suffering to the people of the Republic of Korea through its colonial rule, and expressed his deep remorse and heartfelt apology for this fact. President Kim accepted with sincerity this statement of Prime Minister Obuchi's recognition of history and expressed his appreciation for it."[22] The touchy issue of the demands of the "comfort women" was not brought up on such occasions. In fact, every postwar government "has resisted pressure to issue a formal apology, always limiting Japanese responsibility for what happened to comfort women by oblique references to 'pain' caused during the 'troubled' period of World War II."[23] However, in an indirect acknowledgement of the crime, in 1995 the Japanese government contributed to the Asian Women's Fund, a semi-autonomous organization funded privately, to provide atonement money. The government committed to assist AWF in operational costs as well as fund-raising and claimed to have begun disbursing the funds. With each atonement payment, a letter of apology was attached from the Prime Minister who extended his "most sincere apologies and remorse to all the women who underwent immeasurable and painful experiences and suffered incurable physical and psychological wounds as comfort women."[24] Seeking direct and official apology from the government, few "comfort women" have come forward to accept the token of sympathy. In the Japanese parliament, the Diet, a bill "to promote the settlement of the issue of the victims forced into becoming wartime sex slaves" was introduced in 2001 and reintroduced several times but failed to win support.[25]

Denial and Truth-telling

Even though the government's rhetoric has become more transparent and factual in its acknowledgement of Japan's wartime wrongs, the resistance to coming clean with the truth about the consequences of Japanese occupation and the war has continued. As recently as the 1980s, Japanese authorities were resistant to popular demands for dealing with the past in neighboring Asian countries and reacted slowly and only when the governments of those countries were willing to bring up the issues defying delicate bilateral relations. In 1982, Chief Cabinet Secretary Kiichi Miyazawa made a statement on the issue of revisionist history textbooks indicating that Japan would attend to the problem in the spirit and respect of the 1965 joint communiqués with ROK and China. Spelling out that spirit, Miyazawa states: "Recently, the Republic of Korea, China, and others have been criticizing some descriptions in Japanese textbooks. From the perspective of building friendship and goodwill with neighboring countries, Japan will pay due attention to these criticisms and make corrections at the Government's responsibility."[26] On the other side of the Japanese government's reluctant truth-telling were the pressures of a countervailing democratic movement represented by Japanese groups and citizens, with their counterparts in Korea, China and elsewhere, all determined to reveal the horrific facts of the war. The impact of these grassroots pressures was evident in the government's response to challenges arising from new exposures on the extent of wartime involvement in the case of the "comfort women." No sooner had the Korean government demanded that attention be paid to this issue, the Japanese government had embarked on its own investigation, including hearings by former military personnel and research in Japanese and U.S. archives, and had begun reporting its findings in 1992.[27]

The Korean government's move came in response to the activism of a South Korean professor Yun Chong Ok, the South Korean Church Women's Alliance, the Seoul District Female Students' Representative Council, and other regional groups. In Japan, it is the discovery by Japanese Professor Yoshimi Yoshiaki of incriminating documents in the Library of the National Institute for Defense Studies and the publication and public exposure of those documents that forced the Japanese and other accommodating Asian governments to advance the cause of the aggrieved "Comfort women."[28]

One of the developments towards more transparency on the part of the Japanese government was to support historical research and documentation. In preparation for the fiftieth anniversary of the end of World War II, Prime Minister Tomiichi Murayama announced the establishment of an Asian Historical Document Center "to enable everyone to face squarely the facts of history."[29]

A culture war of sorts may also have contributed to this dialectic of truth-telling. Yamatani Tetsuo's 1979 film, *An Old Lady in Okinawa: Testimony of a Military Comfort Woman*, that was based on the first publicly identified "comfort women" may have encouraged activists to heighten the world's awareness of the plight of these victims.[30] On the other side of the ideological spectrum, a 1998 Japanese film, *Pride: The Fateful Moment*, a sympathetic film about General Hideki Tojo, a war criminal executed following the Tokyo War Tribunal, became a box-office hit that year despite the protest of Japan's neighbors. Shortly after, a comic book with a similar revisionist vein had a runaway sale. The book depicted the Japanese army as the liberator of Asia from Western colonialism suggested that the Rape of Nanjing was exaggerated and Tojo was unfairly treated.[31] The same book created an uproar in Taiwan, for suggesting that Taiwanese women willingly became sex slaves for the occupying Japanese army.[32] The revived nationalism in popular culture has also been reflected in active historical revisionism to socialize Japanese youth.

A resurgence of nationalism manifested in right-wing revisionism of Japan's history has become increasingly vocal since the 1990s. Such organizations as the "Committee for the Examination of History," the "Committee for the Examination of History," and the "Group for the Creation of New History," had been influential in the right-wing factions of the leading parties, especially in the LDP. These groups shared the views that alien influences via the American conquest/occupation had distorted the Soul of Japan, and therefore Japan had to re-evaluate its history, and they argued that Japanese militarism and colonialism was in fact beneficial to Asia. They also entertained ideas of constitutional changes and reclaimed the history curricula in schools to instill Japanese pride in the young.[33] Ever sensitive to the awakening of Japanese nationalism, the failure by the Japanese government to silence the neonationalist voices in Japan has brought loud protests from the governments and peoples in the Koreas, China, Taiwan and elsewhere. In March 2001, during a ceremony marking the anniversary of the unsuccessful Korean uprising of 1919 against the Japanese colonial rulers, South Korean President Kim Dae-jung called on Tokyo "to maintain a correct perception of history." It is the activists in Korea who shouted the loudest against "the refusal of Japanese authorities to ban a controversial junior high school history textbook that glosses over the abuses perpetrated by the colonial regime during its 35-year occupation of the Korean peninsula." Critics have charged that the failure to effectively screen the school textbooks is related to the possible intimidation of Japanese authorities by the extreme right-wing activism.[34] The government's official position on the history textbooks in response to criticisms is predictable and proforma: "During the process of the recent authorization of textbooks, various concerns have been expressed from neighboring countries. However, the authorization was carried out impartially based on the Regulations of Textbook Authorization, including the Course of Study and the 'Provision Concerning Neighboring Countries'."[35] The Asian neighbors were outraged that the Japanese government give approval to a middle-school textbook written by scholars who defended Japan's record in the last world war. The South Korean government first lodged a complaint and then recalled its ambassador from Tokyo. The high-profile dispute over the textbooks was considered a setback to South Korean-Japan relations by officials in both countries after the Japanese government had apologized in 1998 "for inflicting 'great suffering' on Koreans under colonialism."[36]

According to Kwan Weng Kin, revisionist historians like Professor Nobukatsu Fujioka, a key member of the Japanese Society for History Textbook Reform, argue that "the goal of history education as laid down by Japan's Education Ministry is to deepen the love of children towards Japanese history." In Professor Fujioka's words, "Comfort women would not help to foster love towards one nation." Thus, in the textbook the Society produced, the issue of wartime sex slaves is totally omitted and, as a result of pressure from the government, four of the other seven textbooks approved by the education ministry also dropped references to comfort women. The book makes no mention of the 1910 annexation of Korea. Moreover the term "war of aggression" is omitted. It would seem that in avoiding to ask for a full re-write, the government gave it a tacit blessing.[37] The retreat of government officials, in spite of the more apologetic earlier pronouncements, is what intensified the protest from countries like South Korea. The government of President Kim Dae Jung in Seoul issued a statement describing the textbooks as "rationalizing and beautifying Japan's past wrongdoings based upon a self-centred interpretation of history."[38] In 2001 Foreign Affairs Makiko Tanaka comments: "The tense atmosphere and concern in the ROK over this issue has been conveyed repeatedly to Japan in various forms, and as the person in charge of foreign affairs I take this matter seriously."[39] In the meantime, an ethnic Korean living in Japan initiates the publication of a book on the sexual slavery to enlighten readers and Japanese teachers. It is a translated version of a year 2000 publication of the Korean Institute of the Women Drafted for Military Sexual Slavery by Japan.[40] Individuals and groups in Japan, with support from activists in the region and the world at large, have gradually made gains in pressuring the powers that be to be more transparent and truthful about Japan's wars and their consequences.

The battle over history textbooks for middle schools underscores Japan's struggle to redefine its identity. It also reflects the gulf between the nationalists who want to preserve the right to interpret Japan's history and those who desire that Japan come to terms with its past and by doing so become a "normal" member of the international community. In coming to terms with its past, Japanese contemporary politics is distinctively marked by the tensions between truth-telling and denial in a remarkable open debate among Japanese and their neighbors. This ever-present conflict has been raising in turn public demands for collective responsibility and accountability.

Extracted Accountability

One way of assessing the extent of accountability accepted by successive Japanese governments is by measuring the distance traveled between the reckoning of wrongs and the eventual redress and compensation for those wrongs. Obviously acknowledgement should precede accountability, as the perpetrator-state needs to admit wrongdoing before acting on what it would be responsible for. As it turns out, in such war crimes the perpetrator can hurriedly make a settlement ahead of acknowledging the crimes committed during the violence and before the specificities thereof are exposed. Postwar Germany proved that there is no set order to the sequencing of the four apology imperatives I outlined at the outset. Chancellor Adenauer initiated and pummeled through the German political process the landmark reparation legislative acts of the 1950s that set the stage for restitution to Jews and Israelis for decades. Reparations came in short order before the truths of the Holocaust were unveiled layer by layer and definitely before the national debates that allocated responsibilities and guilt, and it was even longer before remorse entered the national public discourse. Japan by comparison did not earnestly take up the thorny issue of dealing with its wartime past until almost forty years after the Germans did, primarily because there was a consensus among the postwar conservative political elite that maintaining the status quo and stability was preferable to voluntarily initiating anything radical.[41] Therefore, just as their acknowledgement was slow in coming, their readiness to be accountable for any wrongdoing of the Japanese state was influenced by a political culture that discouraged guilt or collective responsibility, by the treaties imposed on the Japanese as a defeated nation, by their interpretation of international law, by the pressures of local and international human rights activists, and regional political calculus.

Considering Japan's postwar beginning, which unlike Germany was not impacted by deliberate policies of denazification and democratization by Western Allies, it is easy to appreciate the political consensus that emerged and its reinforcement of the already existing political culture and thereby the reluctance to be accountable for wrongdoing. McArthur's decision not to accuse the Japanese emperor of war crimes along with leaving the existing political structure intact, enabled the carryover of bureaucrats and politicians opposed to change. There is no evidence of guilt among the survivors of the Tokyo War Crimes Tribunal. Moreover guilt as in the Judeo-Christian tradition is less known in Japan than the idea of shame and letting down one's group. Also authoritarianism rooted in its feudal roots, respect to elders and authority grounded in its Confucianism, and the notion of *wa* or cultivating harmony with others can explain the moral minority in Japan who raised soul-searching questions about Japan's past. In Germany, the open debates on reparations and public remorse were facilitated by a diversity of opinions, not to mention the debates between the two ideological blocks of the right and the left. Therefore, the demand for justice and reconciliation in Japan originates mostly outside political circles.

Legal recourse for reparations and apology is initiated by individuals and groups and increasingly encouraged by Asian countries and the international community. Chinese Liu Lianren filed a lawsuit against Japan demanding 20 million in compensation and an official apology from the state for being abducted from his home and forced to work in a Japanese coal mine. At the end of the war Liu Lianren ran away and hid in the mountains for 13 years unaware that the war had ended. In ordering the state to pay damages, Judge Seiichiro Nishioka said that the state "should be held responsible for Liu's suffering as a fugitive after the war. He said the state had failed in its duty to protect the rights of Liu, who was brought to Japan at the Japanese government's behest." In the end it was a bittersweet victory, considering that Judge Nishioka rejected the claim by the plaintiff's lawyers for compensation for wartime forced work. In dismissing the claim, he said that the Meiji Constitution absolved the state of liability for damages and international law did not support individuals seeking reparation for suffering during wartime. It was that same court, in 1998, that recognized the state's exploitation of "comfort women" and ordered payment of 900,000 yen in compensation to nine former Korean sex slaves – a ruling that was overturned later.[42] Included among those seeking legal redress from the Japanese state are Japanese nationals – the so-called war orphans who had been separated from their parents and had lived in Chinese foster homes for decades. The government was accused of failing to bring them to Japan and not assisting them even after they were finally settled in Japan.[43] This is just one of several far-from-settled cases demanding apology and compensation.

To employ Karl Jasper's ethical mode of responsibility in which he makes a distinction between criminal, political, moral and metaphysical guilt requiring different forms of accountability, the Japanese had difficulty in assuming political guilt let alone in considering moral culpability. The creative approach Japanese authorities have chosen when challenged to be accountable has been to set up creative outlets such as the Asian Women's Fund to deal with reparation demands while at the same time allowing the state to skirt around direct state responsibilities. As the press release in 2000 from Chief Cabinet Secretary Hidenao

Nakagawa states: "the government of Japan is painfully aware of its moral responsibility regarding the issue of the 'wartime comfort women' and has been dealing sincerely with this issue through the fund."[44] The government touts the fact it is meeting its moral responsibility to the "comfort women" through atonement projects in the Netherlands, the Philippines, Korea, Indonesia and Taiwan since its establishment in 1995.[45]

Among the factors that inhibited Japanese political leaders from making either major concessions or aggressive initiatives to make comprehensive settlements with classes of war victims, is the convenient belief that treaties reached between Japan and the allies and between Japan and Korea have settled all claims of compensation. Although North Korea, China, the Philippines and Taiwan are not party to any treaty with Japan, Japanese authorities have broadly cited previous treaties to deny compensation to claimants. The two major treaties Japanese courts have been sheltering under are the Allied Treaty and the Korean Treaty. The Allied Treaty's disclaimer reads:

Except as otherwise provided in the present Treaty, the Allied Powers waive all reparation claims of the Allied Powers, other claims of the Allied Powers and their nationals arising out of any actions taken by Japan and it nationals in the course of the prosecution of the war, and claims of the Allied Powers for direct military cost of occupation.[46] In the same way the Korean Treaty states:

> The Contracting Parties confirm that [the] problem concerning property, rights and interests of the two Contracting Parties and their nationals (including juridical persons) and concerning claims between the Contracting Parties and their nationals, including those provided for in Article IV, paragraph (a) of the Treaty of Peace with Japan signed at the city of San Francisco on September 8, 1951, is settled completely and finally.[47]

Japanese authorities have been using such provisions to show claims have been settled. According to Parker and Chew, "neither treaty addresses private claims but only claims in which states are the parties. According to these treaties, the parties have agreed not to take up additional state claims against the other parties."[48] In a report to the Economic and Social Council of the United Nations, a Japanese delegate states, "With regard to compensation for individuals, the Government had fulfilled its obligations under the San Francisco Peace Treaty and other treaties. The right of individuals to seek compensation had been respected, and the matter has been settled."[49] And from then on he continues to assert that Japan has fulfilled its moral obligations by setting up the Asian Women's Fund and financially contributing to it.[50] Non-governmental organizations and advocates of victims have resorted to putting pressure on their governments to be more representative of their demands to remedy past injustice. For example, the Korean Council for the Women Drafted for Military Sexual Slavery by Japan demanded in August 2003 that the government "officially declare [s] that comfort women were not included among the benefactors of the 1965 Korean-Japan Agreement which concluded the compensation issue for Japan's longtime occupation of the Korean peninsula."[51]

Here is an illustration of "ethic of responsibility" in which political leaders pursue prudent politics toward the state's Leviathan ends in apposition with an "ethic of ultimate ends" related to a universalizing moral consensus, as Max Weber brings to our attention in his notable essay "Politics as a Vocation."[52] Two hundred Koreans who were once forced laborers and comfort women feel so strongly about their government's indifference to their legal claims against Japan to such an extent that they have expressed their intention to give up their Korean citizenship.[53]

The legal claims of some lawsuits so far are complex and some have tenuous standing in international law. The guarded jealousy of state sovereignty weighed against the ambiguities and the weaknesses of international law make the struggle of groups and individuals seeking justice exceedingly difficult even as international public opinion is changing. Japanese courts seem to be under more pressure to work with existing international laws and are seeking the legislation of new municipal laws to aid them in dispensing justice as the claims are multiplying. As Laura Hein explains:

> Clearly, some of the most recent rulings demonstrate, however, that judges feel real discomfort about just dismissing the claims, given how much the plaintiffs had suffered at the hands of wartime officials. The growing confusion and angst revealed in these judgments suggest a shift in attitudes among jurists, although this change of heart has not yet been reflected in most of the rulings.[54]

When ten Chinese filed lawsuits in 1999 demanding a formal apology and 1000 million yen from the Japanese state for war crimes committed by Unit 731, a biological warfare unit, "known for its germ warfare experiments on Chinese, the 1937 Nanjing Massacre and indiscriminate bombing over a safety zone during the 1937-1945 war," the Tokyo District Court dismissed their claims. Yet, the court acknowledged the claim by the wartime victims and their families and "urged the government to apologize to the people of China to establish peace and friendly relations with its neighbors."[55] In other words, the court's argument is that apology should be given to the nation at large but not the victims themselves. Judge Ko Ito's conclusion is that " the payment of redress for wartime suffering is a political issue and should be negotiated on the diplomatic level between the states involved and dealt with by a peace treaty."[56]

Considering the various defenses of the legally embattled Japanese state, groups and individual claimants have devised varying legal strategies or have tried in some cases to create a common front. South Korean, Japanese and Dutch civic groups sought compensation in 1999 for their sufferings under hard labor in Siberia and the Dutch East Indies. The three groups reached an agreement at first to cooperate in demanding compensation, but they soon developed separate legal strategies. The Japanese groups wanted a joint appeal to the U.N.Human Rights panel, while the Dutch group sought for Japan to recognize individuals' rights in seeking compensation.[57]

As a final resort, war victims have turned to bringing their lawsuits against Japan to the United States on the assumption that their cause will get wider global attention and that the United States provides a better climate for such cases. In 2000, fifteen former sex slaves from South Korea, China, Taiwan and the Philippines filed a class-action lawsuit against the Japanese government in a federal district court in Washington D.C. A month previously, Chinese nationals sued Japanese companies in California for wartime forced labor. The plaintiffs are allowed to file lawsuits in the United States under the Alien Tort Claims Act under the 18th American law that permits foreign citizens to sue other foreign citizens and entities for international law violations. A year later, 30 surviving former sex slaves brought another lawsuit against Japan in a U.S. court. In both cases, the U.S. government sided with Japan, arguing that the courts did not have jurisdiction and that Japan had already addressed issues of compensation in postwar treaties.[58]

As the international campaign is moving toward the direction of global intolerance to crimes against humanity in the past and the present, the Japanese government is obliged to cope with these challenges. Demands for reparations and apologies for past injustices have become, in John Torpey's words, "a major preoccupation of the one-time victims (or their descendants), of their societies more broadly, and of scholars studying social change as well."[59] Former sex slaves and their advocates have advanced their cause by any means including the arts. Testimonial narratives, exhibitions of art work by victims, and symposia are among these.[60] Even a bill was introduced in the U.S. Congress expressing "the sense of Congress that the Government of Japan should formally issue a clear and unambiguous apology for the sexual enslavement of young women during colonial occupation of Asia and World War II, known to the world as "Comfort women", and for other purposes."[61] The Japanese government has systematically countered and responded to every allegation at all international forums. In reaction to regional and international pressures, the acceptance of accountability has come then in fits and starts. Remorse however is a paradoxical affair that has both failed and succeeded at the same time, mainly because states can be bureaucratically cold while humans believe that expiation can only be realized through sorrow.

Atonement and Public Remorse

An expression of remorse for injury should be at the very center of an apology for reconciliation. While such an expression can easily be communicated between individuals, how can an expression of collective sorrow on behalf of a people or its state be attainable. Tavuchis asserts that remorse or public regrets from the "Many to the Many" can be delivered, but when they are, most of the time they lose their affective force.[62] In the many responses to the lawsuits, to charges of neglect and denial about its war crimes during World War II and before, Japanese authorities have not only employed legally safe language but progressively explicit expressions of sorrow and regret, especially since the mid-1990s. A month before the 50th anniversary of the war's end, on a state visit to China, Prime Minister Tomiichi Murayama set the tone for what is yet to come, the most credible apology to war victims. As noted previously, in a speech during that official visit he makes a claim that Japan had in fact been remorseful all along. In his own words: "Japan has been thus working to forge bonds of mutual understanding and confidence with other Asian peoples, based on the profound remorse for its acts of aggression and colonial rule in the past."[63] An editorial opinion in the *Asahi Shimbun* has a different take on the character of public remorse undertaken by Japanese: "The Japanese perception of the war in the post war period has been anything but commendable. While supporting the pacifism enunciated by the Constitution, the Japanese have been apt to forget their position as aggressors in the war that they waged for their own purpose." That same editorial calls for the Diet to adopt, on the historic 50th anniversary of World War II, a no-war resolution "making clear to the world Japan's remorse for the war and its commitment to peace."[64] Prime Minister Murayama also took advantage of the 50th anniversary to officially establish the "Asian Women's Fund" to atone for the so-called wartime comfort women who, in his words, "suffered emotional and physical wounds that can never be closed" and openly admitted that "the scars of war still run deep in these countries to this day."[65]

The most dramatic of expressions of remorse from the Japanese was given by Prime Minister Tomiichi Murayama on August 15, 1995. A culmination of his efforts and those of the Socialist Party he belonged to, his speech, choice of words, and the setting were indeed significant. In his nationally televised speech from his home, Murayama said:

> During a certain period in the not too distant past, Japan, following a mistaken national policy, advanced along the road to war, only to ensnare the Japanese people in a fateful crisis, and, through its colonial rule and aggression, caused tremendous damage and suffering to the people of many countries, particularly to those of Asian nations. In the hope that no such mistake be made in the future, I regard, in a spirit of humility, these irrefutable facts of history, and express here once again my feelings of deep remorse and state my heartfelt apology. Allow me also to express my feelings of profound mourning for all victims, both at home and abroad, of that history.[66]

Murayama's acknowledgement of "aggression" and his use of the term had no precedent in past apologetic statements from government officials. Moreover his using of the word apology (*owabi*) instead of the overused term of "regret" (*hansei*) received much attention, as it was an expression of deeper remorse.[67] But another observation made about the speech was that it was delivered at his residence right before attending the official ceremony commemorating the 50th anniversary of the end of the war. Delivered at a private space separated from the official site of the ceremony threw doubt on the authoritativeness of the apology. A more sympathetic interpretation of the choice of site would say "by separating the speech from the ceremony ... Mr. Murayama gave his words much more of the force of the state" since the commemorative ritual was for the Japanese where sympathies were being extended to Japanese victims of the war.[68] The private venue of the apology and what seemed like a personal contrition might have diminished the efficacy of the apology. The only other avenue to deliver a much needed legitimate apology, however, could have come from the Japanese parliament, the Diet. And it did after much debate and contention among the major political parties. The Socialist Muruyama failed to persuade the Liberal democrats to pass a resolution similar to the one he was able to deliver two months later. The resolution that was passed by the National Diet was remorseful but not apologetic. It was more a "carefully crafted ambiguity than a sincere apology," as one reporter called it.[69] The resolution read: "Solemnly reflecting upon many instances of colonial rule and acts of aggression in the modern history of the world, and recognizing that Japan carried out those acts in the past, inflicting pain and suffering upon the peoples of other countries, especially in Asia, the Members of this House express a sense of deep remorse."[70] The reactions to the bill inside Japan and in the neighboring countries were negative. Opposition parties either boycotted or opposed the compromise made with the rightwingers of the Liberal Democratic Party. Incidently the text used regret or soul-searching *hansei* instead of *owabi* or *shazi* contrary to President Murayama. The feeble apology actually angered the neighboring countries. One diplomat described the root of that anger as "Japan's determined wriggling not to face up to its guilty past."[71] The Japanese have continuously been touting Murayama's 1995 speech each time international questions are raised over Japan's recognition of its own history. Yet Murayama's famous pronouncement has never been endorsed by the Diet.[72]

Measured against the straightforward criteria of success in an apology process, postwar rapprochement between Japan and its neighbors has been an abysmal failure.[73] The Japanese leadership has been slow to acknowledge the brutal consequences of its colonialism and imperialist wars while at the same time downplaying war atrocities including the exploitation of sex slaves. Unlike Germany that was left with the burden of guilt after the war, the legacies of Hiroshima and Nagasaki were responsible for a culture of victimization that was in return to reinforce the reluctance of the new Japanese elite to acknowledge guilt for Japan's own crimes. Along with postwar policies and the Cold War, that same culture conspired to insulate Japanese leaders from the Asian cries for apology and redress. Furthermore, denial politics and new revisionist interpretations of Japanese history have exacerbated the problem of telling the truth about Japanese war crimes. The official history of Japan's role in World War II and its earlier history stand in marked contrast to the grievances and claims of its Asian neighbors. Thus, the first acknowledgements of Japanese wartime excesses and remorseful pronouncements by government officials were not to be heard until the late 1980s and 1990s, and only after grass roots pressure from within Japan and from its Asian neighbors. Successive Japanese governments responded through selective accountability, careful contrition and contradictory languages of apology as the international challenges grew. This complex politics of memory, identity and reconciliation in Asia raises important questions about the ethics of reconciliation in postwar societies.

The Political Calculus of Apology

In this case of a collective apology we concentrated on the responses, initiatives and resistance on the part of the Japanese state to demands for an official declaration of remorse and compensation. Even though the apology type is from Many to Many, to borrow Tavuchis's mode of apology, it is not one between groups and corporate entities because the victims in every case insisted on the involvement of the Japanese state. Victims seek apology and compensation from the perpetrator-state responsible for the violence and the consequences. A collective apology cannot exclude the state from its moral discourse as the political calculus is unavoidably tied to the "high" politics of the statecentric international order.

Attention so far has been given to the public display of repentance over collective wrongdoing by heads of states and governments. Jean-Pierre Lehman writes, "Prime Minister Junichiro Koizumi could go to Nanjing and, as German Chancellor Willy Brandt did when he came to the Warsaw ghetto memorial, kneel and beg forgiveness."[74] He has other suggestions as well but noticeably Lehman begins with the symbolic speech act. This overemphasis on the performative acts of leaders overshadows the democratic legitimacy an apologetic act should be based upon by representing the victims and their families. The agency of victims is prominent in the initiatives taken by individual citizens, advocacy groups and a few visionary political leaders.

In the apologetic discourse involving Japan and its neighbors there is a continuous conflation between private and public accountability. Did the Prime Ministers Murayama or Koizumi engage in personal repentance or as deputies of their state? Their apologies do not seem to be delegated even as they address distant victims and their representatives.

The discursive distance between victims and perpetrators is far and wide considering that the crimes perpetrated are geographically removed from the Japanese public space and memories. The victims could not face the perpetrators in the way they were accommodated in the dramatic truth commissions in Argentina, East Germany and South Africa. Thus the unraveling of the truths about war and colonial atrocities is revived by individuals and groups who seek proximity with a faceless state in their pursuit of justice. The mostly Asian victims of Japanese-induced crimes seek both apology and reparation. They want at once an apology that stipulates proximity and genuine sorrow, and reparation that is not bureaucratically removed from victims and survivors but authoritative enough to redress wrongdoing in their behalf. These demands have precipitated, so it seems, schizophrenic reactions from political leaders who are caught between a rock and a hard place – between representing empathy themselves and the peoples they represent and the sanctified interests of the state in a statecentric moral order. In 1985 when the Japanese Prime Minister with a number of his ministers made an official visit to the Yasukuni Shrine, the uproar that followed prevented the Prime Minister from making a similar visit the following year. Years later, in 2002 and again in 2003, Prime Minister Junichiro Koizumi defiantly visited the shrine claiming that he would honor the Japanese war dead and at the same time apologize for the victimization of Asians.[75]

The difficulty for deputies in the apology process derives from the inherent conflict between the universal norms of reconciliation that yield new ethical sensibilities and the established habits of state sovereignties. This existing breach of confidence questions the efficacy of speech acts that pass as public remorse. Consequently, unless public apologies are put on record, which once again reinforces the power of institutions and legality in statecentric international law, the efficacy of public apologies are undermined by both victims and perpetrators. That is why the failure of the Japanese Diet to deliver a forceful statement of public apology and an authorization of comprehensive reparation settlements represents the weak side of the Japanese political calculus.

Other than reconciliation, the political calculus of apology between Japan and its neighbors, however, is more discernable as it has to do more with normalization and power politics. The Japanese policy preference is to deal with past wrongs just enough to keep the peace on bilateral terms with these countries, although historically sensitive issues of revisionism and new fears of militarism have precipitated habitual setbacks in maintaining that status quo. Japan desires to become a normal state that would enable it to be a member of the U.N. Security Council and play a role of global leadership in peacekeeping and other areas. Japan is also taking into account its special relations with China marked by mutual economic gain as well as potentially dangerous power rivalry in the region. By avoiding to reach more comprehensive settlements of grievances with its neighbors, critics often charge Japan with undermining its long-term interests.

Notes

1   Maria Rosa Henson, *Comfort Woman: A Filipina's Story of Prostitution and Slavery under the Japanese Military* (Lanham: Rowman & Littlefield Publishers, Inc, 1999), 91. This personal account is a powerful testimony to the suffering, shame and resilience by survivors of the sex slavery. Another testimonial document is *Comfort Women Speak:*

Testimony of Sex Slaves of the Japanese Military edited by Sangmie Choi Schellstede (New York: Holmes & Meier, 2000) that includes three United Nations reports.

2   See Shuko Ogawa, "The Difficulty of Apology: Japan's Struggle with Memory and Guilt." *Harvard International Review* 43 (Fall 2000): 42-46.

3   See Girma Negash, "*Apologia Politica,*: An Examination of the Politics and Ethics of Public Remorse." *International Journal of Politics and Ethics*, 2/2 (2002): 121-125.

4   Donald Shriver, *An Ethic for Enemies: Forgiveness in Politics* (New York: Oxford University Press, 1995), p. 8.

5   Tavuchis explains that authentic expression of sorrow is possible in which "regret, gently but firmly, reminds us of what we were before we erred, what our place was, where we stood in relation to the other, and what we have lost." See Nicholas Tavuchis, *Mea Culpa: A Sociology of Apology and Reconciliation* (Stanford, CA: Stanford Univeristy, 1991), p. 20.

6   Tavuchis, *Mea Culpa*, 109.

7   The German existentialist philosopher, Karl Jaspers, contributed the most insightful ideas to date on guilt and responsibility among individuals, groups or nations by making distinctions between criminal guilt, political guilt, moral guilt and metaphysical guilt. See, Karl Jaspers, *The Question of German Guilt.* (New York: Capricon Books, 1961). See also Andrew Schaap, "Guilty Subjects and Political Responsibility: Arendt, Jaspers and the Resonance of the 'German Question' in Politics of Reconciliation," *Political Studies*, 49 (2001): pp. 749-766.

8   It is worth noting that there is a legal movement in the United States to encourage apologies in order to avert lawsuits and encourage settlement. Several states have enacted statutes to encourage and protect apologies. See Jennifer K. Robbennolt, "Apologies and Legal Settlement: An Empirical Examination." *Michigan Law Review*, 102/3 (December 2003), p. 460.

9   Emmanuel Levinas, *Ethics and Infinity.* (Pittsburgh: Duquesne University Press, 1985), p. 86.

10 Don Kirk, "Koreans Slice Their Fingers in Anti-Japan Rite." *The New York Times*, 14 August 2001.

11 *The Japan Times*, 5 November 2003.

12 Reiji Yoshida, "Prime Minister Pledges Yasukuni Return." *The Japan Times*, 8 April 2004.

13 Mark E. Manyin, "North Korea-Japan Relations: The Normalization Talks and the Cmpensation/Reparations Issue." Congressional Research Service, 13 June 2001.

14 George Hicks, "The Comfort Women Redress Movement," in Roy L. Brooks (ed), *When Sorry Isn't Enough* (New York: New York University Press, 1999), p. 114.

15 Shuko Ogawa, "The Difficulty of Apology: Japan's Struggle with Memory and Guilt," *Harvard International Review* (Fall 2000): p. 43.

16 Ogawa.

17 Ogawa, 46.

18 Aaron Gerow, "Consuming Asia, Consuming Japan: The Neonationalistic Revisionism in Japan," in Laura Hein and Mark Selden (eds), *Censoring History: Citizenship and Memory in Japan, and the United States* (Armnok, N.Y.: M. E. Sharpe, 2000), pp. 92-93.

19 Christine Wawrynek, "World War II Comfort Women: Japan's Sex Slaves or Hired Prostitutes?" *New York Law School Journal of Human Rights*, 19/3 (Summer 2003): pp. 913-922.

20 Statement by the Chief Cabinet Secretary Yohei Kono on the result of the study on the issue of "comfort women." The Ministry of Foreign Affairs of Japan, 4 August 1993.

21 Edward W. Desmond, "Finally, A Real Apology," *Time*, v. 146, 28 August 1995, p. 47.

22 Japan-Republic of Korea Joint Declaration. "A New Japan-Republic of Korea Partnership toward the Twenty-first Century." The Ministry of Foreign Affairs of Japan, 8 October 1998.

23 Harry Sterling, "Japan Refuses to Face Up to its History." *The Toronto Star*, 8 January 2001, Edition 1.

24 Recent Policy of the Government of Japan on the Issue Known as "Wartime Comfort Women." The Ministry of Foreign Affairs of Japan, June 2001. Also see Letter from Prime Minster Junichiro Koizumi to the former comfort women. The Ministry of Foreign Affairs of Japan, The Year of 2001.

25 Tomiko Okazaki. Comment by Upper House lawmaker from Minshuto. *The Asahi Shimbun*, 8 August 2002.

26 Statement by Chief Cabinet Secretary Kiichi Miyazawa on History Textbooks. The Ministry of Foreign Affairs of Japan. 26 August 1982.

27 On the Issue of Wartime "Comfort Women." The Ministry of Foreign Affairs of Japan, 4 August 1993.

28 Hicks, pp. 115-119.

29 Statement by Prime Minister Tomiichi Murayama on the "Peace, Friendship, and Exchange Initiative." The Ministry of Foreign Affairs of Japan, 31 August 1994.

30 Hicks, p. 115.

31 Jonathan Watts, "Japan reclaims 'war hero'." *The Guardian* (London), 23 December 1998, p. 12.

32 Michael Millett, "Japan's Take on History Upsets Neighbors." *Sydney Morning Herald*, 3 March 2001.

33 "Hearts and Minds: Three Questions for Japan." *Korea Times*, 28 June 2000.

34 Michael Millett.

35 Comments by the Chief Cabinet Secretary, Yasuo Fukyda on the history textbooks to be used in junior high schools from 2002. The Ministry of Foreign Affairs of Japan, 3 April 2001.

36 Paul Shin, "Japanese textbook offends Koreans." *Chicago Sun-Times* (Associated Press), 10 April 2001.

37 Kwan Weng Kin, "Japan wages war of words." *The Straits Times* (Singapore), 6 May 2001.

38 Harry Sterling, "Whitewashing history: Japan refuses to come to grips with its military past." *The Gazette* (Montreal, Quebec), 28 May 2001.

39 Comment by Minister of Foreign Affairs Makiko Tanaka on the official Stance Conveyed by the Government of the Republic of Korea on the Decision to Authorize Japanese History Textbooks. The Ministry of Affairs of Japan, 8 May 2001.

40 "Ethnic Korean Leads Publication of Book on Comfort Women," *Korea Times*, 8 April 2002.

41 In Germany the pragmatism of Adenauer and the Christian Democrats as well as the moral political agenda of the Social Democrats made the reparation legislations inevitable.

42 "Family wins 20 million yen for laborer's time on run." *The Japan Times*, 13 July 2001.

43 "Second wave of war orphans hits government with lawsuits." *The Japan Times*, 25 September 2003.

44 Press Statement by Chief Cabinet Secretary Hidenao Nakagawa on the Asian Women's Fund. The Ministry Foreign Affairs of Japan, 1 September 2000.

45 On the Completion of the Atonement Project of the Asian Women's Fund (AWF) in the Netherlands, The Ministry of Foreign Affairs of Japan, 13 July 2001.

46 *Treaty of Peace with Japan*, 8 September 1951, 3 U.S.T. 3169, 136 U.N.T.S. 45, art. 14a, 60. Quoted in Karen Parker and Jennifer F. Chew, "Reparations: A Legal Analysis," in Brooks, pp. 141-142.

47 Korean Treaty, pmbl., 583 U.N.T.S., 60. Karen Parker and Jennifer F. Chew, "Reparations: A Legal Analysis," in Brooks, p. 142.

48 Karen Parker and Jennifer F. Chew.

49 United Nations Economic and Social Council, Committee on Economic, Social and Cultural Rights, 26th session, Summary Record of the 43rd Meeting, E/C.12/2001/SR.43, 27 August 2001.

50 United Nations Economic and Social Council.

51 "Comfort Women Seek Justice Apart from 1965 Korea-Japan Agreement," *Korea Times*, 14 August 2003.

52 For a criticism of Max Weber's most influential essay, "Politics as a Vocation," see Peter Johnson, *Politics, Innocence, and the Limits of Goodness* (London: Routledge, 1988), pp. 150-152. Johnson says "Weber's belief that the problem of political morality is a choice between Christ and Caesar is too simple and reveals a romantic conception of man as isolated, individual chooser," 151.

53 "Comfort Women Seek Justice Apart from the 1965 Korea-Japan Agreement."

54 Laura Hein, "War Compensation: Claims against the Japanese Government and Japanese Corporations for War Crimes." In *Politics and the Past: On Repairing Historical Injustices* (Lanham: Rowman & Littlefield, 2003), p. 133.

55 "Court Rejects Chinese War Victims' Damages Case." *The Japan Times*, 22 September 1999.

56 "Court Rejects Chinese War Victims' Damages Case."

57 "War Victims Unite Efforts to Win Redress from Japan," *The Japan Times*, 12 February 1999.

58 "WW II comfort women face uphill battle in US courts."Channel NewsAsia, Media Corporation of Singapore, 27 June 2001.

59 John Torpey, *Politics and the Past: On Repairing Historical Injustices*. Ed. (Lanham, Md.: Rowman & Littlefield, 2003), p. 1.

60 "Comfort Women's Exhibit Visits U.S.," The Japan Times, 28 December 2000.

61 House Concurrent Resolution 195; 107th Congress, 1st session, 24 July 2001.

62 Tavuchis explains authentic expression of sorrow is possible in which "regret, gently but firmly, reminds us of what we were before we erred, what our place was, where we stood in relation to the other, and what we have lost," p. 20. For others, like Nigerian writer Wole Soyinka, remorse may be nebulous, "nebulous because one can only observe that an expression of remorse has been made," in *The Burden of Memory, the Muse of Forgiveness*, p. 34.

63 "Remarks by Prime Minister Tomiichi Murayama during His May 1995 Visit to China," The Ministry of Foreign Affairs, 4 May 1995.

64 "No-war resolution can help Japan chart future course," *Asahi News Service*, 6 March 1995.

65 "Statement by Prime Minister Tomiichi Murayama on the Occasion of the Establishment of the 'Asian Women's Fund'," The Ministry of Foreign Affairs of Japan, July 1995.

66 "Statement by Prime Minister Tomiichi Murayama 'On the Occasion of the 50th anniversary of the War's End'," The Ministry of Foreign Affairs of Japan, 15 August 1995.

67 Edward W. Desmond, "Finally, a Real Apology," *Time*, v. 146, p. 47, 28 August 1995.

68 Sheryl WuDUNN, "Premier of Japan Offers 'Apology' for its War Acts," *The New York Times*, 15 August 1995, Section A, 1.

69 Ben Hills, "Japan Expresses Remorse but Ducks Apology for War," *Sydney Morning Herald*, 8 June 1995.

70 "Prime Minister's Address to the Diet," The Ministry of Foreign Affairs of Japan, 9 June 1995.

71 Kevin Rafferty, "Japan's 'Feeble' War Apology Angers Neighbors," *The Guardian* (London), 10 June 1995.

72 Kwan Weng Kin, "Japan wages war of words," *The Straits Times* (Singapore), 6 May 2001.

73 A valuable source on reactions by the Japanese elite, personal testimonies, narratives and legal and political analyses is Roy L. Brooks's *When Sorry Isn't Enough: The Controversy over Apologies and Reparations for Human Injustice* (New York University Press, 1999). Also, see my brief analysis on Japanese-Korean rapprochement in "*Apologia Politica*," pp. 128-130.

74 Jean-Pierre Lehmann, "How to avert the risk of war with China," *The Korea Times*, 17 June 2002.

75 "Statement by Chief Cabinet Secretary Masaharu Gotoda on Official Visits to Yasukuni Shrine by the Prime Minister and Other State Ministers on August 15 of this year," The Ministry of Foreign Affairs of Japan, 14 August 1986. "Observation by PrimeMinister Junichiro Koizumi on the Visit to Yasukuni Shrine," The Ministry of Foreign Affairs of Japan, 21 April 2002. "Address by Prime Minister Junichiro Koizumi at the 58th Memorial Ceremony for the War Dead," 15 August 2003.

PART 2

Violence as Injustice

Chapter 5

Power to Destroy, Power to Heal
Violence, State Power and Paradigm Shifts for Peace

Carol Hunter
Earlham College

All the lessons of history in four sentences: Whom the gods would destroy, they first make mad with power. The mills of God grind slowly, but they grind exceedingly small. The bee fertilizes the flower it robs. When it is dark enough, you can see the stars.

Charles Beard[1]

Power and the Destabilizing Effects of Unequal Distribution of Wealth and Power

Power is complex, with both glaringly visible and disturbingly invisible forms, but its definition is simple – the ability to do or act. The guiding question in this essay regarding power is straightforward: what uses of power, what forms of power create a sustainable and just world? This question has a corollary and that is "What are the underlying proclivities and preconceptions that keep us from utilizing these powers more?

I suppose by now most people have read or at least heard of Jared Diamond's *Gun's Germs and Steel*. I'm attracted like a moth to flame to sweeping, comprehensive attempts to understand problems and readily confess to believing nothing less than 10,000 years of history and a global examination of all perspectives is required to say anything of substance. The goal, however admirable, is certainly not within reach of any individual, so I offer these thoughts humbly and gratefully aware that they are only a part of a much wider discussion.

But I raise Diamond's book because he is interested, as I am, in the question of why wealth and power have become distributed as they now are. Inequitable distribution of wealth and power, as the principle author of our Constitution, James Madison, pointed out, is a destabilizing factor in societies.[2] Since the political uses of both violence and nonviolence are defended as tactics to bring about more just/peaceful/stable societies, this issue of an uneven distribution of wealth and power is basic. Diamond's brief conclusion is that it is "a combination of government and religion, together with germs, writing and technology (the guns/steel) that have shaped the historical pattern."[3] To a large extent it is the first agents on his list: government and religion, often working symbiotically that have determined how states have responded to or chosen to use the other agents: disease, writing and technology. States, with their ability to centralize resources, levy taxes, control access to information, raise and maintain armies, wield enormous power: power that can be used to heal or to destroy. States have a great potential to provide goods and services that individuals alone cannot: Public health, public works projects, education of its citizens, and common defense. But that same power of states to centralize information and resources, if not shared, can create a monopoly of power. Thus states can become dictatorial tyrannies keeping masses of people uneducated, devoid of human rights and living in poverty and fear. Diamond uses the word "kleptocracy" which is suggestive of the ability of nation states to take from the masses of poor and concentrate wealth for a few.

States that survive must become expert at marshaling popular support. The most morally satisfying way is to redistribute wealth and power in popular ways: political choice and participation in government, protection of human rights, health care, social benefits, roads, schools, libraries, environmental protection, old age and unemployment insurance, etc. Countries like Canada, Japan, Switzerland, the Scandinavian countries and much of Western Europe come to mind as modern examples. Another way to gain support is to disarm the populace and arm the elite, promising to maintain public order and curb violence. We think of this most often in conjunction with dictatorships in Latin America and Africa. Yugoslavia, Georgia, and Hussein's Iraq are recent examples. Yet another way to gain support is to construct an ideology or religion that justifies the state and its use of power. The United States uses aspects of all three, but has developed some very subtle forms of the latter that merit closer examination. Angela Davis observed at a recent talk at Earlham College, "Ideology is what we take for granted."[4] Academics may well think they might be exempt from this – that their ideology is well thought through and I hope for many of us this is true. But even these attempts may only mask a deeper set of unspoken shared cultural assumptions and it is these that have power because they become normative and authoritative in a society.

The Normative and Authoritative "Myth of Redemptive Violence"

I once asked a class to list some of the widely held, authoritative cultural assumptions of which they were aware. They quickly generated maxims like "If you work hard you'll get ahead" "Bigger is better" "More is better" "Get yours now" "We have the best society in the world" "If you disobey the law, you should accept punishment" "In a land of opportunity, the rich deserve their wealth and the poor have only themselves to blame" "Sex and violence sell" "Individuals are free to do whatever they want"

"You can't do anything without money." Most missed the ironic and disempowering aspects of the juxtaposition of the last two statements.

While the list is revealing, what they missed may be even more revealing. When pushed, some of them could also see that there are numerous aspects of US culture that reinforce the old patterns of racism and sexism: the belief that whites are superior to nonwhites, men are superior to women, citizens are superior to immigrants, etc. (but of course none of them were "guilty.") The persistence of these fractures among people ostensibly part of one nation is enormously significant because it undermines the potential for peace with other nations. If we habitually have groups of people seen as "other" or "inferior," we are that much less likely to be able to embrace the full humanity (with all its differences) of those from other nations, especially if we have reason to see them as "enemies."

Although most students had an awareness of the pervasiveness and even celebration of violence in the culture, none articulated what New Testament scholar Walter Wink calls "the myth of redemptive violence," defined as "the victory of order over chaos by means of violence," a justification of "might makes right."[5] This concept fits Davis' notion that "what we take for granted becomes so embedded culturally that it is normative and authoritative." Historically, redemptive violence has been generally framed with some controls such as "violence as last resort," but as our current "pre-emptive" war with Iraq demonstrates, redemptive violence is being asked to stand alone as an unqualified principle. Once one begins to see it, redemptive violence is woven quietly and almost seamlessly throughout the major cultural carriers: our schools, our holidays, our public monuments, our businesses, the media, the churches. Some brief examples of how this functions will demonstrate how deeply ingrained is the idea that good things come from violence and why it will require a major paradigm shift to begin to think about widespread political use of alternatives such as nonviolence.

What history is taught and the way it is taught plays a central role in perpetuating this myth of violence. The founding sacred story of the United States is the American Revolution, a war fought, we are carefully taught, to give us freedom from the tyrannical British. We believe it was "the only way," never stopping to ask ourselves if there were alternatives (which there were: a quick example is the Philadelphia plan which only lost by one vote, ironically on the grounds that the colonies could never work together, something that war forced them to do). We don't ask if our neighbors to the north in Canada are any less free than we because they never fought the British. Most students are convinced the Civil War or War between the States was a justified war – the "only way" to end slavery; ignoring that the British empire had ended slavery by an act of parliament, our neighbors to the south ended slavery at the time of their revolutions from Spain, and that nearly the only men really eager to fight the war as a war to free the slaves (rather than to defend states rights or the union) were denied that right because of their color, until the deaths became so horrendous that African Americans were armed. World War I is taught as the war fought to make the world safe for democracy; almost no one pointing to the evidence that it did just the opposite with its war profiteering and peace settlement that led to the "good war," WWII, which of course was fought to stop Hitler; never mind the evidence that it was the Japanese that brought us into the war, not outrage at Hitler's final solution, and that some US companies were making tidy profits selling to Hitler.[6]

The loss and sacrifice of war creates a sensitive situation, in which the deaths must somehow be justified to have meaning. Unfortunately, this is frequently done in such a way as to glorify war, increasing the likelihood that it will happen again. Veterans, particularly generals, become the heroes and the ones whose lives we teach and celebrate. Journalist and history teacher Coleman McCarthy has asked high school, undergraduate and law students to identify a list of "famous people." He includes Napoleon, A. J. Muste, Robert E. Lee, Sojourner Truth, Ulysses S. Grant, Adin Ballou, Dwight D. Eisenhower, and Dorothy Day. Where ever he does this, participants score 50% – people know the generals.[7] Why do we know and teach generals and warriors and not those who have worked for peace? How can we learn about options if they aren't taught? The extent to which war reinforces war is pointed out by Howard Zinn who observes that the man with the greatest name recognition in psychology, Sigmund Freud, and the man whose name is synonymous with 20th century physics, Albert Einstein, when asked to explain the persistence of war both used history rather than their own studies of human nature or science as evidence to explain why humans continue to wage war.[8]

Why do we teach that justice can only come from war when we have so much evidence to the contrary? In the 20th century alone more than 150 million people, civilian and military died as a direct result of war. Uncounted is the damage to infrastructure, environment, medical costs and the uncountable human cost of veterans who return home too scarred by what they've been through to transition back to being healthy citizens, spouses and parents. It seems that in the last century, we have given war a more than fair trial at bringing about a better world. The Center for Defense Information gives a figure of $13.1 trillion spent on the Cold War, with an average military expense of $298.5 billion.[9] These costs gain some perspective when we contrast them with the cost and benefit of other possible uses. For instance, the UN World Food Program estimates that it would take just $24 billion to cut hunger in half through direct food aid programs and investments in agriculture and rural infrastructure.[10] Currently there are more than 300 million land mines, causing untold capricious damage around the world. The cost of eliminating all of them is somewhere between 30 and 33 billion dollars.[11] Costofwar.org is a website that keeps a running tally of the cost of the current war in Iraq and what the same amount could purchase if spent for education or immunizations or public services.[12] Money spent for war is money taken away from human services and building infrastructure, so the forces supporting such expenditure must be great indeed. What if the money being spent for military had been used by the state department to create a more secure world using money as a source of power to heal, rather than destroy? How would the world see the US today if we had chosen a foreign policy strategy of creating allies, rather than bombing possible enemies? How and why have we constructed a historical narrative that reinforces the idea that greatness and freedom are dependent upon the effective use of violence?

History of course, get lots of reinforcement from other aspects of the culture: our holidays (Memorial Day, Flag Day, Fourth of July, Veterans Day) try to help a nation find meaning in the sacrifice of so many lives, while encouraging the next generation to be willing to follow in their footsteps. Our monuments (almost every small town has a monument to its war dead; we build battlefield monuments along our roadsides, but where are the memorials celebrating those who brought about change through means other than war; who sacrificed for the good of all, but not with a uniform on? Our national anthem with its "rockets red glare, bombs bursting in air" comes out of war. It seems significant that after 9/11 the patriotic song most frequently sung was "America the Beautiful." This is not just because the melody is easier to sing: the words express love of country, not glorification of war, an important distinction that is getting lost. The role of business in perpetuating war is long and sordid: from J.P. Morgan making millions selling defective rifles with a 600% profit margin to the Union army to Major General Smedley D. Butler's well known expose "War is a Racket" to the Nye commission to our present concerns over the interests and practices of the Carlyle Group, Haliburton and other oil companies in Iraq. Is it accident or design that, as of this writing, every ministry building in Iraq has been devastated by coalition bombs, except the ministry of oil? Political commentator Kevin Phillips points out that what is most disturbing in the current war profiteering is that the beneficiaries have moved beyond the military-industrial complex of which President Eisenhower warned the nation to a "new complex of technology, arms exports, internal security and clandestine operations, with its particular concentration in the crossroads of world oil production and religious prophecy."[13] On the home front, business reaps profits merchandising war games, camouflage clothing, handguns and rifles in department stores. One large chain store even packed Easter baskets with army figures and ammunition along with the holiday candy and Easter bunnies. War is profitable to some in ways that peace is not.

The role of television, videos, computer games and other forms of media in perpetuating violence has received great attention – there is no need to belabor all the ways in which they reinforce the myth of redemptive violence: cartoons, cops and robbers, good guys/bad guys, talk shows, reality shows. The average American watches 3000 homicides every year. Studies show that violence goes up in remote communities when TV comes in. Television serves the interest of those in power – the average now is 3 years of our life spent watching commercials; we are exposed to 3000 a day! We think we can brush them off but studies, like those of Jean Kilbourne, have shown that is not the case.[14] When socialization is sophisticated enough, the beliefs seem invisible. The concept of television "programming" may well be more descriptive than intended.

Another way that the culture subtly reinforces violence is the many ways military language and imagery have become pervasive and are used for non-military events. Newspapers report on "war on spam" or wars between competing companies. One vivid example comes from immunologist Angela Montel describing events in our cells. In a talk she gave at Blufton College, a Mennonite school, she used language common in her discipline to say: "Natural killer cells and t cells will seek out the foreign invaders and deliver a lethal blow through the use of perforin mediated assault." Apparently, we have World War III going on inside. When challenged on the language, she acknowledges the concept could be restated with equal accuracy as "CD16+ and CD 56+ cells and T cells will seek out the unwanted bacteria, viruses, or parasites and will render them incapable of life and propagation through the use of perforin-mediated mechanisms." She admits it doesn't sound as resonant, but also acknowledges she's been "programmed to be energized by the rallying cry of a fight against microbes."[15] The real danger of the militant language is that it programs us to wage all out war on microbes, rather than acknowledging our interdependence on all living things – we fail to acknowledge that a truly successful war on microbes would exterminate us as well. This has a parallel in current political affairs. If the US or any nation is willing to wage all out war against any perceived enemy, including destroying infrastructure, vegetation and soil through chemical agents, and millions of non-combatants/ civilians, we are in danger of wiping out ourselves as well. Reports from the ground in Baghdad confirm that one of the greatest threats to all living creatures, human and otherwise, in Iraq may well be depleted uranium. Contaminated dust settles in the food, water and air that everyone, including US forces are dependent upon.[16]

The same is true for domestic policy. Tilting the balance scales toward the wealthy through tax cuts and legal codes undermines the health of the whole nation. After-tax income has increased 72% for the wealthiest one percent, while decreasing by 16% for the poorest twenty percent in the last twenty years. While gross domestic product continues to climb, the index of social health indicators (housing, health insurance, retirement,) has steadily declined since the 1970s. When these basic safety nets are absent, stability is eroded and drug and alcohol abuse, cynicism, anger, violence, scapegoating, compliance with lower wages and longer hours increases. Lillian Rubin, author of, *Families on the Fault Line*, in her interviews with 162 working class families from all ethnicities, repeatedly heard "we live scared" – scared of job loss, scared of homelessness, scared of loss of health with no insurance.[17] A scared population is neither healthy nor stable. Essayist Barbara Kingsolver observes "Just about any country you can name spends a larger percentage of its assets on its kids than we do. Virtually all industrialized nations have better schools and child care ... "[18] This skewing of resources away from life supporting uses helps maintain the forces of violence. It is not surprising that the "volunteer" army with its promise of employment, steady income, free medical care, not to mention a 2 billion dollar promotional budget, is an attractive option for many poorer income young people. Even so, it is having a tough time keeping up with the current demand for soldiers. Few are re-enlisting, reservists are upset about being called to Iraq, and in a deja vu of resistance among Vietnam soldiers, a significant number of Iraq war soldiers are questioning US policy when they see it on the ground. The US government has taken upon itself enormous power to destroy with both its international and domestic policies.

Diamond's thesis included religion as well as government as instrumental in shaping the historical pattern. Eleven academy awards for *Lord of the Rings* and the current incessant discussion about Mel Gibson's blockbuster *The Passion* (R rated for violence) affirm that the visual portrayal of religious themes is powerful and reinforces the deep attraction that Americans have for religion as a source of meaning and moral basis in their lives. Religion received inordinate attention in the 2004 presidential election, with most of the analysis focusing on the emergence of the "Religious Right" with its concerns about gay marriage and abortion. The Western theological tradition that dominates the US practice of religion, like state power, can be used to heal or to destroy. Important doctrines and ideas that have emerged reinforce the idea of humans as inherently violent and support the use of redemptive violence, but there are also ideas that speak of humans as made in the image of a beneficent God and capable of redemptive love. Religious differences are essential in a free society – something to be celebrated – but the focus here is on the ways in which theology and nationalism too often intersect, reinforcing militarism rather than peace.

Perhaps the greatest boon to the rise of the European nation-state was getting the church to develop and accept "just war theory." St. Augustine's dictum "we go to war that we may have peace" creates a rationale that has convinced masses, who may have reservations about the horrors of war, that war can bring about good.[19] For many citizens, of whatever nation, the lines between fighting all out wars for the country and "fighting fair" (i.e. practicing the second part of Augustine's quote: "be peaceful in warring") have blurred. Robert Tucker pointed out well before our current war on terrorism, that the US tends to believe that "only the criterion of just cause really matters and that if the cause is "great enough, it may be appropriate to disregard some of the ordinary restraints in the prosecution of hostilities."[20] This describes the historical pattern the churches have followed: Regardless of their position about war prior to hostilities, the majority of churches have supported their nation's war effort, including the necessity to win by any means necessary. If people are convinced the cause is just (stop Hitler, contain communism, fight terrorism) they tend to disregard restraints like "is this really the last resort," "will our retaliation be proportional" and "are civilians being protected?" In the best American tradition of pragmatism, adhering to *jus ad bellum* but not *jus in bello* makes sense. It is hard to come up with any war that has been prosecuted according to basic just war tenets, so why pretend? At some point, "proportionality" disappears in battle and one must decide whether to "win at any cost" which justifies using ABC weapons (atomic/biological/chemical) or adhere to one's principles and suffer the possibility of more deaths and loss, or even to accept defeat as the most principled option. The same is true for the principle of "protection of non-combatants and civilians." Given the nature of modern warfare, if one really believes killing children, mothers and grandparents is unethical, rather than "collateral damage," one is left with the same moral dilemma as pacifists: does one respond in kind to violence or does one hold to just war principles and suffer the consequences? At this point, just war theorists may well start looking to nonviolent practioners to see if there are any other strategies than war for combating injustice.

Sometimes it is easiest to see the intertwining of religious and national interests in historical perspective. A little more than 150 years ago Frederick Douglass observed, "slavery could not exist without the support of the churches."[21] From the perspective of most churches, slavery, with its relatively clear Biblical support, was the country's "peculiar institution." Abraham held slaves; Jesus didn't speak against slavery; Paul told slaves to obey their masters, even though the New Testament was written as the Roman Empire, utilizing slave labor, imposed its will on the area. Yet today what was a minority opinion – that the Bible was an anti-slavery document – has become a widely accepted interpretation. But few churches adopted the prophetic theology and hermeneutic of the anti-slavery churches, making the change a cultural one, rather than a substantive reorientation. Today's challenge for Christians is similar: to develop a hermeneutic based on the moral teachings of Jesus that allows the Bible to be read as an anti-war document in spite of all the passages that are traditionally used to support war. Such interpretations however are never going to become mainstream in a nation built on war. Most churches are flying US flags in their sanctuaries and calling for support of our troops, meaning support of the war, not support to bring them home and create a world in which it is less likely they will ever again be called upon to commit atrocities in the name of patriotic duty or doing good. The parallels with the 19th century are sobering: The membership of antislavery churches in the 19th century is comparable to the number of members of peace churches today. Could the current militarism of our nation exist without the support of the churches?

There is one additional condition that makes it difficult for us as a culture to break out of the deceptive cycle of trying to end violence through violence. The most egregious abuses of power are accepted as the way things are. A contributing factor to this state of affairs is our Enlightenment/Reformation understanding of the individual, which often blinds us to systemic issues. We quickly recognize individual agency and accountability; we miss structural issues, as essayist Derrick Jensen points out. "To kill one Indian may be a hate crime ... to dispossess an entire culture may be in the words of the US Supreme court ruling on the preemption of Indian land by settlers in 1823 'supported by reason and certainly cannot be rejected by Courts of law.'" Killing one Indonesian is murder, but when Weyerhaeuser contracts with a military dictatorship in Indonesia, destroying forests and agricultural land which results in starvation and death of thousands, it is sanctioned as legal business practice and in the best interest of the US economy.[22] To kill one African American may be a hate crime. To lock up African Americans at a rate four times greater than South Africa imprisoned blacks during the apartheid years (and a rate 9 times greater than the US white population) is justified as part of keeping the country safe from crime, even though as Angela Davis points out incarcerating ever greater numbers of people (with 5% of the world's population, the U.S. incarcerates more than 20% of the world's total prison population) "the most obvious pattern was that larger prison populations led not to safer communities, but, rather, to even larger prison populations."[23] Stealing a loaf of bread from a grocery store is a crime, but stealing retirement benefits or wages from thousands of people is seen as an inevitable part of business cycles.[24]

We value our individualism, but when the Center for Disease Control reports more than 900,000 cases of child abuse in 2001, resulting in death or serious injury, we have to wonder about our commitment to children and family values.[25] Child abuse is an unacknowledged reflection of a culture built on the myth of redemptive violence. We believe that to discipline a child means to use corporal punishment "for their own good" and then find that those who have been abused by excessive and capricious punishment as children are more likely to become abusers themselves. Our culture is full of distracters, keeping us focused on the details – of ball games or individual politicians, of video games or the price of gas. We miss the overall patterns and have difficulty seeing structural violence because it just seems like economics, or tradition, or the way things are. In short, we have created a culture where we are predisposed by media, holidays, monuments, business, language, history, child rearing and religion to believe powerful cultural assumptions that violence and wars bring good things.

Rethinking Power: The Practice of Nonviolence as an Alternative to the Myth of Redemptive Violence

Martin Luther King's words that "violence multiplies violence and toughness multiplies toughness in a descending spiral of destruction" have never been more insightful or timely. King and a host of others who have experienced first hand the human propensity toward injustice and violence conclude, "Hate cannot drive out hate, only love can do that."[26] Nonviolent love as a force more powerful than hate or vengeance is not a concept or idea that most policy-makers or academicians, habituated to the myth of redemptive violence, tend to take very seriously. But if humans have the power to learn from experience, it would seem that the experience of the last century would predispose us to try something other than the old formula of "if you hit me, I'll hit you back harder." Why do we find nonviolence hard to accept as a serious alternative to domestic and international violence? First, the widespread use of nonviolence requires some new, generally unfamiliar ways of thinking. It requires a massive paradigm shift, something that does not come easily with all the cultural reinforcements for the use of violence already discussed. One aspect of this is rethinking and expanding our ideas of power. The use of violence limits its options to only one understanding of power – "power over" or coercive power – the power of might makes right. Nonviolent political power is predicated on the understanding that political power can "never be exercised without the acquiescence of the people," even in dictatorships and tyrannies.[27] When sufficient numbers of people refuse to cooperate with a government, the government will eventually change or fall. This is the basis for "people power" or "power with" – the power of people acting together. A vivid example still within the living memory of some was what happened in the U.S. when a catalytic number of people refused to continue to cooperate with segregation laws. The system could no longer continue as it had. But in order to develop the power to resist, a third form of power must be fostered –one that Gandhi spent much time cultivating in himself and others – and that is "power within." Power within is the re-orientation of internalized cultural values and re-discovery of the value and interconnectedness of all life in such a way that one finds the courage and power to say "no" to injustice. It sounds simpler than it is. Historian and activist Howard Zinn has commented, "Civil disobedience is not our problem. Our problem is civil obedience. Our problem is that numbers of people all over the world have obeyed the dictates of the leaders of their government and have gone to war and millions have been killed because of this obedience."[28] Gandhi said "the first principle of non-violent action is non cooperation with everything that is humiliating"[29] Sustaining the freedom in that powerful "no" requires strength and courage because it may entail profound suffering. While it is important to remember that there are many variations of pacifism, running the spectrum from non-resistance to selective pacifists, from pragmatic to principled, those actively engaged in nonviolent resistance find that diverse, but nurturing spiritual practices and the development of community are basic to strengthening this power.[30] Nonviolence expands relationships horizontally into community, rather than vertically because nonviolent activists tend to see the world as a "web of mutuality" rather than a "winner take all" competition. The emphasis is on attacking unjust systems, not individuals. This paradigm shift is far reaching.

Stories socialize us, but few of us get stories of non-violence from our parents or communities; most stories are told by marketing conglomerates. Thus we need a massive re-education to learn from those who have been part of the long tradition of protest against injustice, what is possible, and how to navigate a course which neither passively accepts injustice nor participates in the oppression of others; in Camus' phrase to neither be victim nor executioner. What if we gave serious study to these stories in our general education classes and not just marginalized them to peace studies? When one begins to look, it is surprising how wide spread both pragmatic nonviolence and principled nonviolent resistance are.

Nonviolence is found in all parts of the world and has sprung out of all religious traditions. Buddhist pacifists such as Thich Nhat Hanh, and the Dali Lama are well known. Gandhi, of course, is the best known Hindu. St Francis (1180-1226) who in an age of crusades and holy wars, rejected all violence as an offense against the gospel commandment to love and a desecration of God's image in all human beings, and urged tolerance and love for all, including Muslims, is beloved by both Catholic and Protestants. One of the least known but most dramatic and powerful of all nonviolent movements was an Islamic one, led by Khan Abdul Ghaffir Khan (better known by the honorific Badshah Khan (1890-1988)). A Pashtun from the Northwest provinces of India (now Pakistan), he created the Kudai Khimatgars, or Servants of God, which grew into a nonviolent army of over 80,000 to oppose British colonial rule. They were deeply admired by Gandhi, because the Pashtuns, with their reputation for defending honor with violence, could hardly be said to have chosen nonviolence out of a fear of fighting.[31]

Cultural blinders may keep us from seeing the non-violent traditions that have roots in North America. Three quick examples are the Hopi, the Sweet Medicine of the Cheyenne and the Great Peace of the Iroquois. The latter have a vivid story of Deganawida crossing Lake Huron in a stone canoe and learning from Jigonhsasee the Great Peace woman how to overcome the violence that had kept the northeast tribes in fear and warfare. The five tribes (later six) developed a Great Binding Law of ceremonies that creates space for negotiations and recognition of the humanity of the enemy.[32]

Millions of people have engaged in nonviolent action as a pragmatic way of resisting oppressive systems, forcing changes in economic and social institutions, even bringing down tyrannical governments. But nonviolent actions, even when committed for pragmatic reasons (like no guns) or strategic reasons (like the chances are better for a positive outcome) have been undervalued, maybe in part because they are so common we fail to recognize them as such. A key element of the beauty of nonviolence is that anyone can do it – young, old, infirm – it doesn't depend on physical power, but on the power of people united, combined with their ability to think strategically and tactically and to persevere. Many movements for social change utilized nonviolent methods. Women vote today, not because they picked up guns and demanded it, but in response to persistent, nonviolent pressure. The sit down strikes in the auto plants during the 1930s or Caesar Chavez's organization of the United Farm Workers are two other examples among many. George Lakey, nonviolence trainer for the successful 1989 Pittston campaign by US coal miners, tells of an old miner who told him with a sigh "I have to tell you that I prefer the good old days when a strike meant that we could tear things up, beat up scabs, shoot at company trucks – you know, we had a lot of guns and knew how to use them." "But," he admitted, "that stuff doesn't work any more. Go ahead, teach us nonviolent struggle." George calls that "nonviolence as a last resort."[33] A. Philip Randolph's threat of a nonviolent march on Washington in 1941 was sufficient to cause FDR to issue an Executive Order banning discrimination in federally funded defense industries. Randolph was present 22 years later at the well known March on Washington in 1963, a highly visible event, but one backed by years of nonviolent resistance, that resulted in the passage of the Civil Rights Act of 1964 and Voting Rights Act of 1965. Note that working class people have carried out most nonviolent social change movements, a fact that may contribute to their invisibility by those elites in positions of power not directly affected. In any given week there are community-based organizations all across the US who are engaged in nonviolent action: marches, sit-ins, street blockades, boycotts, civil disobedience by hospital workers, hotel works, janitors, and most recently grocery store clerks. But we tend not to celebrate nonviolent successes and thus miss our opportunity to build on them. Civil rights activist and nonviolence advocate Diane Nash observed at a King Day celebration held in Richmond, Indiana (near Dayton, Ohio, home of the Wright brothers) that we celebrate the achievement of the Wright brothers, but we certainly have improved on their original design. Huge resources of time and money have moved us from biplanes that shudder a few thousand feet, barely clearing trees, to jets flying reliably at 30,000 feet and 600 miles per hour. Her analogy was clear. We haven't put the same time, energy and resources into learning how to wage successful nonviolent campaigns.[34] In his book published in 1973, political scientist Gene Sharp listed 198 types of nonviolent actions, including various forms of protest, persuasion, social economic and political non-cooperation, and nonviolent intervention (direct action).[35] Imagine where nonviolence (and the current political state of the world!) could be today, if even half the budget and resources spent on the Cold War had been used to develop these strategies and educate people in nonviolent resistance.

Nonviolent social change is probably best known in its more revolutionary forms: when the goal is a change in governments rather than reform within governmental systems. But only a few examples are well known; Most people have not heard of (much less studied) Kwame Nkrumah's use of nonviolence in Ghana's struggle for independence (1952), the successful Nepalese student struggle for greater democracy, the overthrow of Jorge Ubico in Guatemala (1944) or the prolonged nonviolent campaign for democracy in Taiwan. The strategic shift of the African National Congress back to major reliance on nonviolent action in the 1980s is another example ultimately resulting in a replacement of the white exclusive control of political and economic power with a multiracial democracy. In 1989 alone, 15 nations experienced nonviolent revolutions, most of them independence movements from Soviet and/or communist control. All but China's succeeded beyond anyone's expectations. One of the most dramatic was Otpor, the largely student movement that brought down the Serbian dictator, Slobodon Milosovic in 2000. The revolutions required enormous courage and creativity on the part of the participants, who remained non-violent in the face of brutality, prisons and threats to their lives. Some were killed; but a nonviolent revolution greatly increases the possibilities for rebuilding with justice and stability, since non-violent resistance leaves no swath of murder and destruction to fuel perpetual cycles of revenge.[36]

A common objection to nonviolent action is that it precludes the right to self defense. This reflects a cultural failure to consider options other than "fight or flight" in protecting oneself. Most of us are probably familiar with some examples, but don't always process them as part of this discussion of violence and nonviolence. An example is stories of women who have successfully distracted would be attackers through conversation or feigning illness or other creative means. In fact, experienced nonviolent interveners claim they are safer without a weapon, because it gives them more options. (Protecting oneself from unprovoked attack, of course, is different from voluntarily and courageously exposing oneself to the possibility of injury as part of a strategic plan as men did in Gandhi's famous salt march.) Numerous towns have protected themselves nonviolently from environmental pollution, toxic waste incinerators or from the encroachment of unwanted mega stores that would drive out locally owned businesses. Some urban neighborhoods use nonviolent action to fight the invasion of drug dealers. They march, set up patrols, and prevent drug dealers from using favorite street corners. Gandhi suggested nonviolent civil defense to Switzerland in 1931 and to Britain in 1940. Sweden and Austria have incorporated nonviolent civilian based defense into their national defense planning. These governmental defense planners mainly are interested in resisting invasions and have put research and development funds into creating nonviolent strategies that will prevent a military occupation from succeeding in their countries. Even though this application is among the least known uses of nonviolent action, it has received funding for research because of governmental interest.[37]

Yet another application of nonviolent action that is gaining some visibility is third party nonviolent intervention, mostly through the actions of groups like Peace Brigades International (PBI), Nonviolent Peace Force and Christian Peacemaker Teams (CPT). These groups may simply use their presence as accompaniers and their privilege as outsiders to increase the safety of those receiving death threats. For instance during a wave of killings of lawyers in Sri Lanka in 1989, the national bar association invited PBI to send a team there to accompany lawyers, and while death threats continued, none of those accompanied by PBI was killed. Or groups may observe and monitor as was done with the South African elections in 1994 or the Nicaraguan election of 1990. CPT teams are doing monitoring and accompaniment work in places like Columbia, Iraq and Hebron, often providing some of the most reliable information about what is going on including stories of Jews and Arabs trying to build bridges rather than walls.[38] Christian Peacemaker Teams in Baghdad successfully protected a water treatment plant (that had been destroyed in the first Gulf War) from being destroyed a second time by US bombs, by informing the military of their presence and keeping vigil around it.[39]

This list could go on but the point has been made that we as a members of the global community have options other than dropping bombs. Susan Shear, executive director for Women's Action for New Directions, a supporter of Sensible Multilateral Response to Terrorism (SMART) observes: "We've seen what happens when we go in with guns blazing and bombs dropping: anarchy, anger, retaliation, hunger. It's time to try a different tack: hands extended to build a better world .... Most polls confirm that Americans are nervous and frightened at the prospect of continuing to go it alone in the world. It may be that we can only survive if we join hands with other countries and work to make a sustainable peace – not a never -ending war."[40] Gandhi, as might be expected, saw this more than 50 years ago, and took it further. He wrote "Democracy can only be saved through non-violence, because democracy so long as it is sustained by violence, cannot provide for or protect the weak ... The states that are today nominally democratic have either to become frankly totalitarian or, if they are to be truly democratic, they must become courageously nonviolent."[41] That seems to be a sobering assessment of where we are today – walking a thin line between totalitarianism and the possibility of rule by, of, and for the people. To accomplish the later, we need a cultural shift from using power to destroy to using power to heal, a shift requiring a transformation in our underlying stories, images and assumptions used by our cultural carriers, a shift from the myth of redemptive violence to using the methods of peace to create a just and sustainable peace.

Notes

1   See http://www.wisdomquotes.com/001835.html.

2   See *Federalist Papers #10*. "Factionalism arising from the various and unequal distribution of property" could endanger the new nation. Madison went on to discuss why equality of property was not the way to solve this problem.

3   Jared Diamond. *Guns, Germs, and Steel: The Fates of Human Societies* (New York: Norton, 1999), p. 267. Diamond is a professor of physiology at UCLA Medical School.

4   Angela Davis, Speech at Earlham College, Richmond, IN. 16 January 2004.

5   There are many terms used to describe this phenomenon: combat myth, constructive violence, destructive violence, zealous nationalism, etc. Robert Beck, *Nonviolent Story: Narrative Conflict Resolution in the Gospel of Mark* (Maryknoll, N.Y.: Orbis Books, 1996) opens his book with a very insightful chapter called "Louis L'amour and the myth of constructive violence." Beck uses the term to refer to the mythology expressed so effectively in L'amour's westerns (and in US politics) that violent means are necessary to the creation of just ends, but the term "constructive violence" has broader meanings, as well. Realizing that all language is fluid, but it is the necessary tool for written communication, I have chosen to use the term "redemptive violence," popularized by Walter Wink in his trilogy of books on power, in the hopes that its meaning, especially its connection with hierarchy, domination and "power over" will clarify and distinguish the rough boundaries of this term. The quotes are from Walter Wink, *Engaging the Powers: Discernment and Resistance in A World of Domination* (Minneapolis: Fortress Press, 1992). p. 16.

6   Union Carbide, IBM and Ford are among the best known companies. Banks as well. See Edwin Black, *IBM and the Holocaust: The Strategic Alliance between Nazi Germany and America's Most Powerful Corporation* (London: Crown Publishers, 2001); Charles Higham, *Trading with the Enemy: An Expose of the Nazi-American Money Plot, 1933-1949* (New York, 1983); and Kevin Philips, *Dynasty* (New York, 2003).

7   Colman McCarthy, foreword to *The Universe Bends Toward Justice: A Reader on Christian Nonviolence in the U.S.* Angie O'Gorman (ed). (Philadelphia: New Society Publishers, 1990), ix.

8   Howard Zinn, *Declarations of Independence: Cross-Examining American Ideology* (New York: Harper Collins, 1990), pp. 33-34.

9   Martin Calhoun, Senior Research Analyst, Center for Defense Information http://www.cdi.org/issues/milspend.html (accessed 9 July 1996.) Calhoun also prepared a page of "real totals" which puts total military spending in 1996 at $494 Billion, not $265.6. See also http://www.cdi.org/issues/realtota.html.

10   John Allen, "Compared to war, feeding world's hungry has modest price tag" http://www.natcath.com/NCR_Online/archives/032803/032803h.htm The U.N. World Food Programme home page is www.wfp.org.

11   See International Campaign to Ban Land Mines at http://www.icbl.org/ and information from UNICEF at http://maic.jmu.edu/journal/3.3/profiles/UNICEF.pdf.

12   See National Priorities Project at http://www.costofwar.com.

13   Kevin Phillips, *American Dynasty: Aristocracy, Fortune, and the politics of Deceit in the House of Bush* (New York: Penguin Books, 2004), p. 276.

14   Jean Kilbourne, *You Can't Buy My Love: How Advertising Changes the Way we Think and Feel* (New York: Touchstone Press, 2000).

15 J. Denny Weaver (ed). *Teaching Peace* (Lanham, Maryland: Rowan and Littlefield, 2003) pp. 232-233.

16 The Laka Foundation in Amsterdam, the Netherlands, has done documentation and research on nuclear energy. Several of their responsibly researched articles are available on line at http://www.rimbaud.freeserve.co.uk/dhap99f.html. (Accessed 27 March 2004.)

17 Lillian Rubin, "Family Values and the Invisible Working Class" in Steven Fraser and Joshua Freeman (eds.), *Audacious Democracy* (New York: Houghton Mifflin, 1997), p. 34.

18 Barbara Kingsolver, *High Tide in Tucson* (New York: Harper-Collins, 1995), p. 105.

19 St. Augustine. *Select Letters*, trans. James Baxter (Cambridge, Mass: Harvard U. Press, 1953), Epistle ad Bonif. clxxxix. P. 331. The whole quote is: "We do not seek peace in order to be at war, but we go to war that we may have peace. Be peaceful, therefore, in warring, so that you may vanquish those whom you war against, and bring them to the prosperity of peace."

20 John Howard Yoder, *When War is Unjust: Being Honest in Just War Thinking* (Minneapolis: Augsburg Press, 1985), p. 67.

21 Douglass' speech, "What to the Slave is the Fourth of July?" given to the Rochester Ladies Antislavery Society 5 July 1852 is widely reprinted. See http://douglassarchives.org/doug_a10.htm (Accessed 25 March 2004).

22 Derrick Jensen, *The Culture of Make Believe* (New York: Context Books, 2002), pp. 12-44. The Supreme Court case is *Johnson v. MacIntosh* 21 US 543 1823. Other examples he gives are Occidental Petroleum in Columbia; United Fruit in Guatemala.

23 Angela Davis, *Are Prisons Obsolete?* (New York: Seven Stories Press, 2003), p. 12.

24 A recent editorial in the *Indianapolis Star* reflects this thinking. In response to yet another plant closing (this one an RCA plant in Marion, IN) causing almost a thousand more workers to lose jobs in a state where the average wages are 11.6 % below the national average, syndicated columnist Morton Marcus wrote" Perhaps it is time for us to stop thinking of workers as victims of globalization, but as negligent participants in the erosion of Indiana's economy." His conclusion was that "Hoosier workers [must] become responsible for their own well being." Morton J Marcus, "Workers are Responsible for Themselves" *Indianapolis Star* 25 March 2004, p. A6.

25 US Department of Health and Human Services, Administration for Children and Families, Children's Bureau 2003. "Child Maltreatment, 2001", Washington, D.C.: US Government Printing Office. Available on line at www.acf.hhs.gov/
programs/c/publications/cm01/outcover.htm (Accessed 16 March 2004).

26 Martin Luther King, Jr. *Strength to Love*   (Philadelphia: Fortress Press, 1981), p. 53. From the Sermon "Loving Your Enemies."

27 Gene Sharp, *The Politics of Nonviolent Action: Power and Struggle* (Boston: Porter Sargeant Pub,1973), p. 29.

28 Howard Zinn, *Howard Zinn Reader: Writings on Disobedience and Democracy* (New York: Seven Stories Press, 1997).

29 Thomas Merton, *Gandhi on Non-Violence* (New York: New Directions Publishing, 1964), p. 29.

30 "Non-resistance" refers to the philosophy that under no circumstances is one to offer resistance. Unfortunately, this is often the only public understanding of "pacifism" and it is why those who choose to actively resist injustice, with nonviolent tools, rather than weapons of war generally avoid the confusing term pacifist and use the more explicit "non-violent resistance." Pragmatic nonviolence refers to the use of nonviolence for pragmatic

reasons like it works, or one is out gunned. Principled nonviolence is nonviolence as a way of life as practiced by Gandhi and others.

31 Eknath Easwaran, *Nonviolent Soldier of Islam* (Tomales, California: Nilgiri Press, 2002).

32 John Mohawk, "The Warriors Who Turned to Peace" *Yes! A Journal of Positive Futures* (Winter 2005): 24-27. Mohawk addresses the Haudenosaunee Confederacy from the perspective of how a people who knew only violence developed the power to make peace. See also Chapter 1 "The Original Peacemakers: Native Americans" in James Juhnke and Carol Hunter, *The Missing Peace: The Search for Nonviolent Alternatives in United States History* (Kitchner, Ontario: Pandora Press, 2001).

33 George Lakey, "Nonviolent Action As 'The Sword that Heals'" on line at http://www.trainingforchange.org/_0103_pacifismR.htm (Accessed 22 August 2002). Also available as a pamphlet.

34 Diane Nash, "King Day Celebration." Speech delivered at Earlham College, Richmond, IN, 19 January 2004.

35 Gene Sharp, *The Politics of Nonviolent Action: Methods of Nonviolent Action* (Boston: Porter Sargeant, 1973).

36 Two good texts that contain these stories and more are Peter Ackerman and Jack Duvall (eds.), *A Force More Powerful* (New York: Palgrave, 2000), and Stephen Zunes, (ed.), *Nonviolent Social Movements: A Geographical Perspective* (Malden, MA: Blackwell Pub, 2000).

37 Daniel Hunter and George Lakey, *Opening Space for Democracy: Third Party Nonviolence Intervention* (Philadelphia: Training for Change, 2004) This 600 page training manual for third party nonviolent intervention is full of practical tools and handouts. Numerous ideas in this paper are indebted to this manual See especially "Nonviolence and Guns" p.291 and "Three Applications of Nonviolent Action" pp. 291-292.

38 Art Gish, "Hebron: Building Bridges, not Walls" *Signs of the Times* (Vol XIV No. 1) http://www.cpt.org/archives/signs/2004/winter04.php.

39 Maxine Nash, member of the Christian Peacemaker Team in Baghdad. Talk at West Richmond Friends Meeting House, Richmond, IN, 27 March 2004.

40 Susan Shaer, Executive Director of Women's Action for New Directions 22 March 2004 at http://www.wandorg/news/smart-pressreport.htm. Smart security is an attempt to shift US budget priorities towards more humanitarian ends, shift foreign policy towards a more internationalist approach, working with the UN and NATO, ending the proliferation of nuclear weapons and "pursuing to the fullest extent alternatives to war."

41 Thomas Merton, *Gandhi on Non-Violence* (New York: New Directions Publishing, 1964), p. 45, p. 53. Quoting from Gandhi, *Non-violence in Peace and War* (Ahmedabad: Navajivan Publishing House, 1948). Vol 1: pp. 269, 159.

Chapter 6

The Ethics of Living American Primacy, or, Towards a Global Jim Crow, and Its Discontents

Will Watson

University of Southern Mississippi

As readers familiar with Richard Wright's great 1938 essay "The Ethics of Living Jim Crow" will surmise, the title of this paper registers a contention that global ethics have now entered what must be called an ironic phase. The nature of this ethical irony will, I hope, become clearer as I draw parallels between the "ethics of Jim Crow" and the ethical environment in which we find ourselves, post 9/11, in the age of American hegemony. In his the "Ethics of Living Jim Crow" Wright details the day-to-day deformations of human character condoned by that fiendishly precise code of social disempowerment. In the current moment of American hegemony it is useful to rediscover such a code as an "extra-ethics." This formulation derives from how historians of the New South describe lynching as having been "extra-legal," that is, bearing no formal relation to questions of legality, but rather existing on a plane where racist public sentiment and political necessity exceed the ability of law to represent or restrain them. According to the extra-legal strictures of Jim Crow, all manner of patently immoral and evil behavior was perfectly acceptable as long as the violence and injustice were directed against black folk.[1] Thus Wright used the term "ethics" ironically, to denote the coherent and patently unethical set of social and cultural practices called "Jim Crow" by which black folk were compelled to accept, act out and even internalize the dictates of white supremacy. Although legally proscribed by the Civil Rights Act of 1964 and other such laws, the legacy of Jim Crow for America's moment of post 9/11 tragedy and military "triumph" – over the Taliban and Saddam Hussein – bears considerable examination.

The original Jim Crow laws emerged out of a similar moment over one hundred years ago, ushered into being by the bloody national tragedy of the Civil War, and given greater impetus by the American triumph over Spain in the 1898 war and the resultant rise of the USA as a global empire.[2] One way that Gilded Age Americans came to understand this new global order was to see it as contiguous to and consistent with the practice of white supremacy that had always marked American life. The new empire was literally awash in the rhetoric of racial condescension and white millennialism. In his famous 1899 speech, "The Strenuous Life" Theodore Roosevelt would say of the Philippines, "their population includes half-caste and native Christians, warlike Moslems, and wild pagans. Many of their people are utterly unfit for self-government, and show no signs of becoming fit. Others may in time become fit but at present can only take part in self-government under a wise supervision, at once firm and beneficent."[3]   Even Senator Albert J. Beveridge, an Indiana Progressive for instance, might proclaim that "The Philippines are ours forever," and that "We will not renounce our part in the mission of our race, trustee, under God, of the civilization of the world."[4] Historically, such white supremacy was deeply rooted in American culture, but it was also assuming a new reach and complexity in the post-Reconstruction American South, where de facto segregation practices were being written into laws covering every conceivable public setting. Whether facing nationalist insurrection, as in the Philippines or trying to thread the racial and political labyrinth of Cuba, American soldiers, diplomats and administrators brandished this newly invigorated American color line as a weapon against any and all moral and ethical complexity. Teddy Roosevelt, John Hay and other diplomats forged ahead with a whites-only empire that heeded Kipling's call to "lift up the white man's burden," and thought of themselves as liberating those "new-caught, sullen peoples/ Half-devil and half child" who populated the empire.[5] Again, the ingenuously racist language of Senator Beveridge's call for perpetual American investment of the Philippines is instructive: "What alchemy will change the Oriental quality of their blood and set the self-governing currents of the American pouring through their Malay veins? How shall they, in the twinkling of an eye, be exalted to the heights of self-governing peoples which required a thousand years for us to reach, Anglo-Saxon though we are?"[6] It was white America's racial destiny, in other words to manage and control the non-Anglo Saxons of the world, for their own good.

The drawing of such a color line in Asia, the Pacific and the Caribbean gave domestic white racists further assurance of their inherent superiority and confidence in their supposed right to enforce inequality by legal and extra-legal means, up to and including state-sponsored violence. Jim Crow, in other words, could perfect itself because it underpinned domestic and foreign policy at a time when white Americans had been forced, by the collapse of the Old South and the victory over Spain in 1898, to come to terms with "the Other," that is, with a bewildering variety of cultural practices, social and political arrangements, both in the USA and in the Empire. The rise of the Crow made it easy for white Americans to see the whole world as either "Anglo-Saxon" and thus with them, or "colored" and with their racial others. Such early 20th-century Manichean-ism was a recipe for injustice, intolerance and inequality, and yet it was so clearly in line with deeply held notions of America's supposedly millennial destiny as to avoid the ideological bone yard for ... well, it might still be with us. Let us proceed.

Despite its embrace by American empire builders, history has judged Jim Crow's disdainful paternalism to be repugnant: ethically shameful, socially destructive and even, horror of horrors, politically inexpedient. The American war against the Philippines independence movement (1900-1904), for instance, featured American massacres of non-combatants on a scale presaging those in Vietnam and eventually killed an estimated 200,000 Filipinos and 4,000 American soldiers. Similarly, the Platt Amendment written into the Cuban Constitution of 1900 by racist American diplomats sanctioned the tradition of direct American intervention in Cuban affairs against which Fidel Castro and Che Guevara would define their nation and their philosophy of revolutionary violence less than a century later. In the USA itself, Jim Crow was embodied in the hundreds of lynchings that Ida Wells Barnett decried as *A Red Record* (1895) and led to the formation of the sort of racist "closed society" whose legacy still haunts us.[7] Needless to say, to invoke Richard Wright's formulation, "the ethics of Jim Crow" both at home and abroad were hardly ethical in any recognizable way. Rather the Crow signaled an ethical debauch, a period of ethical collapse, whose excesses and self-contradictions were disguised by a smug rhetoric of national/racial superiority that was all too easily assimilible to notions of American exceptional-ism and national mission.

In our own time, it is increasingly difficult for me to avoid the impression that this rhetoric, and this idea of American destiny, have been resurrected, given an ideological facelift to make them more palatable to the post Civil Rights Act American bourgeoisie and are now humming along every bit as happily as they did when Woodrow Wilson screened the egregiously racist *Birth of a Nation* at the White House in 1915 and proclaimed it "like history writ with lightening." The fall of the USSR catalyzed new, but familiar proclamations of various schema of American ascendancy. George Herbert Walker Bush called for a "New World Order," for instance. Francis Fukuyama crowed about the "end of history" and proclaimed that "there is no alternative" to capitalist social organization. Samuel Huntington considered that the stage had been set for a "clash of civilizations" between the supposedly enlightened, democratic west and the benighted, archaic despotism of, Muslims, Slavs, Hindus and, apparently, everyone else. In this brave new world, the IMF and other Western financial institutions dictated radical free trade "shock treatment" to both developing nations and the former USSR and invoked what Noam Chomsky calls the "Washington Consensus" to pressure the nominally sovereign nations of the Southern Cone and Pacific Rim to privatize nationally owned utilities and open formerly closed currency and securities markets to global speculators, regardless of the dire consequences that resulted for almost everyone not a member of the capital owning class.[8]

The ascension of the USA to the role of the "one true superpower" on the global stage was sacrementalized in blood by the apocalyptic American destruction of Iraq in the first Gulf War, the murderous sanctions and almost daily bombings imposed on that nation over the subsequent decade, and the second round of invasion and massive bombing that began in March of 2003. At home, this violent rite of ascension was matched by what history will most certainly condemn as an ethical lapse of epidemic proportions, as the American people abetted and even cheered the destruction of Iraq. A key reason for this failure of empathy was 9/11, of course, which imparted the final formative touches to the ethics of the new American imperium. The closest analogy to 9/11 in the time of Jim Crow would have to be the destruction of the battleship USS Maine in Havana harbor in 1898. Although the exact cause has yet to be made known, the sinking of the Maine in Spanish waters provoked enough nationalistic anger to make palatable a war of conquest that Gilded Age hawks had longed and planned for since the early 1890's. Their rush to war was underwritten by the yellow journalism and jingoistic bombast of profit-hungry newspaper magnates William Randolph Hearst and James Gordon Bennett, who often played up the humanitarian benefits of the proposed invasion of Cuba, arguing that the Cubans suffered under a cruel and genocidal Spanish regime there, while downplaying the *Red Record* of Judge Lynch, the bloody repression of labor activism and the genocide against Native Americans in their own backyard.

The parallels between 9/11 and the Maine's sinking, thus, are striking. As stage managed by the Bush administration and a too-complacent press and media, 9/11 conferred upon the American people a mantle of self-righteous victim-hood that too often precluded their asking difficult questions about the imperial ambitions of interest groups close to the Presidency, such as the Project for a New American Century, for instance, which included Dick Cheney and Jeb Bush, the president's brother. In this reprise of imperial history, profit-driven CNN and Fox News dutifully stood in for Hearst and Bennett, broadcasting copious amounts of the requisite rhetoric about the suffering of the Iraqi people under the genocidal Hussein regime and decrying that regime's propensity for violating UN resolutions, while neglecting to make much of certain inconvenient facts about the similar, and unpunished, propensity of Israel for doing the same. The media also shied away from any objective measurement of the degree to which Iraqi suffering could be laid at the feet of American-imposed sanctions, and were relatively silent about the wholehearted support of American regimes for Saddam Hussein in the late 1980's, at the very time when he was "gassing his own people," as one heard on everyone's lips in the lead up to the March 2003 war, and filling mass graves with opponents of his regime as an attempt to quash internal resistance to his war against Iran, a war for which Saddam was armed and supplied by the USA.

Even before 9/11, however, a racial rationale for such hypocrisy and brutality had begun to circulate. The Americans' inability to empathize with any of the victims of their decade-long assault on Iraq is exactly contemporary with the entry of such pithy anti-Arab epithets as "sand nigger," "camel jockey" and "rag head" into the American vernacular following Desert Storm. How else to explain that UN reports that US-imposed sanctions had killed 500,000 children were met with indifference? Or the fact that US targeting of Iraqi water-purification and distribution infrastructure constitutes a war crime but went pretty much unreported in the USA for years before 9/11? As would *The Lancet*'s October 2004 study of Iraqi civilian mortality after the USA invasion, which used rigorous epidemiological models to arrive at a likely figure of 100,000 civilian deaths attributable to American arms in the year following the March 2003 invasion. Similarly, around the time of the 2005 inauguration, at the same time as Americans and their President were binging on a Jeffersonian rhetoric of liberty, freedom and respect for individual rights, they were also being encouraged, by the future Attorney General, the Pentagon and the Justice Department to apply rather cavalier definitions of torture and habeas corpus to the widely publicized mistreatment and abuse of prisoners of the terror war at Guantanamo and Abu Ghraib. One was reminded of George Orwell's formulation in "Politics and the English Language": "the words democracy ... freedom, patriotic ... justice ... are often used in a consciously dishonest way," Orwell opines. "That is, the person who uses them has his own private definition, but allows his hearer to think he means something quite different." In the current age, it is difficult to avoid the impression that such "conscious dishonesty" is the lingua franca of the American hegemony.

This catalogue of the hypocrisy and brutality of the American hegemon could continue, ad nauseum, but I want to pause for minute and suggest that none of it – from free market shock therapy on impoverished nations, to "preemptive war on Iraq," to our high threshold of tolerance for genocide and torture – can be said to be genuinely predicated upon what could in any way be called ethics. Rather the ethical content of American hegemony is presaged in the smirking irony of late night talk show banter between celebrities like David Letterman and his bandleader Paul Schaeffer, whose entire shtick often consists of knowing winks and leers about some narcissistic non-fact known to only a narrow circle of media-savvy cognoscenti. Ethics, to continue the analogy, has only an ironic meaning in the age of American hegemony, and not many of us are in on the joke. It seems pretty much self-evident, conversely, that a genuine global ethics would validate cooperation, consent and consensus, and indict a new kind of global social contract.[9] Such an ethical global social contract, in other words, would assure the restraint of those who have power, every bit as much as it compels the governed to obey. In fact, a genuine global ethics would be scrupulously alive to any use of power without the consent of the governed. Ethicists would deem such actions immoral, bad, unethical. American hegemony, however, to apply this code, would give little indication of being consensual or cooperative, especially in a global diplomatic context, for instance, which strikes me as one place where cooperation and consent could be most rigorously defined. Recent American diplomacy, by contrast, has often seemed to work to manufacture a false or ephemeral consensus, a tactical consent, usually through a combination of economic bullying, outright bribery and rhetorical distortion, as when Dick Cheney called the UN Security Council "irrelevant" and dismissed dissenting NATO allies as "the old Europe." The Bush "coalition of the willing" in the 2003 invasion of Iraq was, as a result of this false consensus building, largely a motley crew of developing world nations fearful of losing USAID funding and similarly underdeveloped ex-Iron Curtain countries, such as Poland, that were hungry for cash, recognition, and membership in NATO and other economic-military alliances. The manufacturing of the appearance of consent in this way cannot truly be deemed ethical. Rather, the phrase "coalition of the willing" resembled a sort of Orwellian doublespeak for acts of political and economic bullying and coercion: "Coercion is Cooperation, Blackmail is Diplomacy," Big Brother might proclaim. The bullying of impoverished and isolated developing nations is not ethical. Nor are the American withdrawal from the Kyoto Protocols, and from the International Criminal Court, and the refusal to sign the International Ban on Landmines. All of these things indicate that American hegemony disdains consent, and cooperation, and thus has no dalliance with the discipline of ethics, or, one is more than a little tempted to say, the rule of law. Such hubris does not in any way augur ethical behavior, at least not in the classical sense of such behavior being animated by timeless moral principles or values. American hubris even seems corrosive to any sound definition of ethics, and everyday the corrosion gets worse. For instance, to anyone watching closely at all, the appointment of John Negroponte to Iraq ambassador should reveal the actual meaning of what the "conscious dishonesty" of the Bush administration plans for a "free and independent" Iraq. Iraq will be about as "free and independent" as El Salvador, Honduras and Guatemala were during the days of CIA trained death squads and contras in the 1980s. Negroponte was Reagan's ambassador to Honduras, and, although the smoking gun that would connect him to the death squads may have never surfaced, to the global human rights community, nonetheless, he was America's chief spook and war criminal in the region. It would be hard to find an American diplomat with better credentials for the job of turning Iraq into a 21st-century Middle Eastern version of a banana republic, a place where all the native leaders are thugs and crooks, the real ruling power is American corporate interest, and instead of the rule of law you have American backed paramilitaries and militias that go around "disappearing" – an 1980s-era Latin American euphemism for "kidnap, torture and murder" – anyone opposed to the American-backed kleptocracy.

The groundwork for the Iraqi kleptocracy has been laid by Coalition Provisional Authority (CPA) orders that force open Iraqi markets, and allow for complete foreign ownership of Iraqi property, banks, and businesses, making it difficult for the Iraqi people to ever control their economic destiny. In September 2003, for instance, L. Paul Bremer, Administrator of the Coalition Provisional Authority (CPA) in Iraq, signed four Orders (39-42) which together provide for the full privatization of public enterprises, full ownership rights by foreign firms of Iraqi businesses, full repatriation of foreign profits, the Flat Tax (that darling of the conservative American Right), the opening of Iraq's banks to foreign control, national treatment for foreign companies (which means, for example, that Iraq cannot require that local firms able to do reconstruction work should be hired instead of foreign ones), and (with an earlier order) elimination of nearly all trade barriers ... U.S. corporations that have received billions of tax-payer dollars for reconstruction in Iraq could own every business, do all the work, and send all of their money home.[10]

The CPA orders are reminiscent of the so-called Platt Amendment (1903) to the post-1898 Cuban constitution. The Platt Amendment, written by William McKinley's Secretary of War, Elihu Root, explicitly prescribes that "the United States may exercise the right to intervene for the preservation of Cuban independence, the maintenance of a government adequate for the protection of life, property, and individual liberty, and for discharging the obligations with respect to Cuba imposed by the treaty of Paris on the United States, now to be assumed and undertaken by the government of Cuba."[11] Although repealed in 1934, the Platt Amendment provided for perpetual American occupation of the base at Guantanomo and generally set the island nation on a road whose inevitable endpoint was the mafia-friendly Fulgencio Batista regime in the 1950s – an exemplary kleptocrat! – and its nemesis, Fidel Castro, whose concepts of property were, shall we say, somewhat more egalitarian. Unlike the Platt Amendment, however, the CPA orders *cannot* be rescinded by an Iraqi government. This is a perfect set up for a banana republic, except perhaps we should call it a petrochemical republic! Again, such actions as the Iraq invasion, CPA Orders 39-42 and the appointment of an ambassador many social justice activists feel should be standing before the bar of a war crime tribunal in The Hague; such things betray even the possibility of genuine ethics and moral principles. And though the Project for a New American Century, *The Wall Street Journal* and *The Weekly Standard* may prattle shamelessly about America's millennial moral responsibility to lift up a new edition of the white man's burden and make the world safe for McDonalds and McDonnell-Douglas, history has, nevertheless, served to demonstrate that empire is inherently unethical, not least because it divides the world into democratic and imperial subjects, and too often confers upon the latter only the barest shadow of human rights and civil liberties. Because inequality is unethical, American hegemony cannot be ethical. Never was, never will be. Anyone who held that it could be was either mystified, a la Big Brother, or being lied to, or, as Orwell had it, "consciously dishonest."

Those of us forced to endure the degraded political language of American hegemony increasingly discover an ethical universe where things are a trifle, well, weird. For instance, in what has to qualify as one of the most extreme ironies of recent political history, perhaps the most genuinely ethical government action in the whole sad lead up to the Iraqi War was taken in March 2003 by the Turkish Parliament. Alive to massive popular demonstrations against the war, the Turks were unable to muster enough votes to grant passage of 62,000 American troops across Turkey's border with Iraq. And this was despite what were clearly Washington's attempts to bribe the Turkish government with promises of some $15 billion in military and economic aid! Although aficionados of Kissenger-ian realpolitick will be quick to point out that any and all Turkish action towards Iraq should be seen through the lens of the Kurdish problem, in the global Jim Crow of American hegemony, their style of realism itself could be somewhat passé. Might we not consider the possibility that the Turkish government, merely by expressing the will of the Turkish people, is acting in line with a genuine ethics of cooperation and consent? Should it not be considered that a government that turns down a monstrous bribe from an imperial power bent on inflicting carnage on a geographical neighbor is, even despite itself, acting ethically? Are not the Turks, merely by running the risk of alienating an unethical superpower, acting ethically? Apparently we now live in a world where Turkey – which only a few years back was happily going about the ethnic cleansing of its Kurds and which has never come to terms with the Armenian genocide of 1915 – can teach the USA about the discipline and practice of ethics. And this is a world of American hegemony? Let me suggest that one would not be altogether misguided to conclude that in such a world, the only truly ethical actions might be those that resist hegemony on every front.

Given the Turkish example of such resistance, it might be useful to explore the concept of differing *sets* of ethical standards. Being a literary scholar somewhat comfortable with so-called "multi-culturalism" it is no great stretch for me to accept that there are, in the innumerable variations of the human world, any number of internally consistent and culturally valid codes for judging, in a specific context, what is moral, good and just, and what is not. Local ethical codes condone all sorts of things that seem unethical, even repugnant, to us: female circumcision and child slavery in Africa, dowry murder in India, bigamy in Utah, arbitrage on Wall Street. In Richard Wright's world for instance, white supremacists such as Ben Tillman and Theodore Bilbo, "the White Chief," clearly *could* embrace Jim Crow as an ethical code, embrace it passionately, in fact, because it solaced them for their defeat in the Civil War and assuaged the fears of cultural annihilation pressed upon them by an ascendant modernity. A further tragedy of the Jim Crow world was the extent to which fear and violence in the name of whiteness could compel African Americans themselves to internalize the strictures of the Crow. In his autobiography *Black Boy*, Wright recalls, for instance, being beaten vigorously by his mother when she found out that the deep, bloody gash on his forehead had been caused by his engaging in a rock fight with white boys who replied to Wright's puny gravel sniping with a barrage of broken bottles. For Wright's mother, then, it was clearly ethical to attach more importance to reinforcing the message of white supremacy than to staunching her son's bleeding wound! In the Jim Crow social order, the burden of ethical action, in other words, is reserved for losers in the struggle for resources, respect and status.

Richard Wright will detail the destructive force of such extra-ethics, throughout his career, in his shockingly naturalistic novel of the Chicago South Side, *Native Son*, in his essays on the African independence movements collected in *White Man, Listen* and in his autobiography *Black Boy/American Hunger* (1947), to which I want to turn, briefly, because it further addresses the problem of extra-ethics, not only in terms of Jim Crow, but also through examining another historically specific extra-ethics that was equally important to Wright's life and career: Communism. In Wright's autobiography, he expands upon the biographical sketch in "The Ethics of Living Jim Crow" to depict his later journey north to Chicago and his discovery of racial tolerance in the John Reed Club and the Communist Party. Although Wright's eventual disenchantment with the CP is one of the central events in his intellectual life, the description of the CP in *American Hunger* is complex and ambivalent. Close to the conclusion of that book, Wright describes a CP "criticism-session" convened to discipline an ostensibly errant CP organizer. To Wright, the most striking thing about this proceeding is the way that, before addressing the specific errors of the accused operative, the CP leadership presents a graphic picture of the entire global context of the proceeding. Everything from the struggle to collectivize Soviet agriculture, to the condition of the Chinese Revolution, down to the latest rent strike on the South Side is deemed relevant by the tribunal. By the time the specific issue of the organizer's misdeeds is addressed, the man has no alternative but to forgo any defense of his actions and accept the discipline imposed by the Party. At the trial, the Communist bosses create a world picture that advances an implicit and yet indisputable code of human behavior. In our discussion of ethics and hegemony, Wright's CP criticism session is important because it illustrates how a particular extra-ethics of global hegemony, that of world Communism in the 1930's, exists as a punitive, disciplinary, and inherently ideological discourse. That is, such an extra-ethics is constructed through a narrative of world history that is at once logically consistent and utterly biased. Thus, in describing both Jim Crow and Communism, Wright emphasizes what cultural theorists call the "constructedness" of ethical codes, their historical specificity and the manner in which they represent and reproduce the material interests of a dominant power elite.[12]

In both his 1938 essay and in his later autobiography, then, Wright reveals "Ethics" as a purely ironic category, as an absence. A genuine ethics would condemn and resist the "extra-ethical" disciplinary strictures of the Crow and world Communism alike. Two conclusions can be drawn from Wright's literary irony that should be of use to any critique of American global hegemony.

First, such extra-ethics harmed almost everyone they touched. Both blacks and whites in the USA, and common people in the Communist Block, and Third World were brutalized and stripped of their humanity by these extra-ethical codes. Even in the case of the USA, an argument could be made that the secrecy and suspicion of the Cold War, an extra-ethics that was the *doppleganger* of world Communism, inflicted defeat after defeat upon democracy and civil liberties at home and the prestige of the USA abroad. US Presidents and State Departments repeatedly proved perfectly willing to overlook the depredations of a long list of murderous dictators and other assorted thugs who, purportedly, aligned themselves with *our* extra-ethics against those of the Communists. As Chalmers Johnson argues so persuasively in *Blowback*, the inconsistency between the USA's announced ethics and its brutal self-interested behavior in Asia has fostered the dangerous, unstable world in which events like 9/11 were not only possible, but likely.[13]

Second, extra-ethical codes encourage animosity between disempowered social groups, foreclosing any possibility of a genuine ethos of cooperation and consent between them, often for decades, sometimes perpetually. In particular, Wright's experiences in the Southern working class reveal the bitterness of the racial division of labor between better paid "white man's work" and the degrading underemployment inflicted upon the typical "Black Boy" of Wright's generation. This animosity disguises the relative impoverishment of both groups and compensates the white workers for their impoverishment with what historian David Roedigger has called "the wages of whitness."[14] In fact, since C. Vann Woodward's epoch-making history of the New South in *The Strange Career of Jim Crow* was published in the 1950s, it has become a commonplace to argue that the elites' economic agenda – cheap labor, cheap land and political quietism – was advanced by legal segregation of poor blacks from poor whites. Thus, in the extra-ethical universe of Jim Crow "white is right" regardless of the dire economic and social consequences for unskilled workers and poor farmers of both colors. However, these racial animosities do not harm all parties in Jim Crow society equally; in fact they serve the interest of a third group which benefits from social conflict. I'm speaking, of course, of the all-white class of factory owners and big landowners and bankers whose material interests were well served when race hatred fractured any potential black/white economic and political solidarity.

Again, the parallel between Wright's depiction of the extra-ethics of Jim Crow and those of American global hegemony are striking, for they parallel the way that American hegemony has promulgated a similarly divisive, two tiered set of extra-ethics, this time on a global scale. For might not such ethical monstrosities as the Bush Doctrine, pre-emptive war and the neo-liberal "Washington Consensus" be seen to signal that a new, similarly uneven, historical contest for rights and resources has been naturalized? Made to seem self-evident? Normal? In this anti-ethical universe, where might is the measure of right, anyone not anxious for martyrdom could find him/herself slated for one type of collateral damage or another, be it by less-than-smart bombs in Fallujah, or by the demolition of civil liberties in the imperial center. Neither possibility seems remotely ethical. But that's just too bad, for when might makes right, ethics becomes the responsibility of the powerless. The powerful are judged by less stringent standards. Powerful media personalities such as the gambling-addicted William Bennett and drug addict Rush Limbaugh simultaneously bash the intemperance of lesser mortals and indulge the very vices they decry, with impunity. Corporate leaders such as Kenneth Lay and Dick Cheney may advance a mythical vision of "free markets" and "competition" while they work inside connections to insure that the real markets are rigged in their favor. In this world, much as in Richard Wright's Jim Crow American South, it is the parched Egyptian fellaheen, the cloistered and abused women of Saudi, the underpaid sweatshop workers and dispossessed peasants of Asia and the Southern cone who bear all the responsibility for ethical action. Ethics are strictly for the wretched of the earth, in other words. You must not infringe, they are told, upon the sovereign rights of American corporations and banks to strip your natural resources, supplant your native culture with Hollywood's whorish junk, destroy your domestic agriculture and markets, corrupt your rulers, and gut your pathetic social service infrastructure – schools, hospitals, unemployment relief – to make the payments on first world "development" loans. For non-corporate persons to protest this, for mere people to resist corporate rights, is to be labeled anti-American, certainly, and potentially run the risk of being called "terrorist." Such proscriptions are clearly not ethical, however; they are merely an expression of power, of force.

In the Global Jim Crow system, then, the developed world's spear-carriers *and* the fellaheen of the developing world share the same divisive, punitive, disciplinary extra-ethics, one that is premised upon the maintenance of an elitist power structure and that emphasizes our ostensible "racial" and "religious" differences over our economic similarities. are locked in perpetual animosity. Thus the two similarly disempowered groups find themselves locked in perpetual struggle, if not outright combat, by the artificial scarcities and well-maintained ideological divides of the neo-liberal world order. And that's most of us; don't kid yourself. The second set of extra-ethics is the province of the supranational aristocracies of military and financial power that run the show for all it's worth.[15] If this is so, then American hegemony, like Jim Crow and Soviet Socialism, will have a brief, ignoble and most unethical tenure on the earth. For such unjust, duplicitous systems, regardless of how formidable they may seem, inevitably create the forces that will bring them down and the conditions in which they will crash. I, for one, will not be unhappy to see such a system consigned to the dustbin of history.

Notes

1   Richard Wright. "The Ethics of Living Jim Crow, An Autobiographical Sketch ."*Norton Anthology of African-American Literature.* New York: Norton, 1997, 1388-1396. In Wright's essay, to list a few examples, a black teenager is thrown from a fast moving car because he didn't call the white men who gave him a ride "Sir." A hotel elevator man makes extra tips by charging white patrons a quarter to kick him repeatedly in the buttocks. A bellhop is castrated because he's suspected of having had carnal knowledge of a white prostitute. The narrator is threatened with a gun because he momentarily seems less-than-sanguine about a hotel detective's pinching the buttocks of a black hotel maid. Repeatedly, Wright finds himself treated as a non-person by everyone from white prostitutes to matronly librarians. All these things, and worse, could be perfectly consistent with the "extra-ethics" of Jim Crow, and yet bear no resemblance to any genuine ethical code of human behavior.

2   Stanley Karnow's *In Our Image: America's Empire in the Philippines* (New York : Ballantine Books, 1990) is still the standard account of the USA's Philippines

adventure. See also John B. Judis's *The Folly of Empire: What George W. Bush Could Learn from Theodore Roosevelt and Woodrow Wilson.* (New York: Scribners, 2004) for an account of imperial parallels that differs from mine, and is more comprehensive.

3   Theodore Roosevelt. "The Strenuous Life."
     http://www.historytools.org/sources/strenuous.html.

4   *Record*, 56 Cong., I Sess., pp. 704-712.

5   *Rudyard Kipling's Verse* (New York: 1924), pp 371-372.

6   *Record*, 56 Cong., I Sess., pp. 704-712.

7   As witnessed, among other things, for instance, by the recent indictment of Edgar Killens for his alleged role in the still unsolved murders of three Civil Rights activists in Neshoba County, Mississippi in 1964.

8   Chomsky, Noam. *Profit Over People: Neo-liberalism and Global Order.* New York: Seven Stories, 1998, 19. For succinct depiction of the sinister side of there-is-no-alternative-neo-liberalism, see Greg Palast. *The Best Democracy Money Can Buy.* New York: Penguin, 2004. Chapter 4, "Sell the Lexus, Burn The Olive Tree: Globalization and Its Discontents."

9   Daisaku Ikeda indicates the direction that could be taken by global ethics post-9/11 when he says, "Since it is probably unrealistic to expect self-restraint on the part of the terrorists, those who oppose them must put priority on the exercise of self-mastery – a quality that grows from the effort to consider and understand the position of the 'other.' Equally essential are the courage and vision to address the underlying conditions of poverty and injustice that are enabling factors in terrorism" (Daisaku Ikeda, *2004 Peace Proposa: Inner Transformation: Creating a Groundswell for Peace.* Tokyo: The Sakka Gakai, 2004, 10).

10   Antonia Juhasz. "Capitalism gone wild in Iraq." *Tikkun*, Jan-Feb, 2004.

11   *Platt Amendment.* http://www.classbrain.com/artteenst/publish/article_64.shtml.

12   Richard Wright. *Black Boy (American Hunger): A Record of Childhood and Youth.* New York, Harper/Collins, 1993.

13   Chalmers Johnson. *Blowback: The Coasts and Consequences of American Empire.* New York: Henry Holt, 2000.

14   David Roediger. *The Wages of Whiteness: Race and the Making of the American Working Class.* New York: Verso, 1999.

15   The existence of such a global elite was handily demonstrated by Michael Moore's sometimes scurrilous but always powerfully satirical film, *Fahrenheit 9/11.* The Saudi Ambassador to the USA, Prince Bandar, one might recall, was called "Bandar Bush" by the Bush clan, indicating his symbolic consanguinity with his similarly royal American counterparts. The soft historical analysis and sensationalism of the film notwithstanding, the way Moore gave a face and name to this sort of elite bonding was worth the price of admission a dozen times over!

Chapter 7

The Fist of Pacifism

Angela Gordon
Washington University in St. Louis

Tobias T. Gibson
Washington University in St. Louis

Introduction

Participants in social protest movements have long debated the appropriate nature of tactics employed in their activities. While this debate has led to a number of innovative approaches to social protest, it has not led to a consensus on their suitability. Despite a number of nonviolent opportunities for protest – including mass marches, sit-ins, street theater, direct action, boycotts, and others – a fundamental ideological schism remains between protesters who advocate the use of violence, and those who eschew it.

In some recent American social movements, the arguments over the use of aggressive tactics and violence have often been played out on the world stage. From anti-globalization protests to the environmental movement, there are groups on both sides of the violence debate. Within the environmental movement, for example, there is a huge gulf between the tactics of groups such as the Earth Liberation Front (ELF) and those of individuals (and groups) such as Julia Butterfly Hill. Ms. Hill spent over two years living in a giant sequoia in an effort to prevent loggers from cutting it down; she currently advocates for spiritually-based personal accountability for the environment.[1] ELF actions, by contrast, were responsible for an estimated 55 million dollars in property damage in 2003 alone. The group argues that "any means necessary" should be taken to "take the profit motive out of killing".[2] The environmental movement as a whole has been extremely divided by ELF's violent tactics, with many groups distancing themselves and "their" movement from ELF's actions. This same dynamic is played out within many modern social movements.

This esay is an exploration of the use of destructive behavior and violence within social movements. We begin by briefly reviewing the history and philosophy of pacifism, and the debate within social protest movements over the use of violence. We follow this with an examination of tactics recently employed by demonstrators in opposition to the recent U.S.-led invasion of Iraq. Specifically, we look at the use of violence by participants in the anti-war movement in St. Louis, Missouri, and the debate that accompanied these actions.

History and Philosophy of Nonviolent Protest

Though there are many avenues followed by practitioners of pacifism, historically, three major schools have been identified: Hindu, Christian, and "Revolutionary Secular".[3] In the Hindu tradition, violence is seen as creating a disturbance in the structure of the soul common to all life. Moreover, violence emphasizes the divide between souls, and especially the soul from God. While some separation is inevitable, Hindu philosophy teaches that it should be resisted.[4] According to Mohandas Gandhi, perhaps the most influential Hindu pacifist, God can only act through *ahimsa*, which is identified with love and non-violence. Thus, individuals, like God, must act according to *ahimsa* in order to minimize the divide between their souls and God's.[5]

According to Christian pacifist philosophy, man must act in accordance with the New Testament's teaching of God as love. Thus, like the physical incarnation of God as Jesus Christ, Christian revolutionaries must be humble and practice nonviolence. Due to one's faith, then:

> The Christian can ignore the laws established by the State because he has no need of them for himself; he considers that human life is better assured by the law of love he professes than by the law of violence imposed upon him. The profession of true Christianity which includes the precept of nonresistance to violence and evil relieves the faithful from belief in external authority.[6]

Likewise, Dr. Martin Luther King, Jr. wrote that the "Christian doctrine of love operating through the Gandhian method of nonviolence was one of the most potent weapons available to oppressed people in their struggle for freedom".[7] Thus, for the Christian pacifist, nonviolence is a matter of both faith and pragmatism.

Although most secular revolutionary theory (Marxian, as one example) does not recognize pacifism as an effective means to an end, there have long been currents of peaceful revolution in even the most extreme revolutionary theories of socialism and anarchism. Anarchist pacifist DeLigt writes:

> Every end suggests its own means. To transgress this law inevitably brings about a tyranny of the means. For if these lead away from their intended goal the farther they get away from their objective and the more their actions are determined by them. For example, it is impossible to educate people in liberty by force, just as it is impossible to breathe by coal gas.[8]

Secular pacifists, then, believe that a principled revolution should be undertaken only through principled means, or risk replicating the oppressive techniques of the state.

The Vietnam War Protests and Beyond

Despite the principled objections to violence, there has long been a divide between "peaceful" pacifists and "violent" pacifists. This divide became particularly evident in the effort to end U.S. involvement in the Vietnam War. According to Lewy, as the war progressed, many major pacifist organizations began to support the armed National Liberation Front in South Vietnam. This support, in turn, led to "a compromise with the pacifist values of reconciliation and nonviolence and eventually the open acceptance of the legitimacy of the revolutionary 'struggle of the oppressed.'"[9]

The first group to openly advocate violent pacifism was the Women's International League for Peace and Freedom (WILPF). After WILPF leadership publicly supported armed insurrection, Gene Sharp attempted to rally support for peaceful resistance in a speech at the WILPF biennial meeting. Reports from the meeting state that, "After his speech there was a rush to the microphone, and several speakers denounced Sharp as naïve and stupid for putting his faith in the efficacy of nonviolence".[10] Likewise, in its efforts to denounce U.S. involvement in Central America in the early 1980s, the American Friends Service Committee (AFSC) announced that it supported "the use of force by some oppressed groups in defense of their rights" including violence that is "essentially reactive and aimed at justice and is therefore qualitatively different from the violence of the oppressors".[11] Commentator Rael Jean Isaac opines that "increasingly violence has become the touchstone by which pacifists identify those worthy of their support. The more violent a group, the more just its cause must be – always provided, of course, that the cause is 'progressive.'"[12]

The Civil Rights Movement and the Use of Violence

In some ways, the most dramatic divide between social activists are the tactics they choose to employ in promoting their cause. Perhaps the best example of this comes from the Civil Rights movement in United States in the 1960s. As noted above, Dr. Martin Luther King, Jr. was a Christian pacifist, and the protests he organized and led embodied his beliefs. Marches, sit-ins, the bus boycotts in Montgomery and elsewhere, and the Freedom Rides are all examples of the nonviolent methods used by King and his followers.[13] There were, however, individuals and organizations that thought that King's peaceful approach to creating change was too slow, and that it accommodated society's existing power structure to such a great extent that it limited the effectiveness of the protest. Individuals such as Stokely Carmichael[14] and H. Rap Brown, and organizations such as the Black Panther Party,[15] advocated and prepared for more violent protest.[16] Brown, for example, called on an audience in Cambridge, Maryland to "Shoot him [the honkey] to death, brother. Cause that's what he's out to do to you."[17] In large part, some black activists advocated violent means because they, like the WILPF and AFSC, felt that as long as the motives were progressive, the ends justified the means.

These examples are not isolated. Many anti-war and social justice organizations have, to some degree, embraced or at least condoned violence as a means to social change. There remains a broad schism between individuals and groups willing to use violent means, and those absolutely dedicated to pacifist protest. This divide was again on display in recent peace efforts in the United States, and across the globe, to protest the U.S. government's calls for war in Iraq in 2003. The remainder of this paper focuses on the ideological divide within the recent peace movement, using events in St. Louis, Missouri as the centerpiece of our discussion.

Case Study: St. Louis Citizens Protest the War in Iraq

In the months leading up to and immediately following the initial bombing and invasion of Iraq by the United States in March, 2003, citizens in St. Louis, MO, showed their opposition to the war through a series of public events. These events included rallies, marches, vigils, teach-ins, direct action events, and information sessions. Some were tied to national or global days of protest. Many were organized by a coalition of largely religious organizations called the Instead of War coalition (IOW), or by students at various colleges and universities in the region.

While the majority of the anti-war protesters and events were peaceful, a small group of people advocated more confrontational tactics and engaged in property damage and destruction. These activities were hotly debated in meetings, and through the local Independent Media Center. It is this debate, and the escalating institutional reactions to property damage, that are at the center of this analysis.

Methods and Sources

This analysis of the anti-war movement in St. Louis focuses on five events. These events were chosen based on the following criteria:

- They were organized by the Instead of War Coalition and were publicly announced and advertised,
- They occurred in or immediately adjacent to the City of St. Louis,
- They drew a diverse set of people from the larger St. Louis region, and
- One or both of the authors were present.

As a group, these events demonstrate growing division within the anti-war movement, and confrontation between the movement and civil authorities.

Our narrative is based on personal observations of all events and the planning of several of the them, and on the archived record of debate on the St. Louis Independent Media Center's website. We describe each event briefly, including any acts of violence, and then discuss how the event was viewed by the participants. We will then situate these activities within the larger framework of the national response to the war in Iraq.

For readers unfamiliar with Independent Media sites, some description is necessary. Independent Media (or, IndyMedia) Centers exist in many cities in the United States and around the world. Each center develops its own mission statement, but generally, IndyMedia exists to provide an outlet for "grassroots, non-corporate coverage" of news events.[18] The St. Louis Independent Media Center (STLIMC) describes its mission as follows: "we aim to provide a grassroots and often under-reported perspective on local and regional artistic, environmental, political, activist and social justice issues."[19]

STLIMC is web-based, and allows anyone with internet access to publish articles, photos, or comments to their newswire. Published works range from formal articles written by volunteer staff writers to informal opinion pieces to articles copied from other sources. STLIMC allows instant self-publication; there is no editorial process, and articles are posted to the newswire directly by the author. In addition, participants can comment on or reply to specific published articles. These comments appear after the original piece, as part of a single internet document. Usually, they are informally written, and are sometimes confrontational. All articles are considered open content, and therefore available for reprint, rebroadcast, or academic use.[20] They are archived on the website and form a record of on-going discussion of current events.

During the months prior to the start of the war in Iraq, STLIMC was a hub for information concerning anti-war events. Events were publicized through the website, and discussed at length after they occurred. The articles and comments published on STLIMC's website form the major source for the analysis of the debate over the use of violence in the St. Louis anti-war movement. As much as possible, the events analyzed will be described through quotations from STLIMC writers and participants. For the most part, misspellings and informal grammar are left in the document, except in cases where the meaning is otherwise unclear. Any changes (including ellipses where comments have been excerpted) are in [square brackets].

Relying on a non-traditional source complicates citations. IndyMedia writers do not always provide a name, or provide only an anonymous pseudonym. Writers do not always use the same name or pseudonym every time they publish. Individual articles and comments do not have direct, distinct internet links, but are given either an article number or comment number that is unique. Articles are easier to locate than comments. Therefore, our method of citation is as follows: The main STLIMC internet address is provided in the bibliography. All direct quotations and paraphrased material from individual articles and comments are cited in the endnotes. For articles, the date of publication, article number, and author's name (if given) are provided. For comments, the date of publication, comment number, article number that the comment refers to, and author's name (if given) are provided. All articles and comments referred to in this paper were available on STLIMC's archived newswire at the time this paper was written.[21]

The Events

The five events described in this chapter took place between December 2002, and March 2003. They all occurred in the City of St. Louis, although two events had portions that extended into University City, immediately adjacent to the City of St. Louis. The events are described in chronological order in order to stress the trajectory of violence and response by protesters and civil authorities. Each event will first be described, and then discussed in terms of how it was viewed by participants. The role of violence, both in the events and the debates that followed, is highlighted.

8 December 2002

This rally and march started with a gathering of 1600 people at the Centenary United Methodist Church near downtown St. Louis. Speakers and musicians rallied the crowd inside the church before marching to the Soldiers' Memorial:

> The church was filled with 'Instead of War…Not in Our Names' signs provided by the organizers, banners, and a variety of homemade signs in support of peace and related causes. Not to mention beautiful, *peacefully* [italics added] rowdy people who cheered, clapped, booed, and sang whenever the mood took them. Marchers spread out, with signs and drums, along the entire five blocks from the church to the Soldier's Memorial, where two representatives from Veteran's for Peace did a little speechifying to the assembled crowd. Finally, a bit reluctantly, we had to go home.[22]

The event was the largest event held in St. Louis to this date, and received favorable coverage by local television stations and newspapers.[23]

Although the event exceeded organizers' hopes,[24] not all participants were happy with the event:

> […] everyone was neatly tucked inside a church far away from anyone who didnt already agree with our viewpoints … then we all marched 5 blocks to a secluded (but permitted and paid for) spot downtown where no one was, and therefore, no one was able to hear what we had to say … now, i dont know about you … but when our government bombs people far away […] i get really mad, so mad that the rage fills my body and i want to take my anger out to the streets, the streets full with people and let them know whats going on and what their tax dollars and apathy are supporting … but

instead, on sunday, we literally preached to the choir, and so the bombs will keep falling ... [25]

Most of the complaints were along the same lines, arguing that the event was not inclusive because it was held in a church,[26] that it was too passive, and that it did not address the underlying problems of capitalism and class.[27]

15 February 2003

This event was originally planned as a morning of neighborhood canvassing, followed by a rally at the Pilgrim Congregational United Church of Christ. Over 200 people spent the morning going door to door, asking people to put anti-war signs in their yards and to send postcards to their representatives. They were then bussed to the church, where they entered as a group to join a capacity crowd to listen to speeches.

> Those who came to this house of worship represented a diverse cross-section of the American public: people of all faiths, races and creeds. They crowded the aisles, sat on floor, jammed the vestibule, and stood out in the cold on the sidewalk. All [of] them shared one thing in common: a determination to stop the Bush administration's unilateral and unprecedented decision to wage a preemptive, unprovoked war. [...] Despite the moment of silence, the mood [of] those gathered in St. Louis seemed more defiant than solemn.[28]

The church rally was very similar to the event of 8 December 2002, but was much larger and over-filled, which led to significant crowds standing outside on the sidewalk. The over-size crowd, among other things, eventually led to an unplanned, unpermitted march following the end of the official event:

> The march was amazing. Folks were spilling out of the church, the organizers of the rally were just going to bus them all back home. But there was all this energy and anger left in the crowd. So we just marched. Without leaders, without committees, without permit. It just happened. And all the cops could do was escort us. They weren't prepared to arrest anyone, let alone 500 people.[29]

There are thirty-seven pages of discussion about the march on the STLIMC website. Most descriptions of the march were very positive. Many people felt the same way as "still hyped" (quoted above), and urged planners to learn a lesson from the march and include more participatory, visible activities in future events.

Much of the discussion, however, focused on a few isolated incidents of property damage that occurred shortly after the march crossed the border from the City of St. Louis into University City. Slogans were scrawled in magic marker on storefront windows, and newspaper vending machines were thrown into the streets. Other marchers immediately returned the vending machines to the sidewalks, and both the action of throwing them and the reaction of replacing them were hotly debated on STLIMC's website:

> Who were those misguided, rabble-rousing punks throwing newspaper vending machines into the street? [...] fortunately, it really didn't impress anyone on Saturday. Each one of these 'high-profile' stunts [...] was followed by a group of well-minded protesters attempting to clean up their mess. Look—I'm not trying to prevent anyone from getting their message across. Of course, I'm not. It's all important. But this was a rally for peace and justice. We were united in this vein, but we only became divided (albeit, temporarily) by these acts of vandalism. And whatever critical mass we held on those streets that day could have come to an end with police interference induced by such vandalism.[30]

This is fairly typical of articles and comments that criticizing the property damage that occurred during the march. Many people who wrote in favor of the march itself were disappointed or angry that any form of violence was used.

In response, many writers either defended the property damage or questioned the definition of property damage as violence: "People drew on windows and threw newspaper boxes into the street? Big deal! That's not violence and is minor stuff compared to the violence about to be perpetrated by the state."[31] Others criticized those speaking against the property damage:

> We all want peace, but we might chose different ways to struggle towards that common end. If you prefer to lobby and vote and rally inside churches, that's fine with me, that's your style. If I chose to struggle in other ways, you should also respect that and keep in mind that we have a common goal. There is no one single way to fight for peace. This is all experimental, we're all trying to do it right. Yet, I've noticed that the religiously inclined pacifists are rather quick to write somebody off as 'violent', 'disruptive', 'bad for the cause', whereas anarchists are more willing to accept well-intentioned attempts to struggle in more mainstream ways, as just another form of resistance against this drive for war.[32]

Some were openly dismissive of those upset over the property damage: "you got kids as young as 7-8 years old picking up guns in palestine to fight back for their lives, they've lost everything ... and your worried about someone smashing a goddamned window?"[33]

A recurring theme among these articles and comments is the need to remain united, even though different tactics might be preferred by different groups within the broader movement. A *sense* of unity did remain largely intact, even though *physical* unity had been broken by the breakaway march.

17 March, 2003

Leading up to the withdrawal by the United States of the United Nations Resolution authorizing an invasion of Iraq, the Instead of War coalition (IOW) asked people to be prepared to march on Grand Boulevard the evening following such a withdrawal. IOW had planned (and received permission) to watch President Bush's speech to the nation as a group, and then to march along Grand, on the sidewalks. Organizers decided to carry flags of nations opposed to a war in Iraq, as well a single American flag surrounded by the names of cities and counties that had passed anti-war resolutions.[34] Approximately 1000 people joined the demonstration in opposition to the war:

> The march began on the sidewalk, but a few determined protesters led the push onto the street. Instead of War Coalition 'peacekeepers' attempted to keep everyone on the sidewalk, but eventually gave up when the march flowed onto the street, with hundreds blocking traffic. The march circled back around to Arsenal and Grand, where it began. Many of the protesters went back into the park, but quite a few were determined to stay on the street, in defiance of the war and the police. At some point during the march, about 15 torches were lit, and carried behind banners that read, 'We live under your laws. We ARE at war!' and 'Military Recruiters, Get out of our 'hood! And Exxon, send your own fuckin' troops!' Eventually, the police forced the protesters out of the street, without making any arrests."[35]

This was the most confrontational event to date (other than non-violent direct actions that had taken place in nearby St. Charles, MO). The large number of protesters, the torches, and the defiance of police orders to leave the intersection at Grand and Arsenal combined to create a very tense situation. The peacekeepers eventually convinced people to let them use water to quench the torches, leaving a small number of black-masked protesters wrapped in a banner, blocking the intersection. No arrests were made, and the protesters eventually left peacefully.

In addition, there was a small group of young men jeering at and insulting anti-war protesters. Although police moved them across the street when they physically threatened a demonstrator, the young men eventually followed a woman to her car and sprayed her with mace.[36] There was very little discussion on STLIMC of the use of torches, the takeover of the streets, the blockade of the intersection, or the violence of the counterprotesters. The major reason for this silence, we believe, is that STLIMC's server was down from 16 March to 18 March, 2003. By the time the website was once again available, other events had taken precedence over discussing the Grand march.

20 March, 2003

Following the format of the Grand march, Instead of War organizers had asked people to gather downtown the evening following the first bombing of Iraq by the

United States. Rumors that bombs *would* start falling on the evening of 19 March led approximately 500 people to gather downtown, only to be sent away by organizers after a brief rally.[37] The major event occurred on 20 March:

> On Thursday, March 20, over 1000 people rallied in Kiener Plaza to protest the outbreak of the US war on Iraq. After a short vigil, the demonstrators marched single file past a counter to the [Eagleton] federal building, a few blocks away. 1083 people completely surrounded the federal building, in a symbolic effort to contain the federal government's actions. The crowd returned to Kiener Plaza, where an all-night vigil and funeral procession began. At the same time, over 300 demonstrators marched into the streets, intending to march to Laclede's Landing.[38]

It is this last element of the event that drew the majority of the discussion on the STLIMC website.

During the original rally at Kiener Plaza, people often referred to (by themselves as well as by others) as "anarchists" or "Black Bloc" (and referred to as Black Bloc from this point) passed out small flyers urging people to join an unpermitted march to Laclede's Landing after the main event. Laclede's landing has a number of bars, restaurants, and clubs that bring people to that area of downtown at night.

From the start, this off-shoot was confrontational, with many flaming torches and a large group of people blocking the street. It grew from there:

> On Thursday, March 20, the second night of the U.S. bombing offensive on Baghdad, a large group split off from the planned Instead of War vigil in downtown St. Louis. After one arrest was made in an intersection near the Kiener Plaza vigil, several hundred people marched on the streets of downtown St. Louis winding their way to Laclede's Landing and eventually back to Kiener Plaza. Construction barricades, dumpsters, and dozens of newspaper boxes were dragged into intersections, small fires lit, graffiti written, cop cars spat on, and at least one bank window smashed.[39]

Although only one arrest was made, and STLIMC writers disagree about the amount of property damage that took place, this was the most confrontational and destructive event to date.

The STLIMC debate following this event was extensive and, at times, bitter. One writer addressed his comments "To you who destroy":

> If the movement proceeds peacefully, carefully, and with some logic, it might just work. But if you goons in costumes [Black Bloc 'members' often wear masks] insist on destroying rather than building, you will ruin our ability to make legitimate public statements. You will ruin our credibility. You will impede the possibility that we can get a strong majority of people behind this effort (anyone remember the concept of democracy?). You will get peaceful people around you beaten down by your thuggish counterparts in the polic department. And if you do that – if you get people hurt with your stupidity and thoughtlessness, well then, what are you really but just another part of the problem?[40]

Apparently, the anti-war movement creates strange bed-fellows. A few pro-war writers weighed in with their reactions to property violence:

> Congratulations to you all. You have embarrassed yourselves and damaged the cause you pretend to defend. [...] You mention democracy, well, in a democracy the majority rules and the majority thinks your ideas and your actions are a joke. Thank you. You make it easier for the rest of us to dismiss you.[41]

Most of the negative comments about the property destruction focused on the threats of division within the movement and dismissal of the whole movement by outsiders.

There was also some discussion about whether or not property damage is violence, in part in reaction to the events of 20 March, and in part as a continuation of earlier debates. This best summarizes the comments made by those against the use of violence and property damage:

> I'd also like to take up the argument about the interpretation of violence. When the argument is put forth that the action is justified because it is not really violent, I don't think that is sufficient to justify the action. I think there is an important distinction to be made between what IS violent and what our audience (the St. Louis silent majority) would PERCEIVE as violent.[42]

The response by those either responsible for or defending the destruction of property argued that "*property destruction is NOT an act of violence*"[43] and that more forceful means were necessary.

Protesters also objected to the idea that alienating the general public was necessarily bad. As f00_fighter stated, "im not trying to win anyone over. im trying to STOP THIS WAR! and peaceful protests unfortunatly wont do it."[44] Many writers were elegant and discussed their motivations at length:

> We are sick and tired of the cyclical violence of our corporate police state. [...] To support the perpetuation (reformation) of a violent society by dogmatic calls for nonviolence (complacency) and order is simply to build a raft so as not to drown in the pool of blood [... .] The dogma of nonviolence ideology is exactly this perpetuation [...]. It is a legitimation of the violent state to accept the choices of resistance that *they* offer. We took the streets [...] in solidarity with others in the belly of this fascist beast: the tens of thousands who shut down and continue to shut down San Francisco, Chicago, New York, and DC through civil and uncivil disobedience, shutting down "business as usual" because this is exactly what started the war and what starts all wars.[45]

Others repeatedly pointed at the police as the main source of violence at protests generally, but admitted that "St. Louis police so far have not attacked any of the unpermitted street protests."[46] That was about to change.

30 March, 2003

In response to complaints about earlier, more passive events, organizers had planned an outdoor rally preceded by marches from various parts of the city, converging on Forest Park. Nine feeder marches, representing students, religious congregations, labor unions, women, veterans, children, and others converged on the World's Fair Pavilion to hear speakers and live music, with a total of over 5000 people attending.

From the beginning, police reaction to these marches was different than at past events. The university students' march formed on the campus of Washington University, and walked along a major road bordering Forest Park before joining the artists' group waiting at the St. Louis Historical Society Museum. Permits had been obtained for a sidewalk-only march. While in the past, the police had been tolerant of marches that took over the streets, police repeatedly used officers on foot and in cars to force the students out of the streets and back onto the sidewalk.

The event itself went as planned. The Black Bloc, so heavily criticized for their actions following the event on 20 March, again passed out flyers. This time, rather than an invitation to join a post-event march, the flyer explained the motivations for engaging in violence against property. Rather than limiting themselves to explaining to a self-selected audience on STLIMC's website, the Black Bloc used a mainstream event to spread their message.

Afterwards, as at several other events, a small group splintered off to march to the Central West End, another restaurant district at the east end of the park:

> on sunday march 30th, I went to the peace rally, and then went to march to the central west end afterwards, and ive seen anarchists at these things before and yesterday they were at their most peaceful, there was hardly any shouting (or chants for that matter), mostly drum banging and marching quietly on the street. everyones energy was low due to a cold day, and an unsatisfying rally, and an unending war, so we marched peacefully, and when we were on lindell [a street bordering the north side of the park], all hell broke loose. i witnessed police brutality with my own eyes, i had always heard of it, and seen some on the internet, but this was the first time in my life that it effected me personally, they arrested, beat, and maced people, and after they started arresting and beating the first few people, alot of people backed off (for fear of being beat), but then the police chased after us with guard dogs, mace, batons, and i saw [the] rubber bullet guns but im not sure if they were used.[47]

With minor variations, the eyewitness reports posted to STLIMC are very similar. Seven or eight people were eventually arrested, several with injuries:

> I was one of the people that was arrested last night. [...] While I was under police control my head was slammed into the truck of the police car twice, I was maced, and then called every name in the book by the authorities. I was in the police station and the

entire time I was scared for my life. After getting released I was taken straight to the hospital as I was having trouble remembering my birthday, getting physically sick, and feeling dizzy. After a CAT scan was performed it was determined that I had suffered a concussion, contusions, and a mild stroke.[48]

Although neither author was present at the off-shoot march, the senior author has viewed one of three videotapes made that afternoon and can verify a very large, heavily armed police presence amid a very chaotic scene. Very little was reported through conventional media, other than mention of the arrests, and those involved were advised by the American Civil Liberties Union not to release the video footage to the general media.

Although there is no certainty that the change in police tactics was a direct result of the property damage that occurred ten days earlier, people involved felt a direct connection:

from what i can gather it seems the police force was a bit sore from the successful rally last thursday night [20 March] downtown and found a chance to retaliate. they waited for the group to become smaller so they could strike without fear of a riot, and for the media to leave as well so that public awareness would be minimal.[49]

Once again, the physical rift, representative of the ideological rift, within the anti-war movement allowed civil authorities to suppress those protesters who were not wed to nonviolent methods. Other writers commented directly on what they saw as a change in police attitudes towards the anti-war protests in general:

Yesterdays police action on the later break off march after Sunday's beautiful peace rally at Forest Park set a new precendent of brutality in what I thought was a open, if not positive relationship between those of us who participate in the Anti-War Movement and the St. Louis Police. Yesterdays showing of catastrophic force betrayed many of those who felt that they had a tangible avenue to let their voices be heard on the Streets of St. Louis.[50]

From the escort provided to marchers on 15 February, 2003, to the violence inflicted on marchers on 30 March, 2003, police reactions toward the anti-war community changed radically. While several factors could be involved, including changing sympathies once the war actually started, we believe that the change is related in large part to the increasing levels of property damage and other confrontational tactics accompanying the events of 15 February, 17 March, and, particularly, 20 March 2003. As discussed below in relation to a non-war-related protest event, St. Louis police response to planned demonstrations continued to escalate in the months after the 30 March event. This is not to say that we are trying to blame the victims. Whether or not the police brutality of 30 March was a direct response to the damage to property on 20 March, it was abhorrent and possibly illegal.

The Effects (and Effectiveness) of Violent Protest

A central debate within the St. Louis anti-war community was about the "effectiveness" of different styles of protest. Those calling for pacifist methods frequently cited a fear that the use of violence (against either people or property) would divide the peace movement, making it less effective, alienate the general population, or both. On the other side, people argued that peaceful methods were ineffective, and only a forceful strike against "business as usual" could prevent the war.

Discussions of social movements often note that movement participants are shut out of official avenues of power:

> The key challenge confronting insurgents, then, is to devise some way to overcome the basic powerlessness that has confined them to a position of institutionalized political impotence. The solution to this problem is preeminently tactical. Ordinarily insurgents must bypass routine decision-making channels and seek, through use of non-Institutionalized tactics, to force their opponents to deal with them.[51]

Clearly, this is what both the peace movement in general, and the Black Bloc in particular, were trying to do. Likewise, being locked out of institutionalized avenues of power also motivated much of the Civil Rights Movement, violent and nonviolent.[52] The question is, what tactics are effective at achieving movement goals?

Gamson's small-scale study of differential success rates between groups using violence (violence users) and those avoiding violence or being victims of violence (violence recipients) shows surprising results. Although his sample sizes are small, Gamson found that violence users have a higher success rate than other groups of protesters.[53] In summary, he writes:

> Am I ready to conclude then that violence basically works? Not quite, or at least not in any simple fashion ... . It is easier to say what these data refute than what they prove. Violence should be viewed as an instrumental act, aimed at furthering the purposes of the group that uses it when they have some reason to think that it will help their cause. This is especially likely to be true when the normal condemnation which attends to its use is muted or neutralized in the surrounding community, when it is tacitly condoned by large parts of the audience.[54]

Condemnation of violence among the general citizenry of the United States, however, was not "muted or neutralized" during the time period covered in this paper. While President Bush referred to the anti-war protests as "a beautiful thing", as a demonstration of democracy, he also dismissed the millions of protesters as irrelevant, saying, "You know, size of protest, it's like deciding, well, I'm going to decide policy based upon a focus group."[55] National polls conducted at the beginning of the war showed support for Bush's actions as high as 76 percent.[56] Under these circumstances, when the political establishment is "largely immune to pressure from movement groups", McAdam argues that "tactical innovations are apt to be repressed or ignored rather than triggering expanded insurgency".[57]

That was the situation for the St. Louis anti-war movement, and for the movement throughout the nation more generally. While the Black Bloc and others were able to create more visible, confrontational protest activities, these events did little to change the outcome of the situation. Across the nation, there were thousands of people arrested before and immediately after the start of the war (for example, in San Francisco, where over 2000 people were arrested in the two days following the first bombing campaigns[58]). The war started despite these protests, and continues a year later. Those groups in St. Louis, San Francisco, and elsewhere who attempted to move beyond permitted marches and rallies were eventually worn down by a combination of repression by the civil authorities (such as that following the 30 March event in St. Louis or the use of rubber bullets against protesters in Oakland, CA[59]) and loss of support within the general public. During the massive civil disobedience actions in San Francisco, the *San Francisco Chronicle* stated that the promise of continuing civil disobedience was making it "harder for many people to sympathize with the demonstrators – even for those who support their cause."[60] Again, the ideological and methodological split within the peace movement eroded support for confrontational and violent protesters. In several situations around the country, the physical split that mirrored the ideological split allowed police to deal, sometimes brutally, with smaller groups of protesters.

Discussion and Conclusions

Today, more than a year and a half after the invasion of Iraq, it is difficult to assess the successes of the anti-war movement. If the movement's solitary goal was to prevent the war in Iraq, then the movement was a failure. If, however, one looks at shorter-term goals such as raising awareness of issues, getting out a message, or gaining new supporters, we feel that the movement enjoyed some measure of success.

For the Black Bloc in St. Louis, there were clear successes. Its stated aims included preventing "business as usual," and its members succeeded on several occasions. During at least three events discussed here, the Black Bloc was directly or indirectly responsible for closing down streets during and after official events. They encouraged more "mainstream" protesters to leave the comfort of the sidewalk and take over the streets, and often energized otherwise quiet crowds. They brought broader attention to the anti-war movement by bringing the protests to areas with lots of people, such as the University City "Loop" area and Laclede's Landing. Their willingness to be confrontational and to disobey the rules of protest set by the City of St. Louis did expand the reach of the anti-war message.

Their willingness to use violence, however, had less positive outcomes. It overshadowed more peaceful messages in local mainstream media. The *St. Louis*

Post-Dispatch's coverage of the 20 March event, for example, led with the post-event march: "Dozens of war protesters dressed in black, some carrying torches and wearing masks, marched through the streets of downtown St. Louis late Thursday night tipping over newspaper boxes and blocking traffic."[61] The pro-war writers on STLIMC's newswire made it clear how disdainful they were of the Black Bloc activities. If earlier property damage was indeed a driving force behind the increased intolerance of the peace movement by the St. Louis police force – leading eventually to the brutality following the 30 March event – we then argue that the use of violence by protesters made the anti-war movement less effective in the long run, and may have made future protest more difficult in St. Louis.

One reason for our skepticism is the police response to planned protests in connection with the World Agricultural Forum (WAF) held in St. Louis in May 2003. On the first morning of planned protests, 16 May 2003, police preemptively raided a shared house and the Community Arts and Media Project (CAMP) building, which houses the STLIMC office.[62] Other protesters were arrested while riding in a van or riding their bicycles on the streets long before they reached the protest area.[63]

Since the beginning of the war in Iraq in March, 2003, activities protesting the war have continued. There is still a weekly candlelight vigil. Instead of War has organized small, mostly informational events, and has turned its main focus to the 2004 presidential election and the creation of a Civilian Review Board to review high levels of violence by the St. Louis Police Department. There have been few opportunities to witness protester-police interactions.

On the eve of the first anniversary of the U.S. bombing of Iraq (19 March, 2004), however, Instead of War organized a rally and march as a send-off to a "Peace Train" of protesters going to a large event in Chicago the following day. The main body of protesters arrived by light rail at the Savvis Center Plaza in downtown St. Louis at approximately 8PM. By 7:30, there was already a very large police presence in the area, proportionally larger than at previous events. During a march to the Eagleton Federal Building, Black Bloc drummers used street signs, parking meters, and fire hydrants as drums. At least one large traffic barrier was thrown into the street. The police issued verbal warnings to stop hitting public property, and peacekeepers with IOW tried to stand physically between Black Bloc drummers and the sidewalk "drums." Peacekeepers also repeatedly asked the drummers to stop. The increased presence of both police officers and IOW peacekeepers is perhaps a reflection of their fears of a repetition of the property damage of 20 March, 2003, or the police brutality of 30 March, 2003.

The most dramatic incident of the night occurred when two or three Black Bloc members placed an American flag on the flagstone plaza and prepared to light it on fire. Approximately 20 police officers immediately surrounded them and confiscated the flag, claiming it would be a public fire hazard. Police officers pulled batons out, and IOW peacekeepers restrained and argued with the Black Bloc members, trying to defuse the situation. The night ended without further incidents, and no arrests were made.

The interaction of violence, nonviolence, and civil suppression on the first anniversary of the war shows that the dynamic between pacifist protesters, the Black Bloc, and the police has continued to escalate in St. Louis, with both movement peacekeepers and police attempting to constrain Black Bloc actions to fit a pacifist model of protest.

Our study of the anti-war movement in St. Louis provides not only an example of ideological differences within a diverse social movement, but also demonstrates the value of Independent Media sites as a resource for understanding the motivation of participants in social movements. Black Bloc members, in particular, are wary of talking to strangers about their actions, because of fears of police infiltration. By using STLIMC archives, we were able to document debates within the St. Louis peace movement. These archives show that there was an awareness of the broader philosophical and pragmatic arguments for and against the use of violence. They also allowed us to use participants' own words in both our description and analysis of anti-war events in St. Louis leading up to the invasion of Iraq.

Notes

1   www.ecotopia.org/ehof/hill; www.circleoflifefoundation.org.
2   www.earthliberationfront.com/news/2004/011304r.shtml;
    www.earthliberationfront.com.
3   Mulford Q. Sibley. *The Political Theories of Modern Pacifism: An Analysis and Criticism* (New York: Garland Publishing, 1972).
4   Ibid., p. 2.
5   Ibid., p. 3.
6   Leo Tolstoy. *The Law of Love and the Law of Violence* (New York: Holt, Reinhart, and Winston, 1970), pp. 70-71.
7   Martin Luther King, Jr. "Pilgramage to Nonviolence," in James M. Washington (ed.), *Martin Luther King, Jr. I Have a Dream: Writings and Speeches that Changed the World* (San Francisco: Harper, 1992), p. 59.
8   Bart DeLigt. *The Conquest of Violence: An Essay on War and Revolution* (New York: E.P. Dutton and Company), p. 72.
9   Guenter Lewy. *Peace and Revolution: The Moral Crisis of American Pacifism.* (Grand Rapids, MI: Erdmans Publishing, 1988.), p. 169.
10 Ibid., p. 170.
11 Ibid., p. 173.
12 Rael Jean Isaac. "The Violent Pacifists," in Michael Cromartie (ed.), *Peace Betrayed? Essays on Pacifism and Politics.* (Washington, DC: Ethics and Public Policy Center, 1990.), pp. 167-168.
13 Doug McAdam. "Tactical Innovation and the Pace of Insurgency," in Doug McAdam and David A. Snow, (eds.), *Social Movements: Readings on Their Emergence, Mobilization, and Dynamics* (Los Angeles: Roxbury Publishing, 1997.), pp. 340-356.
14 Carmichael (now Kwame Ture) began his civil rights work as a pacifist, working with the Student Nonviolent Coordinating Committee (SNCC). He wrote (Carmichael and

Hamilton 1967:52): "From our viewpoint, rampaging white mobs and white night-riders must be made to understand that their days of free head-whipping are over. Black people should and must fight back. Nothing more quickly repels someone bent on destroying you than the unequivocal message: 'O.K., fool, make your move, and run the same risk I run – of dying." SNCC became marginalized within the Civil Rights movement following Carmichael's rise to chair, and his increasing calls for violent struggle. He eventually left SNCC to join the Black Panther Party. http://www.spartacus.schoolnet.co.uk/USAcarmichael.htm; http://www.spartacus.schoolnet.co.uk/USAsncc.htm.

15 Bobby Seale. *Seize the Time: The Story of the Black Panther Party and Huey P. Newton* (Baltimore: Black Classic Press, 1991).

16 Although most incidents of violence involving the Black Panthers or other groups, such as the Deacons for Defense and Justice were reactionary in nature, their members were often heavily armed and trained and ready for violent protest and defense See Stokely Carmichael and Charles V. Hamilton *Black Power: The Politics of Liberation in America.* (New York: Vintage Books, 1967.), and Seale, *Sieze the Time.*

17 Peter B. Levy *Civil War on Race Street: The Civil Rights Movement in Cambridge, Maryland.* (Gainesville, FL: University of Florida Press, 2003), p. 140.

18 http://docs.indymedia.org/view/Global/FrequentlyAskedQuestionEn.

19 http://stlouis.indymedia.org/about.php3.

20 http://docs.indymedia.org/view/Global/FrequentlyAskedQuestionEn.

21 Hard copies of the IndyMedia documents may be obtained from the senior author if the archives are unavailable.

22 STLIMC: 12/10/02, April Calvin, Article #4240

23 Jodi Genshaft. "Hundreds Opposed to War Let Their Feeling Be Known at Rally," *St. Louis Post-Dispatch*, 9 December 2002, B1.

24 STLIMC: 12/4/02, Noward, Article #4190

25 STLIMC: 12/13/02, revolutionary, Article #4190, Comment #4288

26 STLIMC: 12/10/02, Marzapan, Article #4280

27 STLIMC: 12/14/02, Me, Article #4190, Comment #4305; 12/14/02, Me, Article #4190, Comment #4306

28 STLIMC: 2/16/03, C. D. Stelzer, Article #4929

29 STLIMC: 2/16/03, still hyped, Article #4888

30 STLIMC: 2/16/03, Michael, Article #4888, Comment #4890

31 STLIMC: 2/16/03, ChuckO, Article #4888, Comment #4896

32 STLIMC: 2/17/03, A. Berkmann, Article #4888, Comment #4939

33 STLIMC: 2/18/03, think about it, Article #4888, Comment #4984

34 STLIMC: 3/17/03, IOW, Article #5969

35 STLIMC: 3/27/03, II, Article #6998

36 STLIMC: 3/19/03, i hate cointelpro, Article #6079; 3/31/03, Macy Red, White and Blue, Article #6079, Comment #7395

37 STLIMC: 3/20/03, Matthew Cunningham, Article #6136, Comment #6138

38 STLIMC: 3/28/03, II, Article #7078

39 STLIMC: 3/22/03, uwi-uwi, Article #6367

40 STLIMC: 3/21/03, Aaron, Article #6214

41 STLIMC: 3/21/03, SLP, Article #6214, Comment #6249

42 STLIMC: 3/22/03, Aaron Michels, Article #6214, Comment #6391

43 STLIMC: 3/21/03, two of your friendly neighborhood anarchists, Article #6214, Comment #6216

44 STLIMC: 3/21/03, f00_fighter, Article #6214, Comment #6216

45 STLIMC: 3/22/02, uwi-uwi, Article #6367

46 STLIMC: 3/22/03, A. Berkmann, Article #6214, Comment #6393

47 STLIMC: 3/31/03, anonymous of course, Article #7387

48 STLIMC: 3/31/03, AJ Cook, Article #7387, Comment #7394

49 STLIMC: 3/31/03, den-e, Article #7327, Comment #7371

50 STLIMC: 3/31/03, Eric Carter, Article #7284, Comment #7374

51 Doug McAdam. "Tactical Innovation and the Pace of Insurgency," p. 340.

52 In writing about ghetto riots, Feagin and Hahn refer to the riots in terms of "politics of violence" and write: "Such a perspective helps explain the timng of collective political violence at the end of decades of civil rights struggle. Black Americans had not been successful in achieving their principal objectives through the political processes of voting, parties, or machine politics. Nor had they fulfilled their goals through rhetoric or nonviolent activities such as sit-ins and demonstrations ... . As a result, violence emerged as the ultimate alternative for many, to be engaged in regardless of the personal consequences." See Joe R. Feagin and Harlan Hahn. *Ghetto Revolts: The Politics of Violence in American Cities*. (New York: The Macmillan Company, 1973), p. 43.

53 William A. Gamson. "The Success of the Unruly." in Doug McAdam and David A. Snow, (eds.), *Social Movements: Readings on Their Emergence, Mobilization, and Dynamics* (Los Angeles: Roxbury Publishing, 1997), pp. 359-360.

54 Ibid., p. 361.

55 See Ron Hutcheson. "Protesters Rarely Able to Get Message to Bush," *Knight Ridder/Tribune News Service*, 21 February 2003, Washington Dateline; Anne E. Kornblut. "Confronting Iraq; President Undeterred by Antiwar Protests," *The Boston Globe*, 19 February 2003, p. A1.

56 Richard Benedetto. "Poll: War Support Continues to Climb to 76% Approval," *USA Today*, 21 March 2003, p. 12A.

57 Doug McAdam. "Tactical Innovation and the Pace of Insurgency," p. 341.

58 Joe Garofoli "Protesters' Tactics Alienating Even Those Against War; Experts Question Effectiveness but Organizers See Success," *San Francisco Chronicle*, 23 March 2003, p. W2.

59 Martha Mendoza. "Police Fire Rubber Bullets at Anti-war Protest at port in Oakland; Nearby Longshoremen Injured," *Associated Press*, 7 April 2003, Domestic News.

60 Joe Garofoli "Protesters' Tactics Alienating Even Those Against War."

61 Susan C. Thomson and Jake Wagman. "Anti-war Demonstrators March Downtown; Students Protest at Washington University; Later, Smaller Group Blocks Traffic in St. Louis; Some are Arrested," *St. Louis Post-Dispatch*, 21 March 2003, p. A10.

62 STLIMC: 5/16/03, protestor, Article #9047 and associated comments; 5/16/03, bring the lawyers, Article #9049 and associated comments

63 STLIMC: 5/16/03, protestor, Article #9047; 5/16/03, digger, Article #9051

Chapter 8

Violence and Non-Violence as Constitutional Argument

An Analysis of the 1963 Civil Rights Demonstrations in Birmingham, Alabama

Neal Allen
University of Texas

On May 3 1963, police officers violently clashed with black civil rights protestors on the streets of Birmingham, Alabama. Police turned their clubs, dogs and high-pressure fire hoses on the protestors, many of whom were children. The two sides of this horrific and momentous conflict were doing several things that day, and in the several days of protest that preceded it. The police were carrying out the law of the city, as interpreted by their boss, Police Commissioner Bull Connor. They were defending the mores and way of life of the White South. They were frightening and hurting individuals who attempted to challenge those mores. The protesters were engaging in civil disobedience to claim what they regarded as their rights as American citizens and human beings. They crucially called attention to the depravity of segregation and the need for national government action.

Both groups were also engaging in constitutional argument, supporting particular visions for the place of government and citizens in the American constitutional order. One group used the resources of government to violently enforce the existing political order, and the other used non-violence to confront and highlight the worst injustices of that political order. The methods of the two sides could not be more different, but their actions shared an important component. They were communicating particular views of the constitutional order, communicating to each other, to the community of Birmingham and the state of Alabama, and through the medium of newspapers and television the rest of the country.

This essay makes the claim that violence and non-violent protest can be understood partly as constitutional argument. I present an interpretation and analysis of the American civil rights movement in the 1950s and 1960s to elaborate how this constitutional perspective can contribute to understanding of political violence, and its effect on American politics. After briefly discussing the constitutional argumentative component of some kinds of political violence, I present a historical narrative in three parts of the place of constitutional ideas in the civil rights movement. First I discuss the role of the *Brown* decision in southern politics of the time, and the decision oriented political conflict outside the judicial system to constitutional questions. Next I discuss the events of Birmingham and their significance for public policy, linking political violence, constitutional argument and policy change. I conclude by discussing the legacy of the violent constitutional argumentation for contemporary American politics, particularly for debates over social issues like gay marriage and the place of religion in politics.

The Concept of Violent Constitutional Argument

The typical image of constitutional argument comes from the judicial process, with lawyers arguing interpretation of the law in front of a judge or panel of judges. The type of constitutional argument given the most media coverage, and the political event most directly concerned with constitutional argumentation, is the Supreme Court process, with lawyers arguing for opposing sides in oral argument, and justices debating each other in published opinions. But what makes the high court's process one of constitutional argument is not just that it is judicial, or even that the Court's rulings are regarded as authoritative judgments about the constitutionality of government actions. The process is one of constitutional argument because the content of the debate is constitutional. Advocates and justices present competing visions of the relationship between citizens and government, and the fundamental organization of politics. The American Constitution is a document that sets this fundamental organization, just as Great Britain's constitution is a set of government decisions and societal norms. Constitutional debate is broader than merely debate over the interpretation of the document, but involves debate over the nature of the fundamental organization of politics. Supreme Court deliberations have such constitutional content, but so do speeches by presidents and legislators, and conversations between ordinary citizens.

Political violence is constitutional argument when the violence is supporting a particular vision of the fundamental political organization of society. This support of a constitutional vision gives substantive constitutional content to violent actions, and includes them in larger debates over the proper relationship between citizens and government. I will later discuss how *Brown v. Board of Education* partially lays the foundation for the Birmingham demonstrations, but it useful here to compare to two events. Both events were conflicts between groups with opposing visions of the relationship between citizens and their government. The states defending their segregated school systems in Brown, as well as Bull Connor's police in Birmingham, were using governmental resources in an attempt to prevent change from segregation to integration. Their integrationist opponents in the courtroom and then the streets were claiming a constitutional right to equal treatment, and that segregation blocked that right. Both conflicts also were partially about the relationship between the national and state governments under the constitution, with the segregationist forces claiming the constitutional prerogative to organize local and regional society.

What separated the two events, for the purposes of this essay, was the means of argumentation. *Brown* and its component debates were characterized by legal and verbal argument, and did not include violence, although attempts to enforce the decision led to violence in places like Little Rock and Boston. The direct action civil rights movement, of which Birmingham in 1963 became a part, had both verbal and non-verbal components. The non-verbal component of civil disobedience through marches and sit-ins made was connected intimately to the verbal component that was expressed in speeches, writings and even the chants and songs of the marchers. The non-violent protests, and the violent reaction by law enforcement that they stimulated, was a case of violent means being used for constitutional ends. Just as Von Clausewitz claimed that war was politics by other means, sometimes violence is constitutional argument by other means.

Many types of political violence are also constitutional argument. The American Revolution was partly the violent expression of the constitutional arguments of the colonists, about representation, taxation and local governance. Hate crimes are a kind of constitutional argument, claiming elite status for certain racial, ethnic, gender, or sexuality groups over others. The Iraq War of 2003 was partially justified as the violent enforcement of a particular international constitutional vision, with the United States and its allies deposing Saddam Hussein because he would not comply with United Nations regulations.

I focus here on the connection between violence, constitutional argument and the American civil rights movement for three reasons. First, the connection between the political violence at the demonstrations and constitutional argument is particularly close, since the demonstrations were part of a constitutional change process initiated by the Supreme Court. Second, this particular violent episode was crucial in causing constitutional change, with one side of the constitutional argument achieving victory. Third, important political debates in contemporary American show the legacy of the violent constitutional argument of May 1963.

Birmingham, Brown and the Supreme Court

The Supreme Court affects American politics, with major decisions like *Brown v. Board of Education*, reorganizing conflict in a particular issue area. The Court changed political conflict into a form that parallels the organization of conflict within the judicial system. Alexander Hamilton wrote in Federalist 78 that American courts "have neither force nor will, but merely judgment," and that the judiciary "can take no active resolution." This limitation to "judgment" channels the Supreme Court's power into the realm of political ideas. The Court can directly affect what kind of ideas are part of settled law, and which ideas are permissible or impermissible as motivations for government action. *Brown* made the idea of segregation impermissible as an organizing principle of American society. But I am concerned in this essay with the Court's indirect effects on political conflict and the place of ideas within such conflict. *Brown* had an indirect effect that initiated a conflict process, of which the violent constitutional argument of Birmingham in 1963 was a part. Both the police and the protesters were caught up in a process of political transformation, and used available means to advance their particular constitutional arguments. This process was partly a result of the judicialization of conflict over racial integration in America.

Judicialization of Political Conflict

I argue that the Court's indirect contribution can be best understood as "judicializing" political conflict. An opinion like *Brown* makes the political process concerning school integration more like a judicial process. Competing groups occupy roles similar to opposing sides in a trial, with political actors polarized into competing camps. Political actors, like politicians, parts of government, interest groups and courts themselves function like participants in an adversarial judicial system.

After the Court, with the issuance of a transformative opinion, judicializes a given issue area, certain kinds of arguments are more likely to be made and be successful than before the opinion. Arguments will be framed in terms of legality, constitutionality, jurisdiction and adherence to core principles. These arguments will be less amenable to settlement through legislative and executive bargaining, and debate participants will gravitate toward categorical solutions that exclude the possibility of compromise. Sometimes issues that have undergone a judicialization process remain unresolved until polarization takes violent form. This judicialization process includes two other phenomena: nodes of conflict and the production of social/political doctrine. Both help to illuminate the place of the Birmingham demonstrations in constitutional politics.

Court-created Node of Conflict

A Court-created node of conflict is a space of contention over a given issue that is brought into existence by a transformative Supreme Court opinion. The issue at hand and disagreement about it are not created by the Court, but are present in politics and society. The Court contributes to the debate over the issue by reconceptualizing the conflict in constitutional terms, framing debates in the form of legal argumentation, integrating the existing debate into part of national political debate, and ensuring further participation in the debate by federal appellate courts.

In developing this theoretical concept I draw heavily on the work of Julie Novkov in Constituting Workers, Protecting Women: Gender, Law, and Labor in the Progressive Era and New Deal Years (2001). Novkov examines the role of lawyers and public interest advocates in the production of the labor regulation doctrine of the New Deal Court expressed in West Coast Hotel. She argues that the decision was the result of a long period of negotiation over values and institutional arrangements. This discursive contestation occurs in what she terms a "node of conflict," the institutional space where negotiation over doctrine occurs. These nodes are created by lawyers and public interest advocates who identify ambiguities and inconsistencies in existing doctrine, especially with respect to changing social conditions, and advocate for new doctrinal understandings. This advocacy creates of kind of rip in the doctrinal fabric, and forces judges to take up a previously settle issue and, in some cases, produce a new doctrinal order. This lengthy passage from Novkov's book lays out the node-creation process:

> How is this doctrine actually produced? Institutionalized relationships and processes operate to transform ideas into doctrine and ultimately in some cases into nodes of conflict. Ideas, expressed from every possible perspective and for every possible reason, enter into the legal system through the narrow gateway of briefs. Lawyers' briefs filter and select the possible lines of argument to allow only those that will be permissible and coherent to the courts. Finally judges determine which arguments are valid and which are not, disagreeing with each other's outcomes and reasoning along the way (Novkov 18).

I propose that a similar process operates in the opposite direction, with the Court initiating the change process. A transformative opinion like *Brown* produces a similar kind of disjunction of settled equilibria and societal understandings, and sets the term of the debate to follow. This Node exists in both ideational and institutional dimensions of the political system. The Court stands in the role Novkov gives to lawyers and public interest advocates, and other authoritative institutions stand in the role she gives to Courts. While reversed, the change process that occurs within a court-created node is like Novkov's process one of negotiation over constitutional values and order. Interested groups will enter the discursive space created by the decision, carrying the debate forward with new arguments and new methods of argumentation. The Supreme Court did not intend in 1954 to create the space for the violence of Birmingham nine years later, but the police and protestors were debating within a court-created node of conflict.

Social/Political Doctrine

The arguments interested groups put forth in response to a judicial opinion will articulate and reveal existing social/political doctrine. This doctrine will have the characteristics of constitutional doctrine, with theories of interpretation, identification of sacred higher law texts, conceptions of institutional design, and logical arguments. These doctrinal positions will support, oppose, or both support and oppose the Court opinion.

The extra-judicial effect of a transformative Court opinion is stimulative of this creative process. In response to the challenge of an argument presented by the judicial branch of the federal government, affected groups will reconceptualize and present to the larger community a justification for their values, laws and political institution. This justification, while built upon an existing worldview, is organized in the form of legal doctrine. With an opinion on constitutionality like Brown, Court stimulates an alternate process of the construction of meaning, which is presented as a competing theory of constitutional interpretation.

Here it is significant not just that in the 1950s the Court stimulated increased opposition to school integration in the South. The form of argument used by Southern defenders was legal and constitutional, opposing the foundations of the Court's integration arguments. White Southern leaders did not merely disagree with Warren's assertion that separate institutions were inherently unequal, or that all citizens were entitled to equal treatment from federal and state government. White southerners presented a developed alternate constitutional doctrine, still working with the constitution as the primary sacred text. Defenders of segregation added to their interpretive theory new sacred texts, like the Kentucky and Virginia Resolutions and the writings of John C. Calhoun. They offered a state-centered creation story to counter the nationalist origins assumed for the Union by the Warren Court in Brown and other decisions applying national standards to state governments. White southerners also grounded their thinking in the concept of interpositition, which was at the core of their understanding of institutional design.

An example of this alternative constitutional doctrine is discussed below. The presentation of social/political doctrine is an important part of the effect of a transformative Court opinion because it allows for a kind of communication between the Court and its adversaries, in a type of discourse that is shaped by the arguments and institutional characteristics of the judiciary. The presentation of arguments in a doctrinal form by Court opponents allows for debate with groups in government and society who support the general issue position of the Court, but for different reasons or from different perspectives.

The presentation of arguments in doctrinal form affects all of the other theoretical concepts in this set that makes up judicialization of political conflict. Contestation over constitutional meaning in judicially-created nodes of conflict occurs in doctrinal form, with the Court opinion serving as both a model and a devil's advocate for competing arguments. This doctrinalization of arguments furthers the dialectical nature of post-opinion debate, with competing groups crafting their arguments in forms grounded in divergent constitutional worldviews that cannot be reconciled through bargaining and compromise. Also while transformative opinions give the Court a vital role in stimulating debate, and influencing the content and form of arguments within that debate, those opinions do not resolve the policy questions at issue. The process of resolution, at least of the particular constitutional and institutional issues raised by the Court, occurs in a broader and less Court-controlled process I call court-induced punctuated change.

Within the conflict over integration that played out in elections and street protests, White southerners constructed an alternate constitutional vision. A useful example of that vision is the editorials of the Richmond News Leader in 1955 and 1956. Written by James J. Kilpatrick, these writings were an explicit attempt to give legal and constitutional form to the reactionary movement of the White South. Powe identifies the editorials as key documents in the development of the Southern resistance: "The political and intellectual problem facing the South was how to explain to itself and the rest of the nation why defying the Supreme Court of the United States was okay" (Powe 58).

The editorials present a constitutional interpretation constructed around the concept of interposition, in which a state "interposes" itself between its citizens and an unjust federal government action. Thus resistance to the Supreme Court decision was not unlawful, but "the highest possible example of fidelity to the compact" (Nov. 23, 1955). According to Kilpatrick's understanding, the moral and legal high ground is occupied by Southern Whites, with their "reverence for law, and our obedience to constituted authority" (Nov. 22). This states' rights-centered theory was justified with reference not just to the nature of the ratification of the Constitution, but to other documents like Jefferson and Madison's Kentucky and Virginia Resolutions, and the writings of Calhoun. The Southern federalist theory is argued against the Court's nationalism; individual rights are confronted by sovereign power.

These editorials follow the form of what I call the production of social/political doctrine. Previously existing regional values are publicly presented as a coherent doctrine that is grounded in legal and historical authority. An interpretation of the Constitution is supplemented by the inclusion of supportive sacred texts into the constitutional canon. A revised founding myth is offered as foundation for opposition to the Court's argument and directives. Thus the Court stimulates an intellectual process the replicates its own process, but using different inputs and ideas.

Not only do the arguments of the Richmond paper's Kilpatrick editorials follow the form of social/political doctrine, they were published in a form clearly meant to be taken as constitutional doctrine. The News Leader published them in a pamphlet called Interposition, and included as supporting materials like Kentucky and Virginia Resolutions, writings by states' rights proponents like Calhoun, John Taylor of Caroline and Littleton Waller Tazewell, governor of South Carolina in the 1830s. These sacred texts were included along with resolutions and reports of the Virginia legislature in support of massive resistance to integration. This pamphlet includes all the components of a social/political doctrine, and was produced in opposition to *Brown*, and to support the movement against the Court's position.

Kilpatrick wrote in 1962 an extended book version of the argument presented in his 1955-56 editorials, called The Southern Case for School Segregation. In the Introduction, he framed his project as the production of constitutional doctrine:

May it please the court:
When this book was conceived, it was intended to be titled "U.S. v. the South: A Brief for the Defense," but it seemed a cumbersome title and the finished work is not, of course, a brief for the South in any lawyer's sense of the word. It is no more than an extended personal essay, presented in this form because the relationship that exists between the rest of the country and the South, in the area of race relations, often has the aspect of an adversary proceeding. We of the South see ourselves on the defensive, and we frequently find ourselves, as lawyers do, responding in terms of the law and the evidence. (Kilpatrick 1962)

Kilpatrick's writings were part of the same constitutional project that included the violent police repression seen on the streets of Birmingham in May of 1963. The Supreme Court, and its allies in the direct action civil rights movement, stimulated the production of an alternate constitutional vision by white southerners who wanted to protect the segregationist social system. In response to a constitutional Court opinion, southern political elites mounted a constitutional defense. The ideas and substantive content behind that defense was better elaborated in the writings of Kilpatrick, but still present in the actions of the Birmingham police.

How Birmingham Changed America

An opinion like *Brown* has the effect of polarizing political conflict on the issue at hand. I find the metaphor of the dialectic useful in understanding this polarization. The Court creates itself or supportive interest groups as thesis, and stimulates production of an antithesis, taking its form and substantive orientation, if not its issue stance, from the thesis. New theses emerge within the debate, responding to the debate initiated and organized by the Court. In some cases a thesis and antithesis come into conflict in a way that creates a new political order. Violence, and its antithesis, non-violent protest, are in a sense the culmination of the dialectical change process begun by *Brown*. Their conflict was dialectical because the two sides were manifestations of a conflict inherent in the issue of racial integration, and their direct opposition was inherent in their orientation toward that issue.

By stimulating and manipulating the form of existing political conflict, a transformative Supreme Court opinion can begin a process of punctuated change that can lead to a new policy equilibrium, and a new constitutional order. In areas like school integration, and societal integration more generally, the necessary role of other political actors keeps the Court from resolving the issue with even a landmark opinion like *Brown*. The Court's role is more stimulative and organizational, affecting the timing, intensity and form of debate. By remaking debate into a form consistent with judicial politics, the Court initiates a dialectical change process that leads to confrontation of competing ideas and doctrinal theories. This confrontation, which in the area of societal integration occurred in the streets of Southern cities like Birmingham and Selma, draws other institutional actors into the change process. These other actors then create a new equilibrium, validating one of the competing positions in the adversarial debate initiated by the opinion. In the case of integration, the new equilibrium was created by the President and Congress with the Civil Right and Voting Rights Acts of 1964 and 1965. This new settlement was buttressed with a particular constitutional argument, best presented by Lyndon Johnson in his post-Selma speech calling the voting rights legislation, that is itself a participant in the judicialized debate initiated by a Court opinion.

The backlash against *Brown* that transformed southern politics can only be understood in the context of the organization of national and state political institutions that protected the South from racial change. All relevant state and federal institutions were deliberately designed to maintain the racial status quo, with blacks relegated to lower-caste status. V.O. Key, in his classic analysis of southern politics in 1949, argues that continued subjugation of blacks was the organizing principle of regional politics.

> Southern sectionalism and the special character of southern political institutions have to be attributed in the main the Negro. The one-party system, suffrage restrictions departing from democratic norms, low levels of voting and of political interest, and all the consequences of these political arrangements and practices must be traced ultimately to this one factor. All of which amounts to saying that the predominant consideration in the architecture of southern political institutions has been to assure locally a subordination of the Negro population and, externally, to block threatened interference from the outside with these local arrangements.[1]

Key was writing of the Solid South, in which only Democrats could win statewide office. Dedicated to white supremacy, the party excluded any progressive ideas on race from public debate. Also the state-level Democratic organizations, and the national legislative nominations they controlled, served the interests of the more racially conservative whites from the "black belts," areas of high black population and thus a greater perceived threat from black empowerment.

White supremacists won all Senate elections in this period, and almost all House elections. Immune from Republican competition, southern Senators and congressmen gained seniority over their colleagues from the two-party competitive North, and thus controlled several key committee chairs. This control of national legislative power enhanced the ability of the more segregationist southern whites to block federal support for integration:

> The critical element in the structure of black-belt power has been the southern Senator and his actual, if not formal, rights to veto proposals of national intervention to protect Negro rights. The black belts have nothing to fear from state governments on the race question ... on the fundamental issue, only the Federal Government was to be feared.[2]

Southern whites could count on their long-serving representatives in Washington to keep integrationist legislation from ever emerging from Congress. The power of the President to unilaterally use the federal government to integrate southern society was limited. The white southern voters could concentrate on economic or other non-racial issues, confident that the federal government would leave their apartheid system alone. *Brown* shattered this equilibrium, with one branch of the federal government committed to transforming southern society.

Eugene "Bull" Connor is at the center of the change process I am suggesting took place after *Brown v. Board of Education*, and his career is a microcosm of the trends in Southern society and politics that led to the violent conflicts of the mid-1960s. Like many of the reactionary segregationist politics that held power in the post-*Brown* backlash era, he had served in public office before the Supreme Court decision. Connor's public stands as police commissioner had always shown the racism inherent in Southern white culture; he had made news for his opposition to a 1938 convention of civil rights activists in Birmingham, and as a delegate to the 1948 Democratic convention he was a leader of the Alabama delegates that walked out in protest of the party's civil rights policy and later endorsed Strom Thurmond's segregationist Dixiecrat run for the presidency.[3] But his success in office and at the ballot box was mostly due to his law-and-order and anti-corruption stances. He finished last running as a reactionary segregationist in the Democratic primary for governor in 1950, and by 1953 Connor's career lay in ruins, as he left office dogged by allegations of corruption and embarrassed by a public trial for being in a hotel room with a women who was not his wife, who happened to be his secretary.[4] Connor's attempts to return to elected office as county sheriff in 1954 and Commissioner of Public Improvements in 1956 ended in defeat at the ballot box.

While opposition to racial integration had always been part of Connor's public image, he put the issue at the center of his mid-1950s attempts to get back into power. He was successful in this quest, riding racist backlash to victory in 1957: "In the wake of the *Brown* decision, Connor sized up the Birmingham electorate correctly in 1957, using the race issue to reclaim his seat at city hall. The police commissioner rode a cresting wave of popularity into the 1960s."[5] This resurgence of Connor's career as a reactionary segregationist is not just reflective of a broader trend in Southern politics, but this resurgence put him at the right place at the right time to play a crucial part in the integration of Southern society.

He took that opportunity to use the resources at his disposal as a government official to aggressively support the existing constitutional order, and to support the hostile orientation toward civil rights for blacks and federal authority that characterized the policies of Alabama governor George Wallace and other prominent white reactionary politicians. When Connor's use of state resources to support the segregationist constitutional vision came into conflict with the constitutional rights-based non-violent protest of the black demonstrators, he escalated the debate to violence. The horrifying scale of that violence helped lead to federal legislation that remade the constitutional order to conform to the arguments of his integrationist opponents.

The 1964 Civil Rights Act had its roots in the violent clashes on the streets of Birmingham, Alabama in May of 1963. When national televisions news coverage brought horrifying pictures into Northern homes of Sheriff Bull Connor unleashing fire hoses, dogs and policemen wielding clubs on the black demonstrators, some of them children, the place of civil rights on the national agenda changed. President Kennedy went on national television to commit himself to a civil rights bill, and President Johnson made passage a kind of memorial to the slain leader. In his history of the Warren Court, Lucas A. Powe finds the genesis of the Civil Rights Act in the Birmingham demonstrations under the leadership of Martin Luther King, Jr., and the genesis of those demonstrations in Supreme Court Action:

> There is no doubt that Birmingham was the catalyst for the Civil rights Act of 1964. Had not the North seen the white south so vividly, a strong civil rights bill would have waited in the womb of time... . *Brown v. Board of Education* had brought out the worst in the American South, and King had learned how to reflect that behavior to the American North to bring out the best in the country.[6]

The national political system responded to the violent constitutional argument of Birmingham not with further violence, but with legislation that settled the fundamental political questions in favor of the black protesters, mandating integration of all public accommodations and banning racial and gender discrimination in employment.

The Legacy of Birmingham as Constitutional Violence

While the most obvious and significant legacy of the violent constitutional argument that took place in Birmingham, Alabama in May 1963 is the Civil Rights Act of 1964, I argue that two other phenomena in contemporary American politics show the lingering effect of the demonstrations. Conflict over constitutional rights and the social order are less violent than they were in 1963, with the nightly news no longer dominated by pictures of protestors being beaten by police officers. Law enforcement has adopted techniques that minimize violence, and debate over core civil rights has mostly moved into governmental institutions like courts and legislatures. But the politics of rights and social values still shows the legacy of 1963, and the continuing power of the losers in the constitutional fights of the civil rights era.

Bull Connor in 1963 occupied a particular vital role in American politics, the conservative defender of the social order. American conservatism has long been characterized by such figures, like William Jennings Bryan in his presidential campaigns at the turn of the twentieth century. National politics from the 1960s forward has been often a battle between such a conservative figure, like Barry

Goldwater in his 1964 presidential run, fighting against a perceived assault on core American values. While in the 1960s the national government took the side of Bull Connor's opponents, forcing integration of Southern society, the role of conservative defender of the constitutional order continued to play a role in national politics.

This conservative role was decoupled from its violent past, but not from its modern origins in white Southern defiance of national social norms. Ronald Reagan began his general election campaign for the presidency, following the 1980 Republican convention, with a speech at the Neshoba County Fair in Philadelphia, Mississippi. Speaking near the site of the murder of three civil rights workers by Ku Klux Klansmen in 1964, Reagan proclaimed, "I believe in states' rights. I believe in people doing as much as they can at the private level." He promised to "restore to states and local governments the power that properly belongs to them."[7] Reagan used the role of conservative defender of the constitutional order to connect himself to the history of Southern resistance to integration and federal intervention. This role is occupied today in American politics by conservative social figures like former Alabama Supreme Court judge Roy Moore, who had a massive stone monument to the Ten Commandments installed in the Alabama judicial building. His action was in the tradition of Bull Connor's violent constitutional argument in 1963. Both used the power of their elected political office to communicate a particular conservative position on a constitutional issue, defying national political norms. The role of conservative defender of the social order is also often occupied by President George W. Bush, in opposing threats to perceived core national values. His public statements opposing the withdrawal of "under God" from the pledge of allegiance and gay marriage show him defending a social order that is valued by American conservatives, especially in the white South.

Another parallel between the violent constitutional argumentation of 1963 Birmingham is the use of government resources to further constitutional argument. But not just conservatives like Judge Roy Moore use their offices to make constitutional claims. Liberal government officials have used the power of their elected offices to support the drive for gay marriage rights. The mayors of San Francisco and New Paltz and Nyack, New York, as well as the county government of Multnomah County, Oregon, have conducted gay marriage. Just as Bull Connor used the coercive power of his police force to make a constitutional claim, these local government officials used the resources of the state to enter a constitutional debate.

Notes

1   V.O Key, Jr. *Southern Politics in State and Nation* (Knoxville: University of Tennessee Press, 1984).
2   Ibid., p. 9.

3   William A. Nunnelley. *Bull Connor* (Tuscaloosa, Ala.: University of Alabama Press, 1991), pp. 31, 34.
4   Ibid, pp. 40-44. Birmingham had an ordinance prohibiting unmarried people of the opposite sex from occupying the same hotel room. Connor was convicted, but the state Supreme Court overturned on appeal. An impeachment attempt stemming from the incident led to a deadlocked jury.
5   Ibid, pp. 184-185.
6   Lucas A. Powe. *The Warren and American Politics* (Cambridge, Mass., Belknap Press. 2000).
7   Earl Black and Merle Black. *The Rise of Southern Republicans* (Cambridge, Mass., Belknap Press, 2002).

Chapter 9

Jack Rocks, Earrings and the Occupation of Moss #3

Emblems of the Struggle for Decency in the Appalachian Coalfields

Fred C. Smith

University of Southern Mississippi

The men did not know where they were going, or how long they would be gone. The previous evening an anonymous phone call had instructed, "kiss your wife and kids goodbye," code words that informed them to assemble at Camp Solidarity near Carbo, Virginia. As the three-vehicle convoy – an old school bus and two panel trucks – traversed the severely graded Appalachian terrain, the men were exposed to alternating scenes of the pristine beauty of early autumn Appalachia and the refuse of the men who lived there. The entourage kept a strict time schedule. Later the reasons for this extremely regimented trip from Camp Solidarity to the as-yet-unrevealed destination would be vividly manifest. But for the duration of the trip the three teams of miners representing West Virginia, Kentucky and Virginia (red, white, and blue, respectively) had time to reflect. Some of them, those from the area, soon deduced where they were going. There was only one Pittston coal facility approachable from this direction, the Moss Preparation Plant # 3. Earlier in the week a United Mine Workers of America (UMWA) leader had conspiratorially asked each one of the men if was able to "do something to help us," and their affirmative answer accounted, in part, for their seats in the vehicles.[1]

Moss Preparation Plant #3 processed eighty percent of all the Virginia coal mined by the Pittston Coal Company; an interruption in its operation would close all the regional Pittston Coal Company mines. The coal preparation facility had been under intense observation by certain people for a number of weeks. Taking advantage of the Sunday afternoon-induced laxness of the Virginia State Police – blue team leader Bo Willis said that the monotonous regularity of the ballet of shift changes between the Vance Security officers and the Virginia State Police at Moss #3 reminded him of the cartoon in which both the sheep-dog and the wolf punched a time clock – these irritated, angry, militant, yet non-violent miners occupied Moss #3. The one hundred miners and one activist minister thus initiated the signature event of a most remarkable series of events in coalfields of Southwestern Virginia. During the Pittston/UMWA negotiations and subsequent strike, the residents of the Virginia coalfields witnessed the attempt of the Pittston Coal Company to destroy the UMWA and the collusion of both the state and federal governments toward that end. This article is a consideration of some of the consequences and causes of those remarkable events.[2]

In 1989, the United Mine Workers of America, wounded in prestige and power, entered the second year of on-and-off negotiations with the Pittston Coal Company. The company remained unimpressed with the strength of the union because of the revealed weaknesses and leadership problems manifested since the resignation of John L. Lewis. The seeds of conflict that were to result in the Pittston strike of 1989 were planted in the transition of power from Lewis to Tony Boyle.

John L. Lewis believed that it was possible for American workers to enjoy the benefits of a middle class lifestyle. When interviewed by a reporter in 1937, Lewis summed up the demands of the United Mine Workers: the right to organize, shorter hours, the prohibition of child labor, equal pay for men and women for the same kind of work, and a guarantee that all who were willing and able to work be employed. When the reporter asked in a follow-up about a "living wage," Lewis exploded. "No!" he thundered, pounding his fist on the table. "Not a living wage. We ask more than that. We demand for the unskilled workers a wage that will enable them to maintain themselves and their families in health and modern comfort, to purchase their own homes, to enable their children to obtain at least a high school education, and to provide against sickness, disability, and death.[3]

Lewis created a pattern that subsequent union leaders tried, generally with little success, to emulate. He was big, beetle-browed, always impeccably attired, and did not shrink from self-aggrandizement. The UMW President was a crafty judge of human character and was not reluctant to use the reputation of others to further the union's aims. After passage of the National Industrial Recovery Act, which included a provision for collective bargaining, he was quick to interpret President Roosevelt's wishes for Appalachian coal miners. The President, he told them, wants you to join the union. In all his speeches, explanations, or arguments he was roaringly eloquent.[4]

The UMW affiliated with the American Federation of Labor (AFL) and was the single most important force in the creation of the Congress of Industrial Organizations (CIO). In 1933, UMW organizers fanned out across the coalfields in an attempt to organize all coal workers under the impetus given by the National Industrial Recovery Act. Provisions of the legislation allowed workers the right to organize and bargain collectively with employers. The UMW also helped organize other mass production industries, particularly auto and steel. Even though Lewis was quick to capitalize on FDR's popularity, he was quick to oppose him when he felt it in his, and presumably the union's, best interests. He opposed FDR's election in 1940. He lived high, talked loud, ruled authoritatively and the coal miners loved him. The typical Appalachia coal mining family might have three pictures in the house: Jesus, FDR, and John L. Lewis.[5]

All future presidents of the UMW and its successor, the UMWA, were judged by the Lewis pattern of bombast, eloquence, Machiavellian manipulation, and iron control. Upon his retirement, Lewis handpicked his successor. The membership expected Tony Boyle to continue the pattern set by Lewis and he did not. Appalachian coal miners are not noted as a particularly docile or obedient or easily convinced group. Maintaining peace and order within such a group, let alone dominating it the manner of John L. Lewis, stretched Boyle to his limits and beyond. Soon Boyle faced trying new circumstances. Diesel engines reduced the demand for coal, hydroelectric power production increased, foreign competition advanced, alternate sources of fuel appeared, and policymakers and businessmen considered the expansion of nuclear reactors for the production of electricity. Increasingly diversified corporations controlled coalmines. Steel companies, airlines, and oil companies protected their positions in the energy market by acquiring coalmines and coal related facilities. Cleaner burning anthracite coal of the Mid-west and Western coal fields challenged the bituminous coal of Appalachia, and the Appalachia miners proved to be a very undisciplined lot. Wildcat strikes, walkouts unsanctioned by UMW leadership, complicated relations and negotiations with coal operators. By 1963, the year Tony Boyle assumed office, the coal miners in general and the UMW in particular had suffered a heavy blow.[6]

Lacking the status and bearing that made Lewis a legendary figure among the miners, Boyle faced an increasingly recalcitrant and truculent membership. He tried to maintain Lewis's course of strict discipline and control of the membership. By 1969, the coal miners in Appalachia were suffering from some of the policies that Lewis himself had initiated in order to rescue the industry from the morass of the post-World War Two era. After the war Lewis had allowed coal operators to mechanize in order to lower production costs; the UMW even financed some of the mechanization. The price of coal, due to the efficiencies of mechanization, had remained almost constant for twenty years, but miners in the Appalachian coalfields paid the biggest price. In 1948, the anthracite coalfields employed 440,000 men; in 1969, fewer than 140,000 were at work in the mines. The U.S. Department of Labor estimated that the UMW's membership had decreased from its all time high of 600,000 to less than 100,000 active miners. Not only was membership in the union falling, mining remained the most dangerous job in America. Coalmine accidents claimed the lives of 307 men in 1968, and 9,000 more were injured. Pneumoconiosis, known popularly as "black lung" had been recognized in Great Britain for twenty years as an occupational hazard; in the United States it had hardly received any attention. Even excluding the "black lung" victims, coal mining was the nations most dangerous industry.[7]

In 1969, for the first time since 1928, the UMW's President faced an election challenge. Joseph Yablonski, a UMW Executive Board Member, citing Boyle's refusal to support West Virginia wildcat strikers in their attempt to get land-mark "black lung" legislation written into the state workmen's compensation package, and charging Boyle with nepotism and fraud, challenged Boyle's re-election. Boyle met the challenge in a rather straightforward manner; he conspired to have Yablonski murdered. The brutal murder of Yablonski and his family, the cumulative effects of wildcat strikes, fraud, Boyle's conviction, declining membership, and the increasing negotiating strength of coal operators stripped the union of much of its prestige and seriously undermined its support in the coal field communities.[8]

Arnold Miller won the presidency twice after Boyle's resignation. At first he was hailed as a more democratic leader and reformer. Soon, however, he became suspicious and quarrelsome and jealous of his control over union employees and local leadership. Amidst growing opposition and suffering from a heart attack, he resigned in 1979. The union vice-president, Samuel L. Church, without the benefit of a union-wide election, assumed the presidency in November 1979.[9]

Delegates to the December 1979, convention of the United Mine Workers of America adopted two positions that seemed to indicate a strong power base for Sam Church. In what many saw as a referendum on Church, the delegates agreed to waive the constitutional requirement for an election and appointed him president. Furthermore, the convention allowed Church to choose his own vice-president, again, without benefit of an election. The second day of the convention saw perhaps an even greater affirmation of the Church administration. The delegates agreed to increase the union's monthly dues from twelve to twenty-seven dollars. The recent expansion of the UMW into the UMWA, an international organization, required funding for an entirely new level of organization. Even more germane to the remarkable events in the Appalachian coalfields of 1989, was the creation of a strike fund. The delegates voted to assess each working member twenty-five dollars a week to finance approved work actions. The Pittston strike of 1989 was financed by the assessment of 1979.[10]

Rich Trumka defeated Sam Church in the election for union president in 1982. The election was not close. In the years to come some people saw the wisdom of Sam Church in raising dues and in creating the strike fund. The UMWA's transition from a local-national to a local-national-international organization required a significant increase in operating funds and without the security of the strike fund, begun under the Church administration, it is unlikely that the union could have successfully conducted the Pittston strike. However, those two measures destroyed Church's ability to win election, in his own right, as union president. In many ways Sam Church and his contributions have been overlooked, while his errors or misjudgments have been magnified. The producers omitted Sam Church from a film extolling the virtues and administrations of previous UMWA Presidents. An acquaintance commiserated with Church over his exclusion from the film and speculated that the dues increase and the strike fund assessment caused him to lose the election. By the time of the Pittston strike the strike fund had grown to over $100,000,000 and provided each striking miner with $200 per week and health insurance. The two things that caused him to lose the election proved to be absolutely essential for the survival of the union. Church brushed off the sympathetic and appreciative remarks with the observation that it did not really matter how he was viewed, he just did what he thought was right.[11]

Until 1982, no President of the United Mine Workers of America, or its UMW predecessor, held a college degree. Rich Trumka held a B.S. degree in Accounting and Economics from Pennsylvania State University and a law degree, emphasis on Labor Law, from Villanova. He satisfied the union requirement that all elected officials have a minimum number of years in actual mining experience by working periodically at a union mine, 1968-74.[12]

By the mid 1980s, the UMWA had some money in the bank, a growing strike fund, and for the moment at least, a relationship with all the unionized coal operators through the agency of the Bituminous Coal Operators Association. The BCOA and its role as contract negotiator for the coal operators made it possible for the union and for the operators to save time, money, and trouble in the negotiations at the end of each three-year contract period. Two aspects of this agreement are of particular relevance to the Pittston strike.

The UMWA brought health and retirement benefits to the membership. In 1946, the UMWA negotiated a multi-employer contract that created a Welfare and Retirement Fund. The fund built eight hospitals in Appalachia, established a number of community clinics, and recruited young doctors to practice in the coalfields. The UMWA is responsible for the quality and access to health care for the entire community. Even non-union coal miners benefited from the establishment of medical facilities. The health and retirement benefits were financed by a per-ton royalty on coal produced by each of the BCOA companies. Compliance with the royalty payment provisions and the payment of benefits to miners or their families was efficiently administered and maintained through procedures standardized within the framework of the UMW agreement with the BCOA.

The second aspect of this arrangement germane to the Pittston strike in particular concerned strikes in general. Miners and operators suffered from wildcat strikes. Sometimes the reason for strikes against mines was never articulated, or if articulated, was insignificant. Coal miners had a long history of strikes and a reputation for being extremely sensitive and volatile. A particularly charismatic miner could fan the flames of imagined or minor personal affronts into a full-blown work stoppage. On the other hand, mining was the most dangerous job in America and many miners felt that mines grossly de-emphasized safety considerations in favor of increased production.

In an attempt to limit the number of strikes and to insure that petty or solvable problems did not erupt into work stoppage, the UMWA and BCOA with the assistance of the Federal Labor Relations Board established specific conditions under which strikes were accepted as bonafide labor practices. The only way the union could conduct a strike against a member of the BCOA was in protest of violations of fair labor standards. Thus, only NLRB recognized and UMWA sanctioned strikes could be carried out for violations of safety standards and non-adherence to carefully articulated work rules. These rules and procedures covered only the relationship between the BCOA and the union. It was in the union's best interest for all coal operators to affiliate with BCOA. Previous experience with the Massey Company had demonstrated the union's vulnerability in individual company negotiations. In 1988, in the midst of negotiations for another three-year contract, the Pittston Coal Company informed the UMWA that it chose not to participate in the negotiations, nor would it continue affiliation with BCOA[13]

The Pittston Strike

So imbedded was the connection between coal strikes and violence against people and property that the entire region recognized at least one symbol that spoke flaming rhetoric, bombastic declarations, flat tires, smashed windshields, and broken bones – the jack rock.[14] Since the advent of pneumatic tires on coal trucks, the jack rock had become a regionally recognized symbol of labor trouble in the coalfields. To residents of Appalachia, labor strikes meant violence – the one was the product of the other. Historically the coal strikes of Appalachia had a long and well-deserved reputation for creating violence and disunity in the community. Among the better known incidences of labor violence in the coal fields – the vast majority of violence perpetrated not by the miners but by company hirelings and state or federal troops – the Latimer Massacre, Cabin Creek, Battle of Blair Mountain, Paint Creek, Matewan, Bloody Harlan, and Buffalo Creek attest to the nature of labor relations in Appalachia. In these uneven battles – miners vs. the company and the government – modern miners employed a homemade weapon, the jack rock. The jack rock would appear in the Pittston strike but in a surprising form.

In these coalfield communities, a miner was a union man or he was not and the choice taken often influenced social, religious, and political associations. Once a person's stance with regard to the union was known, there was little chance for redemption. Often innocent people, people with no interest in or connection to the union or the operator, were injured in the collateral violence of coal strikes. During strikes people in the community had to be circumspect; tempers were high and tensions often brought violent tendencies to the surface. Merchants, in particular, had to adhere to an informal, yet highly stylized, code of expressed attitude and conduct. Open support of a union strike offended the non-union population; non-support made for difficult relations with the UMWA members. The coalfield community had never totally embraced the union in its work actions. Individual communities were more or less inclined to support the UMWA, but the union had yet to ever experience the solidarity of the support of the entire coalfield community. Every strike had initially promised no violence and no destruction of the property of non-affiliated citizens. In every strike this promise was broken. Every work stoppage that had lasted for any significant length of time was accompanied by the ubiquitous jack rock and broken windshields, paint-doused cars, gunfire, and on the part of many coalfield citizens and their families, stark terror.

By April 1989, UMWA miners had been working at Pittston mines for fourteen months without a contract. Since late 1987, when Pittston had informed the UMWA that it chose to opt out of the BCOA, Pittston Group President, Mike Odum had insisted that the nature of the business conducted by Pittston required a change in the working rules mandated by the BCOA agreements. Pittston was a coal exporter, said Odum, therefore, shipping schedules required their coal properties to operate twenty-four hours a day, seven days a week, a clear and egregious exception to BCOA provisions. For fourteen months the UMWA had worked without a contract, a gesture of good will and common sense, the union thought. Surely this indicated the willingness of the UMWA leadership and rank-and-file to be calm, reasonable, peaceful. Perhaps the willingness of the UMWA to work without a contract and to extend the negotiations was a result of the lessons learned in negotiations with the A. T. Massey Company. Also claiming exceptional circumstances, the Massey Company had been allowed to negotiate outside the BCOA. According to Bo Willis, by this time a UMWA staffer, "we got our butts kicked." The UMWA was cautious; it had learned that individual company negotiations spread their own resources too thin. Then Mike Odum let the other shoe drop. Pittston, he said, would no longer contribute to the per-tonnage health and welfare fund. Pittston retirees, in other words, were in danger of losing one of the most prized – and in terms of the price paid in blood and suffering, most expensive – benefits ever achieved by working men and women. Professional health care existed in the coalfields only because the miners, particularly the UMWA, had asked, demanded, and fought for it. The one solid achievement for those fortunate enough to have lived to retirement in the Appalachian mines was the security that came from having health coverage and retirement income. Neither of these benefits were gifts from the coal operators. They were rights well paid for in muscle and blood.

In a 2001 interview, Bo Willis said that Mike Odum did the UMWA a favor when Pittston recused itself from the health and welfare fund. The people of Appalachia, those involved in mining and those not, were alarmed. Now a basic fundamental right, and in the minds of fiercely independent and self-reliant Appalachians, a sacred community trust had been violated. One need only look around in Appalachia and one could see an unusually robust medical community in isolated and economically depressed communities. The doctors, the clinics, the hospitals were there because the UMWA won them for its members. Non-union miners, workers in other occupations, community officials, teachers, preachers, all who lived in Appalachia benefited from the gifts brought to the community by the negotiators of the UMWA. Pittston looked at the union, and saw weakness, irresolution, and an adversary racked by recent sordid history and out of favor with the people. Pittston looked at the union, it should have looked at the community. The quarrel, as Pittston officials would soon find out, was not with a discredited and weakened labor union. Pittston's adversary this time was the entire community. In the eyes of most coalfield residents, Pittston was trying to take away what their fathers had earned; such a breech of trust was not just and it certainly was not decent.

During the months leading to formal declaration of the strike, talk among the UMWA members and the community centered on how things would be different this time. The union officials had insisted that members receive a new round of strike training. Over and over again facilitators indoctrinated the membership in the use of non-violent resistance, particularly the techniques employed by Civil Rights activists in the 1960s.

On 4 April 1989, for no particular specific reason, the UMWA announced that a strike against Pittston was imminent. Richard Trumka said that the strike would "begin in the very near future, just as soon as we have things organized." Pittston Group President Mike Odum seemed not to be very impressed: "We have heard this huff and puff routine for 15 months." Odum went on to say that the company was prepared to keep the mines open should a strike be called. Just about everyone agreed, whether they were miners or not, things were different this time. This strike was going to be different.[15]

Evidence of that difference manifested itself almost immediately. On the announcement of the strike, UMWA District President Jack Stump informed the newspapers that this strike would indeed be different. "We are a new breed of miner, better educated ... we have worked and prepared our people ... we can win a violence-free strike." The strike also looked different. When the strike commenced at 4:00 p.m. on 6 April these "new" miners showed up in a new "uniform;" they all wore camouflage. There was a more significant difference than the obvious ones. This time the company was not contesting labor; it was, so the people thought, attacking the community. The forces in the struggle against Pittston had a "new" miner, a new constituency (the community), and a new uniform. The UMWA also had new sophistication. Bo Willis remembers the transformation:

> It dawned on me in a local meeting one night that the person that was the loudest wasn't necessarily right. I think all UMWA members began to realize that. We began to really listen and to read our contract. It wasn't long before we were no longer as apt to listen to the fellow that shouted the loudest. We were ready to try new ways of doing things.[16]

The "movement" had the manpower and the accouterments, all it lacked were the symbols that accompany all great human endeavors. Such symbols soon appeared: single share stock certificates, yellow ribbons, jack rocks, and jack rock earrings.

The strike began with an almost carnival attitude. Striking miners borrowed the "yellow ribbon" from the popular song by Tony Orlando and soon the yellow ribbons appeared on cars, bridges, bicycles, houses, people, and any amenable animals. Striking miners and non-affiliated community members smiled at the coal truck drivers and waved their yellow ribbons. Miners "sat in the road" a term that signified picket lines and minor traffic flow disruptions. Soon the crowd outside the mines and on the roads connecting them became the venue for homemade music and celebratory intercourse. One observer noted the music, "guitars, banjos and fiddles," and that he did not see a single beer can the whole time.[17]

While the UMWA and the coalfield communities played, laughed, and visited along the entrances to Pittston facilities, the company and the state also marshaled their forces. Pittston hired Vance Security to protect its property and the Commonwealth of Virginia dispatched unprecedented numbers of state police to the area in anticipation of violence and disorder.[18]

This strike was different, it did not resemble those of the past, and it carried the support of the community. There were noticeably few reports of jack rocks and even fewer reports of damage to company vehicles. The miners were quite restrained, a remarkable fact considering that 1,600 miners in Virginia, West Virginia, and Kentucky were out on strike. Despite Pittston's use of strikebreakers to run their operations, the UMWA miners did not block access to company property and company officials made no reports of intimidation.[19]

As the strike picked up steam, more evidence of the "difference" in this strike came as the community, particularly women, supported the UMWA. Fifty women formed an auxiliary unit of a UMWA local in protest of the company's suspension of health and retirement benefits to retirees and widows. These women, many of them wearing miniature jack rocks as earrings joined the UMWA picket line at the Pittston Coal Group headquarters in Lebanon, Virginia. Meanwhile near Carbo, striking miners put up a shelter near the railroad tracks leading into Moss #3 coal preparation plant. Railroad workers refused to cross picket lines and railroad supervisors operated the trains in and out of the facility. Not much coal was getting into the preparation plant, said the strikers. Marty Hudson, assistant to UMWA Vice-President Cecil Roberts, said that union leaders thought that Pittston production was down significantly and that the company had been able to hire no more than a handful of replacement workers: "They have called everyone in Pound and Coeburn. Some UMWA members laid off as long as six years ago have been asked to return to work." As the strike wore on negotiations made no progress; tension, incidents, arrests, and the number of state policemen increased.[20]

Mother Jones (or at least a revitalized memory of her) revisited the coalfields on 18 April. Thirty-seven wives and mothers, calling themselves "The Daughters of Mother Jones," occupied the Pittston company headquarters in Lebanon, Virginia.

Dressed in white blouses, camouflage scarves, blue jeans, each woman waved an American flag and most sported jack rock earrings. This thirty-hour takeover of the company offices represents one of the high points of the Pittston Strike. The women occupied the offices and remained on one side of the lobby marked by a velvet cord. Union supporters brought in food and bedding for the non-violent militants. Upon leaving, the Daughters of Mother Jones and their families and friends held an impromptu rally on company grounds.[21]

Throughout the spring and summer the company and union negotiated with no results, and according to both sides, no hope of results. In the coal fields the number of strikers on picket lines increased, vehicles displaying yellow ribbons positioned themselves in front of company trucks and slowed to a snail's pace, hindering the flow of coal. There was an increase in reported incidents of maltreatment of striking miners by the Virginia State Police and Vance Security. There were some reports of jack rocks and spray paint, but the number and severity of those incidents appeared almost trivial when contrasted with the magnitude of the strike and recent labor history. Union members struck the Westmoreland Coal Company in an attempt to prevent Westmoreland's sale of coal to Pittston. After one week Westmoreland agreed to stop the sales. Local magistrates issued strict limits on the number of pickets allowed at each site. The miners promptly ignored such limits and were just as promptly arrested. By May 9, more than 1,300 striking workers and, significantly, their supporters had been arrested.

Things were indeed different from other strikes. The good humor continued and while any violence or destruction of property is too much, the incidences of violence and destruction were, compared to other strikes, insignificant. Some Virginia State Police dispute the reputation of the Pittston strike as being mostly violence free. Sgt. Joe Peters and Trooper Roger Warden of the Virginia State Police remembered the Pittston strike as violent. Sgt. Peters said that, "jack rocks weren't the worst of it. They were throwing railroad spikes through windshields." For Sgt Peters any gathering of men, or women, or lately even teenagers, wearing camouflage was a cause for alarm. Trooper Warden complained about having to "run the gantlet (*sic*) on Route 652." In response to these complaints, Rich Trumpka called for an end to the wildcat strikes conducted in support of the Pittston action. However, even according to police officials, much if not most of the relatively little violence was perpetrated by the "tourists" and friends of the miners rather than by the UMWA membership.[22]

Jesse Jackson brought his Operation Push to Norton, Virginia; and left no doubt about his support for the union and the community. He was a riveting speaker, second only perhaps, to the UMWA's own Cecil Roberts. Bo Willis enjoyed Jackson's messages, but he remembered Roberts's comments at the Jackson rally: "You can't go to church and find a better preacher than Cecil Roberts!" Coal miners in Pennsylvania sent $71,000 to help the union in whatever way deemed necessary. Volunteers from other labor organizations gathered at the makeshift Camp Solidarity on the other side of Carbo from Moss #3 and Communications

Workers of America (CWA) came from Kentucky to help man the picket lines. Things were very different from other strikes. Local law enforcement officials gave the state police only surly and unenthusiastic cooperation. Women wore jack rock earrings and camouflage scarves and tee shirts. In every town and along every road the men wore camouflage. High school students formed UMWA auxiliaries and left school to support their daddies in jail.[23]

There was also something very different about UMWA's leadership. Trumpka was a lawyer and he used his skills in a way that surprised and alarmed company officials. At the May 10 stockholders meeting of the Pittston Coal Group in Greenwich, CT, company executives, especially group president Odum, were surprised to see about 100 striking miners from Southwest Virginia. The miners held proxies in their hands and they intended to vote them. The next day's tally resulted in a very narrow union loss. Trumka had hired a proxy solicitation firm, the first time in history that any labor union had done so, and almost garnered enough support to win union demands in the boardroom rather than at the negotiating table.[24]

Back in the coalfields things were getting even more interesting. Two Commonwealth Attorneys were shown to have ownership interest in both union and non-union coal operations. Questions concerning their qualifications were forwarded to Richmond. Local magistrates issued restraining orders and a federal judge jailed union leaders and levied huge fines. It is important to note that the arrests, jail sentences, and fines came only from the miners' refusal to abide by the limits on the number of pickets allowed. On 6 June, U.S. Judge Glen M. Williams found UMWA District #28 officials guilty of contempt and ordered them jailed until they "purged themselves of contempt." Jack Stump, one of the jailed UMWA officials leaving the Abingdon, VA, Courthouse in leg-irons told reporters, "The strike's not over." Asked when he planned to give the judge what he wanted, Stump responded, "When the strike's over." Judge Williams also fined the men $13,000 each and proved particularly harsh to the UMWA; he imposed fines calculated to bankrupt the union. In addition to his obvious company bias, Judge Williams was a study in arrogance. He once told Bo Willis in U.S. Federal Court that he (the judge) could do whatever he wanted. When Jesus came back, the judge allowed, he would come back as a U.S. Federal Judge. By 8 May the UMWA had been fined over three million dollars. (A U.S. Circuit Court later overturned all fines.) The leadership of the UMWA District #28 sat in jail in Roanoke and read Taylor Branch's *Parting the Waters*, and discussed the tactics used in the Civil Rights movement; coalfield communities solidified their support for the UMWA and the strike against Pittston.[25]

A Dickenson County resident told the *Coalfield Progress* that people not involved with the coal industry were supporting the UMWA in larger numbers than ever before. The resident stated that in times past business people were very reluctant to express their support one way or another. Now it seemed that the community was bonding together so tightly that business people had become very involved in support of the miners. One businessperson was not at all reticent about showing his support. The sign outside Wayne Resnick's "M&R Groceries" respectfully advised that, for the duration of the strike, no service would be provided to Virginia State Police.

Federal mediators could not bring the two sides closer. Union executives were in jail, the union fines were increasing at an alarming pace and 1,500 union miners were still on strike. The strike was still notably violence free, and was more and more beginning to resemble the style and mannerisms employed in the American Civil Rights demonstrations of the 1960s.[26]

By late June the contempt charges against the District #28 leadership had been dropped and the three had been released from the Roanoke jail. The malefactors had solemnly promised not to do it again. The union and the company were no nearer contract agreements and on 22 June Mike Odum announced that the company was dropping all negotiations and intended to return to full production without UMWA employees. Fines continued to mount. On 28 June, a federal magistrate announced that the union would be fined $100,00 per day until it reduced the number of pickets to ordered totals. All the fines had been levied, not because of the activities of the strikers, but because of the sheer size of picket lines and supporting demonstrations. In short, the magistrate fined the union for the actions of the community in support of the strike. The company still tried to injure the status of the union in public opinion. Mike Odum told a television station that UMWA miners had developed a high-tech jack rock catapult and that union folks hauled it around in the back of a pick-up truck. No evidence of any sort relating to such a device is extant.[27]

Despite the community support, despite the national publicity, despite the rather impressive discipline of the rank and file, and despite the more sophisticated and expert leadership of the UMWA, by summer much of the enthusiasm and verve had diminished. The movement needed another "shot in the arm" and in early September the UMWA began preparations for such a treatment.

The Occupation of Moss #3

In early September union leadership approached certain striking miners in Virginia, West Virginia, and Kentucky and asked if the miner would be willing to be at the disposal of the union for a few days. These conversations were always held one-on-one and conducted in a way that attracted no attention. The miners so interviewed were not told what the union had in mind, they were simply asked about their willingness to help out and informed that they might be gone from home for a while. A few days after the initial conversation some of the miners were instructed to be on call at home on the weekend of 16 September. If someone called and said to "Kiss your wife and kids goodbye" they were to report to a specified place at Camp Solidarity by a designated time.[28]

At the same time that the miners were being individually recruited, other union leaders were planning rallies throughout the coalfields. It was important, they told the rank and file, and the members of the community, that families and friends be encouraged to attend one of the rallies this Sunday. It would show solidarity, encourage the striking miners, and demonstrate once again the peaceful nature of the strike for the sake of decency. On Wednesday company operatives bought 101 individual shares of Pittston stock in the names of 100 miners and Jim Sessions, the marvelously militant, activist, minister who accompanied the UMWA through the gates of Moss #3.

The men on the buses had found waiting for each of them at the gathering place a backpack containing a flashlight, extra batteries, toilet paper, bottled water, toiletries, enough food for ten days, and a plastic sheet. Each vehicle also carried a "team" bag. It contained a bullhorn, walkie-talkies, a radio, extra batteries, a deck of cards, and a Bible. As each man stepped out of his vehicle, he was instructed to raise his hands over his head, stock certificate in hand, and march into the plant.

The miner's vehicles arrived at the entrance to Moss #3 at precisely 4:15, the time that the State Police changed shifts. As the day shift left the property, newly felled trees blocked the roads behind them, thus preventing their hasty repair to the Pittston facility. The trees also impeded the prompt arrival of the replacements – Sunday afternoons often found the relief late.

The two Vance officers looked at the 101 camouflaged resolute men – hands held high and clutching a stock certificate – walking toward the gate. Upon being informed that these men were merely stockholders here to inspect the condition of their property, the Vance officers took refuge in the sanctuary provided by their vehicles. The plant manager was at the plant that Sunday afternoon. Upon being told that the miners were acting in a role as corporate stockholders and were simply inspecting company property and upon realizing that at least three of the occupiers had extensive experience in running the plant and satisfied that there was nothing he could do, the manger left. The Moss Preparation Plant #3 had been occupied by the UMWA. Not a weapon was among them and not a harsh word had been spoken.[29]

The miners gained access to a platform at the top of the structure originally intended for placement of air conditioning equipment. It was a flat space about fifty feet wide and 200 feet long. From the platform the miners could see a bridge over 200 yards away and the flat spaces leading to and flanking the bridge. A look in the opposite direction allowed them to peer into the staging area for Vance Security and Virginia State Police. Most of the attention was given to the police area. Would the police try to evict them? Bo Willis remembers the tension of that first night especially.

About six o'clock in the evening that Sunday, September 17, men on the platform began noticing a gathering of cars and pick-ups and people along the bridge, on it, under it, and adjacent to it. Fearing some sort of police action, the miners trained their field glasses on the crowd and were startled to see children, women, and men all wearing camouflage and yellow ribbons. The various Sunday afternoon rallies had terminated at the bridge above Moss #3. There began a ritual that occurred throughout the occupation of the coal preparation plant. The crowd began to shout to the miners and sing union songs. The miners on the platform responded to the community gathered in support below. People took turns using hand-held radios to communicate with family and friends and binoculars on the platform and at the bridge engaged in identifying loved ones. As darkness fell, the crowd on the bridge noticed that the miners had all trained their flashlights on the wall behind them. There in three-foot-high letters, now visible as the flashlights illuminated the letters against the dark backdrop, were the words: UMWA FOREVER. There was a brief interlude of silence and then an enormous roar of approval engulfed the area around Moss Preparation Plant #3. The miners and the community repeated this ritual every night of the occupation.

The attention garnered by the occupation of Moss #3, according to UMWA staffer Bo Willis, was the most important factor in convincing Secretary of Labor Elizabeth Dole to demand arbitration, a movement that the UMWA had requested from the beginning. With arbitration in place the UMWA and the coalfield community ended the occupation of Moss #3. While in arbitration the strike continued for another four months. It ended in an agreement that really did not please either side completely. It was, as are most good things in America, a compromise. The company arranged some alterations in work scheduling that allowed it to operate more efficiently. The union protected the health and welfare benefits of its retirees. The UMWA entered one of its most popular eras in American history, approaching the acclaim it gained during the halcyon days of John L. Lewis. The UMWA truly became an international union. Australian, Japanese, and even Russian miners honored UMWA rules. The Appalachia communities experienced the heady wine of successful community activism and demonstrated to the rest of the nation the virtue of discipline and the value of decency. Memories of the Pittston strike come easily in Southwestern Appalachia; they most often come accompanied by a smile.

Conclusion

The "thunder in the coal fields" achieved most of its volume from two almost unbelievable and aberrant developments. First of all, the communities in Appalachia coalesced in support of the striking miners – a remarkable development in its own right. Second, these miners, although schooled and socialized in an environment in which strikes, violence and destruction were synonymous, practiced aggressive non-violence. Drawing on and studying such historical antecedents as the United Auto Workers of America and its occupation of the Flint, Michigan, auto plant and the community-building and public relations techniques employed in the Civil Rights Movement, the coalfields became a community and the UMWA became its champion. The remarkable events in the Virginia coalfields of 1988 and 1990 – like all remarkable events – have left ephemera. These objects, unremarkable by themselves, serve as eloquent visual shorthand for memory. In addition to the column-feet of newsprint and the articles in journals and books, the "thunder in the coal fields" leaves testimony in non-verbal objects. There are camouflage shirts, pants, and scarves; there are certificates of one share of stock made out in the name of an ordinary miner; there are yellow ribbons borrowed from Tony Orlando; and there are two kinds of jack rocks. The traditional jack rock is only vaguely noticeable in the accounts of the Pittston strike, but jack rock earrings adorned the women of the community as a badge of honor and an emblem of beauty. The "thunder in the coal fields" was a sort of soothing, friendly thunder. It was dramatic, it was intense, but it did not conceal bolts of lightning violence. Just as women of the coal fields chose to reshape the traditional symbol of violence (jack rock) into a an adornment of their countenances (earrings), the people of the coal fields chose solidarity through non-violence to defend rights won by their fathers.

Stock certificates, camouflage, jack rocks, and jack rock earrings – these disparate elements tell the story of how community and labor coalesced and found common ground in the coal fields of Appalachia – a remarkable story, indeed. However, this tale may have something to offer contemporary society. The pursuit of unity and thus, justice, is often motivated by an appeal to history. The people of the coalfields embraced the UMWA's struggle not because of any political indoctrination or protocol. The people recognized in the Pittston actions an attack on basic decency. The thought of elderly miners having to ask for charity medical treatment – miners who had paid dearly for such benefits – struck the people of Appalachia as decidedly indecent. A man might be a philanderer, a spendthrift, a heavy drinker, and a most conspicuous liar, and still retain a network of close family, friends, and colleagues. He could still, despite all those failures, be decent. The communities in Appalachia would not, could not, and did not cheerfully tolerate people or institutions that were not "decent." During the Pittston strike, the coalfield communities had little difficulty ascertaining which side was decent. It was not decent that old folks should ever have to face the threat of begging for what they had already paid. In finding solidarity with the union miners, the community chose both activism and non-violence. Violence was a part of Appalachian history, but even at its most justified occurrence, violence was not "decent." Deeper in collective community history were memories of how basic or "decent" values emerged and how those attributes were distributed to the community. One of the "decent" values was a veneration, respect, and compassion for the elderly. Those that had spent their lives in labor should at least have the fruits thereof. The community and the UMWA remembered the basic values that made people and institutions "decent." From that memory came a community struggle for decency in which violence was firmly adjudged as not decent. Perhaps, also, from those memories will come other ones that may help shape further non-violent struggles for "decency."

Perhaps a piece of shorthand might come into view as activists plan actions. Activists might remember the earrings that adorned the countenance of women in the struggle for decency in the coalfields. Such visual "short hand" might remind them of the power of community and the struggle for decency that transformed the jack rock from a symbol of violence to an object that enhances beauty. The transition from jack rocks to earrings is more of an intellectual journey than a physical evolution, for the struggle for decency is embedded in the history of values. In retrospect, it is rather remarkable that 100 angry, bitter, and militant coal miners did not vent their outrage on company property. Bo Willis is convinced that he understands how that happened. "The community would not let us tear down the plant. If the we had not had the support of the community I doubt that there would be a thing standing on the site of Moss #3." The community chose the decent things; it chose non-violence out of respect for decency.

Notes

The material for this article comes, mainly, from *The Coalfield Progress, The Roanoke Times and World News*, an interview with Bo Willis, and the marvelous chapter by Jim Sessions and Fran Ansley, "Singing Across Dark Spaces." The special section of *The Roanoke Times and World News*, "Thunder in the Coal Fields," is a remarkable narrative of the history of the Pittston strike and is of prime interest to anyone studying this labor history. The best treatment of the occupation of Moss #3 is, and I suspect always will be, the work by Sessions and Ansley. Both were actors – one in the plant, one by the bridge – and their insights and narrative are winsome, provocative and profound.

1   George (Bo) Willis, interview by Fred C. Smith, Big Stone Gap, Virginia, 17 February 2001. The tape recording is in the author's possession. Jim Sessions and Fran Ansley. "Singing Across Dark Spaces: The Union/Community Takeover of Pittston's Moss #3 Plant," in Stephen L. Fisher, (ed.), *Fighting Back in Appalachia: Traditions of Resistance and Change* (Philadelphia: Temple University Press, 1993), pp. 199-223; "Thunder in the Coalfields," *Roanoke* (Virginia) *Times and World News* 29 April 1990.
2   Bo Willis interview.
3   David M. Kennedy, *Freedom From Fear: The American People in Depression and War, 1929-1945* (New York: Oxford University Press, 1999), pp. 298-99. At this time the UMW had not yet become an international union.
4   Ibid.; Roger Biles, *A New Deal for the American People* (DeKalb: Northern Illinois University Press, 1991), pp. 79, 82, 156-157, 160-63, 170, 188; T. H. Watkins, *The Great Depression: America in the 1930s* (Boston: Little Brown and Company, 1993), pp. 46, 83, 86, 167, 279-82.
5   Biles, *A New Deal for the American People*, pp. 155, 162-163.
6   Maier B. Fox, *United We Stand: The United Mine Workers of America, 1880-1990* (No place of publication given: United Mine Workers of America, 1990), 418-34; Biles, Ibid.

7　Bo Willis interview; *Roanoke Times*, 14 November 1969.

8　Bo Willis interview; *Roanoke Times* 14 November 1969; "The Miners Play Rough: Electing a Union President," *Time*, 2 August 1969; "Leadership Fight Looms Among the Miners" *Business Week*, 7 June 1969 "Lewis Heir Faces Revolt," *Business Week*, 15 November 1969.

9　Bo Willis interview; *Coalfield Progress* (Norton, VA), 22 November 1979, p. 3.

10　Bo Willis interview; *Coalfield Progress,* 14 December 1979.

11　*Coalfield Progress*, 4 April 1989; 14 December 1989.

12　*United Mine Workers Journal*, 16-30 September 1982; Bo Willis interview.

13　*Roanoke Times*, 19 May 1987; Bo Willis interview.

14　A jack rock is constructed by bending two large nails into a 90° angle. When soldered or welded at the joint of the two bends, the instrument has four legs, two of which remain pointed upward no matter how the instrument is thrown or how it lands. The sharpened ends easily punctured truck tires. For heavy duty use, some miners would fashion their jack rocks from re-bar rather than nails, presumably, to better puncture the tires of the giant coal machines. Much of the foregoing and that about community attitudes vis-a-vis the UMWA and labor strikes comes from conversation with historian, Brian McKnight. McKnight is a native of the area, a student of Appalachian history, and currently Visiting Professor of History at the University of Virginia's College at Wise.

15　*Coalfield Progress*, 4 April 1989.

16　Bo Willis interview.

17　Ibid.

18　*Coalfield Progress*, April 6-May 9; *Roanoke Times*, May 9-12; Bo Willis interview.

19　*Coalfield Progress*, April 6-May 9; *Roanoke Times*, May 9-12.

20　*Coalfield Progress*, 18 April 1989.

21　*Coalfield Progress*, April 20; *Roanoke Times*, Thunder in the Coal Fields."

22　*Roanoke Times*, "Thunder in the Coal Fields."

23　*The Norton* (VA) *Post*, 3 May; *Roanoke Times*, Thunder in the Coal Fields," Bo Willis interview.

24　*Roanoke Times*, 11 May, p. 12; *Coalfield Progress*, 11 May; Bo Willis interview.

25　Ibid.

26　*Coalfield Progress*, 6 May; *United Mine Workers Journal* 7 (July-August 1971): 7.

27　*Coalfield Progress*, March–July; *Roanoke Times*, May–July; Bo Willis interview.

28　Bo Willis interview; Sessions and Ansley.

29　*Roanoke Times*, "Thunder in the Coal Fields"; Sessions and Ansley; Bo Willis interview.

PART 3

Beyond Justice and Injustice

Chapter 10

A Case of Communist Indoctrination and American Enticement during the Korean War

Brian D. McKnight
University of Virginia–Wise

During the third week of September 1953, a disturbing story broke nationwide regarding the fates of twenty-three soldiers held prisoner by the Chinese. The men, most of whom had been captured during the initial Chinese offensive in November 1950, had spent more than two and a half years in prison camps scattered throughout North Korea when peace was brokered and prison exchanges began. Shockingly, when freedom was finally offered to these men, they refused to accept it, preferring instead to stay behind Communist lines. For the four months that followed, most of these nonrepatriates stood their ground and refused to return to the United Nations' lines. In response, the United States Army began a program through which it hoped to convince these men to abandon their plans to live in China. Ultimately, two American soldiers did accept repatriation, and although Americans in general reveled in their homecomings, the political culture of the era sought retribution. Before discussing punishment, however, the two men who returned became players in a drama which military and political officials hoped would result in the repatriation of the twenty-one who remained behind. In the end, the efforts failed and those nonrepatriates emigrated to China. In this case, the policy of the United States regarding the remaining prisoners did more to strengthen their resolve than weaken it and teaches our modern nation a valuable lesson about the oft-conflicting natures of liberty and power.

Although the initial reports of these men refusing repatriation shook the entire nation, the news had a particular impact on the men's hometowns – places like Hillsboro, Mississippi; Urania, Louisiana; Wink, Texas; and Cracker's Neck, Virginia. The young men who had left their homes only three years before had become the first Americans to fall victim *en masse* to enemy propaganda. Family and friends questioned their sanity and motives, while military officials began to address one of their great fears. Throughout the conflict in Korea, prisoners of war who had gained release from the Chinese told of systematic attempts at indoctrination. From the first days of capture, their captors began a regiment of pro-Communist lectures with a reward system in place as motivation for steady attendance and frequent participation. That intellectual barrage combined with starvation and a climate of constant fear to produce disturbing results for the U.S. military.

In May 1953, hoping to combat this tactic now becoming known as "brainwashing," the U.S. Army secretly flew more than twenty men who had been recently released from captivity from Tokyo to Valley Forge, Pennsylvania, where they briefly underwent a series of controversial therapies. The degrading nature of the army's experiment failed miserably. Psychiatrists treated the men as if they had been thoroughly convinced by their captors, when in reality, only a decided minority of prisoners seriously embraced Communist ideology. The men themselves were disgusted by the apparent distrust of them by their government – four to the point that they bitterly refused to speak publicly about their experience at Valley Forge.[1] The bad press that followed also embarrassed the army. One unidentified army doctor, referring to the reports of the un-brainwashing activities at Valley Forge, announced, "I don't know where this idea started, but there's one thing for sure – we're not running a damned laundromat here."[2] Despite the reaction of the U.S. Army, it was clear that for the first time in American history, a wartime enemy was not only attempting to win the broad political and physical war, but also to win the ideological conflict one soldier at a time. By late September, the American fear that China might succeed in its indoctrination work became a reality.

In the small mountain town of Big Stone Gap, Virginia, the local newspaper announced that China had reported a neighborhood man, Corporal Edward Dickenson, as one of twenty-three prisoners refusing to be returned to the United States. The fear of this "unconfirmed and unverified" report was evident in the article's cautionary prefaces and addendums.[3] The shock of the news was recorded in the voices of family members horrified by the news. Gladys Peoples of Memphis, Tennessee, mother of Corporal Clarence Adams, saw it as "another Communist trick." Her son was surely being held there against his will and would not "cast his lot" with his captors.[4] Bessie Dickenson felt similarly. "Eddie just isn't that kind of a boy." Like Gladys Peoples, she reasoned that "something has happened to him."[5] The grandmother of Oklahoman Samuel Hawkins blamed the Democrats.[6] Just as families and friends came to grips with the building situation, McCarthy-era America began to cautiously position itself around the issue.

Almost as soon as the Chinese newscaster had read off the twenty-three names, discussion began on numerous fronts as to how the men might be convinced to return to the United States. A leading figure in the Los Angeles area American Legion suggested flying each man's mother to Korea to meet with her son. Ed Dickenson's parents were sure that they could convince their son to return home if only they could talk to him. Portia Howe of Alden, Minnesota, was more proactive. On the day that the name of her son, Private Richard R. Tenneson, was released, she contacted military authorities and suggested that tape recordings from family members be sent to each of the POWs in the hopes that the tapes would make them rethink their decision.[7]

An editorial in a Virginia newspaper placed the contest in larger terms. These twenty-three men represented a moral victory for whichever side eventually won them, particularly for the Chinese. Open sympathy for Communist ideology was dangerous during the early 1950s, if these twenty-three products of a free society eschewed such a concept preferring instead life within an unfree nation, the Chinese might be able to claim one final victory in a war filled with defeats on both sides. Aware of the political importance of getting these men to return to the United States, the Department of Defense developed a plan it hoped would convince the twenty-three to return.[8]

Understanding that the institution of the family held more sway than broad theoretical ideas, the army adopted some of the suggestions already published in newspapers. Following Portia Howe's lead in early October, it encouraged the families of these men to record a message to their loved one which would be delivered by military aircraft to Korea. All of the families participated in this program. Someone from the community brought a portable recorder to Bessie Dickenson's house so she could tape her message. In Rhode Island, a local radio station brought family members, friends, and a priest in to record a message to Richard Corden, who would later be identified as the leader of the nonrepatriates. All of this activity was in vain as the POWs refused to listen to the taped messages.[9]

Some families and friends went further in their attempts to contact their loved one. Aaron Wilson's family drove from Urania, Louisiana, to Washington, D.C., with Otho Bell's wife hoping to secure permission to travel to Korea to speak directly with their family members.[10] William Randall, a native of nearby Olla, Louisiana, stationed in Tokyo, received permission to fly to Panmunjom and try to speak with Wilson. He only got close enough to see Wilson from a distance – the prisoner declined the meeting.[11] Perhaps the most compelling story is that of Portia Howe, mother of Richard Tenneson. As her name symbolically suggests, she was an impressively independent woman. When she heard that her son had refused repatriation, she vowed to travel to Tokyo and bring her son home. The town of Alden, Minnesota, was canvassed with fliers asking for donations to pay for her flight, and after more than $200 was raised, she began her journey. She made it to Tokyo, but no further. While army officials delivered some letters from her to Richard, they would not grant permission for a visit. Though her hopes were elevated when Tenneson accepted the mail, they were dashed when he publicly read his hurtful response to the assembled press corps.[12] In Big Stone Gap, Virginia, the town prepared to welcome three of its young men home who had been prisoners of the Chinese. To Bessie Dickenson, this occasion proved an excellent opportunity to begin her own program of counter-information. She asked the readers of her community to write Ed and ask him to return. Feeling that a groundswell of local support would have an impact on her son, Bessie had the paper publish an address where mail could be sent for direct delivery to the POW camp.[13] By late October, the world had only known of these twenty-three nonrepatriates for a single month, but nearly 300 letters had been delivered to the custodial barracks where the men were housed.[14] It is unknown how many of these letters were opened and read by their intendeds, but the enticement effort would soon glean results.

On the night of 20 October, Ed Dickenson, faking a severe toothache, asked to see a doctor at the neutral camp where the men were being held. Once alone with the doctor at the clinic, Dickenson revealed the real reason behind his complaint. "I want to go home."[15] The news of Dickenson's defection sprinted across the newswires and the unassuming young man instantly became a valuable commodity. Though Claude Batchelor, one of the more doctrinaire members of the group, would later claim Dickenson was one of the least committed of the nonrepatriates, to the Department of Defense and Department of State, he might be able to convince some of the others to leave.[16]

For weeks following Dickenson's walkout, he alternated his time between giving interviews to the army's Counter Intelligence Corps and drafting various pleas hoping to lead his former comrades out of Panmunjom. Though Secretary of Defense Charles E. Wilson had vowed at the first report of the twenty-three nonrepatriates that the men would be looked upon "sympathetically"[17] and President Dwight Eisenhower publicly wondered why more American servicemen had not succumbed to the enemy's indoctrination efforts,[18] Dickenson appeared guarded and distrustful.[19] On several occasions, he predicted that some of the less committed prisoners would follow his lead back to freedom.[20] He also wrote a letter to those remaining behind ensuring them that they "should not have any fear at all of being harmed if you come back." Despite his scrawl, the letter was not the sole product of its author. The army had been impressed with the grassroots support that had come in the form of hundreds of letters to the remaining men and helped make Dickenson's message more appealing. Testing the manly resolve and political commitment of the nonrepatriates, the army enclosed a photo of the recently repatriated corporal in a new uniform with several pretty girls surrounding him and offered a precise calculation of back pay owed one of the men based on his rank and time in captivity.[21]

By late November, Ed Dickenson was offering assistance to the enticement effort by living the good life. He was flown to Washington, D.C., where he reunited with his mother and father after more than three years away from home. The Dickensons spent a couple of days touring the city and basking in the national attention.[22] Although Dickenson's reintroduction to American life appeared ideal and President Eisenhower had even used the parable of the *Prodigal Son* to describe how he hoped the nation would react to a nervous Dickenson, the remaining twenty-two still harbored serious doubts about America's sincerity. An anonymous source reported in early November that only three of the remaining twenty-two men were sincere Communists. The other nineteen remained behind out of fear of reprisals, such as trials for treason, once they returned to America. The informant also relayed that the Chinese captors had compiled "confession" documents that would be sent to the United States Government to be against any man who chose home over China.[23] The grassroots nature of the letter-writing campaign began to backfire in early November. The neutral Indian delegation, which managed prisoners on both sides while negotiations were taking place, threatened to stop the delivery of all mail to the twenty-two. It seems that several misguided, but well-meaning, correspondents had written the men urging them to return and used threatening language to convince them. Some had even enclosed newspaper clippings citing rumors of prosecution if the men did not rethink their decision quickly.[24]

Those who remained behind had time to decide. The two sides had settled on an agreement that would allow interviews by representatives of the Chinese and the U.N. until Christmas, during which the men could be repatriated at any time. After the interviews ended, those who remained would be given one month, during which they had limited contact with the outside, to make their decision. During that final month, they could also leave anytime. On 23 January 1954, any of the twenty-two who remained at Panmunjom would get their wish – to go to China.[25]

There were no changes for the rest of the year, but as 1954 opened, another POW walked out. After a New Years Eve party, Corporal Claude J. Batchelor of Kermit, Texas, walked up to one of the Indian guards and announced that he wanted to go home.[26] Married to a Japanese woman since before the war, Batchelor had received hundreds of letters from her in Japan begging him to leave the Communist compound. For him, however, the choice was not easy. He had been one of the leaders of the progressive (pro-Communist) movement inside the prison, but had recently been eclipsed by a better-educated and more doctrinaire colleague.[27] Despite the fact that American newspapers had recorded Ed Dickenson's happy family reunion and his return home to Virginia, Batchelor left Panmunjom expecting retaliation from the U.S. Army.

On the day before the 23 January deadline for repatriation, Ed Dickenson's leave expired. He reported to Walter Reed Army Medical Center where he was admitted for observation. Although he did not see it at the time, his hospital room was, in reality, a holding cell. The next day, the neutral Indians abandoned their posts at Panmunjom having fulfilled the requirements of their duty. The remaining twenty-one soldiers were free to go with the Chinese. As the clock struck midnight on 23 January in Korea, it reached 10:00 a.m. in Washington, D.C. and military authorities walked into Dickenson's hospital room and placed him under arrest. Charged with "holding unlawful 'intercourse' with the enemy" and "currying favor with his captors 'to the detriment' of fellow prisoners," Dickenson again became a prisoner, this time of his own nation.[28]

Over the course of the months that followed, Dickenson's defense team prepared their case and Claude Batchelor was also arrested on similar charges. Beginning in late April and stretching into early May 1954, in a courtroom at Fort

McNair, the U.S. Army attempted to illustrate how tough it could be on communism. At the same time and only one-half mile north at the capitol, Senator Joseph McCarthy was busy trying to show how soft the army was on communism. In the middle of their fight stood Dickenson, Batchelor, and by this time, twenty-one other soldiers now living in China.

By late May, Dickenson had been convicted and sentenced to ten years in prison. On 30 September, Claude Batchelor was given a life sentence, which was reduced to twenty years within a month.[29] In the meantime, the twenty-one men who had refused to return to the United States had been dishonorably discharged. By 29 July 1955, Ed Dickenson had already been at Fort Leavenworth, Kansas, for more than a year and Claude Batchelor was nearing his first year in custody in Texas. Things too had changed for the twenty-one in China. That day, Lewis Griggs, Otho Bell, and William Cowart arrived in San Francisco, California, seeking to renounce their formerly held communist views and resume their lives in America. Although they were immediately arrested, civilian courts refused to allow the army to prosecute men who were no longer members of the military. Four months later, the three walked out of jail as free men. Two years later, Dickenson's sentence was halved and he again made it home from prison in time for Thanksgiving dinner. And in March 1959, Batchelor, whose sentence had been reduced from life to twenty years, then to ten years, was freed.[30] By the time all of this happened, McCarthy was dead, his philosophy severely weakened, and America had lost interest – all things that should have happened five years earlier.

Notes

1   *New York Times*, 4 May 1953.
2   *The Nation*, 23 May 1953.
3   *Kingsport Times-News* (TN), 24 September 1953.
4   Ibid.
5   *The Post* (Big Stone Gap, VA), 1 October 1953.
6   *New York Times*, 25 September 1953.
7   *Kingsport Times-News* (TN), 25 September 1953.
8   *Bristol Herald Courier* (VA), 27 September 1953.
9   Virginia Pasley, *21 Stayed: The Story of the American GI's Who Chose Communist China – Who They Were and Why They Stayed* (New York, NY: Farrar, Straus and Cudahy, 1955), pp. 36, 86.
10 Ibid., pp. 86, 104-105.
11 Ibid., p. 106.
12 Ibid., pp. 187-188, 192.
13 *The Post* (Big Stone Gap, VA), 1 October 1953.
14 *Washington Post*, 25 October 1953.
15 *New York Times*, 21 October 1953; and Raymond B. Lech, *Broken Soldiers* (Urbana, IL: University of Illinois Press, 2000), p. 197.
16 Lech, *Broken Soldiers*, pp. 218; and *Bristol Herald Courier* (VA), 24 January 1954.

17 *New York Times*, 25 September 1953.
18 *Bristol Herald Courier* (VA), 22 October 1953; and "Prisoner Talks Stalled," *Senior Scholastic*, 4 November 1953, pp. 19-20.
19 *Roanoke Times* (VA), 22 October 1953.
20 *Bristol Herald Courier* (VA), 22 October 1953; and *Washington Post*, 22 October 1953; 25 October 1953.
21 *Bristol Herald Courier* (VA), 24 October 1953; and *Kingsport Times-News* (TN), 25 October 1953.
22 *Bristol Herald Courier* (VA), 22 November 1953.
23 Ibid., 3 November 1953.
24 Ibid., 7 November 1953.
25 *New York Times*, 23 January 1954.
26 Ibid., 1 January 1954.
27 Morris R. Wills and J. Robert Moskin, *Turncoat: An Americans 12 Years in Communist China* (New York, NY: Pocket Books, 1970), 73.
28 *New York Times*, 23 January 1954.
29 Lech, *Broken Soldiers*, 266-267.
30 Ibid., 259-260, 266, 267-268; and Adam J. Zweiback, "The 21 'Turncoat G.I.s': The Political Culture of the Korean War," *The Historian* 60 (Winter 1998), 353, 359.

Chapter 11

From Rollback to Preemption: A Comparison of the Reagan and Bush Doctrines

Robert J. Pauly, Jr.
Norwich University

Introduction

Upon assuming office, any American presidential administration faces three fundamental challenges in formulating and implementing its national security policy. First, a given president and his advisors must define and prioritize the nation's interests at that historical juncture – both domestically and internationally. Second, they must determine the present and potential future dangers most likely to threaten those interests. Third, on the basis of their assessment of all such prospective threats, they must decide what measures to take in order to safeguard US interests at home and abroad while in power. What, in turn, typically renders each of these challenges either extraordinarily daunting, relatively easy to overcome or somewhere in between these two extremes, is the extent to which unanticipated events alter an administration's initial interest and threat calculations over the balance of its term or terms in Washington.

While generally reflective of the above definition, the private formulation and public articulation of American national security policy – or, in some cases, lack of one or both – has varied from administration to administration over the course of the history of the United States generally and since the end of World War II specifically. During the Cold War, for example, most administrations build their security policies toward the Soviet Union around the strategy of containment originally conceived by American diplomat George F. Kennan in the aftermath of World War II and articulated under the pseudonym "X" in the pages of the journal *Foreign Affairs* in the summer of 1947. Although some US Presidents were more forceful than others in dealing with Moscow both rhetorically and practically, each focused primarily on ensuring that the Soviet Union did not extend the physical presence of its military forces far beyond its sphere of influence in Central and Eastern Europe. Only one – Ronald Reagan – elected to shift from containment to a strategy that legitimately sought to "roll back" Soviet influence across the globe, a move that helped to convince political leaders in Moscow (President Mikhail Gorbachev in particular) that they could no longer compete with the United States economically and, ultimately, politically or militarily either. In the end, that realization led to the conclusion of the Cold War by way of the collapse of Communist regimes throughout the Warsaw Pact in 1989-90, the reunification of Germany in October 1990 and the implosion of the Soviet Union itself in December 1991.

Since the end of the Cold War, an equally grave threat to US interests has emerged. It is one posed by transnational terrorist organizations and their state sponsors. The scope of that threat was illustrated on 11 September 2001 when members of a radical Islamic group known as Al Qaeda used American commercial airliners to attack the World Trade Center in New York and the Pentagon on the outskirts of Washington, D.C. on 11 September 2001 at a cost of nearly 3,000 lives – the vast majority of which were those of US civilians. The events of 9/11, in turn, prompted the administration of President George W. Bush to develop a new National Security Strategy (NSS) based upon the willingness to take all necessary action to eliminate dangers to American interests at home and abroad before such threats become imminent. Bush then applied the doctrine of preemption in liquidating the regime of former Iraqi President Saddam Hussein through the conduct of the Second Persian Gulf War in March and April 2003 and the nation-building project that has ensued in Iraq. Above all, Bush's doctrine of preemption represented a shift away from the less assertive security policies of his predecessor, President William J. Clinton, as well as a return to the proactive approach Reagan formulated and applied in the 1980s.

With the above observations providing a necessary contextual foundation, this paper compares and contrasts the Reagan and Bush Doctrines by addressing five related research questions. First, what similarities exist with respect to the foreign policy challenges faced by the Reagan and Bush administrations? Second, to what extent are the Reagan and Bush Doctrines reflective of commonalities in the worldviews of Presidents Reagan and Bush and their respective foreign policy advisors? Third, in what ways are those doctrines comparable as pertains to the expression of rhetorical threats and the willingness of the United States to back such threats with the use of military force? Fourth, given the relative costs and benefits of the Reagan and Bush Doctrines at the domestic and international levels, which has to date proven most effective? Fifth, which elements of each of these doctrines have the greatest potential for use in safeguarding US interests in the future?

The chapter examines the research questions under consideration in the contexts of five sections that unfold in the following manner. The first section examines the formulation, promulgation and application of the Reagan Doctrine from 1981-89. The second section examines the formulation, promulgation and application of the Bush Doctrine from 2001-04. The third section discusses the similarities and differences between the Reagan and Bush Doctrines. The fourth section assesses the relative costs and benefits of the two doctrines. The concluding section reviews the paper's key points, then elaborates on the extent to which the most effective aspects of the Reagan and Bush Doctrines are likely to prove useful in the continuing pursuit of American interests during the post-9/11 era.

Examination of the Reagan Doctrine

Upon assuming office in January 1981, Reagan wasted no time in taking a proactive stance with respect to US-Soviet relations. He did so in the continuing aftermath of Moscow's most aggressive foreign policy initiative since the October 1962 Cuban Missile Crisis – its invasion of Afghanistan on the eve of the start of the 1980 Presidential race in December 1979. After defeating President Jimmy Carter in the subsequent election, Reagan crafted and implemented a strategy that sought to confront the Soviet Union and "roll back" its global influence through two means. First, the Reagan administration engaged in a massive military buildup that included the proposed development of a Strategic Defense Initiative (SDI) to safeguard the United States against the threat of Soviet intercontinental missiles via space-based lasers.[1] Second, it challenged Moscow by supporting insurgencies fighting Soviet-backed regimes in developing world states ranging from Afghanistan to Nicaragua and spent much less money that the Soviet Union in the process. Collectively, these initiatives helped to convince Gorbachev the Soviets could no longer compete with the United States in terms of either economic vitality – and related conventional military reach – or political influence. As a result, Moscow gradually reduced its control over the Warsaw Pact, which led to the proverbial closing act of the Cold War, one that was managed by the George H.W. Bush administration from 1989-1992 and left the Clinton administration facing a new set of threats over the balance of the 1990s.[2]

As is true of most, albeit not all, presidential policies, the first steps in the implementation of the Reagan Doctrine were rhetorical in nature. In his 1981 Inaugural Address, for example, Reagan began that process by laying out in general terms the principals on which the administration would base its conduct, describing the United States as "an exemplar of freedom and a beacon of hope" and stressing that "when action is required to preserve out national security, we will act."[3] Next, the administration had to determine where, geographically, it should confront – and attempt to roll back the influence of – the Soviet Union. That decision was a relatively easy one given that Moscow had extended foreign aid to encourage the establishment of communist friendly regimes in thirty states across the developing world in the 1960s and 1970s, including fourteen that had aligned themselves with the Soviet Union under the auspices of Communist Party leader Leonid Brezhnev's self-proclaimed Brezhnev Doctrine between 1975 and 1981.[4]

Once he had decided to focus on the Soviet presence in the developing world, Reagan articulated that point in a June 1982 speech to the British Parliament in London, noting that "we must be strong in our convictions that freedom is not the sole prerogative of a lucky few, but the inalienable right of all human beings" and calling for "a plan and a hope for the long term – the march of freedom and democracy, which will leave Marxism-Leninism on the ash heap of history as it has left other tyrannies which stifle the freedom and muzzle the self-expression of the people."[5] More pointedly, in a March 1984 address to the National Association of Evangelists in Orlando, Florida, the President left no doubt that the Soviet Union itself was the focal point of the Reagan Doctrine, branding that state as "the focus of evil in the modern world" and warned against the temptation "to ignore the facts of history and the aggressive impulses of an evil empire ... and thereby remove yourself from the struggle between right and wrong."[6]

Once Reagan had launched his rhetorical offensive against the Soviet Union, it was left to his foreign policy team generally and Secretary of State George Schultz specifically to clarify further precisely how the United States planned to convert the President's words into practical action. Schultz did so in the context of a February 1985 speech at the Commonwealth Club in San Francisco, making three critical points in that address. First, he emphasized the potential breadth of the Reagan Doctrine by referring to myriad proponents of democracy in states under direct Soviet control or broader totalitarian influence, including the Solidarity movement in Poland, resistance forces in Afghanistan, Angola, Cambodia and Nicaragua and advocates for change in the Philippines, Chile and South Korea. Second, he acknowledged the need to confront the Soviet Union in particular, noting that, "in recent years, Soviet actions and pretensions have run head-on into the democratic revolution." However, he also cautioned all repressive regimes – Soviet backed or otherwise – that "it is more than mere coincidence that the last four years have been a time of both renewed American strength and leadership and a resurgence of democracy and freedom." Third, he struck a prudential tone with respect to the use of American economic, military and political assets to roll back Soviet influence, explaining that "the nature and extent of our support – whether moral or something more – necessarily varies from case to case. But there should be no doubt where our sympathies lie."[7]

Notwithstanding the utility of Reagan's – and, for that matter, Schultz's – rhetoric, the true test of the Reagan Doctrine was the extent to which the administration would back words with the requisite action to achieve clear practical results. Given the relatively limited scope of this paper, three examples – each of which demonstrates that the administration did indeed follow through credibly in applying the Reagan Doctrine – should suffice: (a) the limited use of US military forces to remove a transitory, but potentially destabilizing, Soviet-backed military junta on the Caribbean island of Grenada in October 1983; (b) the provision of covert assistance (primarily by the Central Intelligence Agency) to freedom fighters attempting to overthrow Soviet-backed regimes in Afghanistan, Angola, Cambodia and Nicaragua from

1985-89; and (c) the application of political pressure on authoritarian American allies in Chile, the Philippines and South Korea to implement democratic reforms from 1986-89.

In October 1983, a military council headed by Gen. Hudson Austin – and supported by both Cuba and the Soviet Union – seized power in Grenada, prompting the Organization of Eastern Caribbean States to request US intervention. The presence of 1,000 American medical students on the island only heightened the sense of urgency within the Reagan administration, which responded by dispatching a contingent of 1,900 US Marines to stage a surprise attack on Austin's Revolutionary Military Council. This limited use of force resulted in the rapid rescue of the students and ouster of the Austin regime. The installment of a democratic government followed and all but a token contingent of American troops had been withdrawn within two months.[8] Most significantly, by using force in a pragmatic manner, the United States sent a clear message that it would not tolerate any further increases in Soviet influence in the developing world and did so at a minimal cost. At the time, Shultz referred to the American initiative as "a shot heard round the world by usurpers and despots of every ideology," noting that "the report was sharp and clear: some Western democracies were again ready to use the military strength they harbored and built up over the years in defense of their principles and interests."[9]

The crisis in Grenada was unique in that it afforded the United States an opportunity to remove a Soviet surrogate through quick and decisive military action. However, in most cases, the Reagan Doctrine engaged in a battle of attrition to reduce Soviet influence in a range of carefully selected states, most notably Afghanistan, Angola, Cambodia and Nicaragua. The strategy was fairly straightforward: to use the provision of limited economic aid and logistical support to opponents of Soviet-backed governments in order to drain Moscow's resources to an extent that would force it to reduce its support for a given regime, if not disengage completely.

In each case, that strategy proved quite effective. In Afghanistan, for example, the CIA funneled covert assistance through Pakistan to a coalition of Islamic holy warriors known collectively as the *mujahideen*. US aid included Stinger ground to air missiles, which were first supplied to the *mujahideen* in 1986 and were critical in counteracting the use of Hind helicopters in Soviet counterinsurgency operations in the ensuing years preceding Moscow's withdrawal in 1989.[10] In Angola, the United States sent covert aid to the National Union for the Total Independence of Angola (UNITA) through Zaire and also used South Africa as a proxy to conduct military operations against the Marxist Popular Movement for the Liberation of Angola (MPLA).[11] Cambodia was similar to Afghanistan in that the US aid helped strengthen a loose alliance of insurgents – the Coalition Government of Democratic Kampuchea (CGDC) – against a communist Vietnamese occupation force. However, the CGDK included a controversial element in the Chinese-backed Khmer Rouge, so American aid through Thailand was confined to the non-communist Sihanoukist National Army (ANS) and Khmer People's National Liberation Front (KPNLF).[12] Lastly, in Nicaragua, US assistance to the Contras, served two purposes: it undermined the Soviet-backed Sandanista government and also helped to weaken the Marxist guerillas that regime was backing in neighboring El Salvador.[13]

Ultimately, the collective economic costs to the Soviet Union in Afghanistan, Angola, Cambodia and Nicaragua were considerably greater than those absorbed by the United States. In Afghanistan, for instance, the Soviets spent $7.5 billion on the war from 1980-88, while the cost of American aid to the *mujahideen* was a modest $3.3 billion.[14] In Angola, Soviet aid totaled approximately $2 billion from 1979-84 alone.[15] American aid to UNITA, which began in 1985, had reached just $300 million by the time the United States and Soviet Union jointly sponsored a peace accord between UNITA and the MPLA in 1988.[16] The relative Soviet and US spending burdens was similar in Nicaragua. From 1982-85, Moscow provided the Sandanistas with $1 billion in military assistance. When the United States funneled its first major installment of $24 million to the Contras in 1983, the Soviets had already supplied the Sandanistas with in excess of $400 that year alone.[17] By the end of 1988, Moscow's annual subsidy to the Sandanistas exceeded $1 billion.[18]

While the principal objective of the Reagan Doctrine was to roll back Soviet influence across the globe, it also provided the United States with an opportunity to encourage peaceful transitions to democracy in nations administered by similarly repressive authoritarian regimes. During his final term, and largely at Schultz's behest, Reagan proved increasingly willing to pressure heavy-handed American allies into adopting democratic reforms. His first initiative of this type was launched in the Philippines, where democratic elections were held under American supervision in 1986. When it became apparent that autocratic President Ferdinand Marcos, a long-time US ally and Reagan friend, had lost Corazon Aquino – whose husband, Senator Benigno Aquino, was assassinated three years earlier – Marcos declared himself the winner nonetheless. Subsequently, Reagan successfully pressured Marcos to leave the country and turn power over to Aquino, a move that, according to Schultz, represented a clear change in policy: from that point on, "support for authoritarian governments that opposed communism could not be taken for granted. The United States supported people who were themselves standing up for freedom and democracy, whether against communism or against another form of repressive government."[19] The Reagan administration went on to prove that its action in the Philippines was not an aberration by vigorously promoting free elections in Chile and South Korea the end results of which were the ousters of authoritarian leaders in both contexts in 1988 – Gen. Augusto Pinochet in the former and President Chun Doo Hwan in the latter.[20]

Examination of the Bush Doctrine

While the Reagan Doctrine was crafted as a means to increase the relative power of the United States vis-à-vis the Soviet Union within the familiar bipolar Cold War system, the Bush Doctrine represented a more profound shift in strategic thinking, one that reflected the changing perception of threats to American interests in the aftermath of the events of 9/11. Bush formally articulated that shift in the context of his administration's first NSS, which was released just over a year after Al Qaeda's attacks on the World Trade Center and Pentagon. The unveiling of the NSS coincided with Bush's rhetorical efforts to confront Iraqi President Saddam Hussein over Baghdad's weapons of mass destruction (WMD) developmental programs and sponsorship of terrorist organizations. Those efforts had commenced publicly with Bush's January 2002 State of the Union address, in which he characterized Iraq, Iran and North Korea as members of an "axis of evil, arming to threaten the peace of the world" through the development and proliferation of nuclear, biological and chemical weapons of mass destruction (WMD) and the direct sponsorship of international and transnational terrorist organizations."[21]

The "axis of evil" address was in itself part of a dozen year diplomatic, economic – and, at times, military – struggle pitting America against Iraq that began when the United States and its allies negotiated a United Nations (UN) sponsored cease-fire with Baghdad at the conclusion of the 1990-91 Persian Gulf War. Most significantly, that settlement stipulated that Saddam discontinue the acquisition and production of WMD and the requisite medium- and long-range missile systems to use such munitions to attack his adversaries and refrain from supporting terrorist groups, agreements that he violated repeatedly between 1991 and 2002.[22]

Iraq's record of defiance prompted Bush to issue a firm set of dictates to Saddam in a speech before the UN General Assembly in New York on 12 September 2002. In the context of that address, the President made three unequivocal points. First, he demanded that Iraq comply immediately with all of the promises it made to the international community at the end of the Persian Gulf War, noting that Saddam had ignored 16 separate UN Security Council resolutions in the previous decade.[23] Specifically, the President emphasized that because it was continuing to pursue the acquisition of WMD and long-range missile systems, Iraq remained "a grave and gathering danger" to international security.[24] Second, he challenged the UN to carry out its responsibilities by impressing upon Saddam the need to disarm in an internationally-verifiable manner, asking members of that body's General Assembly: "Will the United Nations serve the purpose of its founding, or will it be irrelevant?"[25] Third, he pledged that the United States would indeed take action to eliminate the threats Iraq posed to American interests – with the UN's help if possible, but also unilaterally if necessary – noting that "we cannot stand by and do nothing while dangers gather."[26]

Designed in large part as a means to warn American adversaries in general and Iraq in particular that the United States would not tolerate either the development and proliferation of WMD or the state sponsorship of terrorism, Bush's NSS is built around three pledges. First, the United States "will defend the peace by fighting terrorists and tyrants." Second, it "will preserve the peace by building good relations among the great powers." And third, it "will extend the peace by encouraging free and open societies on every continent."[27] At its core, the NSS represented a shift from a reliance on the deterrent containment doctrine of the Cold War to a willingness to use preemptive policy-making when necessary to safeguard American national interests. It was a shift necessitated by the changing nature – and severity – of the threats posed to those interests as evidenced by the events of 9/11. As National Security Advisor Condoleezza Rice, one of the principal architects of the innovative new strategy, has asserted, "some threats are so potentially catastrophic – and can arrive with so little warning, by means that are untraceable – that they cannot be contained ... . So as a matter of common sense, the United States must be prepared to take action, when necessary, before threats have fully materialized."[28]

Most indispensably, Bush's NSS recognizes the increased vulnerability of the United States to attacks by transnational terrorist organizations and their supporters (whether state or non-state actors) as was so clearly – and tragically – demonstrated by the events of 9/11. In particular, the document defines three fundamental national interests – the defense, preservation and extension of the peace through collaboration with the world's great powers at the expense of its terrorists and tyrants – on behalf of which Bush promises to utilize America's unparalleled economic, military and political assets. However, it cleverly frames those interest-based objectives in principled rhetoric, noting that the United States seeks to promote a "balance of power that favors ... political and economic freedom, peaceful relations with other states and respect for human dignity" and also stressing that "today, the international community has the best chance since the rise of the nation-state in the seventeenth century to build a world where great powers compete in peace instead of continually preparing for war. Today, the world's great powers find ourselves on the same side."[29]

Domestic and foreign opponents of the Bush administration, along with some of America's European allies (France and Germany in particular), have derided its NSS as one based all but exclusively on the preemptive use of military force, whether employed unilaterally or multilaterally. But even a cursory reading of the document reveals such criticism to be misguided. It is 40 pages in length and the discussion of preemption encompasses just two sentences in one of its eight sections. Granted, Bush and his advisors placed an emphasis on the use of preemptive measures in light of the dire threats posed by terrorist groups and their state sponsors and heightened public sensitivities to those dangers as a result of the 9/11 attacks, but when taken as a whole, the NSS represents a considerably more wide ranging strategy. As Secretary of State Colin Powell has pointed out:

The NSS made the concept of preemption explicit in the heady aftermath of September 11, and it did so for obvious reasons. One reason was to reassure the American people that the government possessed common sense. As President Bush has said – and as any sensible person understands – if you recognize a clear and present threat that is undeterrable by the means you have at hand, then you must deal with it. You do not wait for it to strike; you do not allow future attacks to happen before you take action. A second reason for including the notion of preemption in the NSS was to convey to our adversaries that they were in big trouble ... . Sensible as these reasons were, some observers have exaggerated both the scope of preemption in foreign policy and the centrality of preemption in US strategy as a whole.[30]

Justifiably, Bush cedes primacy to hard-core security issues over the low politics of the environment favored by his immediate predecessor in the White House (President Bill Clinton) and his opponent in the 2000 Presidential Election (Albert Gore). However, Bush does so by laying out the White House's strategy in terms of the proactive pursuit of eight separate goals, five of which relate directly to hard-core security issues and three more than pertain to efforts to foster economic growth and the construction of enduring democratic institutions in the developing world in general and across the Greater Middle East in particular. Specifically, the administration pledges that the United States will:

- Champion aspirations for human dignity.
- Strengthen alliances to defeat global terrorism and work to prevent attacks against us and our friends.
- Work with others to defuse regional conflicts.
- Prevent our enemies from threatening us, our allies, and our friends, with weapons of mass destruction.
- Ignite a new era of global economic growth through free markets and free trade.
- Expand the circle of development by opening societies and building the infrastructure of democracy.
- Develop agendas for cooperative action with other main centers of global power.
- Transform America's national security institutions to meet the challenges and opportunities of the twenty-first century.[31]

When one considers the range of preemptive, preventive and preventative measures discussed in the previous section, Bush's strategy appears not as a rash reaction to the 9/11 assaults, but as a comprehensive blueprint that takes into account the successes and failures of his predecessors in the White House over the past half-century. One of the means the United States used to weaken the Soviet Union's grip over its Warsaw Pact satellites over the long term, for instance, was by "opening societies and building the infrastructure of democracy" throughout Central and Eastern Europe. The Bush NSS is designed to eventually produce a similar democratization of the Islamic world. In that sense, it is both flexible and visionary rather than ill conceived and illogical. As Powell concludes, "Together, [its eight] parts add up to a strategy that is broad and deep, far ranging and forward looking, attuned as much to opportunities for the United States as to the dangers it faces."[32]

What is most instructive about the Bush administration's NSS is the extent to which it takes an assertive but multilateral stance in discussing the economic, political and military means the United States is prepared to use to preempt threats to American security at home and abroad.[33] The NSS suggests that such threats – most notably the acquisition, production and proliferation of WMD by dictatorial regimes – are best mitigated and eventually eliminated multilaterally through the organization of "coalitions – as broad as practicable – of states able and willing to promote a balance of power that favors freedom."[34] Furthermore, it renders critics' characterizations of the Bush administration's supposed aversion to working with the UN under any circumstances considerably less credible by justifying its doctrine of preemption in globally acceptable legal terms pertaining to a state's right to defend itself.[35]

Much of the criticism of Bush's foreign policy before, as well as during and after, the conduct of the Second Iraq War, rests primarily on the premise that he has acted unilaterally more often than not. Responding effectively to that criticism is relatively easy so long as one defines the term unilateralism first. The narrowest definition of the term would suggest that a given state is acting alone – that is, without the support, of any allies whatsoever, let alone the blessing of the UN Security Council or wider international community. A broader definition, by contrast, might indicate a coalition of less than 10 states acting without the authority of a formal Security Council resolution. Yet, neither of these definitions applies to US action in the context of Operation Iraqi Freedom. In that case, the United States acted with the direct or indirect military, logistical and political support of no less than 50 states. In addition, the Security Council acceded to the former, albeit not to the latter. As Powell explains, "Partnership is the watchword of US strategy in this administration. Partnership is not about deferring to others; it is about working with them."[36]

Moving beyond its general and specific characterizations of the potential security threats the United States must confront (most notably the arming of terrorist organizations with WMD by tyrannical regimes) and the means to use in preempting those threats (collective diplomacy if possible; the multilateral or unilateral use of force if necessary), the NSS also prioritizes American interests regionally. Not unexpectedly, that prioritization places an emphasis on Greater Middle Eastern and South Asian security affairs generally and such long-standing imbroglios as the Israeli-Palestinian conflict and troubled Indian-Pakistani relationship in particular. Significantly, in addressing each of these contentious relationships, the NSS acknowledges the need for the United States to strike a balance between the interests of the disparate ethnic and religious groups involved.[37] It does so in large part in order to avoid deepening the anti-American sentiments that have in the past – and continue at present – to make members of the lower classes of the Islamic world susceptible to the recruitment efforts of regional and global terrorist organizations. Rice, for example, has pointed out, that the Bush administration "rejects the condescending view that freedom will not grow in the soil of the Middle East – or that Muslims somehow do not share in the desire to be free."[38]

Similarities and Differences Between the Reagan and Bush Doctrine

In comparing the Reagan and Bush Doctrines, a range of similarities and differences become evident. The articulation of such similarities and differences, in turn, is best achieved contextually through examinations of four issue areas, those pertaining to (a) the nature of the threats faced by each administration, (b) the rhetoric Presidents Reagan and Bush employed in making the requisite political commitments to confront their adversaries, (c) the means at their disposal to use in safeguarding American interests at home and abroad, and (d) their willingness to take direct military action, whether limited or robust, in order to achieve a given foreign policy objective.

In general terms, the Reagan and Bush Doctrines were similar in that each was developed as a proactive means to reduce, and eventually eliminate, threats posed against the United States by adversaries espousing economic, political and religious philosophies diametrically opposed to those upon which America was founded. Yet, the identities of those adversaries and nature of the threats they posed differed markedly. The Reagan administration was matched against the Soviet Union, which administered a domestic system based upon communism, totalitarianism and atheism, imposed those values on the states of Central and Eastern Europe and sought to proliferate them across the developing world as well. Although the Soviets possessed massive nuclear and convention military arsenals, there was little, if any, chance they would use either to strike American targets either at home or abroad. Instead, Moscow's primary challenge to Washington was one for relative political influence at the global level. The Bush administration, by contrast, had to respond to the most devastating foreign attacks on the United States in its history, which Al Qaeda orchestrated on 9/11. Its foes also advocate an alternate philosophical vision to the American way of life, one based on a primitive form of Islamic fundamentalism that even most Muslims abhor. However, those adversaries possess a direct threat to the United States on a daily basis, one complicated by the potential for collaboration between Al Qaeda and other terrorist groups and state sponsors that are – in some cases – in possession of chemical, biological and, perhaps, chemical WMD.

The parallels between the rhetoric utilized by Reagan and Bush in articulating their respective doctrines are striking. Both, for example, equated the struggle pitting the United States against its principal adversaries – the Soviet Union in the former case and terrorist groups and their state sponsors (especially Al Qaeda and Iraq) in the latter – as a Manichean confrontation between good and evil. In particular, Reagan characterized the Soviet Union as an "evil empire" and Bush viewed and presented Iraq as the most threatening member of an "axis of evil." Additionally, members of the Reagan and Bush administrations each described the challenges they faced in global terms, promising to use all the available means at their disposal to spread America's economic and political values throughout the world as a means to weaken – and, ultimately, eliminate – the proliferation of the alternate ideological visions promulgated by their adversaries. On the other hand, there was also one significant rhetorical difference between the two doctrines. While Reagan expressed a willingness to *prevent* further gains in Soviet political influence in the developing world, Bush stated explicitly that the United States would *preempt* threats to American interests before such threats became imminent.

Notwithstanding the comparably sweeping nature of their rhetoric, Reagan and Bush had a different range of capabilities through which to pursue their objectives in the Cold War and Global War on Terrorism. Above all, those differences reflected the extent of American power relative to that possessed by US adversaries in the 1980s and 2000s. At the start of Reagan's tenure, for instance, the relative power and influence of the United States lagged behind that of the Soviet Union as a result of a loss of American prestige that began with Washington's defeat in the Vietnam War, continued with the James E. Carter administration's naïve approach to foreign affairs and culminated in Moscow's invasion of Afghanistan. In practical terms, the United States had no choice but to maintain a substantial military presence in Western Europe and thus could not afford massive deployments to confront the Soviets and their surrogates directly in the developing world. The Bush administration, by contrast, found itself a considerably more favorable position at the global level, one in which American power was not challenged by any one state or group of states to the extent that it was by the Soviet Union during the Cold War. Despite the marked defense cutbacks of the Clinton years, the Bush administration still possessed the requisite assets to conduct Operation Iraqi Freedom without undermining to a marked degree the broader conduct of the war on terror through a range of economic, judicial, military and political tools.

With respect to the application of their respective doctrines generally and the use of military force in the process specifically, there is one clear similarity between the Reagan and Bush administrations. Both proved willing to use force directly in order to demonstrate that their rhetoric was credible. However, the scope of the force they choose to use was markedly different. The former deployed 1,900 Marines to prevent the Soviets from gaining a communist surrogate in Grenada. The latter took relatively limited military action to eliminate the Taliban regime and thus weaken substantially Al Qaeda's capacity to use Afghanistan as a base to plan future terrorist operations against the United States. But it also conducted a major, albeit brief, war that resulted in the liquidation of Saddam's regime, before commencing a nation-building project in Iraq that will entail the long-term deployment of tens, of not, hundreds of thousands of American troops in that context.

Assessment of Relative Costs of the Reagan and Bush Doctrines

Any foreign and security policy or strategy typically entails a variety of costs and benefits. That was – and remains true – of both the Reagan and Bush Doctrines. Assessing such costs and benefits, in turn, enables one to render a rational judgment as to the relative utility of each doctrine. As was the case with the previous section, this one conducts a contextual analysis in an effort to determine the extent to which the Reagan and Bush Doctrines were effective strategies in terms of the political objectives they have achieved – and at what cost – over both the short and long terms.

The primary short-term benefits of the Reagan Doctrine were threefold. First, the doctrine was the economically austere element of a two-part strategy the Reagan administration used in order to regain the initiative and increase its global power and influence relative to that of the Soviet Union in the Cold War. Combined with SDI, which consumed the vast majority of the financial resources Reagan dedicated to confronting the Soviets, the doctrine helped to convince Gorbachev that Moscow would be unable to generate the requisite resources to continue to compete effectively with the United States. Once Reagan felt he could deal with Gorbachev from a positions of strength, he met with the Soviet leader four times between 1985 and 1988, pressing him to release his control on the states of Central and Eastern Europe and setting the stage for the end of the bipolar struggle between Washington and Moscow on American terms. Second, the doctrine led the Soviet Union to withdraw from Afghanistan in 1989 and eventually discontinue its support for communist regimes in Angola, Cambodia and Nicaragua. Third, it accelerated a broader trend toward democratization in the developing world, albeit one that proved to be of a transitory nature.

Its short-term costs were marginal in economic and military terms, but more troubling politically given that, in order to raise funds to arm the Nicaraguan Contras, the Reagan administration struck a deal with Iran through which it sold weapons to Tehran in exchange for the release of American hostages held by several Middle Eastern terrorist organizations. The Iran-Contra scandal that followed led to considerable public ridicule of the administration and the dismissal of National Security Advisor John Poindexter but did not prevent then Vice President George H.W. Bush from winning the 1988 Presidential Election in a landslide over Democratic opponent Michael Dukakis. The longer-term costs, though somewhat ambiguous, have been particularly problematic of late. Most significantly, once the Cold War had ended, the United States withdrew its support for those insurgencies it had supported in the developing world, leaving that region subject to the emergence of "failing" and "failed" states. Al Qaeda, in turn, used one such state – Afghanistan – as a base for the planning and orchestration of the events of 9/11, which themselves necessitated the Bush administration's development of a preemptive NSS.

The short-term benefits of the Bush Doctrine, the cornerstone of which is the NSS, are threefold. First, through its willingness to confront those regimes that have consistently supported terrorist organizations – most notably the Taliban and Iraq – the Bush administration has weakened Al Qaeda and prevented it from carrying out an attack against the United States since 9/11. Second, by eliminating Saddam's regime, the administration has both reduced the potential threats posed to America – and the broader international community – by Iraq's WMD developmental programs and improved the lives of Iraqis, the vast majority of whom lived in fear of the ruling Baath Party over the previous quarter-century. Third, by taking decisive action against Iraq, the United States sent a clear message to other state sponsors of terrorism – most notably Libya, Iran and North Korea – that Washington views the matter seriously and has the political will to back its rhetoric with the use of force. Libya and Iran have both since agreed to engage in negotiations with the West – the former with the United Kingdom and United States; the latter with Britain, France and Germany – the result of which may be the elimination of their WMD programs. There are also two significant costs. First, by conducting Operation Iraqi Freedom without clear authorization from the UN Security Council or the unanimous support of its European allies, the Bush administration helped to create the most serious break in transatlantic relations in two decades. Second, because of that rift, the United States has had to assume nearly all of the economic and physical burdens for the conduct of the war and ongoing nation-building operations in Iraq – burdens that have entailed the loss of more than 500 American troops and more than $100 billion.

The longer-term costs and benefits of the Bush Doctrine are much more unclear than those associated with the Reagan Doctrine in light of the differing timelines of each. It has been more than two decades since the former was launched, while the latter remains very much a work in progress. Should Al Qaeda carry out another strike or series of strikes on the scale of the 9/11 attacks, for example, it may reduce the extent to which the Bush Doctrine is deemed an effective means through which to conduct the war on terror. Similarly, a further deterioration of the already tenuous state of affairs in Iraq, would call into question the extent to which the human and economic costs are worth the long-term commitment to the democratization of Iraq and the broader Middle East. On the other hand, there were myriad critics of Reagan's proactive approach in the early 1980s whose judgments have since been called into question. Ultimately, the objective of the Bush Doctrine – enhancing American security by eliminating threats to US interests before such threats are imminent – is a prudent and noble one. Whether or not it proves practical over time is a question that, at least for now, is difficult, if not impossible, to answer definitively.

Conclusions

At its core, this paper was designed to compare and contrast the Reagan and Bush Doctrines through the presentation of a four-part discussion. It pursued that objective in the following manner. First, it examined the basis for, and subsequent formulation, promulgation and application of the Reagan Doctrine from 1981-1989. Second, it examined the basis for, and subsequent formulation, promulgation and application of the Bush Doctrine from 2001-2004. Third, it described the similarities and differences between the Reagan and Bush Doctrines with respect to four related economic, military and political issue areas. Fourth, it assessed the relative strengths and weaknesses of the two doctrines over both the short and long terms.

Four fundamental conclusions grow out of the evidence put forward and evaluated in the contexts of the paper's four main sections. First, both Reagan and Bush assumed office at what has since proven a defining point in American history. In each case, they responded by developing foreign policy doctrines that differed significantly from that of their immediate predecessors in the White House. Second, those doctrines were very similar rhetorically but also markedly different in terms of the threats the United States faced at the time and the means through which the Reagan and Bush administrations chose to confront their respective adversaries. Third, with respect to the conduct of a cost-benefit analysis, it is clear that the benefits of the Reagan Doctrine exceeded the costs markedly in the short term. Put simply, Reagan provided the necessary proverbial shove to Gorbachev to conclude the Cold War on American rather than Soviet terms. Notwithstanding the long-term implications of the abandonment of Afghanistan, it is unclear whether a different course of action would have engendered the development of an environment less favorable for the rise of a regime such as the Taliban. It is equally uncertain what effect, if any, such a change would have had on Al Qaeda and the events of 9/11. Lastly, on balance, the Bush Doctrine appears to be a reasonable approach to a security threat perhaps as grave as any the United States has faced in its history. Notwithstanding criticism of the Bush administration's supposed penchant for unilateral action, the strategy is has pursued in the war on terror broadly and with respect to Iraq in particular have, on balance, reduced the threats to American interests at home and abroad.

Notes

1   Michael Turner, "Defense Policy and Arms Control: The Reagan Record," in *Reagan's First Four Years: A New Beginning* (New York: St. Martin's Press, 1988), pp. 175. Turner notes that the Strategic Defense Initiative was the most expensive element of a massive US defense buildup that entailed spending increases of 8.5 percent per year from 1981-85.

2   For a definitive examination of the Reagan Doctrine, see Mark P. Lagon, *The Reagan Doctrine: The Sources of American Conduct in the Cold War's Last Chapter* (Westport, CT: Praeger, 1994).

3   Quoted in Davis W. Houck and Amos Kiewe, *Actor, Ideologue, Politician: The Public Speeches of Ronald Reagan* (Westport, CT: Greenwood Press, 1993), p. 179.

4   Lagon, *Reagan Doctrine*, 46.

5   Ronald Reagan, *Speaking My Mind: Selected Speeches* (New York: Simon and Schuster, 1990), pp. 107-108.

6   Ibid., 112.

7   George P. Schultz, *Turmoil and Triumph: Diplomacy, Power and the Victory of the American Ideal* (New York: Charles Scribner's Sons, 1993), pp. 525-526.

8   Robert Young Pelton and Coskun Aral, *The World's Most Dangerous Places* (Redondo Beach, CA: Fielding Worldwide, Inc., 1995), pp. 294; Shultz, *Turmoil and Triumph*, 323-340.

9   Schultz, *Turmoil and Triumph*, 340.

10 Lagon, *Reagan Doctrine*, 57.

11 Daniel Spikes, *Angola and the Politics of Intervention* (Jefferson, NC: McFarland and Company, Inc., Publishers, 1993), pp. 321-322.

12 Lagon, *Reagan Doctrine*, 66-67.

13 Ibid., 59.

14 Saadet Deger and Somnath Sen, *Military Expenditures: The Political Economy of International Security* (Oxford: Oxford University Press, 1990), pp. 70, 126.

15 Shultz, *Turmoil and Triumph*, 1, 118.

16 Spikes, *Angola and the Politics of Intervention*, 322.

17 G.W. Sand, *Soviet Arms in Central America: The Case of Nicaragua* (Westport, CT: Praeger, 1989), pp. 52, 69-70.

18 James A. Baker, III., with Thomas M. DeFrank, *The Politics of Diplomacy: Revolution, War & Peace, 1989-1992* (New York: G.P. Putnam's Sons, 1995), 59.

19 Schultz, *Turmoil and Triumph*, 608-642.

20 Ibid., 969-982.

21 George W. Bush, "State of the Union Address," *White House Office of the Press Secretary*, 29 January 2002.

22 Steve A. Yetiv, *The Persian Gulf Crisis* (Westport, CT: Greenwood Press, 1997), pp. 184-85. These requirements are set forth explicitly in United Nations (UN) Security Council Resolution 687, which was approved on 3 April 1991.

23 George W. Bush, "Remarks at the United Nations General Assembly," *White House Office of the Press Secretary*, 12 September 2002; National Security Council (NSC), "A Decade of Deception and Defiance: Saddam Hussein's Defiance of the United Nations," Background Paper for President Bush's UN Address, *White House Office of the Press Secretary* (12 September 2002): 4-7.

24 Bush, "Remarks at the UN."

25 Ibid.

26 Ibid.

27 George W. Bush, "National Security Strategy of the United States of America," *White House Office of the Press Secretary* (17 September 2002).

28 Condoleezza Rice, "2002 Wriston Lecture at the Manhattan Institute," *White House Office of the Press Secretary* (1 October 2002).

29 Bush, "National Security Strategy."

30 Colin L. Powell, "A Strategy of Partnerships," *Foreign Affairs* (January/February 2004): 24.
31 Bush, "National Security Strategy."
32 Powell, "A Strategy of Partnerships," 23.
33 Bush, "National Security Strategy." In particular, the NSS states that "[w]e must be prepared to stop rogue states and their terrorist clients before they are able to threaten or use weapons of mass destruction against the United States and our allies and friends."
34 Ibid.
35 Ibid.
36 Powell, "A Strategy of Partnerships," 25-26.
37 Bush, "National Security Strategy."
38 Rice, "Wriston Lecture."

Chapter 12

The 2003 U.S. Invasion of Iraq:
Militarism in the Service of Geopolitics

Edmund F. Byrne

Purdue University at Indianapolis

Edward Said once declared American power to be "one of the main problems (in the Middle East)"; and to address this problem he recommended using "one's mind historically and rationally for the purpose of reflective understanding." Many scholars have done something like this with regard to the US invasion of Iraq in 2003, and some say it fails several criteria of just war theory. But while they reflect on that continuing political violence, the invaders are already disseminating reasons for doing more of the same in other countries, again without reference to their real geopolitical objectives. This illustrates how politically ineffective just war theory is in practice because we routinely direct it to yesterday's war rather than to wars being prepared for with enemy-making rhetoric. There are obstacles to addressing the latter, but it can be done. It could have been done with regard to the 2003 invasion of Iraq, even as its perpetrators were insisting that it was all and only about self-defense against WMDs and/or humanitarian intervention. These reasons were debated in the public arena; but they were incidental to the underlying reasons, one of which grew out of an energy policy that relies too readily on military solutions.

America's energy policy has come to embody a conviction that the country's needs can only be met by means of economic and military preeminence. A key corollary of this policy is that corporate entities with ties to the oil industry are not to be challenged in any meaningful way. So rather than rein in our profligate oil consumption it tolerates marginally adequate refinery capacity and under funds development of alternate sources of energy. As a result, once touted plans to develop synthetic fuels and to recover oil from shale have degenerated into a fraud on taxpayers. Similarly, US auto manufacturers, whose profits depend on truck-based guzzlers, now have the lowest fleet average mpg in decades. As global demand for product accelerates, US leaders have increasingly come to rely on their military might, if necessary, to take control of oil-producing countries like Iraq that are less than fully attuned to America's petroleum priorities. In other words, the U.S. has opted to meet its energy needs by maintaining a geopolitical empire even, when necessary, by force of arms.

Like its predecessors, the George W. Bush administration (the Bush administration hereafter) sees no realistic alternative to this long established policy. Even if they do, they are far too busy accommodating their corporate contributors to worry about the long term economic and environmental consequences of this strategy.[1] Thus at this writing they have posted over a hundred thousand troops and 14,000 oil infrastructure security guards in Iraq, plus some thirty warships and a number of Coast Guard cutters protecting oil tankers in and around the Persian Gulf. The cost of this public service to the oil industry adds to federal expenditures an average of US$4-5 per barrel of oil.

To have openly associated the US takeover of Iraq with geopolitics would have been politically unwise. So the Bush administration associated it instead, in religious-sounding terms, with an open-ended war on terrorism. One result: a disconnect between their purported objectives for invading and occupying Iraq and the geopolitical objectives set forth in the documentary record. The result of this misleading oratory was to gain substantial support for a war that failed the just war test.

In the interest of reflective understanding, then, I propose first to identify covert reasons for invading Iraq and then consider ways to expose such hypocrisy in the future. On a factual level, I will note that the failure of US (and UK) political leaders to state truthfully their reasons for attacking Iraq severely hindered timely assessment of their reasons and intentions, which are key *jus ad bellum* conditions.[2] This points to a flaw in just war theory, namely, that it is rarely applied to realtime decision-making. If it is to have an *ante bellum* role to play, its proponents must be able to achieve reflective understanding expeditiously. But this is now easier to achieve thanks to such new technologies as the Internet. What needs to be examined, though, are not just factual claims but asserted principles as well. This in turn might be done better if we could develop a pragmatic extension of John Rawls's principle-oriented approach which he called reflective equilibrium. Rawls himself, I will show, remained too reliant on leaders to guide us in this task, but other philosophers do offer examples of how to proceed.

Why Iraq was Invaded According to Bush Administration Spin and the US Media

Governments often use strategic deception to achieve their ends,[3] with results largely a factor not of ideology but of available resources. This is now very much the case in the United States, where about the only relevant issue still debatable is whether military[4] or corporate[5] interests are the principal protagonists. It is, then, only by looking behind this context of information dominance that one can discover the real reasons for the US takeover of Iraq in 2003. These originate in policies that date back decades and took focused form during the 1990s in studies and reports prepared for top government officials and their confidantes. President Bush secretly endorsed the recommended military intervention early in his administration; then as it became operational, he claimed noble and even imperative motives for doing so. US media passed the government's misinformation on as truth until the invasion phase of the "mission" was over. Then they occasionally dealt with the oil factor as foreign and Internet media had been doing for months. Business publications in particular addressed such geopolitical considerations, but never so as to question the war's legitimacy. I will review this media bias briefly, then focus on the internal record and some explanations that extra-governmental analysts have put forward.

Throughout the six-month mobilization for the US/UK invasion of Iraq – first labeled Operation Iraqi Liberation, or OIL, then cosmetized as Operation Iraqi Freedom – the popular press took regime change and/or non-proliferation as the obvious purposes. But many countries, including some permanent members of the UN Security Council, believed that whatever danger Iraq posed could be countered without going to war. And humanitarian organizations decried the allies' lack of planning for Iraqi civilian needs. So the Security Council rebuffed US and UK demands that it authorize their invasion, opting instead for extending UN-sponsored searches for weapons of mass destruction in Iraq. The allies simply fell back on an earlier resolution (1441) to legitimize their deploying a quarter of a million troops (mostly American) and their weapons of war. Many anti-war protesters assumed this mobilization was oil-oriented, but Bush administration top personnel denied this, even though many of them have career and investment connections to the oil industry. Few U.S. legislators asserted otherwise; many U.K. members of Parliament did. U.K. prime minister Tony Blair, who himself has close ties to the British petroleum industry, dismissed the oil nexus as a "conspiracy theory," but Parliament and people came to doubt his explanations.

The rhetorical build-up began with President Bush's first State of the Union address, intensified during the period of diplomatic bullying and military relocations, became strident in his second State of the Union address, and culminated in the allegedly preventive invasion. In January 2002, he identified an "axis of evil" consisting of three countries – Iran, Iraq, and North Korea – each of which has oil reserves and purportedly some program to develop weapons of mass destruction (WMDs). The strategy: talk WMDs. The first target: Iraq. In January 2003, Bush declared that he would soon punish the Iraqi government for its recalcitrance. Neither "oil" nor any synonym for "oil" appeared in either address – nor in an hour-long PBS Frontline review of the pre-invasion international debate.[6] Yet there surely was an underlying geopolitical strategy at work. And to argue this point, I will now review the framework within which US media covered relevant events before and during the still only partial "regime change" in Iraq.

Media in the United States assumed from the outset that the self-defense and/or humanitarian reasons circumscribed US reasons for invading Iraq. Meanwhile, they reported some warring over oil elsewhere. The New York Times told about U.S. oil-related interventions in Aceh, East Timor, and Colombia, and in the Persian Gulf (to interdict oil shipments out of Iraq). It noted US and others' interest in the substantial oil and especially natural gas reserves in Russia and in the Caspian Sea region. But few noted the petroleum-oriented reason to invade Afghanistan, even though Unocal wanted to build an oil pipeline there, Bush's special envoy to Afghanistan, Zalmay Khalilzad, was a former Unocal aide, and wars are sometimes fought to secure natural resources such as oil.[7] In any event, at a certain moment the Bush administration's rhetoric shifted from Afghan terrorists to Iraqi weapons. Some saw this shift as a major distraction from the war on terrorism. But Iraq had been the administration's target of choice at least as of 11 September 2001. Its post-Afghanistan placement was for reasons of politics and military logistics.[8]

Over the pre-invasion months, the US media did not completely ignore the advantages of controlling Mideast oil. Indeed, the terms 'oil' and 'Iraq' were occasionally linked with reference to U.S. interests. One commentator even went so far as to say that "Iraq's 'ability to generate oil' [quoting a White House spokesman] is always somewhere on the table, even if not in so many words." And a defender of U.S. imperialism declared Iraq, which "has so much of the world's proven oil reserves," to be "the empire's center of gravity." Once the invasion began, the movement of men and machines dominated the news. Nonetheless, the quick securing of oil fields was reported with zeal. Even the takeover of two oil platforms in the Persian Gulf was labeled "a bloodless victory in the battle for Iraq's vast oil empire." Then a series of articles in The New York Times described technical and political obstacles to reactivating Iraq's oil industry.

Less emotive accounts explained the economic role of Iraqi oil. The US Department of Energy provided interested parties with an "Iraq Energy Chronology: 1980-2002." And business publications told how Western oil companies would benefit from a U.S. takeover of Iraq. The Economist analyzed post-hostilities contracts to develop Iraq's oil reserves and how they might be legally implemented. The Wall Street Journal, among others, reported on secret meetings at which U.S. government bureaucrats and oil executives worked out "production-sharing deals" with expatriate Iraqis, industry assessments of production potential in Iraq, and military strategies for defending vulnerable sources of oil.

Once the occupation was in place, the popular press devoted some attention to Iraqi oil, e.g., regarding reactivation obstacles and secret contracts awarded to companies with close ties to the Bush administration. Time Magazine told readers that the U.S. government often "meddled" in oil-rich countries and discounted Secretary of Defense Rumsfeld's not-about-oil protestations because the U.S. military prioritized protection of Iraq's oil facilities and Rumsfeld had to know from a "little-noted energy study" (discussed below) that "(t)he amount of oil that

Iraq brings to market" is a matter of great geopolitical importance. Consistent with this point of view, the Bush administration sought to facilitate favored US companies' control of Iraqi oil by awarding them lucrative contracts and military protection and issuing Executive Order 13303, whereby President Bush declares these companies exempt from liability for any production- or distribution-related happening and thus in effect above the rule of law.

These stratagems to control Iraqi oil have been undermined by concerted guerilla attacks on petroleum infrastructure and coalition-serving foreign personnel. Oil production as a result has barely reached pre-invasion levels, no doubt a factor in soaring petroleum prices; and some otherwise interested drillers (e.g., British Petroleum) have postponed indefinitely their plans to develop Iraqi fields. In a word, pre-war worst-case scenarios are being realized. These setbacks for the invaders do not negate their motives going in, though, and may well become a convenient rationale for their prolonging the occupation.

Geopolitical Factors That Could Have Inspired the US to Invade Iraq

Official pronouncements and their media dispersal tend to preclude rather than assist one's quest for reflective understanding. In particular, as the above indicates, the American media seldom questioned the reasons the Bush administration gave for invading Iraq. I will do that in the next section, and will conclude that control of Iraqi oil was a high priority reason. Before introducing documentary evidence, though, I will first address two primarily theoretical counter-arguments: one, that imperialist objectives were behind the decision to occupy Iraq, above and beyond any interest in controlling its oil; the other, that, however desirable in principle, oil simply cannot be controlled. After addressing these counter-arguments, I will briefly put Iraqi oil in its historical context.

Efforts to discount the oil-oriented argument included two imperialism accounts, one supportive, the other not. The supportive version avers that the only adequate response to terrorist threats is global domination and that the U.S. as the world's only superpower is obliged to take on this responsibility.[9] The non-supportive imperialism account labels the takeover of Iraq an exercise in neo-colonialism. The neo-colonial thesis is well articulated by the Research Unit for Political Economy (2003), based in India. Their thesis is that the "coalition" forces, especially the U.S., wish to dominate the world not only militarily but politically and economically as well. This objective, they argue, arises out of a number of changed circumstances: the demise of the Soviet Union, which leaves no major enemy to justify heavy defense expenditures; the maturity of developed countries' economies, which reduces the possibility of significant growth; the unreliability of governments in countries where needed natural resources are located; and the threat to dollar-based global transactions if the euro were to become a dominant world currency. For all these reasons, the U.S. is establishing permanent military bases all over the world to facilitate controlling peoples and resources when and as needed. Controlling the world's supply of oil is certainly germane to a quest for global hegemony, and so accordingly is control of Iraq's immense oil reserves; but no less desirable for this purpose is controlling the people of the region whose anti-American attitudes threaten US dominance there.

The non-feasibility argument has taken two forms, one based on military, the other on economic considerations. The *military non-feasibility* of an unbounded war on terrorism has been well articulated by a US Army researcher.[10] *Economic non-feasibility* involves discrediting oil-control assertions on the grounds that oil cannot really be controlled given that the oil industry operates in an open market that runs on supply and demand. This argument proceeds as follows. As demand increases, supply is provided; as supply increases, demand declines. Depending on which factor is predominant, the price of oil will rise or fall. It matters little who produces the world's oil; for, any barrel of oil sold on the open market will bring no more or less than the going price. But this price is affected by the imbalance, if any, between supply and demand. Consumers want more supply and producers want to limit supply and/or stimulate greater demand. Members of the Organization of Petroleum Exporting Countries (OPEC), in particular, sought (until recently) to cap their total output to sustain an economically advantageous price range of $22-28 a barrel. This understood, it is not in OPEC (or, for that matter, non-OPEC) oil producers' interest to have much Iraqi oil on the world market. So in the short run they benefitted from the U.N. sanctions imposed on Iraq's oil and defended by the U.S. and the U.K. after the Gulf War. Inversely, no major consumer would benefit from a war that disrupted Iraq's oil production over an extended period of time. From a global perspective, in any event, a government that wants to assure access to a certain quantity of oil can buy it wherever it is being sold and have it delivered to a designated destination. There is, then, no reason to go to war over oil.

So goes the supply-and-demand argument that neoconservatives combined with their insistence that the sole reasons for invading Iraq were anti-terrorism and non-proliferation. It is fatally flawed, however, in that it disregards financial and geopolitical reality. Consumers want their oil supplied consistently and at an affordable price, and investors (*a fortiori*, speculators) care how much oil a provider controls because that affects its ability to influence price. And to accommodate their interests, specialists continually seek more reliable estimates of proven reserves, the quantity and quality of such reserves, and which entities control them. How, then, could a government responsible for an oil-dependent economy not factor world oil prices into its global strategy? It may proclaim its commitment to "market forces."[11] But such platitudes do not satisfy a country's demand for reasonably priced oil. This is especially the case for the United States, which is the world's largest consumer of petroleum products, much of which comes from the Middle East.

On a global level, OPEC countries (mostly in the Middle East) produce 35-50 percent of the world's oil exports. The United States consumes over twenty-five percent of the world's oil and forty-five percent of its gasoline. It imports fifty-five percent of the oil it consumes, a third of which comes from the Middle East. It runs a massive current accounts deficit largely because of its dependence on imported oil; and because most of the world's oil is sold in dollars, when the value of the dollar declines against other currencies, the price of oil rises. Price, however, is not the only problem facing the United States. Saudi Arabia, for years the U.S.'s principal supplier, will probably not be able to meet the U.S.'s growing demand for oil; so if its demand continues unabated, it will have to secure other sources. So too will other countries, notably rapidly modernizing China. In view of such considerations, one analyst says "(t)he hand on the spigot that regulates production (and therefore price) must be controlled by the United States."[12] Iraq, then, with reserves second only to Saudi Arabia, is an increasingly important source of Mideast oil, how much so depending on what new high-technology explorations find there. These explorations, of course, follow upon the U.S.'s "shock and awe"application of its military strength.

Note also, in this regard, that military strength is now heavily motorized, so itself requires reliable access to oil. As Norman D. Livergood points out, the U.S. and the U.K., among others, have long based their foreign policies and their military strategies on gaining access to oil.[13] To this end they have orchestrated coups, e.g., in Iran, provided arms to warring factions, e.g., in Vietnam, and have intervened militarily, e.g., in Kosovo, Afghanistan, and Iraq, and may do so elsewhere, e.g., in Syria and Iran. The goal? To achieve "full-spectrum dominance" of the world's oil supply, by building and protecting pipelines and developing recovery systems wherever there are reserves available to exploit. All this Livergood attributes to "U.S.-British Imperialism," now operating under the political (dis)guise of their governments' war on terrorism.

Livergood's account of Big Oil's quest to control available resources is credible, though too narrowly focused on British and U.S. oil companies. For, oil, along with other natural resources, is now considered the solution to all sorts of problems because so many industries as well as national economies depend on its availability at a market sustainable price. For decades now, however, most of the world's oil has been located outside these consumer countries' boundaries. So suppliers must go where it is, namely, in or offshore from developing countries. Given these geopolitical concerns, all the wiles of diplomacy from cajoling to military invasion are utilized to assure access to oil.

These geopolitical concerns first surfaced during World War I. The German military was never able to secure an adequate supply of oil, whereas the French and British were supplied by the US. When the war ended, France and Britain divided responsibility for potentially oil-rich Arab lands they took over from the Ottoman Empire, with the British turning Mesopotamia into a protectorate which they renamed Iraq. Later, both Germany and Japan lost World War II largely because neither managed to gain access to a regular supply of fuel for its land, sea, and aerial military vehicles.[14] Since World War II government policy makers have had to consider not only military needs for oil but the disparate effects that oil prices have on home heating costs, transportation and tourism and, inversely, on marginal producers, greenhouse gases, and state tax revenues. As for Iraq's oil, if a lot of it is sold, then (other things being equal) the market price will come down. But neither American nor British oil companies would like this to happen, because that would affect the marketability of their own more expensive product. This oil-glut scenario is less worrisome, though, so long as world consumption continues to increase and the supply from Iraq and other places now being developed remains below capacity.

In short, non-empirical economists tend to view the oil market as a self-regulating system. But in the real world competing interests have social, political, and economic reasons to stabilize both the price and the supply of oil. This is especially true of supply at a time of international hostilities. So controlling the world's oil supply is unquestionably a desideratum of political leaders, especially those with expansionary aspirations. This was the case before, during, and after the invasion of Iraq. To show this I will consider first some policy statements made by or to prior US administrations, then some Bush administration policy statements.

Reasons for Invading Iraq According to US Policy Declarations

The geopolitics of oil provides a framework within which one can begin to reflectively understand why the government of a country like the United States, with its large consumer demand for oil, might well seek to control the supply of oil. It does not follow from this, however, that any US administration did in fact adopt a strategy to bring this about. In particular, such generic information does not constitute evidence that the Bush administration had such a strategy and that this strategy called for conquering Iraq. This requires specific, detailed information that I will now introduce.

Pre-Bush Administration Mideast Geopolitics

Control of oil has long been a key component of US and UK policy towards the Middle East. After World War I, US and especially UK petroleum companies sought such control, and their governments assisted them in this objective. During the decades following World War II, the U.K. and increasingly the U.S. resorted to both hard and soft approaches to controlling Mideast oil.[15] Presidents Roosevelt and Truman bolstered oil company interests in Saudi Arabia. For decades Iran has been the site of successive coups (one instigated by the CIA) to determine who will control its oil. When Egypt nationalized the Suez Canal in 1956, French and British forces aided by Israel intervened militarily to reopen it to oil tankers; then to minimize cold war ramifications, Eisenhower negotiated arrangements with oil-producing countries. In 1972, Iraq nationalized its reserves, three-fourths of which had been controlled by British and US companies. A year later, Egypt and Syria invaded Israel causing it heavy losses of personnel and material. The Nixon Administration replaced Israel's material losses, OPEC responded with an oil embargo. In response, US loans and grants to Israel rose from half a million to over three billion dollars a year, and the pro-Israel lobby became ever more powerful and influential. For, it would henceforth be a key objective of US Mideast policy "to maintain the unfettered supply of oil at reasonable prices."[16]

Under President Carter, the Department of Defense developed a contingency plan that recommended developing a military infrastructure in the Middle East so that US forces could respond rapidly to protect oil reserves in that area.[17] Carter then announced in his last State of the Union address that any "attempt by an outside force to gain control of the Persian Gulf region" would be met by "any means necessary, including military force."[18] Over the next decade this so-called Carter Doctrine inspired a strategy to prevent either side in the Iran-Iraq War from gaining preeminence in the region. So the Reagan Administration supplied arms to Iraq while some of its key operatives – including former Bechtel Corporation CEO George Schultz, Dick Cheney, and Donald Rumsfeld – urged Saddam Hussein to let Bechtel use Export Import Bank funds to build an oil pipeline from Kirkuk to Aqaba. Hussein supported this project until the US broke its silence about his use of poison gas against the Kurds.[19] He thereafter ignored US and UK oil companies; then in 1991 to recoup war-incurred debts he invaded Kuwait. Declaring in an only recently declassified directive[20] that "(a)ccess to Persian Gulf oil and the security of key friendly states in the area are vital to U.S. national security," President George H. W. Bush cited "long-standing policy" in ordering the use of military force to oust the Iraqis from Kuwait; and this objective the Operation Desert Storm coalition quickly accomplished.

For the rest of the decade, including eight years under President Clinton, the U.S. and the U.K. routinely bombed and insisted on sanctions against Iraq. Meanwhile, US Middle East policy was heavily scrutinized by both private-sector and government strategists. Their focus was on what it would take militarily to keep the U.S. preeminent in the post-Cold War world and incidentally protect defense spending against any "peace dividend." Already in the 1990s the US military was spending between $50 and $60 billion a year to defend Middle East oil supplies.[21] Then in early 2001 this strategic planning came together in a resource assessment document that envisioned greatly increased need for oil from Iraq and other countries[22] and an action-oriented document in which the Bush administration was advised to take over Iraq. From among the many preparatory documents that are becoming available, I here consider just two late 1990s analyses of US energy policy, first one by a think tank, then one by a Defense Department strategy unit, each of which contends that the U.S. should intervene militarily to control Iraq's oil.

On 23 March 1998, Anthony H. Cordesman told the US Senate Armed Services Committee that the U.S. needed to take a military approach to controlling the oil resources in Iraq and Iran. This Senior Fellow and Co-Director of the Middle East Studies Program of Washington-based Center for Strategic and International Studies set forth a regrettably prophetic agenda.[23] Problems he identified include: the US's failure to contain either Saddam Hussein or the "regional ambitions and opportunism" of France, Russia, and China; Iraq's UN authorization to increase its oil exports from $2 billion to over $5 billion every six months; the counterproductive results of CIA "destabilization" efforts in Iraq; and the unreliability of any ally other than the U.K. for military support if needed. His proposed solutions are multi-layered. Militarily, the U.S. should "demonstrate the effectiveness of (its) unilateral conventional military options ... maintain an unannounced theater nuclear threat against proliferation," recognize that no comprehensive WMD inspection and verification is possible "short of full-scale occupation." Diplomatically, the U.S. should "gradually assert its own vital strategic interests in terms of declared 'doctrines' rather than relying on UN, Coalition, or Western consensus." In rethinking its regional oil policies, the U.S. should seek "how best to minimize Iraqi influence and control over the regional oil market, ensure surplus production and distribution capacity, and counterbalance any Iraqi favoritism towards French and Russian firms in dealing with petroleum development, production, and distribution." This revised policy, Cordesman added, should support "the maximum regional role for US industry." Relying neither on Iran nor on Iraq for oil, the U.S. needs them to be "important energy suppliers."

Later the same year Cordesman backed up his Senate committee testimony with an extensive set of charts and graphs that show, in particular, (1) that Asia, especially China and India, will account for most growth in energy consumption including oil and gas, (2) that most of this will be exported from the Middle East, and (3) that Iraq's oil production will need to increase from 2.2 million barrels per day in 1990 to 7.8 mbd in 2020. He is especially insistent that the rogue states of Iran, Iraq, and Libya "come fully on-line [in oil production] to avoid over-dependence on Saudi Arabia and possible price rises."[24]

One year later, Department of Defense strategists issued Strategic Assessment 1999 (NDU 1999), its fifth annual reflection on security problems, one of which is identified as maintaining access to the world's oil. Four chapters offer a global overview of problems ahead, seven home in on different regions, five on unstable nations, and four on weaponry needs for such a "turbulent world." In Chapter Three on "Energy and Resources: Ample or Scarce?" US reliance on Persian Gulf oil is deemed minimal for the foreseeable future but this finding is weakened by economists' argument that "(a)ny shortfall from the Gulf would affect all oil consumers equally." Ideally, the major importers from the region would defend it, but these include China and India, with whom the U.S. "is not likely to share decisionmaking."[25] This region, moreover, is "infected by political instability and anti-Western attitudes."[26] So "U.S. forces may intervene in future crises and wars in the Persian Gulf. Energy dynamics will dictate that U.S. forces play a major role in

Persian Gulf security."[27] Chapter Seven, in turn, concludes that "a middle-of-the-road course is most likely" in the Greater Middle East. But if Israeli-Palestinian relations should deteriorate (as they have) and the US military presence in the region is challenged. U.S. policies seeking access to oil at reasonable prices and promoting nonproliferation would be severely tested. An unstable oil market could have several outcomes. It could include angry oil producers, like Iran and Iraq, using force to punish those who might have expanded output, like Kuwait, Saudi Arabia, and the United Arab Emirates. It could also include instability within states dependent on oil revenues and unable to pay debts or subsidies to their citizens; this encompasses all the oil-producing states.[28]

Such, then, were the strategic precedents and proposals regarding Middle East oil that were available to the George W. Bush administration.

Bush Administration Mideast Geopolitics

These precedents and proposals became Bush administration policy, in approximately the following way. Soon after the inauguration there were secret meetings of the National Energy Policy Development Group, a task force established by President Bush on January 29, 2001, which studied Iraqi oilfields and issued a report five months later. U.S. Vice-President Cheney, himself a former oil executive, chaired these meetings; and, assert Judicial Watch and others in a lawsuit, various private-sector individuals, e.g., the then CEO of Enron, regularly attended. If so, the task force's records can be subpoenaed; but the DC appellate court held that the scope of discovery needed to be set first, and the U.S. Supreme Court, on appeal, told the district court to do that. Meanwhile, a task force set up by Vice-President Cheney and working under the joint sponsorship of Rice University's James Baker III Institute and the Council on Foreign Affairs completed a 130-page document entitled Strategic Energy Policy Challenges for the 21st Century. Already available in April 2001 but given a September 2001 publication date, it addresses such energy-related topics as conservation, diplomacy, and alternative sources of energy. Especially noteworthy, however, is its inclusion of military force as a way to stabilize the availability of Iraq's oil resources.

To reach this action item the task force first notes that "political factors" (Arab countries' dismay at the United States' pro-Israel stance) could "block the development of new oil fields in the Middle East," and this would have serious ramifications for a country like the U.S. that chooses not to conserve energy. Indeed, it continues, Iraq has already become an on-and-off "swing producer" to manipulate the market, and Saudi Arabia's "willing(ness) to provide replacement supplies" is unreliable. In order, then, to "eventually ease Iraqi oilfield (investment) restrictions"[29] the task force says:

> The United States should conduct an immediate policy review toward Iraq, including military, energy, economic, and political/diplomatic assessments ... (For,) Iraqi reserves represent a major asset that can quickly add capacity to world oil markets and inject a more competitive tenor to oil trade.[30]

In plain English, this is a call for self-interested control of Iraqi oil which includes a call to arms; and it was so understood by the first readers who became aware of its existence. The military option is not preeminent in this document, but it is the one the Bush administration chose to implement; and companies with an interest in its succeeding (already well represented on the task force) began to plan accordingly. Conveniently, an Independent Working Group cosponsored by the Baker Institute and the Council on Foreign Relations issued a 29-page report in December 2002, setting out "guiding principles for U.S. post-conflict policy in Iraq."[31] As its title suggests, this report assumes there will be military conflict. Its "guiding principles" for post-conflict governance in Iraq take up one-third of the document. Two-thirds is about managing production of Iraqi oil and, to a lesser extent, natural gas reserves. But the working group warns against "U.S. statements and behavior" that would indicate an interest in stealing or controlling Iraqi oil[32] and thus provoke "guerilla attacks against U.S. military personnel guarding oil installations."[33]

Thus guided behind the scenes, the Bush administration's political rhetoric cited only its manufactured jus ad bellum reasons for invading Iraq; and these reasons few American citizens seriously questioned. After "coalition" troops had occupied Iraq, a 1,400-member special forces Iraq Survey Group undertook a search for weapons of mass destruction. Survey group head David Kay reported in October 2003 that they had found none; and the administration began shifting its rhetoric from the WMD pseudo-motive to that of regime change. In January 2004, they reassigned 400 technical experts as Kay resigned and he and others began publicly discussing the import of his group's failure to find WMDs. In the meantime, as noted, President Bush had signed secret decrees that assured to US and UK oil companies unlimited, open-ended control of every barrel of Iraqi oil. This objective was in turn just one part of a plan to privatize all of Iraq's capital assets in order to establish a libertarian utopia.[34] Before foreign investors could be lured to Iraq, however, these privatizations had to be legitimized under international law, and this required authorization by an Iraqi government with internationally recognized sovereignty. To this end, the U.S. set up a coalition-friendly interim council which it replaced in June 2004 with a selected group of regional representatives whose principal task was to arrange for national elections to be held early in 2005. This agenda has been severely hampered, however, by the repeated attacks on coalition-affiliated persons and property, the interim leaders' desire to honor pre-invasion oil contracts with French and Russian companies, and the Shiite majority's insistence that government officials be elected. Behind the scenes, revenue from oil production has been diverted to U.S.-selected projects mostly carried out by US companies with no transparent accounting in place.

Neither U.S. presidential candidate mentioned any of this, perhaps because no less important than controlling the oil is not to appear interested in that oil.

Reflective Understanding and War: A Pragmatic Approach to Reflective Equilibrium

Would it have been possible to apply just war theory in real time to assess whether there were adequate reasons for invading Iraq? This invasion was mounted to achieve a complex set of converging objectives – military, geopolitical, and economic, among others – which were set forth in advance in strategic policy documents. These, however, were not articulated in public discourse. Bush administration spokespersons called this intervention a humanitarian rescue of victims variously identified as US citizens, the Iraqi people, and/or the world at large. Ignoring past US complicity with Saddam Hussein as his weapons provider and longtime advocate, they stressed his villainy as justification for warring against him (and "collaterally," of course, against Iraqi civilians). And they mentioned Iraqi oil only to deny its relevance. But what if (as argued above) Iraqi oil was their target, documentary evidence shows this, and (largely contrary to fact) knowledgeable critics said so openly, often, and before the fact? Under these circumstances, the Bush administration might have contended that gaining control of oil (however cosmetically phrased) suffices for justly warring. No matter, though, because the media remained fixated on the administration's announced objectives.

Such, then, is the challenge that faced anyone who wanted to assess such a war in a timely, rather than retrospective, way. To address this problem, as already suggested, one would need reflective understanding. But how does one achieve this? Not by staying within the parameters of Rawls's approach to reflective equilibrium, which he did not extend to foreign policy. But we might try to open this quest for a coherent set of moral principles to include Edward Said's critique of real-world facts (aimed at reflective understanding).

Many academic philosophers, as will be discussed, would frown on this proposed move; but, I believe, just war theorists should endorse it. Why? Because the gap between ideational critique of moral principles and real-world critique of war-making justifications needs to be bridged if just war theory is to be more than merely an historical tool. But doing so is hampered by an epistemological gap between truth-sensitive and goal-oriented uses of language. For, by way of illustration, ancillary to the geopolitical case that was made in behalf of taking over Iraq in 2003 was a dualistic approach both to foreign policy and to communication that has been traced to the philosophical outlook of Leo Strauss. This outlook invites philosophical critique, not merely as a set of ideas but as facts on the ground.

Late Twentieth Century Philosophers on Political Affairs

A number of neoconservatives associated directly and indirectly with the Bush administration apparently found in Leo Strauss's ideas a justification both for imperialist policies and for concealment of their true motives from the general public. If true as various analysts claim, this represents an approach to justifying state use of military power that was rarely supported by American philosophers in the latter half of the twentieth century. So a philosophical antidote seems required, but it cannot be neatly derived from others' efforts at that time. John Rawls can serve as a starting point, however, and the early twenty-first century work of Jonathan Glover takes us much farther. So I will put Strauss and Rawls in their cultural context, then contrast their respective approaches, and finally go beyond their ideational world to the real world as studied by Glover and others.

Rawls acknowledges that even well-ordered peoples might go to war for realpolitik reasons, yet subscribes to the peace thesis that politically wise statesmen together with an expansion of commerce and trade will build a better world in which such misbehavior no longer occurs. But political wisdom may not be the driving force behind a government's decisions. For, as Rawls learned from World War II, people in power might be motivated by an invidious political philosophy with dangerous implications for the world. And this may still occur wherever power is relatively unlimited. Certain Bush administration ideologues in particular seem to have found reasons for international over-reaching in the views of German-Jewish emigre Leo Strauss, according to whom the Nazi takeover of the Weimar Republic showed how easily a democracy can be turned into a demagoguery. A classicist professionally, Strauss understood Plato's Republic to be a warning about how democracy would turn Athens into an unlivable, anti-elitist dystopia.[35] To appreciate this atypical interpretation, one must look beneath the superficial to the esoteric meaning. For, as Plato advised, the truth is for the few; for the masses, a noble lie will do. Strauss transmitted this modus operandi to his students some of whom later established the neoconservative Project for the New American Century,[36] some associates of which became key proponents of the Bush administration's policy towards Iraq. On their view, evildoers are everywhere, so good – preferably religious – politicians need to use deception in their dealings with friends and enemies alike and, moreover, replace the cautious social science approach that characterized US intelligence gathering with a results-oriented political philosophy. The neoconservatives' agenda has been called into question since the takeover of Iraq. Their elitist-cum-imperialist philosophical view remains very useful, though, to members of the Bush Administration, including the president.[37] And their approach to global affairs is based in part on a political philosophy which extends to areas of policy well beyond where John Rawls thought philosophy could go; so it must be challenged on a philosophical level.[38] To this end I will first describe a mid-twentieth century debate among philosophers about critiquing public affairs, then locate Rawls in that debate, then move beyond.

An apolitical stance dominated post-World War II philosophical attitudes in the United States. When the Nazis came to power in Germany before that war, many scholars fled, some to the United States. Two political philosophers who came here, Hannah Arendt and Leo Strauss, were both dissatisfied with existing forms of democracy – Arendt because they lack collaborative deliberation, Strauss because they risk giving way to mobocracy. But a number of philosopher emigres from Vienna, known as logical positivists, saw no basis in theory for addressing political issues, and many U.S. philosophers at mid-century and beyond adopted this stance.[39]

The Vietnam war intensified the split between non-concerned and concerned philosophers, as they are called. The former, denying that one could arrive at a position on public affairs from philosophical reasoning, reduced doing so to a matter of personal preference. Sidney Hook considered philosophers ill-prepared to speak intelligently about political matters.[40] Herbert Marcuse, however, speaking as American Philosophical Association Pacific Division President in 1969, urged philosophers to abandon their "puritan neutralism" and critique "the language, the behavior, the conditions of the existing society" to "counteract the massive ideological indoctrination practiced by the advanced repressive societies of today."[41] Some scholars did this, especially with regard to the causes of war[42] and just war theory.[43] Their work was primarily retrospective, however, whereas what is needed is guidance regarding real-time decisions.

Rawls moved in this direction in his intra-societal theory, first fully developed in his *A Theory of Justice*.[44] But when he turned to global affairs in his *The Law of Peoples*[45] he held on to his intra-state priorities, organizing his thoughts around a problematic classification of peoples according to how well they govern themselves internally and behave themselves externally. Preeminent in his world are "liberal" peoples, in comparison with whom others are evaluated and, if need be, disciplined. Ideally, he argues, liberal peoples will not bully any well-ordered peoples, liberal or only decent. To be deemed decent, he says, a people must honor group rights; but it should be tolerated even if, other things being equal, it is not committed to individual human rights. Both liberal and decent peoples may go to war but only in self-defense; and, for that matter so may any people, even in a dictatorship, if they honor human rights and are not aggressors.[46] At this point, however, equal access to a jus ad bellum ends. For, only a well-ordered society, and a fortiori a liberal society, is entitled, and at times obligated, to intervene even militarily if another society falls too far short of the ideal by becoming a serious threat to peace in the world (an outlaw society) or by facing debilitating circumstances beyond its control (a burdened society). The standards he endorses, then, for dealing with "non-ideal" situations in our imperfect world are about what an "advanced" nation-state would come up with and put into practice, especially if its military prowess far surpasses that of others even combined. Rawls acknowledges that such might could too facilely declare itself right. But he does not subject his value-laden classification of peoples to serious critique. This lacuna in his work can be overcome, however, if one pushes the boundaries of reflective equilibrium farther than he did. I propose doing just that.

Reflective equilibrium, says Rawls, is achieved by means of a back-and-forth process of fine-tuning principles selected in the fact-oblivious original position in light of one's considered convictions[47] and testing the latter against the principles.[48] Eschewing an ideal reflective equilibrium, Rawls settles for examining the tradition of moral philosophy plus any other views that come to mind.[49] This probably doesn't include judgments about facts; yet Rawls does say that to "understand our sense of justice" we must "know in some systematic way covering a wide range of cases what these principles are."[50]

Rawls's reflective equilibrium has had a mixed reception. Generally speaking, it stands or falls depending on one's view of coherence, that is, consistency among principles or beliefs. Among philosophers, foundationalists fault Rawls's willingness to settle for coherence because, they insist, one ought not endorse norms without having first established them meta-ethically.[51] Some logic-oriented philosophers have, however, sought to systematize the search for coherence.[52] Philosophers attuned to social mores tend to oppose Rawls's approach, but for opposite reasons – either because they believe it unlikely to uproot people's deeply held biases[53] or, inversely, because they fear it would do just that, thereby threatening the traditions and myths that underpin the status quo.[54] Some non-philosophical specialists, by contrast, are using reflective equilibrium to address concrete problems, applying it, e.g., to environmental impact analyses[55] and political affairs.[56] Rawls himself envisions the search for reflective equilibrium as a work in progress ever open to further revision.[57] But in LP, as noted, he does not use this device to elaborate rules for international behavior. Instead he posits rules, envisions their eventual acceptance by all, and in the interim subjects the non-compliant to the discipline of "liberal" nation-states. This amounts to wishful thinking, the mirror image of which is a Hobbesian wolf in civilized sheep's clothing.

The principal weakness in Rawls's approach to global affairs is his reliance on an imperfect institution, the liberal society, to act as interim policing agent until a hoped for realistic utopia has come into being. In Rawlsian terminology, this amounts to confusing the expectations set forth in ideal theory with the realities dealt with in nonideal theory. He does this, however, with full awareness of a liberal society's potential for mischief. Already in TJ, for example, he reasoned that an individual soldier may refuse to carry out orders "if he reasonably and conscientiously believes that the principles applying to the conduct of war are plainly violated."[58] Years later in LP, though contending that neither liberal nor decent peoples go to war against one another[59] he devotes several pages to their jus ad bellum towards others. In particular, they may go to war but "only when they sincerely and reasonably believe that their safety and security are seriously endangered by the expansionist policies of outlaw states."[60] In effect reinstating his earlier view of conscientious objection, he adds that "a liberal society cannot justly require its citizens to fight in order to gain economic wealth or to acquire natural resources, much less to win power and empire."[61] It is not clear, however, if such dissent applies to societies that are not liberal. For, in LP (as already sketched in TJ 58) he puts not individual persons but representatives of peoples behind a veil of ignorance. They adopt rules acceptable to both liberal and typically non-democratic decent peoples. Not all peoples will be compliant, though, so there needs to be global policing of "non-well-ordered peoples"[62] and some limited assistance to "burdened societies."[63] The rules Rawls sets forth in ideal theory are standard fare in international law; but he offers little guidance to those called upon to enforce them in non-ideal theory. In particular, he does not address the pros and cons of humanitarian intervention. He insists that burdened peoples can rise beyond their harsh conditions and ought not depend indefinitely on help from beyond their borders; and he rejects economic exploitation as grounds for going to war. But he provides no reliable basis for precluding global exploitation that is deceptively characterized as noble assistance. This discomforting outcome is due in part to Rawls's not having applied reflective equilibrium questioning to global norms.

Rawls apparently believes that once peoples, or nations, become rule-compliant, the world will consist of satisfied societies. For, "a group of satisfied peoples" will no longer look to religion, territory, or political expansion as operative motives for going to war. He does cite some horrendous counter-indications, but seems to think they are non-recurring hence not fatal to attaining a Kantian end state. The Holocaust will not recur, he says – but it has, e.g., in Cambodia, in Rwanda, and in the former Yugoslavia. Economic needs, he says, can be met through negotiation and trade.[64] But to believe this, he admits, one must assume "the larger nations with the wealthier economies will not attempt to monopolize the market, or to conspire to form a cartel, or to act as an oligopoly."[65] Both European countries and the United States, though, have done just that.[66] Yet Rawls believes democratic peoples will in time "engage in war only as allies in self-defense against outlaw states."[67] And when they do, they will act only to maintain global peace. Meanwhile, in the here and now, they might go to war "to gain economic wealth or to acquire natural resources," or even "to win power and empire." If one does, it is not honoring the Law of Peoples, and becomes an outlaw state.[68] Yes, he continues in a footnote, "so-called liberal states sometimes do this, but that only shows they may act wrongly."

These crucial admissions invite treating non-compliant incidents as merely extra-theoretical aberrations but in fact they generate a conundrum. Rawls relies on liberal democracies to bring outlaw states into compliance with the Law of Peoples; yet he acknowledges that a liberal state might itself behave like an outlaw state. Moreover, its policing function is to be guided, he says, by foreign policy graced with political wisdom and luck. Nothing more, for "(t)hese are not matters to which political philosophy has much to add."[69] In theory, then, his principles of global justice are supposed to help distinguish the fox from the farmer; in practice, a fox adept at spin-control might pass for a farmer until there are no more chickens.

In short, after constructing a global framework to advance peace in the world, Rawls concedes it will fail if the designated peace-keeping states act in destructive ways which are beyond the reach of political philosophy. De facto they do, but he merely regrets such counter-indications even though he himself had warned in TJ[70] that when "counter examples ... tell us ... that our theory is wrong somewhere" we should "find out how often and how far it is wrong." He doesn't do this in LP, but hints that he favors doing so by "relying on conjecture and speculation" to envision changes in political and social institutions,[71] agreeing on rules for a Society of Peoples "when a shared basis of justification exists and can be uncovered by due reflection"[72] doing this through a process that "assumes the reasonableness of political liberalism" which is confirmed by the reasonable Law of Peoples thus developed[73] and by Kantian practical reasoning whereby "the resulting principles and standards of right and justice will hang together and will be affirmed by us on due reflection."[74]

Responding Philosophically to Philosophically Endorsed Political Violence

Given his assertions about how global rules are to be determined, why would Rawls leave a government's activities in the world to its foreign policy, political wisdom, and luck? Why say that political philosophy has little to add, knowing as he does that political violence is routinely rationalized? Perhaps he means there are areas of expertise other than political philosophy that facilitate understanding a government's motives. This said, though, philosophical considerations may also influence a government's motives.

Plato, as Leo Strauss advised his proteges, actually thought a society would be better off with philosophers in charge. But the historical record in this regard is mixed at best. The eighteenth-century French activist philosophers ("philosophes") were "men of letters, writers of books" who sought to bring progress and then perfection to the human condition.[75] When to their ideas power was added, however, the result was the Reign of Terror. This does not prove that philosophy and power are never compatible, but it is a warning that reflecting on ideas is worse than useless if not joined with a moral commitment to human rights.

Similarly, Karl Marx's brilliant analyses of economic exploitation took a turn for the worse when purportedly acted upon by Stalin and Mao Zedong. Similar cautions apply to Nietzsche in the hands of the Nazis, although Leo Strauss thought "a planetary aristocracy" is preferable to "a universal classless and stateless society."[76] And such views are, as noted, an inspiration to Bush administration neoconservatives as they pursue their quest for dominance. So in addition to documenting the connection between oil and their targeting of Iraq, one seeking a full account of motives would need to assess the philosophical underpinnings of their endeavor. For this latter purpose, I take a lesson from moral philosopher Jonathan Glover's *Humanity*.[77]

In this book Glover discredits the alleged principles used to justify the wars, massacres, and other moral disasters of the twentieth century. Having accomplished this in unrelenting detail, he is left with no legitimate rationale for these manifestations of human cruelty. What he finds instead is that blind belief, blind adherence to honor, and blind obedience account for the bestial way in which human beings act towards other human beings. So he recommends that we seek an explanation for such heartless behavior in human psychology so, hopefully, we might ameliorate its consequences in the future.

What, a critic might ask, entitles Glover to report on and analyze this immense body of data? As he himself acknowledges, he did not personally experience the moral disasters he describes but relies on reports by others who did.[78] And many of those on whom he depends for information were themselves reporting what they learned from others. So Glover is twice removed from direct empirical evidence. He nonetheless helps us understand this evidence from a moral perspective that the perpetrators assiduously disavowed. He does not justify the moral perspective from which he critiques the political hypocrisy of mass murderers. But he requires the reader to look without euphemism at the ideological slogans and pseudo-science to which they appealed to justify their systematic killing. In so doing, one is backed into a corner from which neither indifference nor approbation offers an acceptable escape.

To develop a comparable moral critique of the Bush administration's agenda to gain control of the world's oil would far exceed the scope of this essay. But the issue can be stated succinctly by noting that the same antiterrorist rhetoric used to cloud motives for invading Iraq is already being directed towards the other two countries in Bush's axis of evil: Iran and North Korea. While political rhetoric and activity focuses on their respective WMD potentials, oil industry experts are busy determining the extent of their oil reserves and how best to access these. Iran's immense reserves of oil and natural gas are well known. North Korea's, though still mostly undeveloped, have also had the attention of industry experts in recent years. With this geopolitical agenda duly noted, I will suggest in concluding how a practical ethicist might strive for reflective understanding of an event like the takeover of Iraqi oil by questioning the validity of asserted threats on which such military interventions are justified.

With relevant factual information at hand, an ethicist can avoid being taken in by a government's rhetorical deception, apply ethical norms to the strategies being implemented on the ground, and evaluate their justification. First, the ethicist might learn from available strategy proposals that a government's asserted motives for certain impending actions do not accurately reflect the motives set forth in its strategic plans, hence call for some adjustments to salvage reflective equilibrium. If this cannot be done without either ignoring the available evidence or abandoning the moral principles brought to bear in assessing it, the ethicist may have to conclude that the strategy being examined is not morally justifiable.

This type of critique helps clarify the meaning and scope of one's moral convictions. It is not a decision machine, but if done thoroughly it helps sort out likely consequences of a given course of action or, inversely, of doing otherwise. In particular, if the reasons a government puts forward for pursuing a certain course of action do not clearly justify the negative consequences of so acting, e.g., the loss of numerous lives and the expenditure of vast sums of money, one can hardly accept the government's stated reasons without disavowing any expectation of achieving reflective equilibrium about the matter. This conflict between one's moral beliefs and the government's stated reasons is even more likely to occur if one takes steps to neutralize an "Our Side Bias,"[79] notably by asking how really fair and impartial are the reasons a government puts forward in proclaiming its course of action just. Are these grounded in legitimate moral principles or do they depend on unexamined biases which dispel all doubts by laying claim to collective righteousness? As Glover's work makes clear, such unexamined beliefs on a grand scale can impact innocent people's lives in ways that are unspeakably brutal and brutalizing. Whence the importance of going beyond just war theorizing to reflect, in Said's sense, on the unexamined beliefs of active warmongers.

Philosophers, among others, have in recent years been moving in this direction. They have not yet generated a real time critique of reasons put forward for going to war. But they are examining background concepts that seem destined to play a role in military endeavors yet to come. In particular, they have focused on the morality of terrorism as such,[80] not on political talk about an ongoing "war on terrorism." One encouraging exception in this regard is a recent publication[81] in which contributing philosophers and theologians warn that merely saying "they are terrorists" does not justify taking military action against people so labeled or others only incidentally associated with them.[82] What matters, though, is that philosophers and others are beginning to critique political violence in a timely way. And from the congressional speeches of Ron Paul (R-TX) prior to the invasion of Iraq they could learn that one who is well informed and courageous can apply just war theory to evolving belligerence in real time.

Political violence, in short, can become the subject of reflective understanding. To be effective in real time, however, the occasional concerned ethicist or politician must become thousands, indeed millions of people who refuse to be duped by words promoting deeds that surely will not to heaven go. Unarmed opponents of militarism are, of course, at an extreme disadvantage; but U.S. troops did eventually leave Vietnam, and China has changed since Tiananmen Square. So when a critical mass of voices rises in opposition to unjustified violence, the morally blind can no longer rely on the politically deaf for support. In such circumstances, peace becomes at least a possibility.

Notes

1   Leonardo Maugeri. "Not In Oil's Name," *Foreign Affairs* 82/4, (July/August 2003): 165-174; Timothy E Wirth, C. Boyden Gray, and John D. Podesta. "The Future of Energy Policy," *Foreign Affairs* 82/4, (July/August 2003): 132-155.

2   Brian Orend. *War and International Justice: A Kantian Perspective* (Waterloo, Ontario, Canada: Wilfrid Laurier University Press, 2000) pp. 48-50.

3   Roy Godson and James J. Wirtz. "Strategic Denial and Deception." *International Journal of Intelligence and Counter Intelligence* 13 (2000): 424-437; Eric Alterman. *When Presidents Lie: A History of Official Deception and Its Consequences* (New York: Viking, 2004).

4   David Miller. "Information Dominance: The Philosophy of Total Propaganda Control?" *Scoop*, 29 December 2003. Available online at http://www.globalpolicy.org.

5   Oliver Boyd-Barrett. "Imperial News and the New Imperialism." *Third World Resurgence* (June 2003): 44-48, 151-152. Available online at http://www.global policy.org.

6   PBS Frontline (3 March 2003).

7   Michael Klare. *Resource Wars: The New Landscape of Global Conflict* (New York: Henry Holt Metropolitan, 2002).

8   Gilbert Achcar. "U.S. Imperial Strategy in the Middle East." *Monthly Review* 55/9, (February 2004): pp. 28-29; Ron Suskind. *The Price of Loyalty: George W. Bush, The White House, and the Education of Paul O'Neill* (New York: Simon & Schuster, 2004).

9   Michael Ignatieff. "The Burden." *New York Times Magazine*, 5 January 2003, 22-27; Robert Cooper. "The Post-Modern State," in *Reordering the World: The Long-Term Implications of September 11*, Mark Leonard (ed.), (London: Foreign Policy Center, 2002).

10 Record, 2003.

11 See, for instance, Edward L. Morse and Amy Myers Jaffe, et al. *Strategic Energy Policy: Challenges for the 21st Century* (Washington, DC: Council on Foreign Relations Press, 2001), p. 41.

12 Minqi Li "After Neoliberalism: Empire, Social Democracy, or Socialism?" *Monthly Review* 55/8, (January 2004): p. 29.

13 Norman D. Livergood. "The New U.S.-British Oil Imperialism," published online at hermes-press.com/impintro1.htm (orig. 10/29/2001).

14 Daniel Yergin. *The Prize: The Epic Quest for Oil, Money, and Power* (New York: Simon & Schuster, 1991).

15 Ibid,, Parts IV-V; James A. Paul. "Oil Companies in Iraq: A Century of Rivalry and War." Available online at http://www.globalpolicy.org/security/oil/2003 /2003companiesiniraq.htm.

16 Sandra Mackey. *The Reckoning: Iraq and the Legacy of Saddam Hussein* (New York: W. W. Norton, 2002), pp. 171, 228, 338.

17 "Capabilities for Limited Contingencies in the Persian Gulf." U.S. Department of Defense (DOD), 15 June 1979. Referred to informally as the Limited Contingency Study, recently declassified.

18 Steve Kretzmann. "Oil, Security, War: The Geopolitics of U.S. Energy Planning." *Multinational Monitor* (Jan.-Feb 2003), p. 13.

19 Battle 2003; Jim Vallette. "Crude Vision: How Oil Interests Obscured U.S. Government Focus on Chemical Weapons Use by Saddam Hussein," *Sustainable Energy & Economy Network/Institute for Policy Studies* (March 2003).

20 *National Security Directive 54* (NSD 54). A classified memorandum from President George H. W. Bush to key members of his administration on the subject of "Responding to Iraqi Aggression in the Gulf" (15 January 1991). Available online at http://www.washingtonpost.com/wp-srv/inatl/longterm/fogofwar/docdirective.htm.

21 M.A. Delucchi, and J. Murphy. "U.S. Military Expenditures to Protect the Use of Persian-Gulf Oil for Motor Vehicles," UCD-175-RR-96-3 (15). University of California, Davis, CA (April 1996.).; Patricia S. Yu. "Estimates of 1996 U.S. Military Expenditures on Defending Oil Supplies from the Middle East," Oak Ridge National Laboratory, 1997.

22 "The Geopolitics of Energy into the 21st Century: Panel Report." Center for Strategic and International Studies (CSIS), February 2001.

23 Anthony H. Cordesman 1998. "Living With Saddam: Reshaping US Strategy in the Middle East." Testimony to the Senate Armed Services Committee (23 May 1998).

24 ——. "The Changing Geopolitics of Energy." Center for Strategic and International Studies (CSIS), 12 August 1998: pp. 9, 16, 21-22, 53.

25 "Strategic Assessment 1999: Priorities for a Turbulent World." National Defense University (NDU), Institute for National Strategic Studies, 1999. www.ndu.edu/inss/Strategic%20Assessments/sa99cont.html, 51.

26 Ibid., 39.

27 Ibid., 49.

28 Ibid., 119.

29 Morse and Jaffe, *Strategic Energy Policy*, pp. 23, 40, 81.

30 Ibid., 42-43.

31 Edward P Djerejian and Frank G. Wisner. "Guiding Principles for U.S. Post-Conflict Policy in Iraq: Report of an Independent Working Group." Available at http://www.bakerinstitute.org/Pubs/W-Papers.htm.

32 Ibid., 8.

33 Ibid., 16.

34 Naomi Klein. "Baghdad Year Zero: Pillaging Iraq in Pursuit of a Neocon Utopia." *Harper's Magazine* (September 2004): 43-53.

35 Strauss, 1959, 126.

36 Robert Kagan and William Kristol. *Present Dangers: Crisis and Opportunity in American Foreign and Defense Policy* (San Francisco: Encounter Books, 2000).

37 Earl Shorris. "Leo Strauss, George Bush, and the Philosophy of Mass Deception," *Harper's Magazine* (June 2004): 65-71.

38 Peter Singer. *The President of Good & Evil: The Ethics of George W. Bush* (New York: Dutton, 2004).

39 John McCumber. "A Closed Intellectual Community: The Policing of American Philosophy." *Studies in Practical Philosophy* 2/2, (2002): 124-137.

40 Sidney Hook. "Philosophy and Public Policy," in Charles J. Bontempo and S. Jack Odell (eds.) *The Owl of Minerva: Philosophers on Philosophy* (New York: McGraw-Hill, 1975), pp. 76, 81, 85.

41 Herbert Marcuse. "The Relevance of Reality," in Charles J. Bontempo and S. Jack Odell (eds.) *The Owl of Minerva: Philosophers on Philosophy* (New York: McGraw-Hill, 1975), pp. 237-238, 241.

42 Robert Ginsberg (ed.) *The Critique of War: Contemporary Philosophical Explorations* (Chicago: Henry Regner, 1969).

43 Michael Walzer. *Just and Unjust Wars* (New York: Basic Books, 1977); Jean Bethke Elshtain (ed.) *Just War Theory* (New York: New York University Press, 1992).

44 John Rawls. *A Theory of Justice* (Cambridge, MA: Belknap Press of Harvard University, 1971).

45 John Rawls. *The Law of Peoples* (Cambridge, MA: Harvard University Press, 1999).

46 Ibid., 92.

47 Rawls, *A Theory of Justice,* 20.

48 Ibid., 46-53.

49 Ibid.

50 Ibid., 46.

51 Jon Mandle. *What's Left of Liberalism? An Interpretation and Defense of Justice as Fairness* (Lanham, MD: Lexington Books, 2000), pp. 45-55.

52 Folk Tersman. *Reflective Equilibrium: An Essay in Moral Epistemology* (Stockholm: Almqvist & Wakool International, 1993).

53 Onora O'Neill. *Towards Justice and Virtue: A Constructive Account of Practical Reasoning* (Cambridge: Cambridge University Press, 1996), pp. 41, 47; Diana Tietjens Meyers. *Subjection and Subjectivity* (New York: Routledge, 1994), pp. 44-47.

54 Mandle, *What's Left of Liberalism?* 194-204.

55 Anders Melin. "'Reflective Equilibrium' as a Method for Analyzing the Dilemma of Assessing Environmental Impacts – An Analysis of EIAs in the Catchment Area of Emån." Proceedings from the 3rd Nordic EIA/SEA Conference (22-23 November 1999), pp. 141-142, 156-159.

56 J. Vorstenbosch "Reflective Equilibrium and Public Debate: How to Cast the Public's Web of Beliefs Broadly Enough," in W. Van de Burg and T. van Willigenburg (eds.) *Reflective Equilibrium* (Dordrecht: Kluwer, 1998); Neil Levy. "Wider Still: Reflective Equilibrium and the Explanation of Political Radicalization." *International Journal of Politics and Ethics* (June 2001); Andreas Føllesdal. "Rawls in the Nordic Countries." Advanced Research on the Europeanization of the Nation State (ARENA) Working Paper 02/15/2002. Available at http://www.arena.uio.no/publications/wp02_15.htm.

57 John Rawls. *Political Liberalism* (New York: Columbia University Press, 1993), p. 97.

58 Rawls, *A Theory of Justice,* 380.

59 Rawls, *The Law of Peoples,* 8, 90.

60 Ibid., 90-91.

61 Ibid., 91.

62 Ibid., 89-105.

63 Ibid., 105-120.

64 Ibid., 19, 46-47.

65 Ibid., 43.

66 Ibid., 52-54, 98-103.

67 Ibid., 52-54, 98-103.

68 Ibid., 91.

69 Ibid., 93.

70 Rawls, *A Theory of Justice,* 52.

71 Ibid., 12.

72 Ibid., 19.

73 Ibid., 22-23.

74 Ibid., 87.
75 Carl L. Becker. *The Heavenly City of the Eighteenth Century Philosophers* (New Haven: Yale University Press, 1932), p. 35.
76 Strauss, Leo. *What Is Political Philosophy? And Other Studies* (Chicago: University of Chicago Press, 1959), p. 54.
77 Jonathan Glover. *Humanity: A Moral History of the Twentieth Century* (New Haven: Yale Nota Bene, 2001).
78 Glover, *Humanity*, xi, 4-5.
79 Trudy Govier. *A Delicate Balance: What Philosophy Can Tell Us About Terrorism* (Boulder, CO: Westview Press, 2002), p. 85.
80 See, for example, Corlett 2003; John R Rowan, (ed.) *War and Terrorism: Social Philosophy Today* 20 (2004).
81 James P Sterba (ed.) *Terrorism and International Justice* (New York: Oxford University Press, 2003).
82 See also Benjamin R. Barber. *Fear's Empire: War, Terrorism, and Democracy* (New York: Norton, 2003); Singer, *The President of Good & Evil*; John Pilger. "Power, Propaganda and Conscience in the War on Terror," *Znet* (26 January 2004). Available online at http://www.globalpolicy.org.

Chapter 13

Beyond Politics

Helena Cristini
International University of Monaco

What characterizes our era today is how our world is bedevilled by obsolete "isms" and rigid ideologies: positivism, rationalism, modernism, pluralism, capitalism, Marxism, fundamentalism, and so forth and so on. None seem to contribute to settling international, national, and personal conflicts. Disequilibrium and alienation are in ascendancy everywhere and consequently the world has become uprooted wherein no culture is spared; both the west and the east are struck by wars, intolerance or fanaticism. If we asked the question, what is the cause and looked exclusively for the answer in the political or economical realm, we would not find the solution to this malaise. The problem is neither purely political nor merely economic, but is an existential one. That is why several scholars have attributed the origins of this contemporary political, economic and social malaise to secular politics, where legal and religious activities are separated.

Secular politics are not challenged in this article, however as sociological studies indicate it has brought about a secularization of consciousness that entails divorcing the temporal and the spiritual. Personal morality is voluntarily detached from public affairs. The world we live in, is one in which moral crises and subservience to merely political values, is the predominant condition. Hence values are uprooted and this article attempts to redefine secular culture in order to include ethical concerns.

The State of Contemporary Politics and the State of Our World

If one intends to describe the state of politics at the beginning of this twenty-first century, they will be confronted with dismal situation. More and more the state controls economic and social life. As a result, in reality national politics are not concerned with the supreme direction of society, but are characterized by corruption and domestic violence. As for domestic violence, one could wonder if any country exists without it. It is just in this very period in which the state stands alone and supreme that we are witnessing not only its decomposition, but also that man has placed his most valuable possessions in the hands of the state. What is more, on inspection, almost all the words and phrases representing the values of our political vocabulary turn out to be hollow, and this superficial language has become the language of politicians globally.

As for international politics, events have shown that they continue to reflect power politics and are mostly marked by turbulence and violence. A succession of devastating wars has shown no signs of letting up. Up to World War I there had been nine hundred major wars in the history of civilization, but in this war the fatalities were unprecedented in any single war. And this most bloody of centuries was just beginning and was to expand to include literally hundreds of wars and atrocities, both large and small. At the end of the twentieth century, the initial euphoria that followed the collapse of the Soviet Union had given way to the horror of "ethnic cleansing" unfolding in its wake. The ignominious September 11th 2001, marked the beginning of a new era: terrorism, which continues and manifests itself in atrocities against civilians: a disco in Indonesia in Bali on the 12th of October 2002,[1] a train in Madrid on the 11th of March 2004.[2] As Catherine R. Stimpson states:

> the refusal to live peaceably in pluralistic societies [has been] one of the bloodiest problems – nationally and internationally – of the 20th century. No wizard, no fairy godmother is going to make this problem disappear. And I retain a pluralist's stubborn Utopia hope that people can talk about, through, across and around their differences and that these exchanges will help us live together justly.[3]

Nobody knows its unravelling. In the last hundred years not only has the human death toll and world destruction been very great, but the fearful uncertainty that prevails for the future is appalling.

Furthermore, as we begin this technologically advanced century, we can witness that the crisis is multifaceted. For example, we are also facing a world wide environmental problem. As decades of economic pursuits without regard for economical consequences are tallied, we see an unprecedented pollution which challenges our world's future; not to mention the moral disarray that modern man finds himself, especially in the most privileged nations. Western psychiatrists comment that an existential malaise prevails coupled with an awesome feeling of insecurity in rich countries: the consumption of anti-depressants has never been as high[4] in Europe Britain holds the record for teenage pregnancy[5] and France for the suicide rate amongst youngsters.[6]

Problem Statement

Therefore, the crises of the world are not confined to the political area. The background of violence in the dawn of this century is such that political theorists go astray as they attempt to explain its causes. Thinkers such as Plato, Simone

Weil and Gandhi would not hesitate to provide a common answer on the roots of this crisis; we live in a world in which moral crisis and subservience to purely political values is the predominant condition.[7] I would agree with them that the separation of the realm of morality from the realm of political affairs has fragmented our modern culture and has brought along political crisis, and the crisis of political behaviour. One should not be surprised that we are witnessing its consequences. Values are uprooted or allowed to decay, their hierarchy disrupted and their meaning corrupted.[8]

Having exposed the problem of the process of secularization and its associated consequences, one should not be reactionary and wish to return to a prior system of thought, such as the Middle Age one. No system of thought, per se, is perfect. However, following Machiavelli, one cannot prevent oneself from the fallacies that the system of thought has made:

> ... the religion of science (is) a faith in the existence of an objective reason, impersonal and mechanical, harmonious and deterministic, existing entirely apart from individual men and indifferent to their purposes.[9]

The problem does not lie in the fact that Machiavelli introduced secularization into politics, separating the Church and political affairs, rather the problem resides in secularised culture and its belief in progress, rationalism, empiricism, individualism, positivism, and scientism which has distorted the way man sees himself and consequently sees others. The desire for wholeness that man has always yearned for cannot be fulfilled in the scientific, rationalistic, and technocratic environment that is ours. In this environment, the self of man can only become an ego interested in ephemeral mundane pursuits and selfish interests.

Therefore, we must acknowledge that the current crisis does not limit itself to politics and economics, but extends to a society that no longer provides the necessary values that man needs for making peace with himself and others. Man creates culture and culture creates man, but culture and society need to be re-aligned with an injection of the *right* set of values. The culture we have inherited is one filled with a scientism crazed by disappointed idealism.[10] Man's belief in himself has become weakest at the very time when his control of the environment is greatest. We need to overcome the myth of omnipotence and learn that the proper use of science is not to conquer the world, but to live in it peaceably. So as Chateaubriand explained, what is needed, in the face of our crisis, is "a second innocence, less assured but more sublime than the first one."[11]

Hence, the purpose of this article is to contend that the expansion of secularisation through colonialism and globalization due to its universal nature was very influential on political theory, and has left man estranged to himself and others. Modern man finds himself in a state of exile lacking direction, as the words of Yeats describe:

Turning and turning in the widening gyre
The falcon cannot hear the falconer
Things fall apart, the centre cannot hold
Mere anarchy is loosed upon the world
The blood dimmed tide is loosed
And everywhere the ceremony of innocence is drowned
The best lack all conviction
While the worst are full of passionate intensity
Surely some revelation is at hand
Surely the Second Coming is at hand.[12]

Therefore, this work proposes that contemporary man's problem is not mainly political, but existential, and aims to highlight some of universal values, which have been conveyed by the most important world religions. From Ph.D. research in India, I found that religions are used as sources for universal values as the etymology of religion comes from the Latin "ligare" or to link, to connect. Considering that contemporary man is feeling disoriented in a world that often lacks meaning, some universal values of religion could be used to reconnect man to himself. Through this article I aim to promote true spiritual philosophies, and not to proselytize one way or another, since religion remains human; all too human. As Vivekananda explained:

It is very good to be born in a church, but it is very bad to die in the church. Temples or churches are simply the kindergarten of religion to make the spiritual child strong enough to take higher steps, those first steps are necessary if he wants religion.[13]

Research Hypotheses

In the light of man's modern predicament, I propose a threefold hypothesis: First, most political conflicts arise from individual dissatisfaction. Second, secular culture does not provide the in depth morality or meaning that man needs to give his life purpose and direction. As ethics are the foundation of any political philosophy, such a situation has a definite impact on political philosophy and on politics, whether international or domestic. Third, the secularization of culture should merit a careful reassessment and be imbued with spiritual values in order to bring any real change in politics. Awareness of these issues needs to be disseminated through the medium of education to the entire culture.

Examination of Modern Man

Before redefining secular culture, it seems imperative to examine modern man's ethos. The story of Icarus seems to best define modern man. In the story, Icarus, the son of Daedalus, was escaping from the minotaur. While doing so, he became arrogant and soared too high. The sun melted the wax that fastened the wings to his body causing him to fall and perish in the sea. Chantal Delsol in her book, *Le Souci Contemporain*[14] (Contemporary concerns), suggests that we imagine Icarus falling back in his maze, bruised but alive. She explains that today we find ourselves in a similar situation. For several centuries we believed that we could escape from the maze of mediocrity and radically transform man and his society, either by the philosophies of progress and of positivism, or through the ideologies that predicted a radiant future. But through the human disasters in Eastern Europe, Africa and the Middle East, the Caribbean and North East Asia, coupled with the reappearance of poverty and illiteracy, along with the epidemics in the world we have come to the profound realization, that these hopes are in vain.

As mentioned earlier, to worsen the problem, the political and social environment of modern man is full of violence: international, national and domestic. Conflicts and strife, along with civil wars continue to prevail whether in the so-called "developing countries" or in the developing nations. On the way to development and modernity, we have lost our spiritual bearings. From a historical point of view, one could state that the values of humanism and scientific progress stood as surrogates for spirituality, and therefore were seen as the highest values man could refer to. Western man at the eve of the twenty first century is like Icarus' grandson. He wonders into which world he has fallen and is in a state of exile and lacking direction. The minautor was to Icarus what barbarism, misery, and separation are to modern man. Modern man is all at sea without a lifebelt. Modern man has no political norms and is unaware of the distinction between good and bad. In a cultural and social world, it is – meaning that takes the place of fixed parameters. A man equipped with meaning can allow himself to wander and to err. Nietsche explained that if you know the why of a problem, the how is easier to find.[15] At the present time, metaphorically speaking, advances in technology have outpaced the human spirit with material progress leaving the ethico-socio-cultural realm behind. As Bertrand Russell explains:

> ... our present predicament is due, more than anything else to the fact that we have learnt to understand and control to a terrifying extent, the forces of nature that lie outside of us, but not those that are embodied in ourselves.[16]

Hence modern man's ethos is fragmented and divided; modern thought does not formulate any morality despite, paradoxically, an obsession with it, and this is the condition that leads to the main hypothesis.

Ego as a Cause of Conflict

Common features of Judaism, Christianity, Islam, Jainism, Buddhism, and Hinduism are that most problems arise from the ego. In relation to political or social problems all contend that they are focused on an ego-centred perspective.

India's native religions (Hinduism, Buddhism and Jainism) emphasize the human possibility to overcome the ego, which is the source of all conflicts, and to achieve moral perfection that disentangles the person from the clutches of the ego. Samdong Rimpoche, president of the Buddhist parliament whilst interviewed in exile, gave a very thorough account of the source of conflict as well as the way to tackle it:

> Problems arise from selfish motivations, therefore, you can't say that problems are purely political or economic since these particularly political or economical problems are created by persons. Problems come with the individual, who will have an approach to everything, which discriminates between self and others with self-interest duly protected and the interest of others sacrificed. However, this kind of approach always creates a problem. That is at the centre of every conflict which you may call political, economical or spiritual.[17]

As for the other religions, all advocate getting out of the cocoon of "the little self" in order to reach ultimate freedom. All indicate that the ego is both the root of separation and unrest within oneself, and with others. This alienates the individual. Interestingly in Latin separation is *diabolos* giving connotations of an evil spirit.

How to Reform the Ego

Islam says that, "he who knows himself, knows his Lord," and Christianity through Saint Augustine, asserts *noverim me, noverim te*, which means, to know myself is to know thee.[18] Similarly, Hinduism, and Buddhism insist on understanding one's self-centred nature in order to come upon the state of awareness. Therefore all religions believe that the true knowledge of the self leads to wisdom, and they all advocate stepping out of the bureaucracy of the ego. For instance, all the religious mystics explain that the fear of someone else seems to generate uncertainty as to who one is. Man needs to adopt an auto-discipline for sacrifice of the ego, to which all religious philosophies prescribe. To achieve that realization one needs to exclude oneself spiritually from society, something that mystics from all religions have done, resulting in the same conclusion that the ego must be reformed.

Solitary refuge is not the only way that one can reform oneself, says Islam. The individual can also choose a high value or environment that can help him to spiritually or psychologically orientate his evolution. The individual self can be weakened to the lower qualities of value experiences (selfishness, hatred, violence), choosing high value order elevates the self. The higher the scale an experience is, the more fulfilled the self becomes. A high value experience not only enriches but also elevates the individual person. The self can only fructify in a society that praises high thoughts and noble actions. The self not only has the duty to self-reform but also to reform society. However, society has the duty to provide the conditions and climate for ensuring the self the required freedom to develop. A society or culture where spiritual values are put aside, cannot provide the required environment for both inner and outer peace, and will only bring fragmentation of the individual self, alongside social and political conflicts.

Organic Society

Society is a living organism, one in origin and purpose though manifold in its operation. Before examining how education and culture could be reformed to impact on society, we need to understand that it is the ego that holds an important responsibility in having caused the individualistic conception of our society. Interestingly enough an organic perspective was found not only in the Hindu, Buddhist, and Jain religions but also in the Semitic ones. Since the individualistic conception of society has shown too many loopholes and contradictions, let us see how an organic perspective could help develop society as a whole. As Radhakrishnan explains:

> The moral advantages of the spiritual view of society as an organic whole, are receiving greater attention. A living community is not a loose federation of competing groups of traders and teachers, bankers and lawyers, farmers and weavers, each competing against all the rest for higher wages and better conditions. If the members of the different groups are to realise their potentialities, they must share a certain community feeling, a sense of belonging together for good or evil.[19]

The service of our fellow man is an obligation or a duty. Surprisingly Western law is based on the notion of "right," whereas in the orient it rests on the concept of duty. So any kind of service is equally important to the whole. There can be no freedom, explains Radhakrishnan, in any section or class in a society whilst others are in bondage. Man is a whole and all his activities have an overarching unity.[20]

As for Hindu ethics, there has always been an acceptance of different paths to the divine "truth is one, the wise call it by many names" (Rg Veda).[21] What is more, in the Hindu scheme, the cultural forms are the highest and the economic the lowest, for the cultural and the spiritual are ends in themselves and are not pursued for any other sake.

The basic approach of the Indian philosopher Radhakrishnan is that we ought not to banish eternal values from life but embrace the concept of organic unity. The Hindu holy text, the Vedanta, explains that there is one unity running through all these developments be it spiritual, moral or social and that once people comprehend this world-view, they will understand that universal values must pervade society and our everyday life. It is in that sense that idealist thinkers, like Plato and Gandhi, maintained that religion and politics are not opposed to each other. Individuals need to be morally advanced for better administration, and for a better world community. Hence the urgency to reform culture and education in order to reform Man. The statement that society is the greatest where the highest truth becomes practical becomes relevant. To Gandhi, truth is the experience of a deeper moral life, whereas harmonious life implies an agreement between word and deed. Simone Weil, the French genius, religious thinker and philosopher, situated at the intersection of Christianity and everything that was not Christianity, attempted to promote an organic approach to culture and denounced the one-sided and fragmented approach of our modern culture. She explained the co-existence of modern culture and contemporary modern crisis:

> ... for the Greeks, science, art and the search of God were united, for us they are separate. Hence, the world we live in is one in which a subservience to purely political values is the predominant condition. Values are uprooted or allowed to decay, their hierarchy disrupted and their meaning corrupted. A total disequilibrium prevails.[22]

Why should politics which has justice for its goal, demand less attention than art and science which have the goals of beauty and truth? We hardly ever look at politics as a high type of art. The reason is simple; for centuries we have been accustomed to look at politics as a technique of acquisition and conservation of power. Nonetheless, power is not an end. By nature and essence as well as by definition, it constitutes a means for service in the promotion of the common weal. A nation is linked to the cultivation of a cultural ethos. Weil explains how these qualities emanate as they transcend. A nation linked to cynicism, nihilism, materialism, reason or rationality will eradicate the possibilities of true improvement and success. Hence, the greatness of a nation is linked to the cultivation of qualities that stem from the absolute. Therefore the transformation of man will necessitate responsibility of the self, and responsibility of culture and society to make possible such a huge transformation: one of attitude and actions and deeds which cover all types of human relations.

A Revolution

To tackle the loopholes of the fragmented, limited culture, we need a more holistic approach. As Franklin D. Roosevelt said, "More than an end to war, we want an end to the beginnings of all wars,"[23] and as Martin Luther King said "scientific power has outrun our spiritual power, we live in an age of guided missiles and misguided men."[24] Likewise, with this research, the solution lies on one hand, in the transformation of the individual, and on the other hand, in the transformation of society. The real revolution needs to start from within. As for the outside one, the educational system and the culture will have an immense role to play if it is to impregnate the spirit with perennial and wise values. A chicken and egg situation ...

Culture

The question is what type of culture can provide the proper climate for the individual self to grow and also inspire politics whether national or international? For universal and permanent values of religion to thoroughly penetrate human existence, they need to be prevalent in the educational system: the arts, media, politics and economics. They need to cover all the expressions of man. The state needs to cease being at the centre of the social, economic and political life. Furthermore, the contemporary culture that has spread throughout the world through liberal order, based on progress by the means of money, technology and science, is one that is secular, and whether social or cultural, has caused serious damage to civilization.

The main result lies in the break of social links. The individualistic ethic, hand in hand with the so-called humanism, is poles apart from spiritual enthusiasm. It is noteworthy that the English word enthusiasm is derived from two Greek words "en" and "theos" which means God within. As a result, man fails to realise freedom, solidarity and wisdom. Man is an impatient species avoiding any suffering, craving short-term gratification and living in a place where mind and body have become strangers to each other. The modern world imbues an intellectual cowardliness in man, which translates itself through the refusal to designate goodness. Instead, a morality of complacency prevails, permanently identifying with what one likes, therefore entailing an ethic of relativism. Society, whether economical, political or social is in the process of waiting for certainty; what follows from this situation is that people then resort to *ersatz* like sects, fundamentalist religious convictions, political extremism or radicalism, and all types of addictive behaviours. This civilisation does not have a culture that defends human dignity. Man is in exile, disconnected from himself and from others. Once again, man needs to reckon with his tragic condition and put meaning back into his life. Culture and its environment have a role to play in transforming this situation. One should start with the premise that moral sensitivity is educable and human nature is perfectible. Let us see how education could be reformed to produce such a change.

Education

A good and worthy education can teach responsibility to oneself and others. Parents, teachers, educators have a role to fill in teaching the child and preparing the teenager. In Christianity one of the precepts of Jesus Christ is, "Hoard up for yourself treasures in heaven, because where your treasure is, there will be your heart".[25] The treasures, for instance, that Judaism advocates can be found through education and studying:

> Education is the seed and root; civilisation is the flower and fruit. If the cultivator sows
> good and wholesome seed his community will reap sweet and wholesome fruits, if bitter

and poisonous, then bitter and poisonous. Our cultivator, our culture-maker is the teacher.[26]

Education instead has itself become greatly misguided because the educator has forgotten his true mission, and lost the compelling force and spiritual power of ascetic self-denial. First, state education should not conceal the treasures that lie in Hindu, Buddhist, Judaic, Christian, Muslim, Jain, cultures and other ancient civilizations since they represent the treasures of human thought. The United Kingdom already teaches the six main religions in its school curriculum.[27] Due to the incredible communication revolution, and worldwide networking in a pluralistic society, every reader can now have access to the writings of mystics of all religions through translations of the works. Considering Christianity alone we could quote several of the church fathers, in particular the Greek who are poorly known, the pneumatophors of the desert, the Rhenan mystics, the Kabbalists and the alchemists. Or we could also quote all the most famous names of Sufism, as of the Vedanta, of Vishnuism and of Tantrism along with all the Taoist philosophers. Among all our contemporaries, it seems fair to add some of the independent thinkers like Simone Weil, Huxley, Hesse, Berdaiev, and Harendt. Along with the esoterists, their laborious work has shed light on forgotten and misunderstood fields such as journeys of self-initiation; sacred sciences; the structure of the myths from traditional societies; the meaning of symbols, of rites; dreams of the imaginary and of the Enlightenment techniques.

It is impossible to quote all of the names. However, René Guenon for his innovative doctrines and Frithjof of Schuon for building a bridge between Islam and Christianity should be quoted. Louis Massignon and Henri Corbin have contributed to galvanize Sufism and Karl Jung gave respect to alchemy again. Ananda Coomaraswamy has explained with a rare spirit of synthesis the meaning of the Asian art and mythologies, and Mircea Eliade provided a definite Yoga analysis. Jean Herbert translated the essential part of the message of the Indian seers, Juleus Evola explored the Tibetan Buddhism. D.T. Suzuki has revealed Zen to the West like Marcel Granet with the Chinese thought, so many other names could be provided. What is paradoxical is that the twentieth century, which we thought agnostic and materialistic has left us a huge spiritual wealth. Could we derive an obvious desire for a second birth out of it?

Orientation of the Education System

Gandhi, Simone Weil, Hindus, Buddhists, and Muslims all believe in a reorientation of education. Historically, education has provided a sense of false grandeur in all subjects whether in history, in literature, in art or any other discipline. As a result, each educator has begun to revere the militarist and the capitalist, instead of directing them and correcting them. What is more, he has indirectly degraded his great function into mechanical and bureaucratic herd-teaching. A vicious circle has been set up. "From bad seed, bad fruit; thence worse seed, worse fruit; until the end in Armaggedon."[28]

Such an educational task is not an easy one, considering the heavy social pressure that opposes it. For instance, with respect to history, historical facts need to be not only exact but they need to be displayed in their true perspective relating them to what is good and what is bad. Being fed with knowledge of false grandeur they are incapable of discerning good from bad. The result is terrifying: teenagers and adults come to admire without loving their hearts. The spirit of truth, of justice, and of love need to be introduced into education since they are integral eternal concepts and belonging to goodness. The transmission of false grandeur throughout the centuries is not particular to history. It is also a general law, which governs literature and art. Simone Weil in *Uprootedness* explains that there is a kind of domination of literary talent through the centuries that answers to the domination of political talent in space. These dominations are of the same nature, all temporal, and all belonging to the fields of matter, force, or power. In whatever subject, history, philosophy, literature or political science and arts, the notion of goodness is despised, shaping young adults to be filled with cynicism and disdain.[29] As for practical politics, political science as we know it, the spiritual is put aside.

Among children and adults, the truth that talent has nothing to do with morality is commonplace. Talents and ability, in the narrow sense of the term, have become the sole criteria for personal advancement; and virtue is not taken into account in evaluating persons particularly in educational institutions. What else can they conclude but that virtue is a distinctive characteristic of mediocrity? Even the word virtue is derided. A child who sees glorified cruelty and ambition in history lessons, selfishness, pride and vanity in literature lessons, and all the discoveries that have transformed men's lives in science lessons, is informed neither about the method of discovery nor about the effect of the transformation. How can he admire goodness? In this atmosphere of false grandeur, it is in vain to even wish to find genuine goodness. Hence confusion prevails.[30]

It is true that talent has no link with morality, but this is because there is no grandeur in talent. As stated previously, there are real links between perfect beauty, perfect truth and perfect justice. A mysterious unity links them because good is one. As far as art and science are concerned, they have also lost their purpose. Art should have beauty and science truth for its purpose; after all truth and beauty dwell on the level of the impersonal. But instead, the modern conceptions of science and art are responsible for the contemporary monstrosities. To that effect, let us ponder on one particular passage in the Vedas:

Science came to the 'man of knowledge' and said: Take me and guard me as a secrets' trust; and give me not unto the crooked ones, impure, evil-minded, un-Self-controlled, jealous, cruel, full of greed and lust. Impart me only to the good and pure, the gentle-minded and benevolent; then, shall I grow in power to help the world.[31]

As this quotation displays, science is divorced from the sense of absolute since the effort of scientific research, as it was understood since the sixteenth century, has not had the love of truth as its motive. The spirit of truth possessed by Gandhi, Radhakrisnan, Tagore, and the other religious or spiritual philosophers referred to in this article are mostly absent in the values of any field of the current education system.

The acquisition of any knowledge allows one to get closer to the truth when it is about the knowledge of something we love. Truth, Simone Weil explains, is not an object of love. Truth is a spark of reality. The object of love is not the truth but the reality. To wish truth, is to wish a direct contact with a reality; it is to love it. Instead of referring to love of truth, we should refer to the spirit of truth as the inspirational fount of our educational system.[32]

For example, and more concretely, the tone and the nature of teaching should be changed. War glorification and national boasting, self-conceit, contempt and decrial of other nations, and expression of triumph over them should all be eliminated. Instead, the more truly refined and civilized spirit of humanism should be diligently inculcated as a reaction against the horror of the senseless butchery of wars and conflicts.[33] This spirit of humanism has begun to manifest itself in the higher thought and feeling of the best and wisest persons of all nations. Moral disarmament must precede physical disarmament. War and conflict can only be abolished or reduced in direct ratio to the abolition or reduction of war mentality. This is possible only by systematic cultivation of a peace-mentality and organizing for peace through diligent right education, of youth as well as the general public. Right education is the foundation of all well being, all good and the use of well-planned spiritual instruction as the most potent instrument for the moral regeneration of mankind. That is to say humanism, inter-nationalism and inter-religionism go together; they are only aspects of each other.

Another Concept of Science

Since the Renaissance, the purpose of science is to identify and observe objectively without recourse to "good" or "bad". Force and matter isolated in themselves with no relation to anything else, provide nothing that human thought can love. Hence a total incompatibility results in a secular attitude in all fields, as well as the phenomena of irreligiousness and false religiosity. In parallel, the greatest problems of the day relate to spiritual as opposed to material adjustment. In this world, there is the knowledge and there is the power to refashion society. But there is not the will to do so and people have no ideal towards which to aim as a whole. People know a little of the methods of supporting life but not how to live, nor what to live for ... Science has become the servant of man's lust for power. We need to discover what is good for mankind, and then see to it that the power that knowledge gives is used for that end. Only a new moral outlook can tell us what is good for mankind: what to live for, what is the meaning, purpose, and aim of life and how to live. Impulsion from within is far better, far more effective, than compulsion from without. As prevention is better than cure, so education is better than legislation. Thus high is the value and purpose of education. In other words, as it is said in the Vedas:

> The spiritual and the temporal powers, both need each other; neither can maintain itself and prosper if not helped by the other. But should the militarist grow perverse and try to overbear the scientist, it is the latter's duty to restrain and curb the former; and he can do so; for science is the parent of the sword, knowledge, which makes, can break the things of war.[34]

Hence the need is urgent to break the fences off between science and religion. Instead, force is therefore sovereign – whether in science or whether in political science. Force is absolutely sovereign and justice is totally unreal; however, justice is real in men's hearts. Because they love justice, justice is a reality in this world and it is science that is wrong; or in what concerns us, it is political science that is wrong. The remedy is to again take into account the spirit of truth found in all the spiritual and ethical traditions quoted above. The spirit of truth can reside in science only if the motive of the scholar is to love one another. This is the objective we give ourselves in the universe in which we live.

A Pedagogy of Peace

We urgently need to bring back these abstract notions to our particular concern and to confront in political philosophy that which can be reflected in international and national politics. Only a society imbued with the spirit of truth can bring back the notion of the public good through the sense of duty and responsibility towards others at all political levels. With a stress on the inside work of the self, added to an education system that has inner life as its pedagogy, we can see how this spirit of truth can be a spur for action in all fields. It may also constitute a trigger for a new kind of people filled with generosity whose inspiration is not drawn from the past or from the present, but from the eternal to shape the future. "Salvation will come from the creative minorities," said Arnold Toynbee;[35] they are the ones who will convey the essential values and the living fire of the lulled crowds. It is through the means of the culture system and through education that the formation of a "supramental" mentality needs to be propagated. A totally secularised instruction is harmful to the formation of "supramental" mentality, one of inner perception. Education is a powerful device to bring back the indispensable values that are today lacking in our societies. With a redefined education, political science and the individual shall find again a sense of self-responsibility and a sense of duty towards the self and others.

Notes

1   David Irons. "Global Terrorism: Why Bali?" *San Francisco Chronicle*, 16 October 2002, A2.
2   Gail Collins. "The Day after Madrid's Terrorism Attack." *New York Times*, 12 March, 2004, Editorial.
3   Myron W. Lustig and Jolene Koester. *Intercultural Competence* (Boston: Allyn and Bacon, 2003), pp. 58.
4   George Monbiot. "Dying of Consumption." *Guardian*, 28 December 2000, 34.
5   Olga Craig. "No Sex Please." *The Telegraph*, 11 January 2004, sec. A.
6   UNICEF. *Official Summary: The State of the World's Children* (New York, Oxford University Press, 2002), p. 231.
7   Simone Weil. *The Simone Weil Reader* (New York: Moyer Bell Limited, 1977), p. 169.
8   Weil, *Simone Weil Reader*, 204.
9   Niccolo Machiavelli. *The Discourses* (New York, Harper and Row, 1961), p. 231.
10 J. V. Ferreira. *Nemesis* (Bombay, Ramrakhiani Publications, 1983), p. 45.
11 Jacques Maritain. *Primauté du Spirituel* (Paris, Librairie Plon, 1927), p. 171.
12 W.P. Yeats. The collected Poems of W.P. Yeats (London, Macmillan and Co, 1952), p. 112.
13 Swami Vivekananda, *Jnana Yoga* (Calcutta, N. Mukherjee, 1937), p. 98.
14 Chantal Delsol, *Le Souci Contemporain* (Paris: Editions Complexes, 1996), p. 9.
15 Edward Schillebecks, *La Politique n'est pas tout* (Paris: Les Editions du Cerf, 1988), p. 46.
16 Yionel Fernandes, *Its Vital Concerns* (Bombay, Somaya Publications, 1996), p. 231.
17 Samdong Rimpoche, interview by Helena Cristini. Sarnath, India, 9 May 1996.
18 Saint Augustine, *The City Of God* (New York: Modern Library, 1958), p. 137.
19 S. Radhakrishnan, *Indian Philosophy* (London, George Allen and Unwin, Ltd., 1930), p. 213.
20 Radhakrishnan, 214.
21 Ibid., 98.
22 Weil, *Simone Weil Reader*, 53.
23 A.J. Toynbee, *Change and Habit* (London, Oxford University Press, 1966), p. 266.
24 Toynbee, 268.
25 B. Marie Duffe, *De L'Ethique en Politique* (Lyon, Faculté de Théologie de Lyon, 1991), p. 181.
26 René Samuel Sirat, *La Tendresse de Dieu* (Paris, Nil Edition, 1996), p. 129.
27 *School Curriculum and Assessment Authority, Religious Education* (London, New House, 1995).
28 Henri Madelin, *Dieu et Cesar* (Paris, Desclée de Browver, 1970), p. 98.
29 Weil, 37.
30 Ibid., 38.
31 Radhakrishnan, 206.
32 Weil, 145.
33 Ibid., 146.
34 Mircea Iliade, *A History of Religious Ideas* (London, Saint James Place, Vols. 1-3, 1979), Vol. 3, p. 132.
35 Toynbee, 287.

Conclusion

No Clash, But Dialogue Among Religions and Nations

Towards a New Paradigm of International Relations

Hans Küng
President, Global Ethic Foundation

Many readers of my earlier books may be surprised by the present topic. I have chosen it not only because of the present political situation, but because it reflects the ultimate phase of my long odyssey in theology. It started in the fifties with Justification: The Problems of Christian Existence. Then it went on, as I believe in a rather consistent way:

- In the sixties with The Church, The Council: Reform and Reunion, and Infallible? An Inquiry
- In the seventies, the new foundation of a Christian theology with On Being a Christian, Does God Exist?, and Eternal Life?
- In the eighties (after the big clash with the Vatican on papal infallibity) with Christianity and World Religions and writings on religions and world peace
- Culminating in the nineties with Global Responsibility: In Search of a New World Ethic and Global Ethic for Global Politics and Economics – and in the first years of the new century with research into the new paradigm of international relations. I did not give up anything I had written (e.g., On Being a Christian), but I tried to expand constantly the fields of my research.

Let me introduce my present topic by way of a little story. Before I started my first American lecture tour in 1963, a Jewish colleague from America visited me in Tübingen and asked me, "What is the topic of your lectures?" My answer was, "The Church and freedom." "Very interesting," he said, with a charming smile. "I know that there's a Church, and I know that there's freedom, but I didn't know that you could have the Church and freedom together!"

But now, exactly 40 years later, when I prepared my lectures for the United States this time, I was also asked about the topic and said. "America and the New Paradigm of International Relations". And the answer in Europe was, "We know that there is a new American administration, and we know that there is a new paradigm, but we didn't know that you could have the American administration and the new paradigm together!"

In 1963 I was able to convince a few people that the Church and freedom can go together. And I hope that now I shall also convince you that America and the new paradigm can and should go together. But let me now start in a very un-American way – from history.

The Clashes of Nations

Let me begin with three symbolic dates that signal the new paradigm in international relations that is slowly and laboriously establishing itself: its announcement (1918), its realization (1945), and finally its breakthrough (1989).

First Opportunity

1918, the First World War, supported on both sides by the Christian churches, ended with a net result of around 10 million dead, the collapse of the German Empire, the Habsburg Empire, the Czarist Empire and the Ottoman Empire. The Chinese Empire had collapsed earlier. Now there were for the first time American troops on European soil and, on the other side, the Soviet Empire was in the making. This marked the beginning of the end of the eurocentric-imperialistic paradigm of modernity and the dawning of a new paradigm. That new paradigm had not yet been defined, but had been foreseen by the far-sighted and enlightened thinkers, and was first set forth in the arena of international relations by the United States of America. With his Fourteen Points, President Woodrow Wilson wanted to achieve a "just peace" and the "self-determination of the nations," without the annexations and demands for reparations which some in Congress wanted. President Wilson has been ignored too much in the United States and even denigrated by Henry Kissinger who often polemicized against "Wilsonianism."

The Versailles Treaty of Clémenceau and Lloyd George prevented the immediate realization of the new paradigm. That was "Realpolitik," a word used first by Bismarck, but its ideology was developed by Machiavelli and it was the first time put into political practice by Cardinal Richelieu. Instead of a just peace, there emerged a dictated peace in which the defeated nations took no part. The consequences of this approach are well known: Fascism and Nazism (backed up in the Far East by Japanese militarism), not sufficiently opposed by the Christian churches, are the catastrophic reactionary errors which two decades later led to the Second World War, which was far worse than any previous war in world history.

Second Opportunity

1945 saw the end of the Second World War with a net result of around 50 million dead and many more million exiled. Fascism and Nazism had been defeated, but Soviet Communism appeared stronger and more formidable than ever to the international community, even though internally it was already experiencing a political, economic and social crisis because of Stalin's policy.

Again, the initiative for a new paradigm came from the USA. In 1945 the United Nations was founded in San Francisco and the Bretton Woods Agreement on the reordering of the global economy was signed (foundation of the International Monetary Fund and the World Bank). In 1948 came the Universal Declaration of Human Rights, along with American economic aid (Marshall Plan) for the rebuilding of Europe and its incorporation into a free trade system. But Stalinism blocked this paradigm for its sphere of influence and led to the division of the world into East and West.

Third Opportunity

1989 saw the successful peaceful revolution in Eastern Europe and the collapse of Soviet Communism. After the Gulf War it was again an American president who announced a new paradigm, a "new world order," and found enthusiastic acceptance all over the world with this slogan. But in contrast to his predecessor, Woodrow Wilson, President George Bush senior felt embarrassed when he had to explain what this "vision thing" for the international order should look like. No change in Iraq, no democracy in Kuwait, no solution for the Israel-Palestine conflict, no democratic change in other Arab States. And in the present moment the doubts also in the United States increase that the so-called "war against terrorism" can be our vision for the future. So today the question arises: over the last decade, have we again forfeited the opportunity for a "new world order," a new paradigm?

We should not give up hope. And especially committed Christians, Jews, Muslims and members of other religions should work for the new paradigm. After all, despite the wars, massacres and streams of refugees in the twentieth century, despite the Gulag Archipelago, the Holocaust, the most inhuman crime in the history of humanity, and the atomic bomb, we must not overlook some major changes for the better. After 1945, not only has humanity seen numerous grandiose scientific and technological achievements. But many ideas set forth in 1918 that had been pressing for a new, post-modern and overall global constellation were able to better establish themselves. The peace movement, the women's rights movement, the environmental movement and the ecumenical movement all began to make considerable progress. There emerged a new attitude to war and disarmament, to the partnership of men and women, to the relationship between economy and ecology, among the Christian churches and the world religions. After 1989, following the end of the enforced division of the world into West and East and the definitive demystification of both the evolutionary and the revolutionary ideology of progress, concrete possibilities for a pacified and co-operative world have begun to take shape. In contrast to European modernity, these possibilities are no longer eurocentric but polycentric. Despite all the monstrous defects and conflicts still plaguing the international community, this new paradigm is in principle post-imperialistic and post-colonial, with the ideals of an eco-social market economy and truly united nations at their core.

Despite the terrors of the twentieth century there is "still perhaps something like a hesitant historical progress." Over the last century, the formerly dominant political orientations have been banished for good. For one, imperialism has no scope in global politics after de-colonization. Moreover, since the end of the South African apartheid regime, racism, a consistent policy of racial privilege and racial discrimination, is no longer the explicit political strategy in any state. Likewise, in the lands of Western Europe from which it originated, nationalism has become a non-word and for many people is being replaced by dialogue, co-operation, and integration.

The Dialogue Among Nations and Religions

The movement is now tending toward a novel political model of regional co-operation and integration, and is attempting to peacefully overcome centuries of confrontation. The result, not only between Germany and France first, not only in the European Union, but in the whole area of the OECD (Organization for Economic Cooperation and Development, founded in 1948 and developed in 1960), including all of the Western industrialized countries (the European countries, the USA, Canada, Mexico, Australia, New Zealand, and Japan) is half a century of democratic peace. That truly is a successful paradigm change! There are wars in Asia, Africa, South America and in the Islamic world (e.g. El Salvador, Guatemala, Nicaragua, Colombia, Israel-Palestine, Sudan, Yemen, Algeria, Gulf, Bosnia and Kosovo), but nobody could anymore imagine a war between Germany and France or the United States and Japan.

So after this all too brief historical tour I want to move to the fundamental definition of the new paradigm of international relations. I have received much stimulation and support in a discussion within the small international "group of eminent persons" which was convened by UN Secretary-General Kofi Annan for the UN year of "Dialogue of the Civilizations" 2001, an endeavor which produced a report for the UN General Assembly, "Crossing the Divide. Dialogue Among Civilizations," Seton Hall University, 2001.

On the basis of the experiences in the EU and the OECD, the new overall political constellation can be sketched briefly as follows. Here, ethical categories cannot be avoided. In principle, the new paradigm means policies of regional reconciliation, understanding and co-operation instead of the modern national politics of self-interest, power and prestige. In specific, the exercise of political action now calls for reciprocal co-operation, compromise and integration instead of the former confrontation, aggression and revenge. This new overall political constellation manifestly presupposes a change of mentality, which goes far beyond the politics of the present day. For this new overall political constellation to hold, new approaches to international politics are needed.

For one, new international organizations are not enough here; what is needed is a new mind-set. National, ethnic and religious differences must no longer be understood, in principle, as a threat but rather as possible sources of enrichment. Whereas the old paradigm always presupposed an enemy, indeed a traditional enemy, the new paradigm no longer envisions or needs such an enemy. Rather, it seeks partners, rivals and economic opponents for competition instead of military confrontation, and uses "soft" power (diplomatic influence and political persuasion, cultural influence and prestige) instead of "hard" military power.

This is so because it has been proven that in the long run national prosperity is not furthered by war but only by peace, not in opposition or confrontation but in co-operation. And because the different interests that exist are satisfied in collaboration, a policy is possible which is no longer a zero-sum game where one wins at the expense of the other, but a positive-sum game in which all win.

Of course this does not mean that politics has become easier in the new paradigm. It remains the "art of the possible," though it has now become non-violent. If it is to be able to function, it cannot be based on a random "post-modernist" pluralism, where anything goes and anything is allowed. Rather, it presupposes a social consensus on particular basic values, basic rights and basic responsibilities. All social groups and all nations must contribute to this basic social consensus, especially religious believers, but also non-believers and adherents to the different philosophies or ideologies. In other words, this social consensus, which cannot be imposed by a democratic system but has to be presupposed, does not mean a specific ethical system, but a common minimum of ethical standards, a common ethic, an ethic of humankind. This global ethic is not a new ideology or "superstructure", imposed by the west to the "rest," but brings together the common religious and philosophical resources of all of humankind. For instance the Golden Rule you find already in the Analects of Confucius but also in the writings of Rabbi Hillel (before Christ) and of course in the sermon on the mount, but also in the Muslim and other traditions. "What you do not wish done to yourself, do not do to others." And a few very basic directives you find everywhere in humanity: Not to murder, not to steal, not to lie, not to abuse sexuality. I shall come back to this point.

Global ethic should not be imposed by law but be brought to public awareness. A global ethic is simultaneously orientated on persons, institutions and results. To this degree, a global ethic does not just focus on the collective responsibility to the relief of any responsibility the individual may hold (as if only the social "conditions," "history," and the "system" were to blame for specific abuses and crimes). Instead, it is focused in a particular way on the responsibility of each individual in his or her place in society and specifically on the individual responsibility of political leaders.

Free commitment to a common ethic does of course not exclude the support of law but rather includes it, and can in some circumstances appeal to law. Such circumstances include cases of genocide, crimes against humanity, war crimes and aggression contrary to international law, as in former Yugoslavia. Meanwhile, following the ratification by more than 60 nations the International Criminal Court

(ICC) is now established to which such violations can be brought, specifically when a signatory state is unable or unwilling to inflict legal penalties on atrocities committed on its territory.

As you know, the U.S. – which was always in favor of international agreements and especially of the International Criminal Court – tried to sabotage it, together with Israel. I therefore come to my third and probably the most delicate part, and I could easily and comfortably stop my essay here or evade in my third part in generalities. I know of course that I am a foreigner but I am not a stranger, having taught many semesters in American universities. I also know that I have not to give you advice on foreign policy but that you expect from me to express my personal concerns which are certainly shared by more and more American men and women and also by more and more columnists in the New York Times and the Washington Post. So I hope you will forgive me my frankness!

A Realistic Vision of Peace

It is notorious that it is the second Bush administration which opposes also other important international agreements like the Kyoto agreement to reduce global warming, the Comprehensive Test Ban Treaty, the Anti-Ballistic Missile Treaty, the implementation of the Biological Weapons Treaty, and so forthetc. These are sad facts for all admirers of American democracy: the present administration of the only remaining superpower seems to many people not only in the Islamic world, but also in the Asian and African worlds and in Europe, to disrupt a policy in the new paradigm. So I cannot avoid comparing the new paradigm with the political reality after 11 September 2001, given that beyond any doubt the fight against terrorism had to be started and the monstrous crime in New York and in Washington could not remain unatoned for.

After the war in Afghanistan and the illegal and immoral war in Iraq – two wars which have brought anything else than peace to both countries – the decisive question is more than ever: what international commitment are we to make? And should we simply continue the fight against terrorism in this style? Can armed forces solve the terrorist problem? Can a bigger NATO stop terrorism? And should European nations now furnish and finance what would amount to a "foreign legion" in the service of the Pentagon? My concern is not the alternatives of the past, but the alternatives of the future. Have we any alternatives at all, as long as foreign policy is above all military policy and billions are being spent on sinfully expensive new weapon systems and transport planes instead on kindergartens and schools, healthcare and public services at home and on fighting against poverty, hunger and misery in the world? Are there still any opportunities at all for the new paradigm outside the OECD world as well?

I think that there are, and I want to indicate them cautiously: not with seemingly firm predictions, but in the mode of "It could be that ... ." I shall do this in full awareness of all the real uncertainties of the future, which today often bring about fundamental changes more quickly than before, changes which are however not always for the worst – as we have seen in the changed attitude of the Bush Administration regarding the United Nations. I shall adopt so to speak the realistic anti-Murphy principle: "What can go wrong need not always go wrong." And as an admirer of the great American tradition of democracy and the demand for human rights, I would plead for peace politics – even in face of the campaign against terrorism which has to be not only a military, but also a political, economic and cultural fight.

It could be that the present American administration, too, will realize that those who think that they can win the fight against evil all over the world are self-righteously condemning themselves to eternal war, and that even the sole remaining superpower and a self-designated police force of the world can carry out a successful policy only if it does not act unilaterally in a high-handed way but has real partners and friends, not satellites, practicing therefore the "humility" in dealing with other nations G.W. Bush promised before his election.

It could be that the United States, more shrewdly than former empires, will not over-extend its power and come to grief through megalomania, but will preserve its position of predominance by taking into account not only its own interest but also the interests of its partners. The attempt to organize a messy world to our liking, is hubris; and also for empires – remember the French, the British, the German, the Japanese, the Russian empire – pride goes before the fall.

It could be that the Bush administration recognizes that the peace in Bosnia after 8 years continues to depend on 12,000 foreign troops, and that peace-building in Iraq will be much harder and take much longer – a long-term occupation and nation-building that cannot be effectively pursued alone or under an exclusively US umbrella. Winning peace is so much more difficult than winning a war.

It could be that the American President, whose budget surplus has decreased in the past year by four trillion dollars and who in the future must again reckon with deficits, will once again reorient his budgetary policy and instead of being primarily concerned with military policy and oil will be concerned with a more successful economic policy, which has also in view further Enron-style bankruptcies, Arthur Anderson crimes, stock market disasters and a recession and Wall Street crash which is still possible.

It could be that the present American administration, because it does not want to alienate the whole Islamic world, will take more interest in the causes of Arab and Muslim resentment towards the West and the United States in particular; that instead of being concerned only with the symptoms it will be more concerned with therapy for the social, economic and political roots of terror; that instead of spending yet more billions for military and policing purposes it will devote more means to improving the social situation of the masses in its own country and those who lose out all over the world as a result of globalization.

It could be that the superpower USA would also act out of enlightened self-interest to prevent the international sense of law from being shaken, as it is when the only superpower sets different standards from those which apply generally in international law, because by doing this it helps those powers which do not want to observe the standards of international law and precisely in this way encourages terrorism and the breakdown of international rules governing the use of force.

It could be – to say only one word on the Israeli-Palestinian conflict as the main source of terrorism – that a new majority of the Israeli people replaces leaders who provided Israelis with neither peace nor security but with an economy which teeters on ruin, and will elect more peace-minded political leaders with the vision and ability to lead the country out of the morass and – not without American pressure – implement the "Road Map," supported by the U.S., the EU, the UN and Russia: withdrawal from all occupied territories and recognition of the State of Israel by all Arab states, with normal political and economic relations. This would make possible an autonomous and viable (not dismembered) state of Palestine, preferably in an economic union with Israel and Jordan, which could be a real blessing for the whole region and especially for Israel.

Indeed, it could be that then even the radical Palestinians, who apply the same logic of violence, will stop their bloody terrorist activities, and that the Palestinians will realistically restrict their "right to return" to symbolic return for some particularly hard cases – in exchange for new settlements and financial compensation. In the long run only the recognition by Israel will lead to a less authoritarian and corrupt and more democratic administration in Palestine.

I am sure, nobody will accuse me of anti-Semitism. In my memoir, *My Struggle for Freedom*, everybody can read how I struggled for the approval of the epoch-making Declaration of the Second Vatican Council in favor of the Jews. And in my volume *Judaism: Between Yesterday and Tomorrow*, I presented a comprehensive sympathetic view of Judaism, its history, the challenges of the present and the possibilities for the future. I therefore felt very proud to receive an honorary degree from Hebrew Union College in Cincinnati in 2000.

I feel now confirmed in my view by the blistering and encouraging article by the former speaker of the Israeli Parliament, Avraham Burg, published in Israel and translated and republished in the famous New York Jewish magazine, *The Forward*, the editorial of which says that despite Burg's vehement language his idea is basically right. As a respected Israeli Labor politician of impeccable Orthodox credentials, he writes:

> The Jewish people did not survive for two millennia in order to pioneer new weaponry, computer security programs or anti-missile missiles ... We were supposed to be a light unto the nations. In this we have failed. It turns out that the 2,000-year struggle for Jewish survival comes down to a state of settlements, run by an amoral clique of corrupt law-breakers who are deaf both to their citizens and their enemies. A state lacking justice cannot survive ... the countdown to the end of Israeli society has begun.

Burg is therefore in favor of two states which is the only alternative to a racist state. And he thinks that this is not exclusively Israeli or Jewish business: "Israel's friends abroad – Jewish and non-Jewish, presidents and prime ministers, rabbis and lay people – should choose as well. They must reach out and help Israel to navigate the road map towards our national destiny as a light unto the nations and a society of peace, justice and equality."

Here particular demands would be made on the three prophetic religions, Judiaism, Christianity, and Islam, not to support uncritically the official politics of their respective governments but to show their prophetic role: "Recompense no one evil with evil," says Romans 12: 17. This New Testament saying is today addressed to those Christian crusaders in America and elsewhere who look for evil only in the other, thinking that a crusade hallows any military means and justifies all humanitarian "collateral damage."

"An eye for an eye, a tooth for a tooth," is written in Exodus 21: 24. This saying from the Hebrew Bible on the limitation of damage is addressed to those Israeli fanatics who prefer to take two eyes from their opponent instead of just one, and would like to knock out several teeth, forgetting that that Gandhi said, "An eye for an eye makes the world go blind."

"And if they incline to peace, do thou incline to it," is written in Surah 8: 61. This saying from the Qur'an is addressed to those Palestinian warriors of God who today would still like to blot out the state of Israel from the map and try to sabotage all peace initiatives.

Conclusion

Peace among the religions is a presupposition of peace among the nations. Let me therefore conclude with a few elementary remarks on a Global Ethic which in the age of globalization is more urgent than ever. Indeed, the globalization of the economy, technology, and communication needs also the globalization of ethic in coping with global problems. The two fundamental demands of the 1993 Chicago Declaration, confirmed by the 3rd Parliament of the World's Religions in Cape Town 1999 and taken up in the Manifesto "Crossing the Divide" for the United Nations Year of Dialogue among Civilizations, are the most elementary ones that can be made in this regard, yet it is by no means a matter of course.

The first is the principle of Humanity, the demand for true humanity. Now as before, women and men are treated inhumanly all over the world. They are robbed of their opportunities and their freedom; their human rights are trampled underfoot; their dignity is disregarded. But might does not make right! In the face of all inhumanity our religious and ethical convictions demand that *every human being must be treated humanly*. This means that every human being – man or woman, white or colored, young or old, American or Afghan – has to be treated not in an inhuman, even bestial way, but in a truly human way.

The second fundamental demand is the Golden Rule: "There is a principle which is found and has persisted in many religious and ethical traditions of humankind for thousands of years: What you do not wish done to yourself, do not do to others ... This should be the irrevocable, unconditional norm for all areas of life, for families and communities, for races, nations, and religions."

On the basis of these two fundamental principles four ethical directives, found in all the great traditions of humanity, have to be remembered:

- You shall not murder, torture, torment, wound; in positive terms: have reverence for life; a commitment to a culture of non-violence and reverence for life.
- You shall not lie, deceive, forge, manipulate; in positive terms: speak and act truthfully; a commitment to a culture of truthfulness and tolerance.
- You shall not steal, exploit, bribe, corrupt; in positive terms: deal honestly and fairly; a commitment to a culture of fairness and a just economic order.
- You shall not abuse sexuality, cheat, humiliate, dishonor; in positive terms: respect and love one another; a commitment to a culture of partnership and equal dignity of men and women.

But let me conclude now. I started with the lack of vision after 1989. I hope it became clear what this vision really could be. It is not a vision of war – "Sweet is war only to those who do not know it," the sixteenth-century humanist Erasmus of Rotterdam said – but a vision of peace. Let me summarize it in the following four propositions:

- There will be no peace among the nations without peace among the religions.

- There will be no peace among the religions without dialogue among the religions.

- There will be no dialogue among the religions without global ethical standards.

- There will therefore be no survival of this globe without a global ethic.

Select Bibliography

Adler, David Gray and Louis Fisher. "The War Powers Resolution: Time to Say Goodbye." *Political Science Quarterly* 113/1 (1998): 1-20.

Ahmed, Nafeez Mosaddeq. *Behind the War on Terror: Western Secret Strategy and the Struggle for Iraq* (New Society Pub., 2003).

Al-Shaybani, Muhammad ibn al-Hasan. *The Islamic Law of Nations: Shaybani's Siyar.* Majid Khadduri, trans. Baltimore, MD: The Johns Hopkins Press, 1966.

Alterman, Eric. *When Presidents Lie: A History of Official Deception and Its Consequences* (New York: Viking, 2004).

Anscombe, Elizabeth. "War and Murder," in *War and Morality*, Richard A. Wasserstrom, ed., Belmont, CA: Wadsworth Publishing Co., Inc., 1970. pp. 42-53.

Aquinas, Thomas. *Political Writings*. R.W. Dyson, trans. Cambridge, UK: Cambridge University Press, 2002.

Barber, Benjamin R. *Fear's Empire: War, Terrorism, and Democracy* (New York: Norton, 2003).

Baxter, James. *St. Augustine: Select Letters*. Cambridge, MA: Harvard U. Press, 1953.

Becker, Carl L. *The Heavenly City of the Eighteenth Century Philosophers* (New Haven: Yale University Press, 1932).

Bhatia, H.S. *International Law and Practice in Ancient India*. New Delhi, India; Deep & Deep Publications, 1977.

Bhattacharya, K.K. *Public International Law*. Allahabad, India: Central Law Agency, 1982.

Boisard, Marcel A. "On the Probable Influence of Islam on Western Public and International Law," *International Journal of Middle East Studies*, 11/4 (July 1980): 429-450.

Bontempo, Charles J. and S. Jack Odell (eds.) *The Owl of Minerva: Philosophers on Philosophy* (New York: McGraw-Hill, 1975).

Briody, Dan. *The Halliburton Agenda: The Politics of Oil and Money* (New York: Wiley, 2004).

Brisard, Jean-Charles, and Guillaume Dasquié. *Forbidden Truth: U.S.-Taliban Secret Oil Diplomacy and the Failed Hunt for Bin Laden*, L. Rounds, et al., (trans) (New York: Thunder's Mouth/Nation Books, 2002).

Brown, Anthony Cave. *Oil, God, and Gold* (Boston: Houghton Mifflin, 1999).

Buch, Maganlal A. *The Principles of Hindu Ethics*. Baroda, India: "Arya Sudharak" Printing Press, 1921.

Byrne, Edmund. "The Post-9/11 State of Emergency: Reality versus Rhetoric." *Social Philosophy Today* 19 (2004).

——. "The Depersonalization of Violence: Reflections on the Future of Personal Responsibility." *Journal of Value Inquiry* 7, (Fall 1973): 161-172.

Calhoun, Laurie. "The Metaethical Paradox of Just War Theory," *Ethical Theory and Moral Practice,* 4, (2001): 41-58.

Carmichael, Stokely, and Charles V. Hamilton. *Black Power: The Politics of Liberation in America*. New York: Vintage Books, 1967.

Chambour, Raafat. *Les Institutions sociales, politiques et juridiques de l'Islam*. Lausanne, Switzerland: Éditions Méditerranéennes, 1978.

Chatterjee, R.K. *The Gita and its Culture*. New Delhi, India: Sterling Publishers Private, Ltd., 1987.

Crépon, Pierre. *Les Religions et la Guerre*. Paris: Éditions Albin Michel, 1991.

Davis, Angela. *Are Prisons Obsolete?* NY: Seven Stories Press, 2003.

De Greiff, Pablo and Ciaran Cronin (eds). *Global Justice and Transnational Politics* (Cambridge, MA: MIT Press, 2002).

DeLigt, Bart. *The Conquest of Violence: An Essay on War and Revolution*. New York: E.P. Dutton and Company, 1938.

Delsol, Chantal. *Le Souci Contemporain* (Paris: Editions Complexes, 1996).

Diamond, Jared. *Guns, Germs, and Steel: The Fates of Human Societies*. New York: Norton, 1999.

Donagan, Alan. *The Theory of Morality*. Chicago, IL: The University of Chicago Press, 1977.

Doswald-Beck, Louise. "The Civilian in the Crossfire," *Journal of Peace Research,* 24/3 (Special Issue on Humanitarian Law of Armed Conflict, Sep. 1987): 251-262.

Drury, Shadia B. *Leo Strauss and the American Right* (New York: St. Martin's, 1999).

Duffe, B. Marie. *De L'Ethique en Politique* (Lyon, Faculté de Théologie de Lyon, 1991).

Durrany, Mohammad Khan. *The Gita and The Quran: A Comparative Study (An Approach to National Integration)*. Delhi, Nag Publishers, 1982.

Eagleton, Thomas F. *War and Presidential Power: A Chronicle of Congressional Surrender*. New York: Liveright, 1974.

Easwaran, Eknath. *Nonviolent Soldier of Islam*. Tomales, California: Nilgiri Press, 2002.

El Fadel, Khaled Abou. "The Rules of Killing at War: An Inquiry into Classical Sources," *Muslim World*, 89/2 (April 1999): 144-157.

Elliot, Jonathan. *Debates on the Adoption of the Federal Constitution in the Convention Held at Philadelphia in 1787*. New York: Burt Franklin Reprints, 1974.

Elshtain, Jean Bethke. *Just War Theory.* New York, NY: New York University Press, 1992.

Elshtain, Jean Bethke. *Women and War.* New York, NY: Basic Books, 1987.

Fernandes, Yionel. *Its Vital Concerns* (Bombay, Somaya Publications, 1996).

Ferreira, J.V. *Nemesis* (Bombay, Ramrakhiani Publications, 1983).

Fiala, Andrew. *The Philosopher's Voice: Philosophy, Politics, and Language in the Nineteenth Century* (Albany: SUNY Press, 2002).

Fisher, Louis. *Presidential War Power.* Lawrence, KS: UP of Kansas, 1995.

Flori, Jean. *Guerre sainte, jihad, croisade: Violence et religion dans le christianisme et l'islam.* Paris: Éditions de Seuil, 2002.

Ford, John C. "The Morality of Obliteration Bombing," in *War and Morality,* Richard A. Wasserstrom, ed., Belmont, CA: Wadsworth Publishing Co., Inc., 1970. pp. 15-41.

Gamson, William A. "The Success of the Unruly," in Doug McAdam and David A. Snow, eds., *Social Movements: Readings on Their Emergence, Mobilization, and Dynamics,* pp. 357-364. Los Angeles: Roxbury Publishing, 1997.

Gause, F. Gregory. "Sovereignty and its Challengers: War in Middle Eastern Inter-State Politics," in Paul Salem, ed., *Conflict Resolution in the Arab World: Selected Essays.* Beirut, Lebanon: American University of Beirut, 1997, pp. 197-215.

Ghosh, Jagat J. *Indian Thesis on War and Peace.* Raniganj, Dist. Burdwan (W.B.), India: Mahima Ranjan Sarkar (Rajashree Press), June 1972.

Ginsberg, Robert (ed). *The Critique of War: Contemporary Philosophical Explorations* (Chicago: Henry Regnery, 1969).

Glover, Jonathan. *Humanity: A Moral History of the Twentieth Century* (New Haven: Yale Nota Bene, 2001.

Govier, Trudy. *A Delicate Balance: What Philosophy Can Tell Us About Terrorism* (Boulder, CO: Westview Press, 2002).

Grotius, Hugo. *Law of War and Peace.*

Hallett, Brian. *The Lost Art of Declaring War.* Urbana, IL: UP of Illinois, 1998.

Hamidullah, Muhammad. *Muslim Conduct of State.* Lahore, India: Sh. Muhammad Ashraf, 1945.

Hartigan, Richard Shelly. *The Forgotten Victim: A History of the Civilian.* Chicago, IL: Precedent Publishing, Inc., 1982.

Hartle, Anthony E. "Atrocities in War: Dirty Hands and Noncombatants," *Social Research,* 69/4, (Winter 2002).

Hayden, Patrick. *John Rawls: Towards a Just World Order* (Cardiff: University of Wales Press, 2002).

Henkin, Louis. *Foreign Affairs and the U.S. Constitution, 2nd ed.* Oxford: Clarendon Press, 1996.

Hook, Sidney. "Philosophy and Public Policy," in Charles J. Bontempo and S. Jack Odell (eds.) *The Owl of Minerva: Philosophers on Philosophy* (New York: McGraw-Hill, 1975), pp. 73-87.

Howard, Michael. *War in European History*. Oxford, UK: Oxford University Press, 1977.

Hunter, Daniel and George Lakey. *Opening Space for Democracy: Third Party Nonviolence Intervention*. Philadelphia: Training for Change, 2004.

Ibn Kudamah, Muwaffak al-Din. *Le Précis de Droit d'Ibn Qudama*. Henri Laoust, trans. Beirut: Institut Français de Damas, 1950.

Ibn Tymiya, Ahmad ibn 'Abd al-Halim. *Le Traité de Droit Public D'Ibn Taimiya: Traduction annoté de la Siyasa sariya*. Henri Laoust, trans. Beirut: Institut Français de Damas, 1948.

Iliade, Mircea. *A History of Religious Ideas* (London, Saint James Place, Vols. 1-3, 1979).

Indian Traditions and the Rule of Law Among Nations. All India Seminar, University of Delhi, India, March 9-11 1960.

Isaac, Rael Jean. "The Violent Pacifists," in Michael Cromartie, ed., *Peace Betrayed? Essays on Pacifism and Politics*. Washington, DC: Ethics and Public Policy Center, 1990.

Jensen, Derrick. *The Culture of Make Believe*. New York: Context Books, 2002.

Johnson, James Turner. *Can Modern War Be Just?* New Haven, CT: Yale University Press, 1984.

——. *Morality and Contemporary Warfare*. New Haven, CT: Yale University Press, 1999.

Juhnke, James and Carol Hunter. *The Missing Peace: The Search for Nonviolent Alternatives in United States History*. Kitchner, Ontario: Pandora Press, 2001.

Kagan, Robert, and William Kristol. *Present Dangers: Crisis and Opportunity in American Foreign and Defense Policy* (San Francisco: Encounter Books, 2000).

Keegan, John. *The Face of Battle*. New York, NY: Penguin Books, 1976.

Kelsay, John. *Islam and War: A Study in Comparative Ethics*. Lousville, KY: Westminster/John Knox Press, 1993.

Khadduri, Majid. *The Islamic Conception of Justice*. Baltimore, MD: The Johns Hopkins University Press, 1984.

Klare, Michael. *Resource Wars: The New Landscape of Global Conflict* (New York: Henry Holt Metropolitan, 2002).

——. *War and Peace in the Law of Islam*. Baltimore, MD: Johns Hopkins Press, 1955.

Kielmansegg, Peter Graf, Horst Mews, and Elisabeth Glazer-Schmidt (eds). *Hannah Arendt and Leo Strauss: German Émigrés and American Political Thought after World War II* (Cambridge: University of Cambridge Press, 1997).

Kilbourne, Jean. *You Can't Buy My Love: How Advertising Changes the Way We Think and Feel*. New York: Touchstone Press, 2000.

King, Martin Luther, Jr., *Strength to Love*. Philadelphia: Fortress Press, 1981.

——, Pilgrimage to Nonviolence. In James M. Washington, ed., *Martin Luther King, Jr. I Have a Dream: Writings and Speeches that Changed the World*. San Francisco: Harper, 1992.

Kingsolver, Barbara. *High Tide in Tucson*. New York: Harper-Collins, 1995.

Küng, Hans. *A Global Ethic for Global Politics and Economics* (London: SCM Press, 1997).

——. *Global Responsibility: In Search of a New World Ethic* (New York: Crossroad Pub. Co, 1991).

——. The Catholic Church: A Short History (New York: The Modern Library, 2001).

——. Tracing the Way: Spiritual Dimensions of the World Religions (New York: Continuum International Publishing, 2002).

Küng, Hans (ed). Globale Unternehmen – globales Ethos. Der globale Markt erfordert neue Standards und eine globale Rahmenordnung (Frankfurt/M, 2001).

—— (ed). *Yes to a Global Ethic* (New York: Continuum International Publishing, 1996).

Küng, Hans and Helmut Schmidt (eds). *A Global Ethic and Global Responsibilities: Two Declarations* (London: SCM Press, 1998).

Lawrence, Bruce B. "Rethinking Islam as an Ideology of Violence," in Paul Salem, ed., *Conflict Resolution in the Arab World: Selected Essays*. Beirut, Lebanon: American University of Beirut, 1997. pp. 27-40.

Levi, Werner. "International Law in a Multicultural World," *International Studies Quarterly,* 18/3,(Dec. 1974): 417-449.

Levy, Peter B. *Civil War on Race Street: The Civil Rights Movement in Cambridge, Maryland*. Gainesville, FL: University of Florida Press, 2003.

Lewy, Guenter. *Peace and Revolution: The Moral Crisis of American Pacifism*. Grand Rapids, MI: Erdmans Publishing, 1988.

Lustig, Myron W. and Jolene Koester. *Intercultural Competence* (Boston: Allyn and Bacon, 2003).

Machiavelli, Niccolo. *The Discourses* (New York: Harper and Row, 1961).

Mackey, Sandra. *The Reckoning: Iraq and the Legacy of Saddam Hussein* (New York: W. W. Norton, 2002).

Madelin, Henri. *Dieu et Cesar* (Paris: Desclée de Browver, 1970).

Mahabharata: 1. The Book of the Beginning. J.A.B. van Buitenen, ed. and trans. Chicago, IL: The University of Chicago Press, 1973.

Mahabharata: 2. The Book of the Assembly Hall and 3. The Book of the Forest. J.A.B. van Buitenen, ed. and trans. Chicago, IL: The University of Chicago Press, 1975.

Mahabharata: 4. The Book of the Virata and 5. The Book of the Effort. J.A.B. van Buitenen, ed. and trans. Chicago, IL: The University of Chicago Press, 1978.

Mahabharata: A Shortened Modern Prose Version of the Indian Epic. R.K. Narayan, ed. Chicago, IL: The University of Chicago Press, 1978.

Mandle, Jon. *What's Left of Liberalism? An Interpretation and Defense of Justice as Fairness* (Lanham, MD: Lexington Books, 2000).

Mann, James. *Rise of the Vulcans: The History of Bush's War Cabinet* (New York: Viking Press, 2004).

Marcuse, Herbert. "The Relevance of Reality," in Charles J. Bontempo and S. Jack Odell (eds.) *The Owl of Minerva: Philosophers on Philosophy* (New York: McGraw-Hill, 1975), pp. 231-244.

Maritain, Jacques. *Primauté du Spirituel* (Paris: Librairie Plon, 1927).

Mavrodes, George I. "Conventions and the Morality of War," *Philosophy and Public Affairs,* 4/2, (winter 1975): 117-131.

McAdam, Doug. "Tactical Innovation and the Pace of Insurgency," in Doug McAdam and David A. Snow, eds., *Social Movements: Readings on Their Emergence, Mobilization, and Dynamics.* Los Angeles: Roxbury Publishing, 1997.

McCumber, John. "A Closed Intellectual Community: The Policing of American Philosophy." *Studies in Practical Philosophy* 2/2, (2000): 124-137.

McQuaig, Linda. *It's the Crude, Dude: War, Big Oil, and the Fight for the Planet* (Toronto: Doubleday Canada, 2004).

Menon, Ramesh. *The Ramayana: A Modern Retelling of the Great Indian Epic.* New York, NY: North Point Press, 2001.

Merton, Thomas. *Gandhi on Non-Violence.* New York: New Directions Publishing, 1964.

Meyers, Diana Tietjens. *Subjection and Subjectivity* (New York: Routledge, 1994).

Miller, Richard B. "Aquinas and the Presumption Against Killing and War," *The Journal of Religion*: 173-204.

Mohawk, John. "The Warriors Who Turned to Peace," *Yes! A Journal of Positive Futures* (Winter 2005): 24-27.

More, S.S. *The Gita: A Theory of Human Action.* Delhi, India: Sri Satguru Publications, 1990.

Mukherjee, Bharati. *Kautilya's Concept of Diplomacy: A New Interpretation.* Calcutta, India: Minerva Associated (Publications) Pvt. Ltd., 1976.

Mukundan, Anayath Pisharath. *The Congruencies of the Fundamentals in the Quran and the Bhagavat Geeta.* New Delhi, India: Samkaleen Prakashan, 1990.

O'Gorman, Angie, ed. *The Universe Bends Toward Justice: A Reader on Christian Nonviolence in the U.S.* Philadelphia: New Society Publishers, 1990.

Olivelle, Patrick. *Dharamasutras: The Law Codes of Apastamba, Gautama, Baudhyana and Vasistha.* Oxford, UK, Oxford University Press, 1999.

O'Neill, Onora. *Towards Justice and Virtue: A Constructive Account of Practical Reasoning* (Cambridge: Cambridge University Press, 1996).

Orend, Brian. "Kant's Just War Theory," *Journal of the History of Philosophy,* 37/2, (April 1999): 323-353.

Orend, Brian. *War and International Justice: A Kantian Perspective* (Waterloo, Ontario, Canada: Wilfrid Laurier University Press, 2000).

Phillips, Kevin. *American Dynasty: Aristocracy, Fortune, and the politics of Deceit in the House of Bush*. New York: Penguin Books, 2004.

Picco, Giandomenico, Hans Küng, and Richard von Weizsäcker (eds). Crossing the Divide: Dialogue among Civilizations (South Orange, NJ: 2001).

Radhakrishnan, S. *Indian Philosophy* (London: George Allen and Unwin, Ltd., 1930).

Ramaswami, Justice v. "A General view of International Law in Ancient India," in H.S. Bhatia, ed., *International Law and Practice in Ancient India*. New Delhi, India; Deep & Deep Publications, 1977. pp. 11-16.

Raven-Hansen, Peter. "Constitutional Constraints: The War Clause," in *The U.S. and the Power to Go to War: Historical and Current Perspectives*. Eds. Morton H. Halperin and Gary M. Stern. Westport, CT: Greenwood Press, 1994.

Rawls, John. *The Law of Peoples* (Cambridge, MA: Harvard University Press, 1999).

——. *Political Liberalism* (New York: Columbia University Press, 1993).

——. *A Theory of Justice* (Cambridge, MA: Belknap Press of Harvard University. 1971).

——. "The Justification of Civil Disobedience," in Hugo Adam Bedau (ed). *Civil Disobedience: Theory and Practice* (New York: Pegasus, 1969).

Riker, Walter. "Rawls's Decent Peoples and the Democratic Peace Thesis," in John R. Rowan (ed). *War and Terrorism: Social Philosophy Today* 20 (2004): 137-153.

Rowan, John R. (ed). *War and Terrorism: Social Philosophy Today* 20 (2004).

Rubin, Lillian. "Family Values and the Invisible Working Class," in *Audacious Democracy*. New York: Houghton Mifflin, 1997.

Russel, Frederick H. *The Just War in the Middle Ages*. Cambridge, UK: Cambridge University Press, 1975.

Said, Edward. "Power, Politics, and Culture," in Gauri Viswanathan (ed). (New York: Pantheon Books, 2002).

——. *The Politics of Dispossession* (New York: Pantheon Books, 1994).

Saint Augustine. *The City Of God* (New York: Modern Library, 1958).

Sawant, Ankush R. *Manu-Smriti and Republic of Plato: A Comparative and Critical Study,* Bombay, India: Himalaya Publishing House, 1996.

Seale, Bobby. *Seize the Time: The Story of the Black Panther Party and Huey P. Newton*. Baltimore: Black Classic Press, 1991.

Schillebecks, Edward. *La Politique n'est pas tout* (Paris: Les Editions du Cerf, 1988).

School Curriculum and Assessment Authority, Religious Education (London: New House, 1995).

Sibley, Mulford Q. *The Political Theories of Modern Pacifism: An Analysis and Criticism*. New York: Garland Publishing, 1972.

Sidgwick, Henry. "The Morality of Strife," *International Journal of Ethics*, 1.1, (October 1890): 1-15.

Singer, Peter. *The President of Good & Evil: The Ethics of George W. Bush* (New York: Dutton, 2004).

Sirat, René Samuel. *La Tendresse de Dieu* (Paris: Nil Edition, 1996).

Smock, David R. *Religions Perspectives on War: Christian, Muslim and Jewish Attitudes Toward Force*, United States Institute of Peace, revised edition 2002.

Sterba, James P. (ed). *Terrorism and International Justice* (New York: Oxford University Press, 2003).

Strauss, Leo. *What Is Political Philosophy? And Other Studies* (Chicago: University of Chicago Press, 1959).

Sullivan, B. Todd. *Getting Intentions Right in War*, Indiana Center on Global Change and World Peace, Occasional Paper No. 17, Bloomington, IN: Indiana University, May 1993.

Suskind, Ron. *The Price of Loyalty: George W. Bush, The White House, and the Education of Paul O'Neill* (New York: Simon & Schuster, 2004).

Tersman, Folk. *Reflective Equilibrium: An Essay in Moral Epistemology* (Stockholm: Almqvist & Wakool International, 1993).

The Bhagavad Gita: Krishna's Council in Time of War. Barbara Stoler Miller (trans.) (New York: Bantam Books, 1986).

Thomas, Troy S. "Prisoners of War in Islam: A Legal Inquiry," *The Muslim World*, 87/1, (January 1997): 44-53.

Tolstoy, Leo. *The Law of Love and the Law of Violence*. New York: Holt, Reinhart, and Winston, 1970.

Toynbee, A.J. *Change and Habit* (London: Oxford University Press, 1966).

Vidal, Gore. *Dreaming War: Blood for Oil and the Cheney-Bush Junta* (New York: Thunder's Mouth Press/Nation Books, 2002).

Vivekananda, Swami. *Jnana Yoga* (Calcutta: N. Mukherjee, 1937).

Vorstenbosch, J. "Reflective Equilibrium and Public Debate: How to Cast the Public's Web of Beliefs Broadly Enough," in W. Van de Burg and T. van Willigenburg (eds). *Reflective Equilibrium* (Dordrecht: Kluwer, 1998).

Walzer, Michael. *Just and Unjust Wars*. New York, NY: Basic Books, 1977.

Weaver, J. Denny, Ed. *Teaching Peace*. Lanham, Maryland: Rowan and Littlefield, 2003.

Weil, Simone. *The Simone Weil Reader* (New York: Moyer Bell Limited, 1977).

Wells, Donald A. "How Much Can 'The Just War' Justify?" *The Journal of Philosophy*, 66/23, (Dec 1969): 819-829.

Wink, Walter. *Engaging the Powers: Discernment and Resistance in A World of Domination*. Minneapolis: Fortress Press, 1992.

Yeomans, Matthew. *Oil: Anatomy of an Industry* (New York: The New Press, 2004).

Yeats, W.P. *The collected Poems of W.P. Yeats* (London: Macmillan and Co., 1952).

Yergin, Daniel. *The Prize: The Epic Quest for Oil, Money, and Power* (New York: Simon & Schuster, 1991).

Yoder, John Howard. *When War is Unjust: Being Honest in Just War Thinking.* Maryknoll, NY: Orbis Books, 1984.

Zinn, Howard. *Declarations of Independence: Cross-Examining American Ideology.* New York: HarperCollins, 1990.

——. *Howard Zinn Reader: Writings on Disobedience and Democracy.* New York: Seven Stories Press, 1997.

Index